Fat Chance:

Surviving the Cholesterol Controversy and Beyond

Dennis Willmont

Willmountain Press
496 Pine Street
Marshfield, MA 02050
781-837-3455
Willmountain.com

Library of Congress Control Number: 2005910464
ISBN: 0-9741257-3-3

Editing: Susan L. McCarthy

All illustrations by author.

Photography by Sally Neeld, saneeld@earthlink.net.
Cover Design by Sandy Conner, sandy@sconner.com.

The purpose of Willmountain Press is to serve as an axis between Heaven and Earth in the presentation of Body/Mind/Spirit unity in ancient Chinese energetic healing systems with a focus on acupuncture.
Website: Willmountain.com.

This book is dedicated to my friend Neil Doré, for whom I wish it could have been written earlier.

Reviews

"*Fat Chance* is a treasure chest of little known facts and scientific correlations assembled by a very wise healer. Dennis Willmont offers both his scholarly explanation and more common, traditional wisdom in his new, user-friendly handbook that should be read by all patients, health professionals and lay people who recognize the important role diet plays in maintaining health and preventing disease. Everyone will surely benefit from this authors' extraordinary depth of knowledge about an essential component of well being. Certain to become an indispensable resource, this book dispels age-old myths, reveals blatant commercial bias and ultimately guides readers toward a safe, healthful and conscious use of dietary fats and oils. I highly recommend it!"

> — William Spear, international educator, author and lecturer on macrobiotics, *Intuitive* Feng Shui®, complementary and integrative medicine, global ecology and personal transformation. His work includes studies on the effect of the environment on health; the relationship between diet and disease; the role of emotional factors in wellness; the care and support of patients dying of cancer and AIDS, and the care and support of survivors of disasters, especially children, in the Ukraine, Sri Lanka and the U.S. He is the President of the Fortunate Blessings Foundation located in Litchfield, Connecticut where he maintains a private practice.

"Dennis' book not only has all the information we need on the oils we presently use and how they are produced, but also integrates how they are seen from the eyes of both Western and Chinese Medicine. This is the best and most complete book on oils I have ever read."

> — Lino Stanchich, Macrobiotic teacher, Health and Lifestyle Consultant.

"A compelling integration of Traditional Chinese Medicine and contemporary nutrition, Dennis Willmont's *Fat Chance* translates perfectly where so many other East-West books have failed. The comprehensive and helpful dietary information regarding good fats vs. bad fats is expertly and thoughtfully presented in concise, understandable fashion. I found the book easy to read, interesting and extremely helpful as a nutritional source guide. Beyond my first enjoyable read, I am certain I will often be pulling this book off my shelf for nutritional reference!"

> — Mark Mincolla, Ph.D., Nutritional Councilor, Author, Host of "Natural Health and Healing Show" on WATD 95.9 in Marshfield, MA.

"*Fat Chance* is the latest of Dennis Willmont's probing works. His indictments of the edible oil industry show how information can be manipulated for profit at the expense of public health. He also criticizes the current cholesterol fad that blames cholesterol as the cause of heart disease in order to sell the public harmful cholesterol-lowering drugs! Instead, he provides simple life-saving alternatives that anyone can practice at a fraction of the cost.

In addition, the entire classification system of fats and oils can be very impenetrable, confusing, and unreliable. Dennis has tackled this topic with surgical precision and presented it rationally and clearly. I wholeheartedly recommend this book for anyone to read, re-read, and pass on to their family and friends."

> — James P. Doyle, D.O., L.Ac. Dr. Doyle ran one of the four medical offices in the US where acupuncture was first practiced in 1973, his office acting as teaching clinic for the first accredited acupuncture school in the US.

"I enjoyed reading Dennis' book and find it a valuable reference. It is thorough, well researched, and contains a wealth of information about the quality, nature, and uses of vegetable oils in our diet. I recommend this book to anyone interested in diet and health."

> — Denny Waxman,
> Internationally recognized teacher, counselor, and writer on health, natural healing and macrobiotics; Founder and Director of The Strengthening Health Institute.

Table of Contents

Table of Contents

Table of Contents

Dietary Fats and Oils

Definition

Dietary fats and oils, technically called lipids, are extremely important foods. **Seventy percent or more of US deaths involve deficiencies, excesses, or imbalances of lipids, the understanding of which are only obscured by the entrenched "beliefs" of the medical community.** The difference between fats and oils is that oils are derived from plants and are liquid at room temperature, whereas fats are mostly derived from animals and are solid at room temperature. [a] The importance of fats and oils is, however, largely misunderstood due to the powerful and manipulating influence of the food industry on both the medical profession and the general public. Technical terms like saturated, unsaturated, monounsaturated, polyunsaturated, cholesterol, and low- and high-density lipoproteins are used to differentiate between different kinds of fats and oils. People are led to believe that saturated fats and cholesterol are "bad" and polyunsaturated oils are "good." On the common sense level and accurate therapeutic levels, however, these differentiations are not as significant as others and, worse, they can lead people into useless and harmful dietary habits.

Three more fundamental differences in categorizing healthy and unhealthy lipids are whether they are:

1) Natural or man-made
2) Essential or unessential to health
3) Containing *trans*-fatty acids or other toxic chemicals made from artificial processing

Natural fats and oils are those that can be obtained from natural plant or animal products without interfering with their innate qualities, as is often done in the extracting, refining, and cooking they undergo in modern society. More harm is done to human health through the industrial processing and overcooking of fats and oils than could EVER be done with the simple consumption of saturated fats and cholesterol. The $280 billion processed food industry obscures this simple fact because highly processed foods are more profitable to sell than fresh ones. This industry can easily afford to lobby government institutions that then support the spin that industry puts on fat and oil nutrition.

---

[a] The exception to this rule includes tropical oils such as Coconut and Palm Kernel oils. Another difference is that oils tend to be more unsaturated and fats tend to be more saturated. Animal fats tend to be long-chain saturated fatty acids; while Coconut oil and Palm Kernel oils are mostly medium-chain saturated fatty acids. This difference in chemistry accounts for entirely different physiological functions in the human body.

1

Dietary Fats and Oils

According to Mary Enig, internationally renowned nutritionist and consultant to individuals, industry, and state and federal governments:

> The American Heart Association (AHA), the National Heart, Lung and Blood Institute's National Cholesterol Education Program, the National Cancer Institute's Cancer Prevention Program, and the US Department of Agriculture's Dietary Guidelines...are misguided and not sufficiently knowledgeable about the chemistry of fats and oils.[1]

According to Enig, any research findings that are contrary to current, government-supported dogma must be carefully hidden within the reports in order to secure future funding from an industrial/medical complex with a highly motivated financial agenda. For example, the Center for Science in the Public Interest (CSPI) waged the campaign against naturally saturated fats and oils that gave a false green light to the incorporation of the *trans*-fatty acids that now play such a dominant role in the fast-food industry, an industry that is responsible in large part for the significant decline of health in Western society and the development of degenerative disease. In the 1950s, a false premise was invented that cholesterol and saturated fats were major causes of chronic disease in the modern world in order to protect the fledgling margarine and shortening industry from its critics in the scientific world who were instead implicating the industrial hydrogenation of fats and oils.

When Ancel Keys announced in the late 1950s that hydrogenated vegetable fats were the most significant cause of coronary artery disease, a public relations campaign was mounted to divert public attention instead to saturated fats. Since then the belief has been that saturated fats are bad for health and polyunsaturated fats are good. The problem with this argument is that the public is left with only these relatively sophisticated terms to choose between while the more important difference between *natural* and *unnatural* polyunsaturates was brushed aside. In 1965, the American Heart Association (AHA) sided with industry over the public by encouraging the consumption of partially hydrogenated fats. By 1984, the National Institutes of Health Cholesterol Consensus Conference and its clone, the National Cholesterol Education Program, followed suit. Other large organizations, including the International Food Information Council (IFIC) and the American Dietetic Association (ADA), the largest dietetic and nutrition organization in the US, are also involved in supporting this scam due to their agendas in pushing the industrial-grade food oils and ignoring well-established information as to the disease-causing effects of the *trans*-fatty acids. Not until 2001 (over fifty years later) did the AHA modify their position slightly by warning against *trans*-fatty acids while continuing to promote hydrogenated oils and margarines.[2]

For example, in their 2003 "Controlling Your Risk Factors" and in their 2001 "Eating Plan For Healthy Americans," the AHA specifically recommends margarine over other lipids: "Choose liquid or tub margarine instead of butter" and "use margarine with liquid vegetable oil as the *first liquid ingredient*." Further adding to this misinformation, they state in the same pamphlet (#58),

"... liquid or tub margarines...are low in...*trans*-fat." As we shall see later, this is an impossible contradiction in terms. One of the most significant ways in which *trans*-fat is made is through the production of margarine!

Probably the most vicious and inaccurate fat and oil scam was the war on Coconut oil waged by the American Soybean Association (ASA) in the 1980s. In spite of efforts by research professionals and the media to set the record straight, public sentiment was so firmly sided with the ASA that people refused to listen to scientific truth. Even doctors and medical organizations were swayed. The war against Coconut oil was started by the ASA in order to eliminate competition from imported tropical oils. Their claim that Coconut oil causes heart attacks because it is a saturated fat is totally unfounded. Coconut oil is a plant-derived saturated fat that does not go rancid as polyunsaturated oils do because it is highly stable. Coconut oil has also been used as a staple food for thousands of years in the tropics where, until the introduction of western industrialized food, degenerative disorders such as heart disease, cancer, diabetes, and dental cavities were virtually unknown. Countries with the highest tropical oil consumption such as Costa Rica and Malaysia have much lower serum cholesterol levels, obesity, and heart disease rates than western nations.

In 1986, the ASA instructed the wives and families of soybean growers to create a lobbying effort against tropical oils in favor of refined soybean oil. Soon the Center for Science in the Public Interest (CSPI) joined in with the help in 1988 of recovering heart attack patient and millionaire Phil Sokolof, who ran full-page newspaper advertisements declaring that food companies were "poisoning America" through their use of tropical oils and saturated fat. In response to this campaign, tropical oils were falsely given such a bad name that they virtually disappeared from sight. Instead, **hydrogenated margarine and refined vegetable oils, conceivably the most health-damaging dietary oils in existence, became commonplace by the early 1990s.** By 2003, the AHA was still recommending the avoidance of coconut ("choose from all vegetables and fruit except coconut")[3] in favor of refined unsaturated fatty acids (UFAs) and margarine. The resulting proliferation of hydrogenated fats and refined vegetable oils has cursed the public because the only way to avoid these synthetic foods is to prepare food from scratch. However, good quality unrefined vegetable oils are not commonly available in grocery stores either. The unfounded aversion to all saturated fats has even spread to MUFA advocates such as the proponents of the Mediterranean Diet. They incorrectly consider Coconut, Palm, and Palm Kernel oils "notorious" because they are among the few plant oils that contain a large amount of saturated fat.[4]

Lipids

Fatty Acids

In order to sort through this confusion about lipids, we need to get an overview of the different terms used to describe them and then separate myth and manipulative dogma from scientific fact. There are three different classes of lipids: (1) sterols (including cholesterol), (2) phospholipids (including lecithin), and (3) triglycerides (including both saturated and unsaturated fats). Triglycerides are the most abundant form of lipids and flow through the bloodstream to be deposited in adipose tissue (fat cells) where they store energy. Energy molecules, adenosine triphosphate (ATP), initially come from sugar. Excess sugar poses a threat to the body, which can overwhelm it with too much energy. Since only so much sugar can be stored as glycogen at any given time, the liver converts the rest into triglycerides. The fatty acids in triglycerides, because they are digested more slowly than carbohydrates, are able to store the ATP away for later use. Most excess fat stored in the body is the result of eating sugar and not fat!

On the chemical level, triglycerides are comprised of three fatty acids joined together by a molecule of glycerol. Fatty acids, in turn, are formed from three simple elements—carbon (C), hydrogen (H), and oxygen (O)—linked together in a chain. The carbon element forms the backbone of this chain with the hydrogen atoms sticking out on the sides and one end like the legs and tail of a millipede. The two oxygen atoms are attached to the "head" end of the chain where they combine with an additional hydrogen atom. The "tail" end is called a methyl group and the "head" end a carboxyl group. This differentiation between the head and tail gives the fatty acid molecule a unique and significant property and function. The methyl group, the fatty "tail," dissolves in oil but not in water, while the carboxyl group, the acid "head," dissolves in water but not in oil.

Figure 1: Simple Fatty Acid Chain

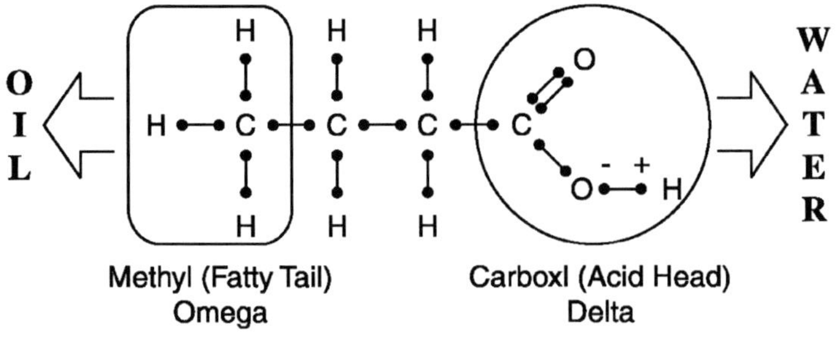

Methyl (Fatty Tail)
Omega

Carboxl (Acid Head)
Delta

This dual property of fatty acids allows them to dissolve in the watery bloodstream. The carboxyl "acid" head of the fatty acid chain gravitates to the watery part of the blood medium while the fatty "methyl" tail sticks out and floats on the surface periphery. This inherent polarity within the fatty acid molecule enables it to bridge between different types of organic environments and transport both nutrients and toxins back and forth between them. In so doing, the fatty acids also generate electrical potentials, move electric currents, and facilitate membrane function. They are, in fact, the main components of membranes including the skin of the body as a whole, the membranes around organs and tissues, the membranes of cells, and the membranes of intra-cellular organelles. In addition, the essential Omega 3 (w3) and Omega 6 (w6) fatty

4   Dennis Willmont © 2005; All Rights Reserved

acids produce substances (the prostaglandins) that act like hormones in regulating and coordinating different parts of the body. These two functions of lipids (regulating what passes in and out of the cells and coordinating local areas of the body with each other through prostaglandins) make dietary fats and oils one of the most important substances for living systems. In fact, the basic direction toward either health or disease depends greatly on the physiological role that lipids play.

Fatty acids are also responsible for transporting the fat-soluble Vitamins A, D, E, and K. In fact, without enough fat in the diet, one can easily become vitamin-deficient since these vitamins cannot be absorbed efficiently without fat. Fat-soluble vitamins also play important roles as antioxidants (AOs), where they protect against degenerative disease including coronary artery disease and cancer. For example, Vitamin A can be derived either directly from animal sources or converted indirectly from the beta-carotene found in green and yellow fruits and vegetables. Vitamin A is critical for healthy skin, immune function, reproduction and cell division, the development of bone and tooth enamel, and vision (especially night vision). Vitamin D also functions as a hormone and is not widely available in food, but instead depend on cholesterol for its formation. Vitamin E, necessary for maintaining cardiovascular health, is found in many natural foods including whole-grain products, wheat germ, nuts and seeds, unrefined vegetable oils, green leafy vegetables, egg yolks, and liver. Vitamin K is found in leafy green vegetables (especially the cabbage family), dulse, and liver and is also made by the beneficial bacteria in the intestine. Vitamin K is necessary for blood clotting and helps the absorption of calcium into the bones to promote bone density.

Fatty acids are further divided by the length and shape of their chain. Straight chains are saturated while crooked chains are unsaturated. If the chain is bent once it is called monounsaturated, if it is bent more than once it is called polyunsaturated, and if it is bent many times, like the essential Omega 3 fatty acids (w3s), it is called super-polyunsaturated. Saturated, unsaturated, and polyunsaturated lipids all occur in different chain lengths. They are generally classified accordingly as long-chain triglycerides (LCTs), short-chain triglycerides (SCTs), or medium-chain triglycerides (MCTs). Chain length has to do with whether the fatty acid will be used for developing structure or function in the body. The longer the chain length, the more the fatty acid will incorporated into body structure (as fat storage or membrane construction) while the shorter the chain length, the more it will be burned or oxidized as energy.[a]

The chain length of fatty acids found in triglycerides is generally from two carbons long to twenty-four or more. For example, the chain length of vinegar (acetic acid) is only two carbons in length; one of the fatty acids in butter (butyric acid—40 percent) is four carbons long; the fatty acids in meats and fish are at least fourteen carbons long; and the stearic acid in beef fat has an 18-carbon chain. Long-chain fatty acids (LCFAs) contain from fourteen to

---

[a] This is an important consideration for Coconut oil, which burns energy easily and cleanly because of its medium length chain.

twenty-four carbons and are found in all fats and oils. These are the most common fatty acids in nature since they provide the most economical form for storage and structure. All of the short-chain fatty acids (SCFAs) and medium-chain fatty acids (MCFAs) are saturated. SCFAs contain only two to six carbons and can only be found in nature as vinegar and butter. MCFAs contain from eight to twelve carbons. They are also relatively rare but can be found naturally in some tropical plants such as Coconut oil, Palm oil, and Palm Kernel oil. Coconut oil contains 64 percent saturated MCFAs, which are predominantly used for energy production. They are not stored in the body as body fat or as deposits in arteries as you have been led to believe.

Bending of the fatty acid chain is caused by decreasing its hydrogen saturation and results in oils that are more liquid. Straightening of the fatty acid chain is caused by increasing its hydrogen saturation and results in fats that are more solid. The shorter the chain and the more unsaturated the fatty acid, the softer the oil and the lower its melting point will be. Even when the chain-length is the same, the degree of saturation will affect the consistency of the oil. For example, polyunsaturated oils (PUFAs), like sunflower oil are liquid at room temperature; and monounsaturated oils (MUFAs) like olive and peanut oils are liquid at room temperature, but begin to solidify and become cloudy or semi-solid in the refrigerator. In contrast, the longer the chain and the more saturated the fatty acid, the harder the fat and the higher its melting point will be. For example, saturated fat like lard is even solid at room temperature. Nevertheless, SCFAs are soft and fluid while LCFAs become thick or even waxy. An example of monounsaturated, polyunsaturated, and saturated fatty acids of the same chain-length (eighteen carbons) but different consistency is given below.

Figure 2: Carbon Bonds in Fatty Acid Chains

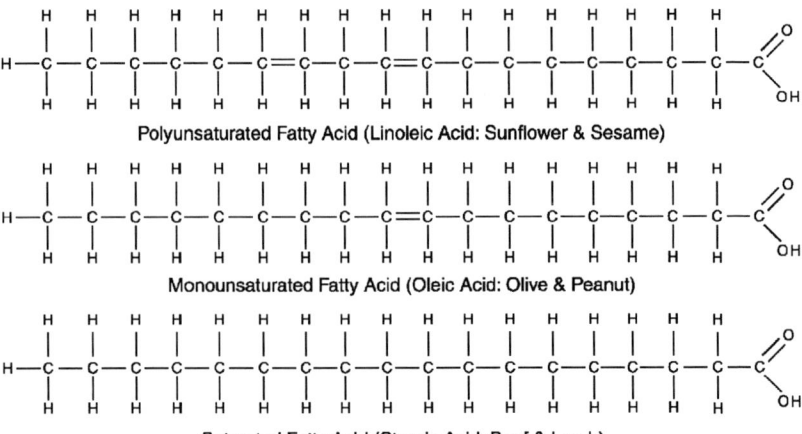

Polyunsaturated Fatty Acid (Linoleic Acid: Sunflower & Sesame)

Monounsaturated Fatty Acid (Oleic Acid: Olive & Peanut)

Saturated Fatty Acid (Stearic Acid: Beef & Lamb)

Bending of the fatty acid chain creates a weak link in the carbon chain and makes unsaturated fatty acids less stable than saturated fatty acids.

Unsaturated fatty acids need to be protected from this vulnerability by making a deliberate attempt to isolate them from destructive forces, especially those of heat, light, and oxygen. The straightness of the fatty acid chain results from the integrity of its carbon molecule backbone where each carbon connects directly with another on the inside as well as with two hydrogen molecules on the outside, the two legs of the millipede. Since the carbon molecule has the capacity to make four bonds, it shares one of these bonds with the carbon on each side of it, while the two hydrogen molecules in the two outside "leg" positions use up the other two bonds. In this case, all of the "leg" positions are filled in with hydrogen molecules. The fatty acid chain is then "saturated" with hydrogen and unable to hold any more. A typical example of a short-chain saturated fatty acid (SaFA), the butyric acid found in butter, is depicted below.

Figure 3: Straight Fatty-acid Chains: A SaFA

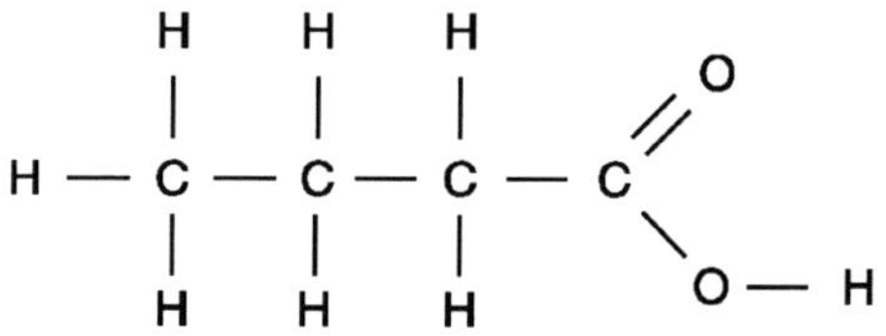

If two, as in the monounsaturated fatty acids, or more of these hydrogen molecules are missing, the fatty acid chain is said to be unsaturated, that is, not all of the possible hydrogen molecules are present. When the hydrogen molecules are missing, the carbon molecules on the inside of the chain must compensate by creating a double bond, which they share with each other in order to compensate for the two missing hydrogen molecules.

Figure 4: A Single Double Bond Pattern (MUFA)

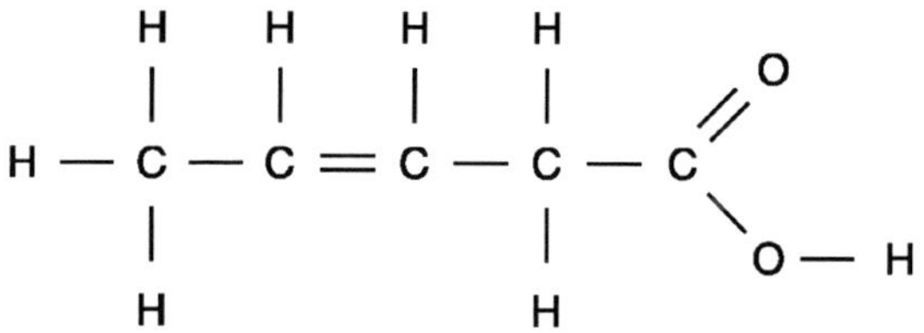

If there were eighteen carbons in the chain of the above example and the double bond was positioned after the ninth carbon molecule from the methyl (left) end, it would be classified as oleic acid, Omega 9 (w9), of which Olive oil is representative as in Figure 2.

The two possible configurations for the unpaired hydrogen molecules in a double bond are *cis-* and *trans-*. The *cis*-configuration results when the hydrogen molecules are on the same side of the fatty acid chain. This position causes the chain to bend, take up more space, and become less dense, and is the single most important factor in making the *cis*-configuration less stable and more active than the saturated fatty acids, which are relatively stable and inert.

Dietary Fats and Oils

The *trans*-configuration results when the hydrogen molecules line up on opposite sides so that the fatty acid chain remains straight. *Trans*-configurations are mostly caused through industrial modifications that try to make unsaturated vegetable oils act like saturated animal fats. Nevertheless, they are only reflections of natural fatty acids. Instead of contributing to the health and well-being of the living organism, they are one of the primary contributors to degenerative disease.

Figure 5: *Cis*- and *Trans*- Configurations

Cis-Configuration   *Trans*-Configuration

The Sterols
Cholesterol: A Definition

Cholesterol is a very sticky and extremely hard waxy lipid that melts at 300°F but is soluble in triglycerides and is absolutely essential for health. While cholesterol can be obtained externally from animal foods, especially organ meats, but also from eggs[a], meat, dairy products, fish, and shellfish, the body can easily make its own supply on demand from more simple substances such as the breakdown of carbohydrate, fat, and protein by the liver, intestine, adrenal glands, and sex glands. Even the placenta can make cholesterol in order to produce enough progesterone so that pregnancy will go to term.

For most people (70 percent of the affluent world population) cholesterol levels are regulated homeostatically in the body. More cholesterol is produced when dietary intake is low and less is produced when it is high. Consumption of sugar and refined carbohydrates push the body to produce more

---

[a] Modern eggs contain more cholesterol than homegrown barnyard eggs. Nowadays, cooped chickens are fed large amounts of antibiotics to keep them safe from epidemics as well as unnatural diets that contain less of the important, but easily perishable, Omega 3 and 6 essential fatty acids (EFAs) and more oleic acid (OA). There is also less of the necessary EFAs in modern eggs to transport and metabolize the cholesterol properly in the body. An organic egg has much more Omega 3s than a commercially raised egg as can be seen in the Omega3:Omega 6 ratios: 1:1 for an organic egg and 1:19 for the commercially raised version. In addition, the plant sterols normally part of a natural chicken's diet, which reduce the cholesterol content of eggs by up to 35 percent, are removed. Beta-catotene is replaced in the yolks with cheap artificial dye and the eggs are now as unhatchable as they are nutritionally void.

cholesterol. [a] Polyunsaturated oils, especially the EFAs, have an inverse relationship with cholesterol at the level of the membranes and can decrease tissue cholesterol levels. Polyunsaturated fatty acids increase membrane fluidity, which, in excess, creates an additional need for cholesterol in the membranes in order to maintain their strength and rigidity. SaFAs, on the other hand, because they tend to make the membranes harder, tend to cause cholesterol to be pulled out of the membranes and into the bloodstream where they raise serum cholesterol levels. Stress also increases cholesterol production because cholesterol is a precursor to the stress hormones involved with the kidneys. Because coffee consumption robs the Kidneys to feed the Heart[b] and in so doing places the entire Body/Mind in an artificial state of fight or flight stress, it is also implicated in raising cholesterol levels. Once made, cholesterol can not be broken down in the body and can only be removed through the stool by the action of bile acids and dietary fiber. **Without sufficient fiber, 94 percent of cholesterol is simply reabsorbed.**

In general:

1) PUFAs circulate cholesterol from the body to the membranes
2) SaFAs circulate cholesterol from the membranes to the body
3) Stress circulates cholesterol from the liver to the body
4) MUFAs balance the flow of cholesterol between the membranes and the liver.

Function

While many companies in the food industry have allowed the anti-cholesterol propaganda to limit the cholesterol composition of their products, cholesterol remains an essential lipid with many functions absolutely necessary to the healthy functioning of the body and mind. These functions include fat digestion; the formation of scar tissue, membranes, and skin; the formation of Vitamin D; the creation of many hormones; and the optimization of infant brain development. Cholesterol also acts as a surrogate antioxidant (AO) that protects the heart.

Bile acids needed for the emulsification of fats and oils are made from cholesterol in the liver, stored in the gallbladder, and used by the body to aid in the digestion and absorption of fats and oils and the absorption of the fat-soluble vitamins. The body uses cholesterol as a raw material for the healing process and forms a major part of the scar tissue formed to heal wounds. In this capacity, cholesterol also plays an important part in the healing of injured arteries. The problem is that the plaque used to create this healing can also thicken into atherosclerosis in the circulatory system or into tuberculosis in the

---

[a] All refined food produces free radicals. Free radicals destroy tissue so the body has to produce more cholesterol to heal the damage.

[b] Kidney and Heart are capitalized here to indicate that they refer to the broader definitions of the "organs" as understood in Chinese medicine. The idea that coffee "robs the Kidneys to feed the Heart" will be explained in detail on p. 40.

lungs. The trick to preventing and healing these diseases however is not to reduce the amount of cholesterol but to heal the source of the injuries—usually the destructive effect of eating refined food.

Membranes are made of phospholipids and cholesterol, which provide flexibility and structure. Cholesterol regulates the stiffness and flexibility of cell membranes and is added to membranes that are too loose, and removed from membranes that are too stiff. The more unsaturated fatty acids are in the body, the looser the membranes become and the more cholesterol is needed to stiffen them up. In contrast, SaFAs harden membranes so less cholesterol is needed to balance them. Alcohol also loosens the membranes and makes them more fluid so that more cholesterol is called for in order to stiffen the membranes. When the alcohol wears off, the membrane hardens, so that this membrane cholesterol is pulled back into the bloodstream in order to reestablish normal membrane fluidity.

Cholesterol acts in a similar way to protect the skin from infection caused by foreign organisms and against the wear and tear of the elements as well as to heal skin tissue and prevent dehydration and cracking. Cholesterol in the skin is also the precursor of Vitamin D. Vitamin D is the sunshine vitamin that regulates calcium and phosphorus metabolism. Vitamin D starts out as cholesterol in the skin and then goes to the liver and kidneys, where it assumes its role in regulating the metabolism of these minerals.

Cholesterol is also the building block for many important hormones including estrogen, progesterone, and testosterone and is also an important ingredient in mother's milk where it is used for proper brain development. Infant formulas, on the other hand, contain very small amounts of cholesterol, if any. Cholesterol can also act as an AO to counteract the free radical proliferation that is such a significant factor in the development of coronary artery disease. This lack of natural AOs caused primarily by refined foods creates high levels of oxidized cholesterol in low-density lipoprotein (LDL) and high-density lipoprotein (HDL) transport vehicles. Cholesterol is not the problem in coronary artery disease any more than trees are the cause of forest fires. Cholesterol is an important and necessary substance that helps more than it hinders. The "cause" of so-called cholesterol problems lies much deeper and will be explained further in this chapter as well as in the chapter on "Heart and Circulatory Disease" and then later in the section on "Natural Cholesterol Regulation." In summation, cholesterol helps to:

1) Improve fat digestion
2) Protect the skin from dehydration, cracking and infection
3) Heal wounds through the formation of scar tissue
4) Regulate the stiffness and flexibility of the membranes and skin
5) Form Vitamin D
6) Create many important hormones
7) Optimize infant brain development
8) Act as a surrogate AO

The Phospholipids

Function

Phospholipids (PLs) regulate the cell membranes, a process so essential that life could not exist without it. Phospholipids, like the triglycerides, are comprised of fatty acid chains attached to a glycerol molecule. The only difference between phospholipids and triglycerides is the number of these fatty acid chains. Triglycerides have three chains and phospholipids have two. This difference changes their solubility. Triglycerides are only fat-soluble while phospholipids are both water and fat-soluble. These qualities make phospholipids spread out easily over water surfaces. Phospholipid molecules also take up more space than straight-chain SaFA molecules, an attribute that makes phospholipids important components of cell membranes and cell structure. Their expansive action not only prevents the cell membranes from hardening, it also allows other important materials to move easily in and out of the cell.

Phospholipids form membranes around cells, the intracellular organelles, including the nucleus and nucleolus, and even the mitochondria where the enzyme ATP is converted to energy. They help decide which materials go in and out of the cells, including oxygen, which is held by the glycerol molecule that holds the two fatty acid phospholipid chains together. This oxygen is required to protect the cells against external pathogens. Phospholipids also form the envelopes surrounding fats, fat-soluble vitamins, and cholesterol so that these materials can remain water-soluble in the bloodstream where they are transported in and out of areas in need. This function is particularly important in cholesterol, which must be coated in temporary phospholipid membranes in order to go back and forth between the liver and the cells in conjunction with LDL (low-density lipoproteins) and HDL (high-density lipoproteins). LDL carries cholesterol from the liver in a centrifugal motion to the cells, while HDL carries cholesterol in a centripetal motion back to the liver.

Lecithin

Lecithin is the best known of the PLs. The name "lecithin" is derived from the Greek name for "egg yolk" from which this supplement was first isolated. As a PL, lecithin keeps cholesterol and triglycerides soluble in the blood so they can reach all parts of the body. Lecithin forms part of the two major vehicles for this transportation, HDL and LDL, and constitutes 22 percent of their composition.

Lecithin also supplies choline to the liver where it becomes an important component of bile, which helps break down fats into small droplets increasing their surface area so they can be more easily and quickly digested. In the same way it also helps keep cholesterol soluble, isolated from arterial linings, and protected from oxidation. These emulsifying actions also help prevent and dissolve gallbladder and kidney stones. In addition, choline helps make the neurotransmitter acetylcholine, which is used for brain and nerve function. Lecithin also helps the various liver functions in general, especially its detoxification functions, which keep us from being poisoned by the breakdown products of our body's own metabolic processes. Cancer results from these types of liver dysfunction over the years and decades.

While all unrefined seed oils contain some lecithin, their richest commercial source is organic, unrefined, non-GMO soybean oil, which also contains a supply of both essential fatty acids, the Omega 3s and Omega 6s. Other commercial sources of lecithin contain only the Omega 6s. In fact, soybean oil was the only commercial source of both of these EFAs until flax and hemp oils came on the market. Hempseed and its oil as well as Rice bran and Rice Bran oil are also good sources of lecithin. Commercial feeds produce eggs and meat with low levels of both lecithin and EFAs and are now insufficient for optimum health. Nevertheless, our body can make lecithin on its own if there is a sufficient amount of EFAs, choline, and phosphate in our diet. Lecithin is removed from refined oils. Legumes, including bean sprouts, are a good source of choline. The best dietary source of phospholipids is Krill oil.

The Triglycerides

Triglycerides (TGs) are the most common fats found in the body, and constitute 95 percent of the fats people eat. Sugar is metabolized into saturated triglycerides so that it can be stored in the body. Short-chain saturated, unsaturated, and monounsaturated triglycerides are used in the body for energy in contrast to the EFAs, which it reserves for more important structural and metabolic functions. Triglycerides function to provide a layer of insulation around the body, which protects the internal organs from shock and injury and keeps people warm during the winter but makes them excessively hot during the summer.

Triglycerides are also important in the storage of energy reserves. Excess sugars are converted into the less harmful TGs where they can be stored away for future use by all the internal organs including the brain. Even though the brain requires glucose for its energy, glucose can be made from glycerol. Since triglycerides are made from fatty acids and glycerol, triglycerides, including the necessary EFAs, also constitute one of the body's major storehouses of reserves. In acupuncture theory, the Reserve Qi[a] is *the* most important type of Qi. Reserve Qi is stored away in the internal organs for times of need, and is responsible for nourishing exceptional organs like the brain, Gallbladder, Heart[b] and circulatory system, reproductive organs, the skeleton, and the bone marrow. The Reserve Qi in acupuncture is, at least in good part, formed from these important triglycerides and EFAs.

TGs can also cause problems. According to Udo Erasmus, an internationally recognized expert in fats and oils and a pioneer in safe and healthy food oil production:

---

[a] Pronounced "chee."

[b] Gallbladder and Heart, here and elsewhere, are capitalized to indicate that they refer to the broader definitions of the "organs" as is defined in Chinese medicine.

Excess high blood TG levels increase our risk of heart disease. They are produced by overeating and by high dietary intake of refined sugars, sticky saturated fats, and too few antioxidants. Under these conditions, TG fatty acids oxidize and damage the inside of our arteries. High blood TG levels may also increase the tendency of blood cells to clump together. Excess stored TG fats (in overweight and obese people) correlate with high blood cholesterol and TG levels. All increase our risk of coronary artery disease, high blood pressure, heart and kidney failure, cancer, and other degenerative diseases.[5]

Excess serum triglyceride levels can be decreased through exercise and by up to 65 percent by taking Omega 3 from flax as well as the Omega 3 derivatives—EPA and DHA from fish and marine animal oils like krill. These foods can also decrease cholesterol levels by 25 percent. Generally speaking, nutritionally balanced Omega 3-rich diets are extremely important in keeping people free from cardiovascular and other degenerative diseases.

Fat Families

The four major classes, or families, that triglyceride fatty acids are divided into are determined by the straightness or bend in the fatty acid chain which in turn is determined by the number of double bonds made by the carbon molecule in the interior "backbone" of the chain. The straighter the chain, the more "saturated" with hydrogen atoms it becomes. These straight chains are called saturated fatty acids (SaFAs); those with only one bend or double bond are called monounsaturated fatty acids (MUFAs); while those with more than one bend or double bond are called polyunsaturated fatty acids (PUFAs). *Trans*-fatty acids are straight chains that have become saturated mostly through artificial methods, such as by the industrial application of high temperatures to naturally formed unsaturated fatty acids.

No purely saturated or unsaturated fats and oils are found in nature. They always exist in combinations of the three natural families of triglycerides. Purely saturated fatty acids would be as hard as wax and would be indigestible. Foods comprised of predominantly long-chain saturated fats, while being more stable, are more difficult to digest and tend to accumulate more easily in fatty deposits. In contrast, foods predominantly comprised of unsaturated oils are easier to digest but easily become rancid and need more care in their handling and storage in order for their beneficial and healthy properties to be actualized.

While animal foods "tend" to be more saturated, they also contain some unsaturated fatty acids. For example, beef fat is 55 percent unsaturated, lard is 56 percent unsaturated, and chicken fat is about 70 percent unsaturated, while the plant-based Coconut oil contains hardly any unsaturated fat and as much as 92 percent saturated fat, much more than any animal source. Coconut oil, however, is a MCFA, a quality that gives it the best of both the saturated stability, and the unsaturated easily digested, energy producing worlds. Each of these types of fat families affects the body differently and offers different benefits to health. They should, therefore, be consumed in a wide variety. Exclusive use of any single type should be avoided. The best sources of natural oils are found in whole foods such as whole grains, legumes, seeds, nuts, and certain fruits such as the olive and avocado. Oils that can be bought and poured from the bottle are always refined in the strict sense because they are separated from the whole food that was their source. This means that many of the nutrients essential to digesting the oil have been discarded. Liquid oils, therefore, should be used sparingly and with respect.

Saturated Fatty Acids

SaFAs are found in all food fats and oils, especially hard fats. The length of a SaFA chain determines its melting point and solidity. The longer the chain of a SaFA fatty acid, the greater the tendency will be for its molecules to stick together. This aggregation makes it harder and gives it a higher melting point, factors that enable it to be cooked or stored without as much destruction as the UFAs, but also can contribute to health problems in our heart and arteries when eaten to excess. People whose diets are high in the long-chain SaFAs found in beef, mutton, pork, and dairy products tend to develop sticky blood platelets, which readily form blood clots in the arteries. When Ancel Keys studied fat consumption and diet in Finland, the European country with the most coronary heart disease and the shortest life spans, he noted that meals often consisted of "great mounds of butter" and "glasses of rich milk" even among the adult population. He noted that Finnish loggers would smear a quarter of an inch of butter on huge slabs of cheese "and eat them with beer as an after-sauna snack."[6] While such an extreme excess of SaFA consumption may contribute to coronary heart disease, hardly any studies have actually found a significant association between these factors whereas many more have not.[7] The body also uses long-chain SaFAs to build cell membranes.

Short-chain SaFAs (up to 8 carbon atoms) are liquid at room temperature; medium-chain SaFAs (up to 10 carbon atoms) are liquid at body temperature; and long-chain SaFAs (above 10 carbon atoms) are solid at body temperature. Shorthand names for fatty acids designate the chain-length followed by a colon and then the number of double bonds. For example, the shorthand name for Butyric Acid, 4:0, shows that it is a short-chain, four carbon molecule with no double bonds making it a SaFA. Other common SaFAs and their shorthand names include: Butyric Acid (4:0), Caproic Acid (6:0), Caprylic Acid (8:0), Capric Acid (10:0), Lauric Acid (12:0), Myristic Acid (14:0), Palmitic Acid (16:0), Stearic Acid (18:0), Arachidic Acid (20:0), Behenic Acid (22:0), and Lignoceric Acid (24:0).

Being easy to digest, short-chain SaFAs, such as the caprylic acid found in Coconut oil, should be included in the diets of people suffering from liver and digestive ailments. Medium-chain SaFAs, such as those found in Coconut oil, are not stored as fat, but are used by the body to produce energy, a factor which makes them popular with athletes before workouts. Coconut oil is the safest oil to use in cooking and is the least vulnerable of all the dietary oils to destruction by oxidation and free-radical formation. Being a MCFA, Coconut oil does not promote the stickiness that leads to blood clot formation or raise blood cholesterol levels. One of the author's clients actually lowered their serum cholesterol by 60 points in only three months by eating Coconut oil with a whole foods diet.

Long-chain SaFAs are converted in the body from excess refined sugar. In order to prevent the glucose in excess sugar from spilling into the urine (as in diabetes), the pancreas moves the glucose into the cells by secreting insulin. If the amount of glucose in the cells is greater than that needed for energy, the extra glucose is converted into saturated fat, which then gets stored away in the cells, organs, and adipose tissues. These fatty acids can interfere with normal essential fatty-acid functions, and increase the cholesterol in our blood. For example, the mitochondria, which is used inside the cells to produce energy, breaks down the glucose into a type of vinegar (a simple SaFA) that can be used as a building block for cholesterol. **Sugar consumption in excess of what is needed for energy is converted into saturated fatty acids and cholesterol.**

Sugars and starches are often hidden in soft drinks as well as in many kinds of deserts such as canned fruits and juices; jams and jellies; cookies, cakes, and pies; candies and confections; ice creams and shakes; and Ketchup which contains a huge amount of sugar. When they form more than a small part of our diet, even the consumption of sweet fruits can lead to fat production. We then become obese like bears that stock up on fruit to build up their store of fat for the winter.

Unrefined, complex carbohydrates like whole grains do not provide the excess energy that turns into fat as refined carbohydrates and simple sugars do unless "we live sedentary lives without exercise, eat for social reasons when we're not hungry, or eat compulsively for psychological reasons."[8] Weight gain has more to do with refined sugar and refined starch consumption than with eating fat!

Figure 6: Long-Chain Saturated Fatty Acid Contents

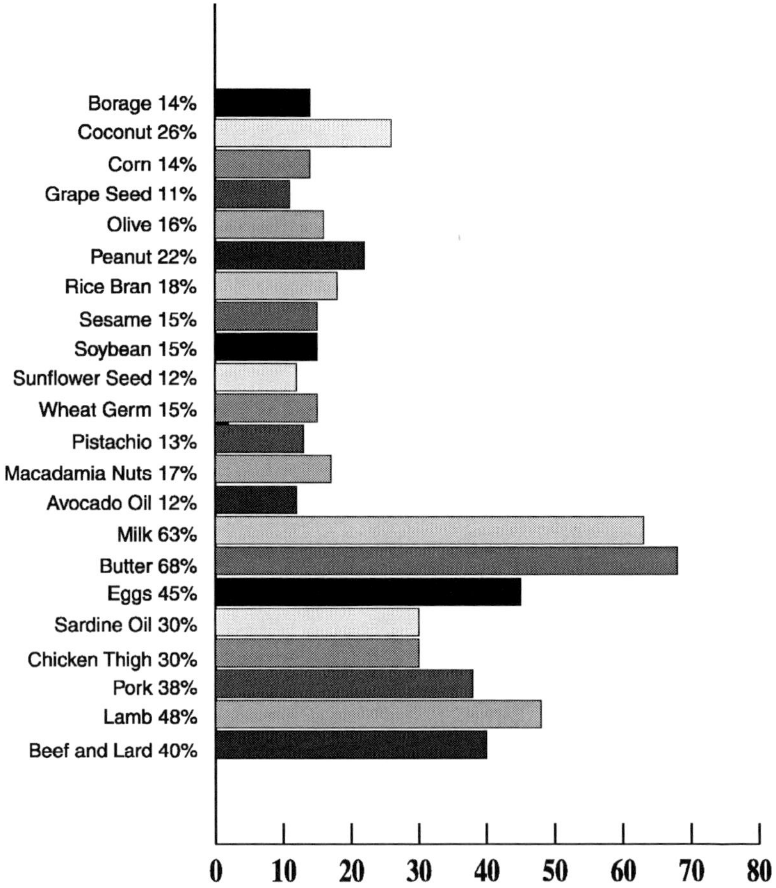

Item	%
Borage	14%
Coconut	26%
Corn	14%
Grape Seed	11%
Olive	16%
Peanut	22%
Rice Bran	18%
Sesame	15%
Soybean	15%
Sunflower Seed	12%
Wheat Germ	15%
Pistachio	13%
Macadamia Nuts	17%
Avocado Oil	12%
Milk	63%
Butter	68%
Eggs	45%
Sardine Oil	30%
Chicken Thigh	30%
Pork	38%
Lamb	48%
Beef and Lard	40%

0   10   20   30   40   50   60   70   80

Monounsaturated Fatty Acids

The dietary value of the monounsaturated fatty acids fluctuates according to fashion. They have risen from a neutral oblivion in the 1970s to a state of prominence in the 1980s, only to fall again to a state of questionable worth in the 1990s. Nevertheless, MUFAs are the mainstay of the Mediterranean Diet as well as fashionable weight-loss diets like the Hamptons Diet, which recommends using MUFAs almost exclusively with the exception of Omega 3 supplements.[9] Even the National Cholesterol Education Program and the AHA now recommends an 80 percent MUFA content in our diet.[10]

The reasons for these endorsements are because MUFAs are in between the SaFAs and PUFAs in terms of stability and function. They do not turn rancid as easily as the PUFAs when used in cooking. Even more importantly, they do not readily create oxidized LDL during their metabolism and so do not lead so easily to atherosclerosis, heart attack, or stroke.[11] In terms of stability and hardness, the MUFAs fall between the SaFAs and the PUFAs. The most important MUFA, oleic acid (OA), melts at 55°F, considerably below body temperature, and so helps keep our arteries supple. While oleic acid can be made from saturated fatty acids in the skin, it is also found in the membranes of plant and animal cell structures. Commercially, it can be obtained from plants and animals. The highest common plant sources of MUFAs are Macadamia oil (81 percent), Hazelnut oil (75 percent), Olive oil (72 percent), Canola oil (62 percent), Peanut oil (47 percent), Rice Bran oil (42 percent), Sesame oil (41 percent), and Pumpkinseed oil (36 percent).

While animal foods are all high in MUFAs, the highest common animal sources are beef (55 percent), pork (50 percent), and eggs (45 percent). While the MUFA, oleic acid, is thought to increase the incorporation of Omega 3s into the cell membrane and possibly decreasing the incidence of breast cancer,[12] excessive use of OA can, however, interfere with the conversion of the essential fatty acids to prostaglandins, which are important hormone-like substances in the body. Higher monounsaturated fat consumption has also been associated with an increased risk of breast cancer.[a]

Shorthand names for MUFAs include the position of their solitary double bond by the letter "w" (meaning "omega") followed by a number designating the position of the double bond on the molecular chain. Most MUFas are w9s because the double bond is nine carbons from the Omega (tail) end of the molecule. The shortest MUFA, Palmitoleic Acid, however, has its double bond seven carbons from the Omega end. Common MUFAs and their shorthand names include Palmitoleic Acid (16:1w7), Oleic Acid (18:1w9), Gadoleic Acid (20:1w9), and Erucic Acid (22:1).

---

[a] V. Pala and others. "Erythrocyte membrane fatty acids and subsequent breast cancer: a prospective Italian study." In *Journal of the National Cancer Institute* 93 (14):1088-95.

Figure 7: Monounsaturated Contents

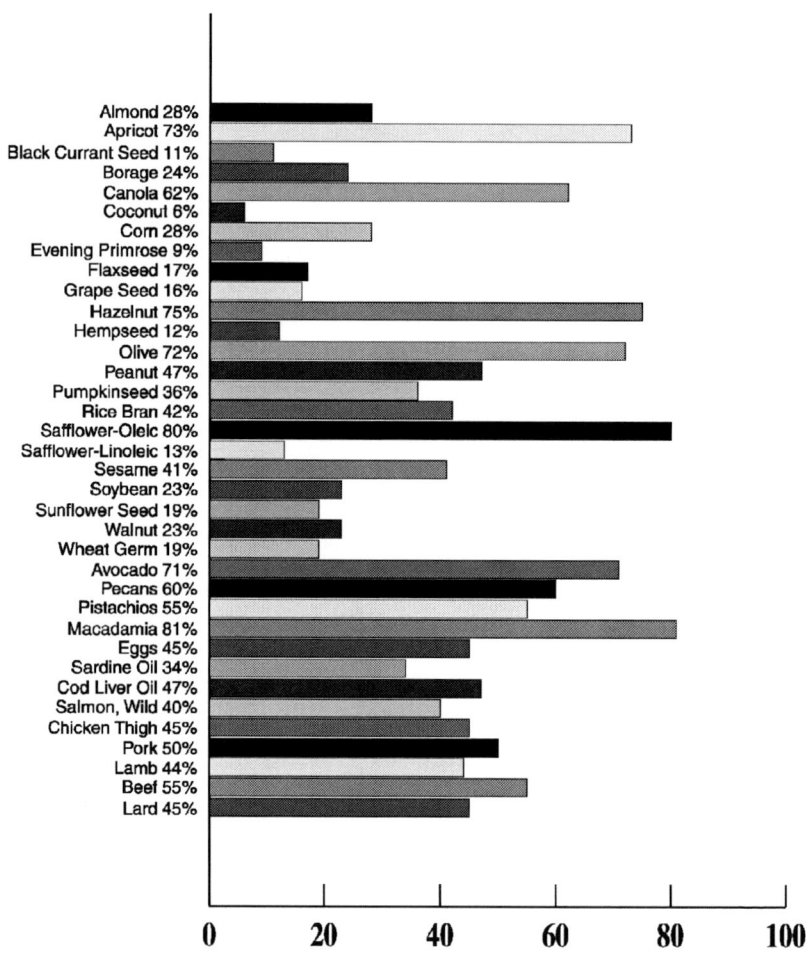

Unsaturated Fatty Acids

In general, PUFA consumption should outweigh SaFA consumption by a factor of at least two to one. The biggest problem with the polyunsaturates, other than their fragility, is that many of them now are completely unnatural and form the basis of many health problems, especially degenerative diseases such as coronary artery disease, diabetes, and cancer. What makes these oils so potentially dangerous is the industrial refining process used to extend shelf life and other non-health issues (margarine and shortening are examples), and the excessive use of heat in cooking. These health-destroying practices convert the natural fatty acids in polyunsaturates into harmful "conjugated" fatty acids[a] and *trans*-fatty acids. Up to 20 percent of the fatty acids of margarines and shortenings, for example, contain *trans*-PUFAs.

Like life and death, the synthetic *trans*-PUFAs are mirror images of the natural health-building EFAs. The EFAs create health and the *trans*-fatty acids create disease because the synthetic *trans*-fatty acids are only convenient substitutions made by the fat and oil industry for the real and essential natural product. Manufacturers are legally allowed to advertise *trans*-PUFAs as "high in polyunsaturates," an action which totally misleads the consumer who believes they are getting one thing (the health benefits of natural unrefined polyunsaturates) when, in fact, they are getting another (a leading contributor of degenerative disease). As of January 2006, manufacturers now have to state the content of *trans*-fats in their products on the label. However, there is a loophole in this law that enables them to state that there are no *trans*-fats in even the MOST *trans*-fat-containing products.[b]

Unrefined polyunsaturates are beneficial to health primarily because of the essential fatty acids they contain: the Omega 3s, alpha-linolenic acid (LNA), and the Omega 6s, linoleic acid (LA). Manufacturers also take advantage of this diversity in natural oils in promoting the health benefits of PUFAs as if the consumer was getting both kinds. In reality, LNA is generally not contained in commercially available polyunsaturated oils. To make this important distinction even more clear, the Omega 3s should be called super-unsaturated (SUFAs) to distinguish them from the Omega 6s. LA and LNA form the base from which all other natural PUFAs and SUFAs are produced in the body, including gamma-linolenic acid (GLA), arachidonic acid (AA), and docosapenetaenoic acid (DPA) from Omega 6; and stearidonic acid (SDA), eicosapentaenoic acid (EPA), and docosahexaenoic acid (DHA) from Omega 3.

---

[a] Conjugated fatty acids (CFAs) are unnatural, industrially made fatty acids formed when double bonds between the carbon atoms shrink from three to two atoms apart and thus the chemical properties of the fatty acid are greatly changed. While CFAs are found naturally in the meat and milk fat of cud-chewing animals, they are also made commercially through hydrogenation. They are not required for human health and are known to interfere with the conversion of Omega 6 essential fatty acids to prostaglandins. While they are currently being touted for their AO properties and ability to improve degenerative conditions, contradictory findings show a dose-related worsening of these conditions. This means that, to be effective, the dose has to be high enough to counteract the supposed benefit. While conjugated fatty acids do have AO activity, there are hundreds of more natural and safe AOs that are equally effective or better. In addition, the natural forms of CFAs are not very abundant. Butter, the richest natural source, does not contain enough CFAs to be either effective or harmful.

[b] See the section called "Hydrogenation and the *Trans*-Fatty Acids" in the "Oil Production" chapter below.

19

Essential Fatty Acids

Essential fatty acids were not known until the 1930s. Chemically, the distance from the methyl (tail) end of the fatty acid molecule, where the double bond is inserted, determines the difference between the Omega 3s and Omega 6s. Omega 3s insert their double bond three carbons from the methyl, or tail (Omega), end and Omega 6s insert theirs six.

Figure 8: Double Bonds in Bent Fatty Acid Chains

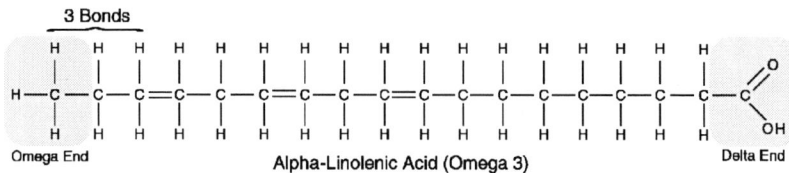

Alpha-Linolenic Acid (Omega 3)

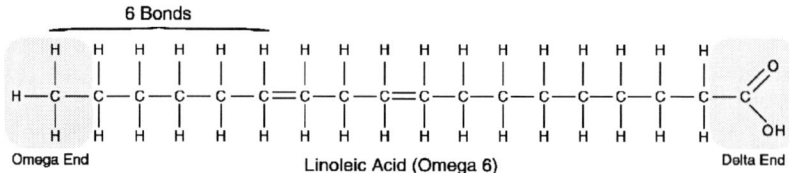

Linoleic Acid (Omega 6)

Plants are able to produce essential fatty acids, but not humans. Because we are not able to make these ourselves but have to rely upon food to get them, and because they are so important for health (they are the derivatives of the hormone-like prostaglandins), they are called "essential fatty acids." The position of the double bond from the methyl end in chemistry, called the omega position, is used to name these two essential fatty acids—the Omega 3s (w3s) and Omega 6s (w6s). The shorthand names for the Omega 6s and their derivatives include: Linoleic Acid (18:2w6) followed by Gamma-linolenic Acid, or GLA (18:3w6), and Arachidonic Acid, or AA (20:4w6). Linoleic Acid is the parent FA of this group and is normally converted in the body into the two SUFAs GLA and AA through enzyme activity. Shorthand names for the Omega 3s and their derivatives include: Alpha-linolenic Acid, or ALA (18:3w3) followed by its derivatives Stearidonic Acid, SDA (18:4w3); Eicosopentaenoic Acid, EPA (20:5w3); Docosapentaenoic Acid, DPA (22:5w3); and Docosahexaenoic Acid, DHA (22:6w3). The Omega 3s are also converted to their derivatives through enzymatic action. Flaxseed oil (14 percent LA and 60 percent LNA) and Hempseed oil (55 percent LA, 20 percent LNA, and 2 percent GLA) are nutritionally unique in that they contain both of these Omega 3 and Omega 6 EFAs.

EFAs function to:

1) Generate electrical potentials
2) Attract and transfer oxygen
3) Regulate genetic expression
4) Strengthen immunity
5) Prevent allergies
6) Stimulate growth
7) Transport cholesterol (LNA)
8) Lower elevated triglycerides up to 56 percent (LNA)
9) Produce hemoglobin (LA)
10) Help fatigued muscles to recover from exercise

EFAs function to generate electrical potentials across membranes, a phenomenon that enables them to transmit messages along the cell membranes to other cells. These measurable bioelectric currents resemble the Qi of acupuncture and are important in nerve and heart functions as well as growth, vitality, and mood. Both LA and LNA transfer oxygen across the alveolar membranes in the lung and into the blood plasma and the red blood cells to the hemoglobin so that all the cells, as well as the energy-producing mitochondria within the cells, can be oxygenated. This ability of LA and LNA to hold oxygen also serves as a barrier to foreign organisms such as viruses, fungi, yeasts, and bacteria, which cannot thrive in its presence. Yin and Yang deficiency symptoms for LA and LNA are listed below.

Deficiency Symptoms Of LNA and LA

	Omega 3 (More Yang)	Omega 6 (More Yin)
Similarities	Growth retardation	Growth retardation
	Behavioral changes	Behavioral disturbances Learning impairment Mental deterioration
	Dry skin	Eczema
	Heart and circulatory problems	High blood pressure, high triglycerides , sticky platelets
	Susceptibility to infections, failure of wound healing, arthritis-like conditions	Immune dysfunction
	Sterility in males, and miscarriage in females	Weakness, low metabolic rate

	Omega 3 (More Yang)	Omega 6 (More Yin)
Differences	Excessive water loss through the skin accompanied by thirst, drying up of glands, loss of hair	Tissue inflammation, edema
	Liver and kidney degeneration	Motor in-coordination, tingling sensation in arms and legs, impairment of vision

Omega 3s

FAs that contain three or more double bonds are called super-unsaturated. These include the Omega 3 LNAs. Some are beneficial while some are synthetic toxins. LNA is five times more fragile than LA and needs to be very carefully protected against the destructive actions of light, heat, and oxygen. The function of LNA is to:

1) Increase stamina and vitality
2) Speed healing
3) Enhance immune functions
4) Treat bacterial infections, including staph and malaria
5) Produce smooth and velvety skin
6) Instill a feeling of calmness
7) Reduce arthritic pain
8) Reduce inflammation, water retention, platelet stickiness, and blood pressure
9) Inhibit tumor growth
10) Reverse premenstrual syndrome
11) Lower blood triglycerides

Since permanent learning disabilities can occur with LNA deficiency during fetal development and early infancy, LNA can also be said to nourish the *Hun*, which, according to acupuncture theory, is the spirit of the Liver[a] and is responsible for the development of rational perspective. In its polar Yin-Yang relationship to the *Po*, the spirit of the Lung, the *Hun* incarnates into the body during the first one hundred days of infancy. In contrast, the *Po* is responsible for physical instinct and incarnates into the body during the period from conception to birth. Together the *Hun* and *Po* comprise important Yin-Yang aspects of one's True Nature, that is, the Spirit-Essence, or *Jingshen*, which splits apart at birth into its Water (*Jing*-Essence)[b] and Fire (*Shen*-Spirit) aspects. The *Hun* supports the Fire-related *Shen*-Spirit while the *Po* supports the Water-related *Jing*-Essence. Disturbances of the *Hun* include many psycho-emotional disorders having to do with the expression or inhibition of the self; especially those associated with anger, psycho-emotional tension, and denial and are related to mania, depression, and bipolar states. These are exactly the same mental conditions related to the deficiency of Omega 3s. While Flaxseed oil is the richest source of LNA (50-65 percent), LNA can also be found in Hempseed oil (20-60 percent), Pumpkin Seed oil (as much as 15 percent or as little as none), Soybean oil (1 percent), Walnut oil (between 3 and 7 percent), perilla, micro-

---

[a] The capitalized use of the word "Liver" refers to all of the functions of the liver according to acupuncture theory as opposed to the more limited functions of the physiological organ.
[b] *Jing*-Essence is synonymous with the Reserve Qi.

algae[a] and cereal grasses, and dark green leaves (50 percent of the small amount of oil they contain).

The main derivatives of LNA are stearidonic acid (SDA), eicosapentaenoic acid (EPA), and docosahexaenoic acid (DHA), which are used by the body to produce the Prostaglandin 3s, which, in turn, are responsible for many positive health benefits. SDA is found separately in Black Currant Seed oil, while EPA and DHA are found separately in the oils of cold-water fish and marine animals like krill.

The optimum daily requirement of LNA is between 1 and 2 teaspoons of oil per day. The proportion between LNA and LA should be one measures of LNA to every two of LA. In healthy individuals ground flaxseed can be used in place of the oil in the proportion of three tablespoons of flaxseed to every tablespoon of Flaxseed oil—a proportion of three to one.[b]

Figure 9: Linolenic Acid Contents

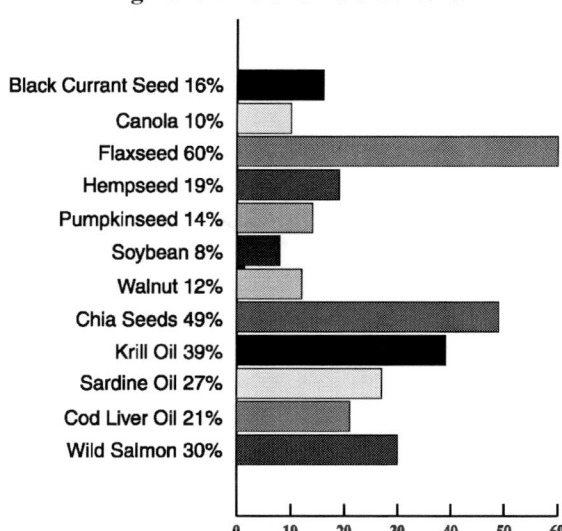

Omega 6s

The Omega 6 LAs are called unsaturated simply because they contain two double bonds. They are what are usually referred to as "polyunsaturated" and form this group's most common part. Like the Omega 3 LNAs, the LAs

---

[a] Twenty percent of the fatty acids found in chlorella are comprised of Omega 3s. Blue-green algae is another source of Omega 3. It contains a high Omega 3 ratio of 4:1, but only 1/3 to 1/6 the recommended daily requirement of 8 grams per fifty pounds of body weight for adults.
[b] According to Erasmus [p. 281], 1 tablespoon of flaxseed equals 1 teaspoon of Flaxseed oil. Since 3 teaspoons equal 1 tablespoon, 1 tablespoon of Flaxseed oil will be the equivalent of 3 tablespoons of flaxseed.

also have natural as well as non-natural, man-made representations that interfere with biological functions.

With the exception of new genetically modified "high oleic" varieties, the richest sources of LA are found in Grape Seed oil (72 percent), Sunflower Seed oil (68 percent), Walnut oil (68 percent), Wheat Germ oil (60 percent), Flaxseed oil (60 percent), Hempseed oil (59 percent), Corn oil (57 percent), Soybean oil (53 percent), and Sesame Seed oil (43 percent). Other common sources include Peanut oil and Pumpkinseed oil. While the daily requirement of LA is higher than any of the forty-five other known essential nutrients, it varies with each person according to their physical activity, stress, nutritional background, and individual differences. An optimum amount might be one tablespoon per day, but males tend to need more than females and obese people may require even more. The more saturated fat and Olive oil one consumes, the more LA one needs. LA also lowers cholesterol.

The main derivatives of LA are arachidonic acid (AA), found separately in animal products, especially pork, eggs, and dairy products; gamma-linolenic acid (GLA), which is found separately in Hempseed oil, Evening Primrose oil (9 percent), Borage oil (20 percent+), and Black Currant Seed oil (15 percent) as well as micro-algae [a] and cereal grasses; and docosapentaenoic acid (DPA), found separately Krill oil as well as in the oils of cold-water fish and marine animals. The body makes the Prostaglandin 2s from AA, which are important for disease functions as well as stress-related survival conditions.

The optimum ratio of w3s to w6s should favor the Omega 3s by a factor of about 1:2, the ratio found among the Japanese.[13] However, because w3 has decreased since the 1850's by one-sixth while w6 consumption has doubled, most people need to make up the difference by taking more of the w3s on a daily basis for six months until the deficiency is corrected. Therefore, the optimum ratio should be reversed (2:1) during this period. At that point, the w3s should be re-combined with w6s in the optimal 1:2 w3:w6 ratio so as to avoid a rebound w6 deficiency.

---

[a] Spirolina is one of the richest sources.

Figure 10: Linoleic Acid Contents

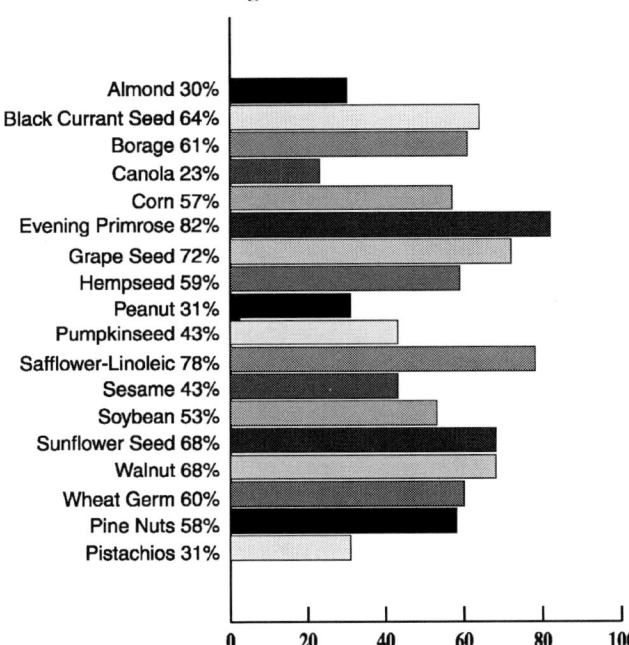

Almond 30%
Black Currant Seed 64%
Borage 61%
Canola 23%
Corn 57%
Evening Primrose 82%
Grape Seed 72%
Hempseed 59%
Peanut 31%
Pumpkinseed 43%
Safflower-Linoleic 78%
Sesame 43%
Soybean 53%
Sunflower Seed 68%
Walnut 68%
Wheat Germ 60%
Pine Nuts 58%
Pistachios 31%

0   20   40   60   80   100

Prostaglandins

Prostaglandins, also known as eicosanoids or leukotrienes, are special hormone-like substances made from essential fatty acids, their precursors, through precision enzyme-controlled reactions, which are in contrast to the random oxidation of oils that produce rancid oils instead. The functions of prostaglandins are to maintain homeostasis in the body. Prostaglandins

1) Allow substances to move in and out of the cells
2) Regulate muscle tone, blood pressure, tension in the coronary arteries, and platelet stickiness

There are three important classes of prostaglandins: Prostaglandin 1 (PGE_1) and Prostaglandin 2 (PGE_2), which are made from LA, and Prostaglandin 3 (PGE_3), which is made from LNA.

PGE_1 helps prevent heart attacks and strokes caused by blood clots in the arteries by keeping the blood platelets from sticking together, thus relaxing the blood vessels, improving circulation, lowering blood pressure, relieving angina, and even potentially slowing down cholesterol production. PGE_1 also produces a sense of well-being by improving nerve function; stimulating the kidneys to remove sodium and excess fluid from the body while regulating calcium metabolism; making insulin work more effectively; helping control arthritis by decreasing the inflammation response; and destroying invading organisms by improving the function of T-cells in the immune system. Finally, PGE_1 prevents the release of arachidonic acid (AA) from the cell membranes.

PGE_2 functions in polar opposition to PGE_1 and is made from AA. PGE_2 initiates clot formation by promoting platelet aggregation and also leads to water retention and high blood pressure by inducing the kidney to retain salt. PGE_1 relaxes the body for civilized, sedentary living, while PGE_2 tightens it up for the fight or flight conditions of jungle survival. The sequence in which PGE_1 and PGE_2 are made from LA is as follows: LA produces gamma-linolenic acid (GLA), which produces dihomo-gammalinolenic acid (DGLA). In turn, DGLA produces not only PGE_1 but also arachidonic acid (AA), which then goes on to produce Docosapentaenoic Acid (DPA) and PGE_2.

Figure 11: Prostaglandin Sequence From LA

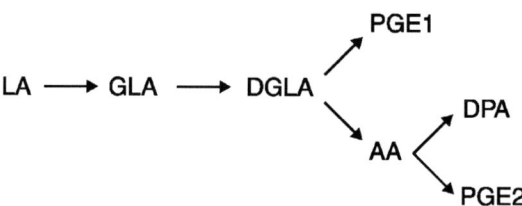

The body converts DGLA slowly to AA in order to protect against the constricting effects of PGE_2. However, animal products contribute to this constriction and the cardiovascular, inflammatory, and kidney diseases that can result when this tendency goes to the extreme because they also contain AA. Therefore, reducing animal food consumption is important in lowering high blood pressure.

PGE_3 is made from LNA, which produces stearidonic acid (SDA), which produces eicosatetraenoic acid, which produces eicosapentaenoic acid (EPA). EPA then goes on to produce PGE_3 as well as docosahexaenoic acid (DHA).

Figure 12: Prostaglandin Sequence From LNA

PGE_3 is important because the EPA it is derived from controls the constricting effects of PGE_2. EPA prevents AA from being released so that the PGE_2s are not made. Krill oil and Fish oil, which contain EPA separately, help prevent degenerative cardiovascular disease, water retention, and inflammation because they bypass the steps where LNA is converted to EPA and, therefore, directly inhibit the production of AA and its offshoot, PGE_2. Dark green vegetables, such as kale, collards, wheat- and barley-grass products, seaweeds, and micro algae, also inhibit the production of PGE_2s. This shortcut is necessary when the enzymes[a] needed to convert EPA from LNA are absent. In the same way, GLA supplements bypass the initial stages of LA conversion and go directly to the production of PGE_1.

Many factors exist, however, that block the conversion of GLA from LA and SDA from LNA including:

1) Saturated Fatty Acids
2) Cholesterol
3) *Trans*-fatty acids
4) Moderate to large amounts of alcohol
5) Lack of insulin
6) Viral infections
7) Non-steroidal and steroidal anti-inflammatory drugs
8) Radiation
9) Cancer
10) Zinc deficiency

About 20 percent of the population cannot convert Omega 6 into GLA effectively, hence the rest of the steps in this chain are never completed and the all-important PGE_1 is never produced. These people, therefore, MUST supplement GLA through diet. Evening Primrose oil (EPO) is a good way to obtain this GLA, which is ten times more effective than linoleic acid in producing PGE_1. Borage oil is also good and contains 2½ times more GLA than EPO. The only type of linoleic acid that can make this conversion is what is known as *cis*-linoleic acid, the natural oil in its unadulterated state. The 72 percent Omega 6 (linoleic acid) found in EPO is just this type of *cis*-linoleic acid and is in stark contrast to the processed and hydrogenated forms, which, in the body, turn into biologically inactive *trans*-fatty acids, where they behave as if they were saturated fats and produce EFA deficiency states in a wide variety of tissues, including the brain, heart, and lungs. Some of these deficiency states lead to:

1) Faulty immune function
2) Poor skin
3) Wounds not healing properly
4) Inflammatory disorders and arthritis
5) Failure of normal brain development
6) Dried up tear glands and salivary glands
7) Abnormality of the heart and circulation
8) Failure to reproduce, especially in males

---

[a] Enzymes are protein molecules that catalyze chemical reactions in the cells, which would otherwise not occur at the typical low inter-cellular temperatures and pressures.

Prostaglandins regulate every cell and organ in the body moment by moment including the activity of certain key enzymes on the local level as opposed to the over-all level as hormones do. There are at least thirty different kinds of prostaglandins. PGE_1 and PGE_3 are beneficial, while many others are detrimental and often involved in the inflammatory process. PGE_1 dilates blood vessels and lowers arterial pressure so as to inhibit thrombosis and platelet aggregation; inhibits cholesterol synthesis; inhibits inflammation in arthritis; activates T-lymphocytes; prevents liver damage and withdrawal symptoms in alcohol-addiction; and inhibits abnormal cell proliferation.

Yin-Yang Fatty Acid Perspective

To understand the relationship between the three triglycerides (saturated, monounsaturated, and polyunsaturated fatty acids) more comprehensively, we can arrange them according to Yin and Yang. The SaFAs are the most Yin because they are more dense and hard and contribute more to structural formation in the body. PUFAs are the most Yang because they are more expanded and soft and contribute more to the functional processes in the body. In between these two polar extremes are the MUFAs, which share properties of both Yin and Yang, structure and function, and tend to create balance and stability between them

Figure 13: Yin-Yang and the Triglycerides

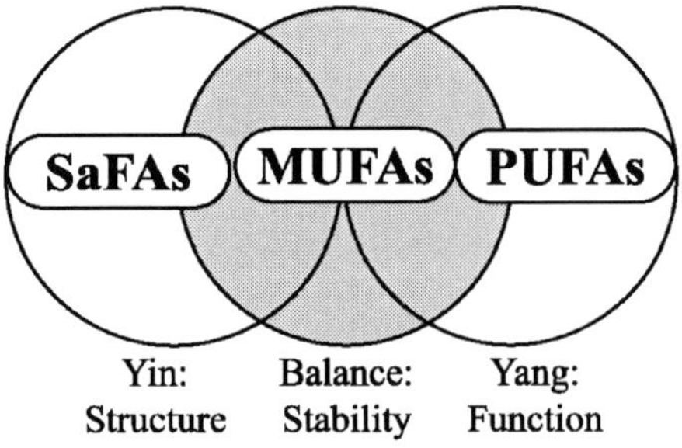

| Yin: | Balance: | Yang: |
| Structure | Stability | Function |

SaFAs

SaFAs represent one of the two most condensed varieties of energy stored from sunlight in all life forms. Sugar, the simplest form of this energy, is converted into SaFAs for storage when the amount contained in the body is more than what is required for immediate energy. This stored energy is contained within SaFAs for later use in times of need. In plants, both simple sugars and complex sugars in the form of carbohydrates are converted into SaFAs as well as cellulose, the second most condensed form of stored energy. Of these two forms, cellulose is the most extreme Yin form of the plant and manifests through its hard and woody structure.

SaFAs are also needed to strengthen tissues in the human body, especially the peripheral tissues (including the skin, membranes, and blood vessels). When overly used, however, SaFAs build up in the body as fat deposits that block organic function. In excess, SaFAs make the body too Yin. Nevertheless, because of their importance in the development of structure, especially peripheral tissue structure in animals, SaFAs are found in ALL fats and oils.

Ironically, SaFAs are most prominent in animal tissues. Animal tissues are characterized by activity in contrast to the inactivity of plants. Therefore, animals are more Yang and plants are more Yin. Since animals move around, they need to carry their condensed energy packages with them wherever they go in the stabilized form of the Yin SaFAs. In contrast, plants do not move around and need to contain their more Yang and active polyunsaturated energy packages with cellulose. Cellulose is even more Yin than SaFAs.

Animal sources of long-chain SaFAs (LCSaFAs) range between 14 percent for farmed Salmon at the lowest to 48 percent for lamb at the highest with an average long-chain SaFA content of 30.66 percent, more than twice the average amount found in plant sources. Plant sources of LCSaFAs range between 5 percent for Canola oil at the lowest to 22 percent for Peanut oil and 29 percent for Chia Seeds at the highest with an average of 12.3 percent. Peanuts and Chia Seeds contain almost as much SaFAs as the average animal source. The reason has to do with their energetic signature. Peanuts are underground legumes that use SaFAs for structure and protection against the pressure of their underground environment. In contrast, Chia Seeds grow in the Yang arid and hot desert and need the extra SaFAs to guard against dehydration and to protect the large amounts of EFAs they also carry. Most other high vegetable sources of LCSaFAs contain less than 10 percent.

Figure 14: Average SaFA Content in Plants, Fish, and Animal Sources

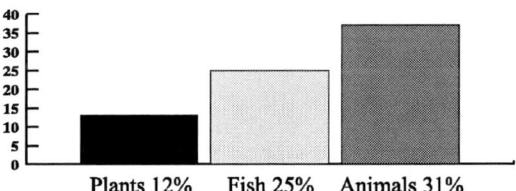

Plants 12%   Fish 25%   Animals 31%

29

Figure 15: High and Low SaFA Content of Plant Sources

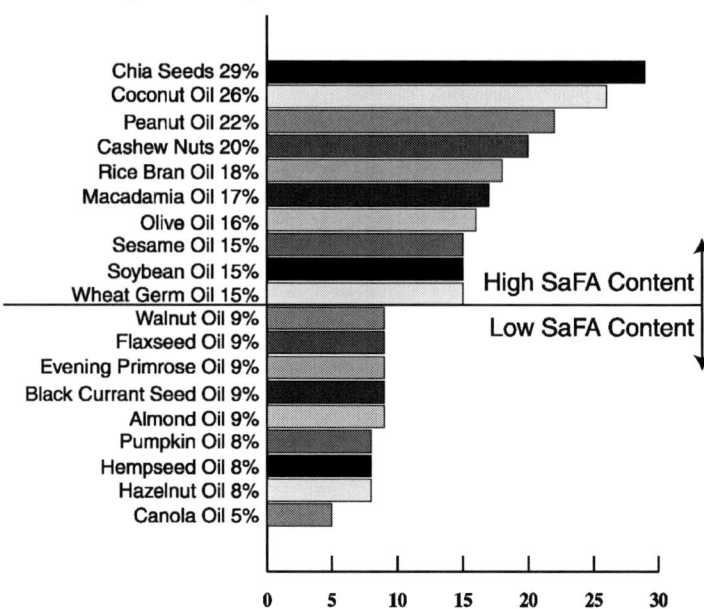

PUFAs

In polar Yin-Yang contrast to the SaFAs are the Yang PUFAs. Because plants are able to convert most of their carbohydrates and sugars into cellulose, they only need to create a relatively small percentage of SaFAs for structural purposes while reserving the most dominant role of their FAs for the functional-based PUFAs. Plants do not move around like animals do, so they need more PUFAs, which can satisfy their functional needs. Plant sources of PUFAs range between 2% for Coconut oil and Macadamia oil at the lowest to 80% for Walnut oil at the highest with an average of 47%, more than three times the amount found in animal sources. Fish oils, at an average of 41%, are somewhere in between, but much closer to the plant sources.

Figure 16: Average PUFA Content in Plants, Fish, and Animal Sources

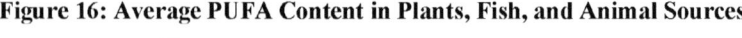
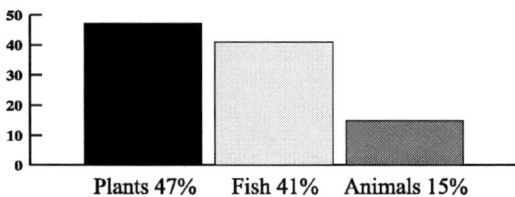

Figure 17: High and Low PUFA Content of Plant Sources

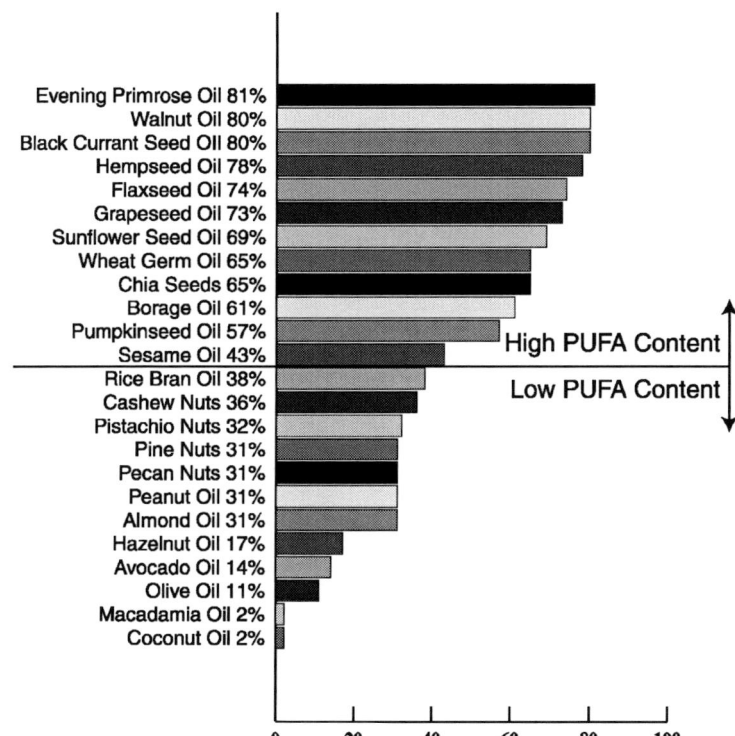

MUFAs

Plant sources of MUFAs range between 6% for Coconut oil and Chia Seeds at the lowest to 81% for Macadamia oil at the highest. Most of the highest plant sources of MUFAs are obtained from the fruits and nuts of trees because trees are the hardest and most Yin expressions of the plant realm. Exceptions to this rule include Canola oil and Peanut oil. Canola oil has been genetically modified from Rapeseed oil to change its FA content. Peanut oil is the only source of edible oils that grow underground. Because peanuts grow underground, they exhibit less of the Yang characteristics of other oils and therefore contain only a moderate amount of PUFAs and no Omega 3s (the most Yang of the PUFAs). The fact that they grow underground also means that, while they also contain one of the highest SaFA contents of the vegetable sources (in reflecting their Yin underground habitat), they need less of the structure-providing Yin of the SaFAs and more MUFAs (more than twice as much) for the balance needed in their underground habitat. All in all, these needs give Peanut oil the most equally balanced triglyceride range, which is the most equally balanced of all sources (PUFA 31%, MUFA 47%, and SaFA 22%).

Dietary Fats and Oils

Among vegetable sources of MUFAs, Sesame Oil (at 43% PUFA and 41% MUFA) and Rice Bran Oil (at 38% PUFA and 42% MUFA) have almost identical proportions of PUFAs and MUFAs. This feature perhaps accounts for their exceptional polyunsaturated stability. Some fish oils also display this balanced PUFA/MUFA characteristic, especially Sardine Oil (31% PUFA and 34% MUFA) and Wild Salmon (30% PUFA and 36% MUFA).

Figure 18: High and Low MUFA Content of Plant Sources

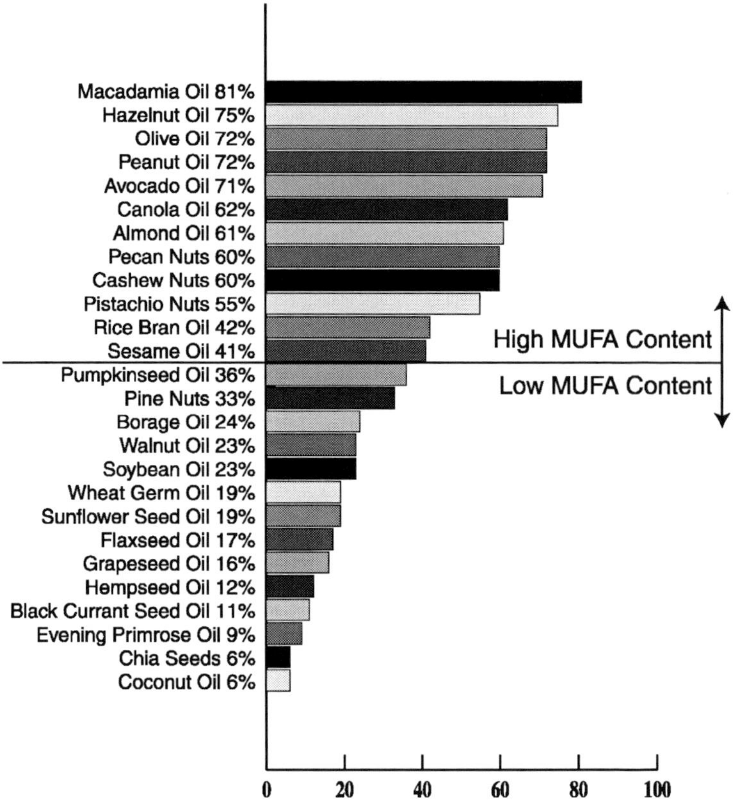

Figure 19: High and Low MUFA Content of Fish Sources

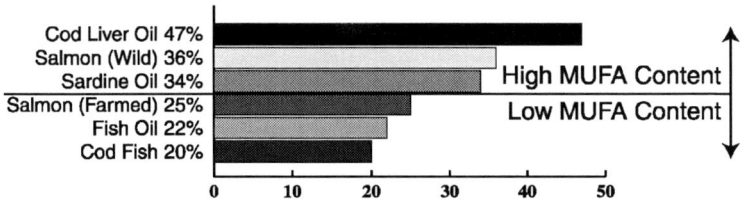

Figure 20: High and Low MUFA Content of Animal Sources

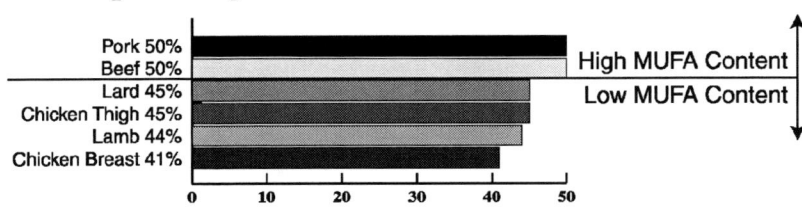

The chart below demonstrates that the moderate MUFA percentages of plant, fish, and animal sources are all relatively equal. Animals contain slightly more MUFAs than plants and fish because they need more balance in going back and forth between their structural and functional polarities.

Figure 21: Average MUFA Content in Plants, Fish, and Animal Sources

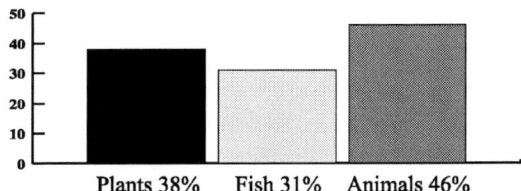

Plants and fish display a similar range of triglyceride proportion. They both need less SaFAs for structure than animals, slightly less MUFAs for balance and stability, and much more of the dynamic PUFAs to help them function to overcome their relatively less dynamic environments. Animal fat, in contrast, needs less of the dynamic PUFAs and more of the stabilizing and consolidating properties of the MUFAs and SaFAs because the movement and activity of the animals needs to be grounded.

Figure 22: Triglyceride Percentages in FA Sources

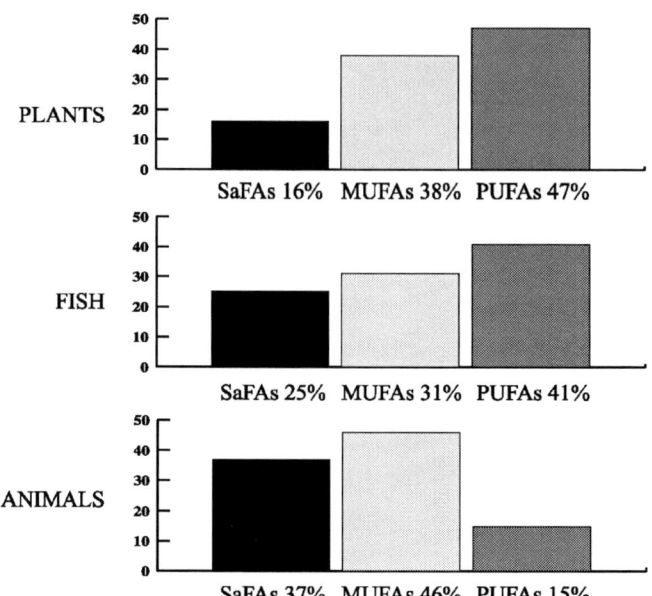

PLANTS

SaFAs 16%   MUFAs 38%   PUFAs 47%

FISH

SaFAs 25%   MUFAs 31%   PUFAs 41%

ANIMALS

SaFAs 37%   MUFAs 46%   PUFAs 15%

Complex Yin and Yang Fatty Acid Dynamics

Everything can be classified according to Yin and Yang. Among the triglycerides, the SaFAs are Yin, the PUFAs are Yang, and the MUFAs are in between and share the Yin and Yang characteristics of both Yin and Yang extremes. Another concept that explains a deeper relationship between things according to Yin and Yang principles describes not the balanced and stable aspects of Yin and Yang but the more dynamic aspects where, at their extremes, Yin and Yang change into their opposites. Here, Yin changes to Yang and Yang changes to Yin in the same way that night turns to day and day turns to night.

In terms of the three triglycerides, this dynamic interpretation of Yin and Yang defines further Yin-Yang variations of each of the two polarized triglycerides, the Yin SaFAs and the Yang PUFAs. Therefore, we can find Yin within Yang and Yang within Yang aspects of the PUFAs and Yang within Yin and Yin within Yin aspects of the SaFAs.

Within the SaFAs, these two polarities are determined by chain-length, which in turn determines the function of the SaFA. Long-chain (LC) SaFAs are Yin within Yin because they are the hardest and most dense triglycerides. In contrast, the medium-chain (MC) SaFAs (like Coconut oil) are Yang within Yin because they do not contribute to structure but to function instead, a rare phenomenon among the SaFAs. Medium-chain SaFAs are defined by having 6 to 12 carbon atoms in their chain. They are basically fat-soluble, but the longer the chain-length becomes, the less water-soluble and more Yin they become. In contrast, when the chain-length gets shorter (under 6 carbons) the molecule gets more Yang and can easily be dissolved in water. We can see this property in the common 2-carbon SaFA, vinegar. We use this water-soluble (Yang) property of vinegar to help digest (that is, make more Yang) the fats and oils we use in salad dressings where the most Yang SaFA (vinegar) helps to dissolve and digest more complex Yin oils.

The PUFAs also have these dynamic Yin-Yang characteristics. The Omega 3 (w3) EFAs are Yang within Yang as they exhibit the most functional and expanding characteristics, especially in regard to the prostaglandin derivative they create—PGE_3. In contrast, the Omega 6 (w6) EFAs are Yin within Yang, especially in regard to some of the derivatives they create—AA and PGE_2 in particular, which create constriction, clotting, water retention, and platelet aggregation.

Table 1: Yin and Yang Within the Triglycerides

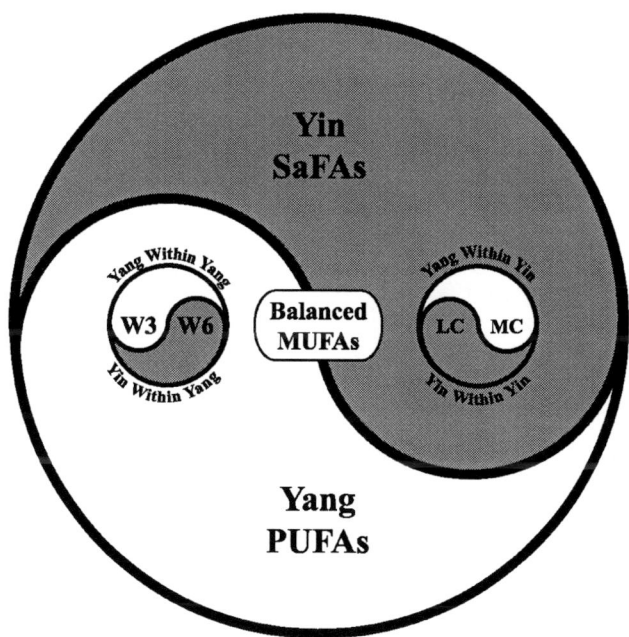

35

Fats and Oils in Chinese Medicine

Yin-Yang

Another way of looking at how lipids regulate body function is according to Yin-Yang polarity in Chinese Medicine. According to this perspective, fats and oils help to regulate the Liver, which in acupuncture theory also regulates the flow of Qi between polar extremes. The Liver corresponds to the spring season, which governs the balanced expansion of an organism into its surrounding environment. A young plant, for example, must hurry to develop its stem, leaves, and flowers in the spring so as to maximize its potential of bearing seeds during the short summer season, especially in polar and temperate regions. At the same time, the plant must not expand too fast without risking death from sudden cold or frost. In acupuncture, the Liver organ, the spring season, and the Wood Phase of the Five Phases[a] governs/symbolizes this type of external growth. Lipids feed the Liver with nutrients having the same capacity to expand or contract and, thus, form an important physiological basis for these Liver functions.

Examples include the polar, Yin-Yang, complimentary/antagonism between saturated and unsaturated fatty acids; between long and short-chain fatty acids; between the water and fat soluble ends of fatty acid chains; between the LDL transporting cholesterol centrifugally to the skin, body cells and their membranes and the HDL returning this cholesterol centripetally to the liver; between the prostaglandins, especially between PGE_1 and PGE_2 but also between PGE_3 and PGE_2; between the Omega 3 and 6 fatty acids; and between the essential fatty acid group as a whole and the saturated fatty acids.

---

[a] The Five Phases represent five different aspects of Yin-Yang polarity. The Winter season represents Maximum Yin and correlates with the Water Phase; the Summer season represents Maximum Yang and correlates with the Fire Phase; the Spring season represents Growing Yang and correlates to the Wood Phase; the Fall season represents Growing Yin and correlates to the Metal Phase; and the two solstices and two equinoxes represent Balanced Yin and Yang and correlate to the Soil Phase.

Table 2: Yin-Yang of Lipids

Expansive: Yang	Contractive: Yin
Relaxes & Softens	Tenses & Hardens
Provides Energy	Builds Structure
Unsaturated	Saturated
Fat Soluble End	Water Soluble End
Short-chain Fatty Acids	Long-chain Fatty Acids
LDL[a]	HDL
PGE_1	PGE_2
PGE_3	PGE_2
Omega 3s	Omega 6s
EFAs	SaFAs

SaFAs, especially long-chain SaFAs, tend to aggregate together to form stability and firmness. At the extreme of this Yin-Yang polarization, SaFAs create clumps that clog the flow of Qi, Blood, and Fluids in the body, including the arteries, organs, and interstitial spaces. In contrast, unsaturated fatty acids tend to disperse. SaFAs help to balance UFAs by keeping them separate in the membranes so they do not form undesirable chemical reactions with one another. What causes this difference between these two fatty acids is the presence of the double bond in the UFA, which kinks the molecule into the *cis*-configuration so that it becomes more difficult to align, less prone to aggregate, and more apt to become liquid (melt) at lower temperatures than SaFAs. The tendency for UFAs to disperse makes them move apart and spread out over surfaces where they help provide the fluidity needed in cell membranes, make and break bonds with one another, and transport materials in and out of the cells.

---

[a] While LDL is Yang because of its centrifugal nature, the cholesterol it attracts makes the exterior of the body parts (skin and extremities) rigid (Yin). In contrast, the HDL (Yin) brings the cholesterol back to the liver (Yin) along with Vitamin D, which makes the bones firm.

Figure 23: Molecular Space Differences in Fatty Acids

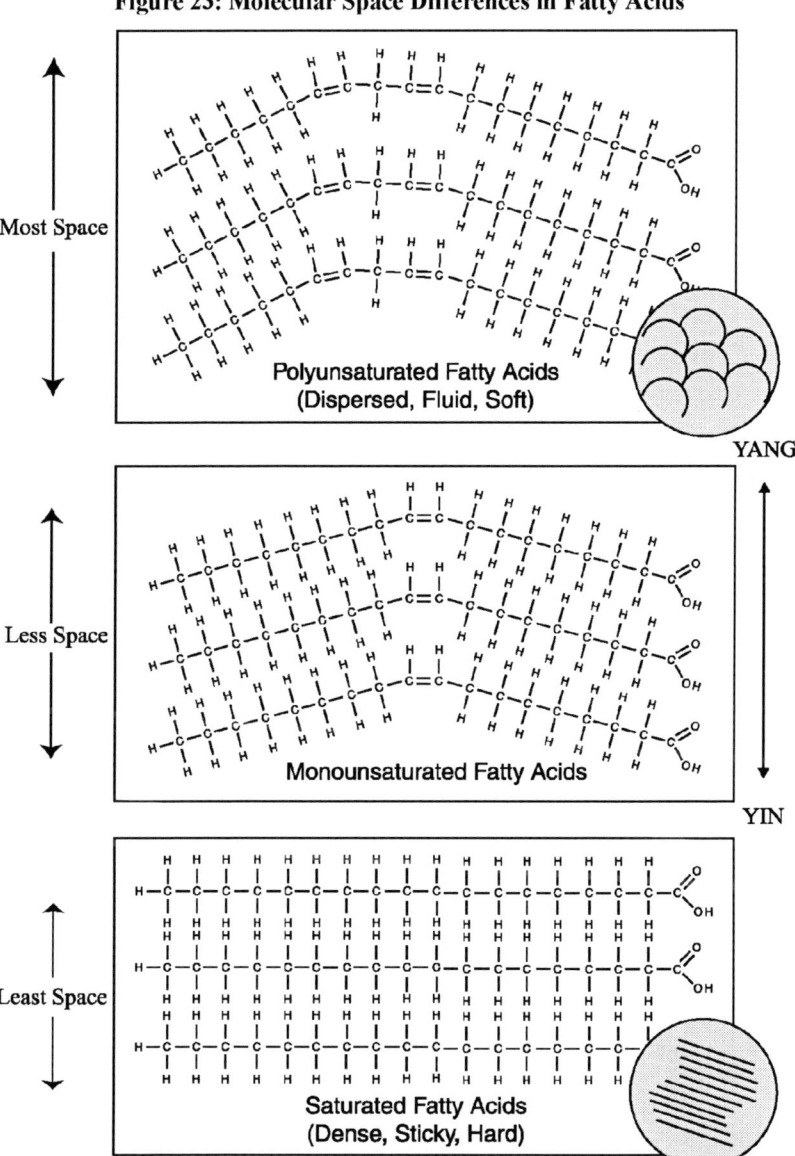

Most Space

Polyunsaturated Fatty Acids
(Dispersed, Fluid, Soft)

YANG

Less Space

Monounsaturated Fatty Acids

YIN

Least Space

Saturated Fatty Acids
(Dense, Sticky, Hard)

The Yin-Yang structure of lipoproteins, which are water-soluble on the exterior and fat-soluble at the interior, enable them to carry fat, cholesterol, and other fat-soluble molecules, like the fat-soluble vitamins, through the bloodstream to different areas of the body according to the place and time they are needed.

Cholesterol itself is a hard, waxy material used to provide structure to the skin for wound healing, rigidity, and shape to the membranes, as well as the manufacture of different hormones and Vitamin D from the skin. Cholesterol is transported from the liver via LDL to the skin and the cell membranes when they need more structure depending on how many unsaturated phospholipids are available. The more the unsaturated phospholipids there are, the more cholesterol must be transported to the membrane to provide structure. Cholesterol and phospholipids work together to provide just the right amount of stiffness or flexibility to the membranes.

When cholesterol is carried back to the liver via HDL, it carries precursors of Vitamin D with it before being sent on to the kidneys where the Vitamin D finally plays an active role in regulating the metabolism and absorption of calcium. Stress causes more cholesterol to be placed into the bloodstream from the liver because the adrenal hormones created in response to stress are made from cholesterol. In acupuncture, the kidneys and adrenals form Yin-Yang aspects of the same Kidney organ. The Kidney organ is the one where the brunt of "fright or flight" stress is placed and is most vulnerable to coffee consumption because coffee "robs the Kidney to feed the Heart." This aphorism means two things: (1) coffee robs the Reserve Qi stored in the Kidneys so that one will be more awake and communicative (aspects of the Heart in acupuncture theory), and (2) cholesterol is robbed from the Kidney process of storing reserves and making bones strong (both functions of Vitamin D). The misplaced cholesterol that should be carrying the Vitamin D to the kidneys and bones is transported to the heart and the blood vessels to make them hard instead.

Series 1 and 2 prostaglandins are also in Yin-Yang polarity with one another. PGE_1 encourages relaxation, recuperation, and health, while PGE_2 stimulates the tension necessary for survival and competitive stress. PGE_2 is constrictive and causes platelets to aggregate and eventually form clots in the blood vessels, and causes the kidneys to retain salt, leading to water retention and high blood pressure at the extreme. PGE_1, in contrast, dissolves the clots, relaxes the blood vessels, and lowers blood pressure, while relaxing the kidneys so that excess fluid can more easily be removed from the body.

Within the essential fatty acid group, the Omega 3 and 6s also have opposite Yin-Yang effects in the body. For example, the Omega 6s enhance tumor formation and growth, while the Omega 3s inhibit them. Generally, however, essential fatty acids are more dispersive than other fatty acids and are important in carrying materials to the surface of the skin, intestinal tract, kidneys, lungs, or cells. This ability enables them to disperse fat-soluble concentrations of substances into the body where they are needed as well as to carry toxins to the surface of the cell, skin, intestinal tract, kidneys, or lungs where these substances can be discarded. LNA is the most strongly dispersing essential fatty acid and helps disperse deposits of excess SaFAs and cholesterol.

Another important Yin-Yang polarity between the EFAs and SaFAs has to do with the storage of light and oils in the body. In this regard, the expansion and contraction associated with EFAs and SaFAs is reversed.

Normally Yang is at the surface of the body and Yin is at the interior. However, these polarities can reverse during times of seasonal variance. In the winter (the most cold season—Yin), the preponderance of the Yin cold temperature of the external environment necessitates that the body conserve its Yang heat within. EFAs are Yang. Omegas 3s are the most Yang and are mostly derived from tiny seeds or sea creatures with hard, shiny coatings like flaxseed, hempseed, perilla seed, chia seed, or Krill. Therefore, they help contain the body's heat within the interior during the Yin winter season. In contrast, during the summer (the most hot season—Yang, the Yin Body Fluids need to be contained at the surface so they are not lost through perspiration or evaporation. SaFAs are Yin, especially the long-chain SaFAs. Therefore, they help contain the body's Yin during the Yang summer season.

This process works with light as well as with heat. Because the wavelengths of sunlight resonate with the electrons in the double bonds of EFAs, EFAs are able to absorb light through the photosynthesis of plants, for example, and to deliver this light to humans through its consumption. Nature compensates for this phenomenon by producing more EFAs in plants and animals in polar and temperate zones where their exposure to the sun is limited than in tropical zones where more SaFAs are produced in plants and animals and sunlight is more extreme. In fact, the double bonds in fatty acids decrease from five to zero from the poles to the equator. This means that light intensity decreases double bonds in fatty acids. Humans absorb the fatty acids produced in their environment through the locally produced food they eat. People living in polar and temperate regions and eating food produced there have more EFAs in their bodies, while people living and eating naturally in tropical regions have more SaFAs. The further north seeds grow, the more their oils will contain the highly unsaturated EFAs. Mediterranean regions mostly produce monounsaturated fatty acids like Olive and Almond oils, while the tropics mostly produce SaFAs like Coconut and Palm oils.[a]

When people eat foods, especially fats and oils that are produced in opposite climate zones than where they live, they thrive less well. Natives of Polar Regions such as the Inuit are able to thrive in areas of decreased sunlight, while Europeans wintering there suffer neurotic, psychotic, and suicidal tendencies. The traditional Inuit diet consists of substantial amounts of EFA rich foods, such as fish and marine animals that contains (EPA and DHA), which are able to supply them with the "liquid" sunshine they need in their extreme seasons of total darkness. Because of the lack of sunlight, SaFA-fed brains become depleted of EPA and DHA during the winter. SaFAs and MUFAs collect in the external parts of the body (the skins of many tropical fruits are extremely hard in order to protect them against dehydration from the sun) because they resist destruction by light, while UFAs tend to concentrate deep inside the inner organs such as the brain, adrenal, and reproductive glands

---

[a] SaFAs are generally Yin. However, because the Yang EFAs tend to decrease in tropical regions, SaFAs in the plant world compensate by making medium-chain SaFAs, like Coconut oil, more Yang.

where their fragility is protected from sunlight. The Omega 3 fatty acids especially store sunlight and provide the body with sufficient sunlight stored within their chemical bonds to thrive in the sunless polar winters of the Arctic regions. Even in temperate regions, imbalance between SaFAs and EFAs, or insufficiency of EFAs, can lead to Seasonal Affective Disorder where depression sets in during the colder months when light from the sun is less available and individual lifestyle makes it even more limited.

EPA and DHA are highly dispersive, have extremely low melting points (-65° to -47°F), and will not harden or aggregate. These qualities make them extremely useful in preventing SaFAs, platelets, and fibrinogen from sticking together and clogging the arteries. They can also lower cholesterol level, LDL, and high triglycerides (by up to 65 percent) and very low-density lipoprotein by 50 percent.

Liver Correlations

In acupuncture, as well as in Western medicine, dietary fats and oils are closely related to the health of the Liver. Natural dietary fats and oils nourish the Liver and its Yin-Yang functions, while imbalances among the fatty acids or consumption of unnatural, refined, hydrogenated, and partially hydrogenated fats and oils, with their accompanying toxic effect on health, poison the liver. In acupuncture, the Liver Meridian, along with its Yin-Yang, husband and wife, Coupled Meridian, the Gall Bladder, encompass more diverse areas, tissues, and other organs than any other meridian in acupuncture. These areas include the groin, flanks, lower back, genitourinary system, reproductive system, digestive system, respiratory system, heart and circulatory systems, as well as the throat, ear, eye, head, and skin. Head disorders of the Liver, including dizziness and psycho-emotional problems, are also related to lipid imbalance.

Table 3: Comparison of Liver and Fatty Acid Disharmonies

Liver Disharmonies	Fatty Acid Disharmonies
Spirit (*Hun* & Rational Perspective)	LNA prevents learning disabilities and mental deterioration.
Psycho-Emotional	EFA deficiency causes neurotic, psychotic, and suicidal tendencies.
Immunity (Circulates the Yang Qi)	EFAs stimulate immune function through Vitamin A and through their ability to hold oxygen and prevent infection); LNA kills malaria and treats bacterial infections.
Growth	LNA increases stamina and vitality and prevents low metabolic rate; LA prevents growth retardation.

Liver Disharmonies	Fatty Acid Disharmonies
Cancer	EFAs regulate tumor formation (w6s enhance while w3s inhibit); lecithin helps detoxify the liver; EFAs prevent liver degeneration; *trans*-fatty acids cause cancer.
Skin (Hot Liver Blood)	EFAs regulate the skin & membranes, facilitate wound healing, and regulate toxin discharge at the skin; the balance of SaFAs and EFAs determine the presence or absence of skin cancer; EFAs nourish the skin through Vitamin A and prevent eczema-like skin conditions; LNA and LA prevent dry skin.
Muscle Problems (the Liver controls the tendons, ligaments, and fasciae)	EFAs regulate stiffness or flexibility; LNA prevents motor in-coordination
Bone Problems (the Gall Bladder nourishes the bones and controls them through a point on its meridian, G39, classified as the "Meeting Point of the Marrow")[a]	EFAs regulate Vitamin D and osteoporosis through cholesterol production; stimulate bone and tooth development through Vitamin A; promote bone density through Vitamin K.
Headaches and Dizziness (stemming from Liver excess, deficiency, or Yin-Yang imbalance, called "Wind" in acupuncture theory)	The balance of natural fatty acids regulates Liver Qi and prevents headaches & dizziness.
Eye Problems (the Liver controls the Eyes)	EFAs benefit the eyes through Vitamin A; LNA prevents vision impairment.
Ear Problems (the Gall Bladder Meridian circles the ear)	Fatty deposits in the ears cause some ear problems. Tinnitus is often caused by Deficient Liver Yin.
Throat Problems (blocked Liver Qi affects the throat)	Weak immunity causes sore throats.

---

[a] By treating the marrow, G39 stimulates the growth of bones. This point is located three body inches above the outer ankles.

Liver Disharmonies	Fatty Acid Disharmonies
Heart and Circulatory Disorders (the Liver feeds the Heart through the Five Phase Nourishing Cycle); therefore, weak Liver Qi helps create weak Heart Qi; Excess Liver Fire over-inflames the Heart; and Liver and Gall Bladder mucous helps create fatty deposits in the Heart and arteries.	EFAs regulate blood pressure through PGE_1 (lowers) and PGE_2 (raises); regulate clogging of the arteries through PGE_1 (dissolves clots) and PGE_2 (forms clots); maintain cardiovascular health through Vitamin E; LNA prevents high blood pressure and sticky platelets; PGE_1 prevents heart attacks; *trans*-fatty and conjugated fatty acids greatly contribute to coronary artery disease.
Respiratory Disorders (the Lung Meridian follows the Liver Meridian in the daily cycle of Qi; Stagnant Liver Qi causes the Lung Meridian to be deficient; the Lung, in acupuncture theory, circulates the Defensive Qi responsible for immunity); in addition, the Gall Bladder Meridian spreads the Yang Defensive Qi to the surface	EFAs and Coconut oil strengthen immunity.
Digestive System (according to acupuncture theory, excess Liver Qi weakens the digestive system)	Fatty acids strengthen digestion through the production of bile from lecithin.
Reproductive System (the Liver Meridian flows through the genitals)	Fatty acids stimulate reproduction through Vitamin A; EFAs prevent sterility in males and miscarriage in females.
Genitourinary System	Fatty acids regulate adrenal hormones in stress through cholesterol production; regulate water metabolism through PGE_1 (removes) and PGE_2 (retains); EFAs prevent kidney degeneration.

In addition, the disease categories of the Liver in acupuncture can be divided into seven different subcategories that describe Liver disharmonies in a Yin-Yang continuum, including (1) Cold Stagnating the Liver Meridian, (2) Deficient Liver Yin, (3) Deficient Liver Blood, (4) Stagnant Liver Qi, (5) Liver Wind, (6) Arrogant Liver Yang (Deficient Yin with apparent Yang excess), and (7) Blazing Liver Fire (a totally excess and toxic condition). These categories also correspond to imbalances in dietary fat and oil consumption.

Table 4: The Yin-Yang of Liver Disharmonies

Yang	Disharmonies	Description	Oil Disharmonies
7	Blazing Liver Fire	Splitting headaches, dizziness, red face and eyes, dry mouth, deafness, ringing in the ears, insomnia, constipation, scanty urine, hypertension, eye and ear disturbances	EFAs instill calmness, benefit the eyes, and strengthen digestion; LNA reduces inflammation and returns cholesterol and fat soluble vitamins to detoxify the Liver; PGE_1 produces a sense of well being, relaxes the Body/Mind, helps insulin work more efficiently, and decreases the inflammation response.
6	Arrogant Liver Yang	Mixtures of Deficient Liver Yin and Blazing Liver Fire	LNA relaxes the Liver by softening the entire system.
5	Liver Wind	Uncontrollable and/or sudden movement or rigidity, trembling; difficulty in speaking, exaggerated stiff neck, spasms and convulsions, twitching, unconsciousness; stroke	EFAs regulate the Yin-Yang balance of the Body/Mind and instill calmness, regulate tension and flexibility in the muscles & tendons; PGE_1 produces a sense of well-being, relaxes the Body/Mind, and lowers blood pressure.
4	Stagnant Liver Qi	Depression, frustration, anger; a sensation of a lump in the throat, groin, breast, or flank; PMS; nausea, vomiting, and diarrhea	EFAs & lecithin instill calmness and help strengthen digestion & reproduction; LNAs reverse PMS; PGE_1 relaxes the Body/Mind.
Yin			

Yang	Disharmonies	Description	Oil Disharmonies
3	Deficient Liver Blood	Pale face, dizziness, hazy vision or spots in the eyes; flank pain, numbness in the tendons and muscles, spasmodic movement; irregular or insufficient menses, anemia; chronic hepatitis; nervous disorders; hypertension	EFAs instill calmness, regulate the tension and flexibility of the muscles & tendons, benefit the eyes, and strengthen immunity; LA helps produce hemoglobin; PGE_1 produces a sense of well being and lowers blood pressure.
2	Deficient Liver Yin	Red cheeks, fever in the afternoon, heat in the palms and soles, dizziness; eye problems; depression, nervous tension; menopausal complaints	EFAs prevent psycho-emotional disorders, instill mental calmness, benefit the eyes, strengthen the reproductive system, and lower Fire; LNAs reduce inflammation and reverse PMS; PGE_1 produces a sense of well being, relaxes the Body/Mind, helps insulin work more efficiently, and decreases the inflammation response.
1	Cold Stagnating the Liver Meridian	Swelling, pain and distension of the groin from hernia or pelvic inflammatory disease	EFAs radiate heat from the center of the body; strengthen the reproductive system; LNAs reduce inflammation; PGE_1 decreases the inflammation response.
Yin			

The Liver in acupuncture also relates to dietary fats and oils through three more general functions relating to its association with the Wood Phase and the spring season. These include: (1) its defensive role in protecting against foreign invasion from either microorganisms or other people or groups, including its ability to circulate the expanding Yang Qi to the surface of the body at the level of the skin, organ, and cellular membranes; (2) its ability to regulate the harmonious flow of Qi throughout the body while maintaining a balance between relaxation and alert tension; and (3) its ability to store the Reserve Qi as one of the so-called Solid Organs.

Since the spring season is the time of expansion into the external environment for the organism, the Liver regulates the circulation of the Defensive Qi, which protects the organism against the invasion of noxious foreign and climatic elements. This function serves to promote a barrier or boundary that one uses to extend oneself into the environment on both the physical and psycho-emotional levels. When this boundary is extended too bruskly, there is an excess of anger and an inability to feel compassion for the need of others to share a common space. In contrast, when this boundary is unable to be extended sufficiently into the surrounding space, there is a collapse of identity accompanied by depression. When one's boundary can not be harmoniously regulated, the result can lead to severe addictive and psycho-emotional disturbances. These two Yin and Yang movements of the Liver directly correspond to the transport of cholesterol in the body. LDL circulates cholesterol to the body and the Body/Mind periphery in response to anger and stress while HDL transports cholesterol back to the Liver in response to relaxation and well being.

LA and LNA also protect against foreign organisms like viruses, fungi, yeasts, and bacteria by absorbing the necessary oxygen that these organisms need to thrive in. SaFAs, phospholipids, and cholesterol work together in forming strong and flexible barriers at the membrane level. EFAs can be used to treat addictions, including those to tobacco, alcohol, drugs, sex, and violence. EFAs do this by relaxing the person and increasing the amount of tension they are able to bear and the amount of space they feel they have in which to deal with stress. This added space makes it easier for them to control the anger and frustration as well as the wild mood swings, irrationality, fear, and violence that are the psycho-emotional source of their addictive behaviors. **People who change their diet to include whole foods and EFAs have a 400 percent better chance of rehabilitating themselves from addiction than if their diet stays the same!**

In acupuncture theory, each organ/meridian corresponds to a different type of whole grain. For the Liver the whole grain is wheat. Certain individuals, mostly those who consume refined grains such as white flour or hybridized wheat[a] as well as the rest of the "Four Whites,"[b] can temporarily develop the classical signs of schizophrenia simply by eating foods containing

---

[a] Hybridized wheat has been created to withstand the onslaught of modern chemical agriculture and creates an allergic response in sensitive individuals. More ancient and heirloom varieties of wheat like spelt or the Egyptian kamut, or wheat in its sprouted form, will not create this type of allergic response and will target healing of the Liver instead.

[b] The "Four Whites" is a term coined by the author to represent the four categories of refined food in modern society: white flour (or refined grain), white sugar (or refined concentrated sweeteners), "white" oil (or refined vegetable oil), and "white" salt (or refined salt).

wheat products. By first avoiding hybridized wheat, and then the "Four Whites" altogether, these individuals can regain the health of their Liver and the psycho-emotional balance that goes with it.

The Liver in acupuncture also regulates the spread of Yang Qi from the interior to the exterior. One of the ways this process occurs at the level of dietary fats and oils is through cholesterol. The liver creates cholesterol on demand from carbohydrate, fat, and protein. While most people are able to self-regulate this production physiologically, it can be upset, however, by the balance between total available cholesterol and UFAs as well as alcohol consumption, stress, and anger. Alcohol throws the Liver out of balance by loosening the membranes (barriers) so that more cholesterol must be sent to them followed by the need to remove this cholesterol rather quickly once the alcohol wears off. The degree of harmony with which this process takes place determines the relative stiffness or flexibility of the membranes as well as one's psycho-emotional bearing. The balance between PGE_1 and PGE_2 also affects the health of the Liver. Both of these two prostaglandins are made from LA, but serve different Yin-Yang functions. PGE_1 relaxes the body, while PGE_2 tightens it up.

The storage of Reserve Qi that the Liver provides as one of the Solid Organs corresponds to the storage of energy reserves in the body where excess sugars are converted into the less harmful TGs and stored away for future use for all the internal organs including the brain. Phospholipids are also important in nourishing the brain while brain nourishment is one of the functions of Reserve Qi.

Table 5: Liver and Dietary Oil Functions

	Liver Functions	Oil Functions
1	Protects against foreign invasions and forms a protective barrier against the world; extremes result in a mindset of overprotection, armoring, and defensiveness.	Serves as a barrier of immunity to foreign organisms; forms membranes & skin through phospholipids & SaFAs; helps heal addictive behaviors & severe psycho-emotional disturbances (EFAs).
2	Regulates the harmonious flow of Qi.	Regulates the circulation of cholesterol to (HDL) and from (LDL) the liver to the skin, membranes & cells; regulates the stiffness and flexibility of membranes and, therefore, the entire Body/Mind; regulates relaxation and tension through the balance between PGE_1 & PGE_2.
3	Stores Reserve Qi.	Stores the reserves of energy through triglycerides and nourishes the brain through phospholipids.

Another important reserve stored in the Liver as well as other organs is simply called the Yin Qi in acupuncture. Yin is defined as the shady side of a hill and is associated with darkness, cold, rest, passivity, and responsiveness, as well as inward and downward movement. In contrast, Yang is defined as the sunny side of a hill and is associated with brightness, heat, action, excitement, and stimulation, as well as outward and upward movement. Liver Yin, more specifically, is the nourishing, cool, and moist aspect that keeps the Liver Yang in check. Liver Yin deficiency is very similar to Liver Blood deficiency but with the addition of heat signs such as agitation, red tongue and cheeks, heat in the palms and soles, night sweat, and a fast pulse. Acupuncture theory explains this condition through the saying that when the Yin fails to love the Yang, it floats away to the exterior. Deficient Liver Blood is associated with dizziness; impaired vision; numbness, or weak tremors in the limbs; dry skin; and scanty menses.

Table 6: Comparison Between Liver Yin and EFA Deficiency

Liver Yin Deficiency	EFA Deficiency
Dry Skin	EFAs moisten dry skin.
Numbness or Weak Tremors in the Limbs	These symptoms are most exaggerated in Multiple Sclerosis, which can be successfully treated with EFAs.
Dizziness	EFAs lower Fire; PGE_1 produces a feeling of well being, relaxes the Body/Mind, and helps insulin work more efficiently.
Impaired Vision	EFAs improve impaired vision.
Scanty Menses	EFAs prevent sterility in males and miscarriage in females.

Fats and Oils in Chinese Medicine

Coronary Artery Disease and Cholesterol

During the second half of the twentieth century, medical procedures to prevent deaths from heart attacks improved tremendously. Death rate fell from about 40 percent per year in 1958 to 2.1 percent by the early 1980s. These results, along with the first implantation of an artificial heart, signify a triumph of modern technological civilization. From a larger perspective, however, they represent a degenerating trend toward the increasing mechanization of life. Short-term surgical success makes it too easy to ignore the long-term and underlying causes of heart problems. Connections between these causes and the important values of human life are then overlooked. While the medical profession gets stronger from these successes, the people lose faith in their own ability to maintain health. Instead, they are taught to believe that health is a commodity that must be bought at a price higher than most anyone can afford; commodities that include heart surgeries and bigger health insurance plans. Real health is not something that can be purchased; it is something that is earned in the process of becoming human. When gullible people place their faith in someone or something else other than themselves, they can be manipulated into believing things that go against their common sense and intuition. Heart surgeries, including bypass surgeries and angioplasties, fit this category because nothing can take the place of a whole, healthy, human heart. When faith in oneself and the Order of the Universe are replaced by faith in mechanical, conventional medicine, the end of humanity is near. Ironically, the beginning of the degeneration of science into religion also begins with this step.

Treating the cause of heart problems is different and more important than mechanical, medical manipulation. The misguided faith in conventional medicine results in many people rushing needlessly into heart surgery, which, in this context, may even do more harm than good. In fact, *current heart surgeries may be unnecessary as much as 85 percent of the time.* In spite of these technical advances, 25 percent (almost 70 million) people still suffer from coronary heart disease in the US while over 42 percent of all deaths result from cardiovascular disease.[14]

Medical Studies

At the University of Sao Paulo, Brazil, Whady Hueb and his associates on the medical faculty did a study of one sector of the 6-8 percent of people who refuse surgery and followed them for two to eight years. For those with obstructions in only one or two of their coronary arteries, the annual death rate in the follow-up period was 0 percent. For those with obstructions in all three of their coronary arteries, the death rate was only 1.3 percent per year.[a] Overall, they found that the chance of surviving eight years *without* surgery was 89 percent. Professor of medicine, Thomas A. Preston at the University of

---

[a] Hueb, W., et al. In *American Journal of Cardiology* 63:155-159.

Washington, claims that 50 percent of all bypass surgeries in the US are unnecessary and are, in fact, no more effective than a placebo.[a]

At least four important studies verify these facts. One of the first of these was the Veterans Study of 1977, which, after comparing bypass surgery patients with those treated medically for eleven years at thirteen different Veterans Administration hospitals, concluded that the survival rates between the two groups were identical.[b] In other words, *bypass surgery had no impact on long-term survival.* The results of this study, in spite of its appearance in the prestigious *New England Journal of Medicine,* has had no influence on the frequency of the operation. Top name surgeons attacked the study, blaming the results on second-rate surgery performed at the VA in spite of the more obvious interpretation that this is *the* typical setting in which ordinary patients are treated.

The second comparison study, the Coronary Artery Surgery Study (CASS), was designed to incorporate these top surgeons. In spite of raising the quality of the surgeons in this study, the same types of groups were followed for ten years with the same results as with the second-rate surgeons. Again, bypass surgery failed to help the survival rates of patients. The most important finding from this study was that patients are able to do without surgery *if* the function of the left ventricle is normal.[c]

The third and last large randomized study ever conducted on the comparison between bypass surgeries and medical treatment was the European Coronary Surgery Study Group in 1977. In 1983, professor E. Braunwald summarized these studies, again in the *New England Journal of Medicine,* stating, "I believe that this operation should...be restricted...rather than [offered] as a panacea for coronary artery disease."[d] Nevertheless, the bypass surgeries continued. While a significant 60,000 bypass surgeries were performed in the US in 1975, over six times as many (380,000) were performed by 1990.

Another study, sponsored by the National Institute of Health and published in 1989, concluded:

> Most American cardiologists have assumed that angioplasty or bypass surgery is necessary to prevent recurrent...heart attack and death caused by the coronary artery...obstructions that...persist after successful...clot dissolving therapy. The *results*...indicate that this is not the case.[15]

This study, as well as the previous studies, however, has no bearing on the amount of surgeries performed. The obvious reason, of course, is the financial gain to be made from these surgeries. Another important reason, however, has to do with liability. Since responsibility for healthcare in modern times is placed

---

[a] Preston, T. In *MD* February, 1985, 104-114.

[b] The Veterans Study. In *New England Journal of Medicine* 311:1311-1339, 1977.

[c] Alderman, E.L., et al. In *Circulation* 82:1629-1646 1990.

[d] Braunwald, E. In *New England Journal of Medicine* 309:1181-1184 1983.

on the physician, they must assume the liability as well. In such a legal environment, why would a physician or health-care practitioner want to take this risk for a non-surgical heart-risk patient when they can much more safely commit the patient to surgery? Ironically, only when faced with surgery will the patient waive the doctor's responsibility.

Prevention of Unnecessary Heart Surgeries

According to Dr. Charles McGee, whenever possible, patients with heart problems should be evaluated by second opinion clinics, where the condition of the left ventricle can be evaluated. This condition can be determined by either an echocardiogram or a nuclear medicine isotope scan. *If the left ventricle is pumping normally, surgical procedures will not improve the chances of survival.* When the left ventricle fails, blood backs into the lungs and causes shortness of the breath and coughing. When the right ventricle fails, fluid backs up into other areas of the body and causes swelling in the ankles, buttocks, or abdomen (ascites). When chest pains can be controlled through other means, heart surgery is unnecessary. Dr. McGee recommends the following precautions against heart surgery, along with reasonable alternatives:

1) Monitor the rhythm of the heart
2) Receive magnesium by injection
3) Do not use a treadmill or angiogram if the left ventricle of the heart is pumping normally[a]
4) Do not use a treadmill test after recuperating from a heart attack
5) Measure the function of the left ventricle with an echocardiogram or isotope scan
6) Load up on AOs or follow the Pritikin, Ornish, or Macrobiotic diet programs as alternative options
7) Have surgery only if chest pains cannot be controlled[16]

Angiograms

The coronary angiogram is a diagnostic procedure used to determine whether atherosclerotic plaque is built up and where it is located, and to what extent in the planning of surgical procedures. The coronary angiogram is also used as a major sales device in the clinical setting to promote heart surgery. A dye injected through a catheter flows through the arteries to the heart where it becomes visible on an X-ray. Angiograms were first performed in 1963 and are now well used throughout the world. Problems interpreting angiograms are twofold: (1) When either the catheter or dye contacts the arteries, they can go into spasm and give a false reading of arterial constriction; or (2) the degree of obstruction varies according to the angle of the camera that takes the X-ray picture. There is also a slight .01 percent chance that the person will die from

---

[a] The angiogram test will most likely be the inaccurate kind. See "Angiograms" below.

the procedure, which can trigger a potentially fatal heart rhythm from the simple presence of the dye in the artery.

Only ten years after the first angiograms were performed, reports of these inaccuracies were beginning to be published. The actual arteries of patients who died after bypass surgery did not look like the ones on the angiograms used to plan the surgeries. Then there were the disagreements between experts as to the meaning of the X-ray pictures. For example, in 1976 at Massachusetts General Hospital an artery was read as being 100 percent blocked by one expert and 0 percent blocked by another. These same experts that cannot agree with themselves or each other recommend that surgery should only be performed on arteries that are more than 50 percent obstructed. Patients with less than 50 percent obstruction should not be operated upon. Patients and surgeons alike depend on the accuracy of these readings. Nevertheless, in 1979, *the American Heart Association reported that individual radiologists substantially disagree with their own previous readings as much as 32 percent of the time.*

In 1984, another study compared standard preoperative angiogram readings with ultrasound readings taken directly on coronary arteries during bypass surgery. The authors found so many differences between these two different readings that they were forced to conclude the following:

> The physiologic[al] effects of the majority of coronary obstructions cannot be determined accurately by conventional angiographic approaches. The result of these studies should be profoundly disturbing to all physicians who have relied on the coronary angiogram to provide accurate information regarding the physiologic[al] consequences of...coronary stenosis (obstruction).[a]

The results of these studies show that the standard angiogram is too inaccurate to be relied on for surgical procedures on the heart. While the fact that these results stand unopposed, their use continues to increase dramatically. Angiograms and heart surgery are lucrative businesses with basic bypass surgeries banking $25,000 to $75,000 each and surgeon's salaries running an easy $1.5 million a year. No wonder they do not want to give it up. According to McGee:

> Medical schools [today] continue to teach how to perform and read the ordinary angiogram, never mentioning its lack of accuracy.... Most American doctors have probably never heard of these studies.[17]

In 1977, B. Greg Brown first described a more reliable form of angiogram, called the quantitative angiogram. Pictures are taken with two cameras to achieve a three-dimensional effect and the data is interpreted by

---

[a] White, C.W., et al. In *New England Journal of Medicine* 310:819-824 1984.

computer. This method produces a margin of error of only 1 percent.[a] In the mid-1980s, a few university medical centers for research used this method. Even today, most doctors and the general public have almost no access to it. Most people are unaware of the differences in reliability between the two procedures and *assume* that the standard, inaccurate angiogram is as reliable as the quantitative angiogram. Unless a person is ready and willing to undergo heart surgery, or a decision has been made to manage the person medically after non-invasive tests have been made, these reports suggest that there is no reason to submit to a standard angiogram.

Bypass Surgery

After testing for heart disease is completed, conventional medicine will recommend either medical treatment or surgery. The most common surgical procedures are bypass surgery and balloon angioplasty. Bypass surgery, otherwise known as Coronary Artery Bypass Graft (CABG), or cabbage as it is commonly referred to in medical slang, involves grafting arteries or veins from other locations in the body to replace any, or all, of the three major arteries flowing out of the heart thought to be constricted with arterial plaque.

Several complications could arise from this extremely invasive surgery, including the usual surgical complications noted by McGee:

> Post-operative infections, failure of the breast bone to grow back together, chronic pain in the incision, abnormalities in the heart's rhythm, heart attacks, strokes, leaking at the sites where bypass graft vessels are attached, bleeding at other sites, transfusion reactions and poor wound healing.[18]

Other complications include pain from cut nerves, additional obstruction, brain damage, and death. In addition AIDS and/or other serious infections have occurred from blood transfusions. The machine that takes over the function of circulating the blood during surgery must be primed with several pints of blood or other fluid. Arthur Ashe, for example, the former professional tennis star, died of AIDS-related pneumonia in 1993 from the infected blood he received during his 1977 and 1983 bypass surgeries. Since then a saline solution, which does reduce the risk of infection, is used to prime these machines, *but* after surgery this alternative leaves patients markedly anemic.

One of the reasons given for the reduction of angina pains after surgery is the increased blood flow to the heart muscle. However, nerves cut during surgery that carry pain signals from the heart grow back in six to twelve months when this pain may return.[19] Since the cause of arterial obstruction is ignored, the obstruction process continues after surgery, but now in a weakened and compromised patient. The obstruction in *native* arteries increases rapidly in some patients, while the grafted veins obstruct even faster. This obstruction only stands to reason since grafted arteries come from areas of the body where

---

[a] Brown, B.G., et al. In *Circulation* 55:329-337 1977.

arterial pressure is much less than the natural coronary arteries surrounding the heart. These grafted arteries are much smaller and have significantly less muscular power and volume capacity to pump blood than the arteries they replace. Once these sub-standard blood vessels have been grafted onto the heart, all of these factors combine and contribute to the speed of further plaque accumulation. Veins that have been grafted to replace arteries are even more problematic since they do not have muscles inside them as arteries do. The muscles in arteries help regulate the flow of blood between the heart and other areas of the body. According to McGee, "Post operative angiograms sometimes have shown cabbage grafts to be totally obstructed within two weeks after surgery."[20] While it is true that these grafts may temporarily save lives, they should, of course, be avoided and, better yet—prevented, whenever possible.

Various degrees of brain damage can also follow heart surgery because, while the heart is temporarily stopped during surgery, blood flow to the brain is substantially reduced. A 1974 Swedish study showed that 12 percent of bypass patients suffered from more severe cases of brain damage such as strokes while marked disturbances on intellectual tests given two months after surgery appeared on *all* the other patients.

Deaths from bypass surgery have certainly decreased since the 50 percent mortality rate at the University of California Medical Center in Sacramento during the late 1970s. Yet, while cardiac surgeons routinely tell prospective patients that the death rate is only 1 percent, the actual studies measuring death rate tell a different story. In 1991, for example, five major teaching hospitals participating in a study in Philadelphia found the death rate for expert surgeons involved in teaching surgery ranged from this low of 1 percent all the way up to 9 percent.[a] The Veterans Study in California, where the range for ordinary surgeons was measured, was 5.7 percent. Of course, the lower death rate percentages usually involve less complicated cases. In turn, less complicated cases usually need surgery less. One wonders how an ordinary or beginning surgeon with obviously higher death rates and more general mistakes gets to be an expert. The crude but true answer, published in the 1989 *Journal of the American Medical Association,* is that they *practice* on patients who are *less likely* to need surgery *if at all.*

Once surgery has been performed, it is important for the person to proceed with natural healing techniques with even more vigor than he or she would in lieu of surgery because their health is now much more compromised. They should not become complacent when their surgeon tells them they will be fine, unless they are willing to meet up with him behind closed doors again.

Angioplasty

Angioplasty, the second major form of heart surgery, involves the insertion of a balloon through a catheter into selected arteries to increase blood-flow volume in the obstructed area. Sometimes an inflatable metal *stent* is used

---

[a] Williams, S.V., et al. In *Journal of the American Medical Association* 266:810-815 1991.

to prevent rapid re-obstruction. Possible complications include heart attack, rhythm problems, and death.

Heart attack from angioplasty can be induced in three ways: (1) the balloon can remain inflated too long and shut off blood circulation to the heart; (2) the arteries can go into spasm from contact with the catheter or the balloon; or (3) the artery can crack open when the balloon is inflated. While the current death rate is only about 2 percent, these rates can be much higher in hospitals with less experienced staff. Worse case scenarios can range between 5.5 and 20 percent with an added 22 percent for other significant "complications."

The more pressing questions concerning these procedures, however, are (1) how much are they really helping and (2) who are they really designed to help? While they may prolong life in some cases, these procedures certainly do not make patients stronger or healthier. More often, patients who start with heart surgery continue to need follow-up procedures as time goes on. According to McGee, "It is not unusual to see patients who have had three or four balloon procedures followed by a cabbage, all within four or five months, all failing to help."[21] *If it were not so easy to correct these problems with sound, whole food nutrition and simple way of life changes, it would be easier to accept the overall weakening of the general public that is produced by reliance on these conventional practices.*

Cholesterol Theory and Coronary Artery Disease

Blood cholesterol appears to be rising even in young people. A 1981 California study showed that cholesterol levels of six-year-old children ranged from 113 to 260 mg (with a mean of 190) in contrast to 100 to 150 mg for children in traditional societies where heart disease is uncommon. Factors said to raise cholesterol are the consumption of refined sugars and starches, excess body fat, smoking, and stress.

Emotional stress, in particular, causes the steepest rise in cholesterol (from 10 to 50 percent). The body uses cholesterol produced in the liver and adrenals to make a variety of stress hormones. In addition to elevated cholesterol levels, stress itself can provoke a heart attack by constricting the coronary vessels so they go into spasm. In fact, Dr. Michael Marmot, a British physician, found that Japanese immigrants accustomed to the American way of life, but preferring Japanese food, had twice as much coronary artery disease as those who maintained their cultural traditions but preferred American food. Dr. Marmot's study suggests that there is something peculiar to Japanese society and lifestyle besides diet that prevents coronary artery disease. The great emphasis that Japanese place on the cohesion, achievement, and social stability of the group most likely protects them from the psycho-emotional stress that would otherwise lead to heart attacks. This cultural and collective identity is in stark contrast to the typical American emphasis on individualism and ambition as well as social and geographic mobility. These American characteristics make it more difficult to achieve stability in life without accumulating a great deal of personal stress. In turn, this stress, compounded with the constant change in the American way of life, makes it more difficult to feel in control of one's life. Issues of control, according to acupuncture theory, are fundamental to the Heart Spirit. When one loses a grip on this control, the Heart Spirit is no longer comfortable in the Heart, a significant factor that, when compounded by the lack of significant connections to other people,[a] may influence its departure and the incidence of a heart attack.

On the other hand, the harmful effects of stress can be reduced by a healthier diet. For example, stress during the two world wars was at an all time high. And yet, people during this time period experienced a lowered incidence of coronary artery disease. Many other factors besides decreased fat and cholesterol consumption, especially decreased consumption of protein and sugar and increased consumption of minerals, vitamins, EFAs, and fiber, account for this finding. Weston Price did a large epidemiological study in the 1930s of traditional people around the world and found that degenerative disease appeared in the otherwise healthy population after a single generation of introducing refined food.

In terms of diet, factors that lower cholesterol are:

1) Removal of refined foods from the diet
2) Addition of Vitamin C, niacin (B$_3$), zinc, magnesium, chromium, selenium, iodine, and fiber, all preferably in the form of whole foods
3) Decreased intake of animal products; the addition of fresh, UNREFINED, highly unsaturated oils from krill, fish, or flax; losing weight (also lowers TG levels)
4) Quitting smoking and coffee
5) Lowering of stress
6) The addition of herbs, essential oils, acupuncture, and exercise

Because of its stimulatory effect on the metabolism, Coconut oil lowers the cholesterol-elevating effects of animal fat. Being a medium-chain fatty acid, Coconut oil is burned almost immediately upon consumption and is not, therefore, stored as body fat or used by the body to raise cholesterol levels even though it is a SaFA.

Serum Cholesterol

Cholesterol and fats play an important part in the build-up of atheroscerotic plaque. For the last forty years the medical establishment has taught that the presence of HDL level (50-75 mg/dl) in the blood indicates that cholesterol is being removed from the arteries. HDL moves cholesterol back from the body-at-large to the liver, while LDL circulates cholesterol from the liver to the body. Therefore, the establishment reasons that LDL (above 120

---

[a] One of the main purposes of the Heart Spirit is to connect with the external world, especially on the social level. See the author's *The Twelve Spirit Points of Acupuncture* for a more detailed explanation.

mg/dl) indicates that the body is being over-loaded with cholesterol and that this excess is deposited in arterial plaque to increase the risk of high blood pressure, heart attack, and stroke. The fact that the average cholesterol is much greater for Americans (220 mg/dl) than people in poor countries (120 to 160 mg/dl) where coronary artery disease is rare *tends* to support this interpretation.

Because cholesterol is a lipid only found in animal foods, it is then assumed that high levels of cholesterol derived from animal fats, and other SaFAs by implication since animal fats are largely saturated, are the cause of coronary artery disease. These ideas first began from the interpretation of a set of curious Russian experiments in 1908 where *vegetarian* rabbits were force-fed a *carnivorous* diet high in protein from meat, milk and eggs. Two significant conclusions derived from this experiment were that high dietary cholesterol created high blood cholesterol and that high blood cholesterol was the cause of coronary artery disease.

The Framingham Heart Study started in 1948 and is recognized as the longest running and most influential heart study in the world. In 1983, the Framingham Study claimed to have identified high blood cholesterol as the highest of three primary risk factors in the development of coronary artery disease, including high blood pressure and smoking as well as diabetes and obesity.[22] In 1984, the National Heart, Lung, and Blood Institute (NHLBI) of the National Institute of Health (NIH) conducted a ten-year survey (the Lipid Research Clinics Coronary Primary Prevention Trial, or LRC) of 3,806 men between the ages of 35 and 59 who had high serum cholesterol levels. The project director defined this study as "the turning point in cholesterol-heart disease research." Based on interpretations of this study, the researchers concluded that elevated serum cholesterol was not just an associated risk factor for coronary artery disease, it was *the direct cause.*[a][23]

The interpretation that LDL creates arterial plaque also came from this study as well as the conclusion that diets high in animal fat were bad for the heart. In the early 1970s in conjunction with the Framingham Study, Drs. Edward Kass and Frank Sacks of Harvard Medical School and their colleagues, including Dr. William Castelli, then current director of the Framingham Heart Study, compared people eating the macrobiotic diet in Boston with those eating the Standard American Diet (SAD) from the Framingham Study. The therapeutic style of macrobiotics these people were eating contained fresh, mostly cooked, whole foods, no animal foods, and very little vegetable oils. The results of these comparisons, published in the *American Journal of Epidemiology*, the *New England Journal of Medicine*, the *Journal of the American Medical Association*, the *Journal of the American Dietetic Association*, and *Atherosclerosis* showed that THE MACROBIOTIC COMMUNITY

---

[a] The *director of the study* himself, as well as medical critics of the cholesterol approach to coronary artery disease, negated these findings soon after they were published because of serious flaws in the design of the study. This topic is discussed in more detail in the "Political Maneuvering..." section of "The Anti-Cholesterol Argument" section of this chapter.

HAD THE LOWEST SERUM CHOLESTEROL VALUES EVER REPORTED FOR A GROUP LIVING IN MODERN SOCIETY **and was similar to those of people where heart disease is *unknown*.**[24]

Four other medical studies around the world later made claims that diets low in animal food, saturated fat, and cholesterol, and high in polyunsaturated vegetable oil were good for the heart. For example, between 1957 and 1972, the Nutrition Department of the New York City Department of Health sponsored a fifteen-year "Anti-Coronary Club Trial," which claimed that the coronary disease rate for those consuming a diet high in polyunsaturated fats and low in total fat, saturated fatty acids, and cholesterol was two-thirds that of a control group on the Standard American Diet.[a] Another study, the Oslo Study, claimed that death rates from heart attack and stroke could be lowered 47 percent by controlling the intake of cholesterol and smoking.[b] In 1980, the Seven Countries Study of 12,000 men was published purporting that diets with low consumption of animal food and other saturated fats led to lower cholesterol levels and lower incidence of coronary artery disease.[c]

HDL/LDL

A 1982 conference held by the NHLBI, the Multiple Risk Factor Integration Trial (MRFIT), announced that heart attacks were still being reported in people with cholesterol levels below 200. The director of this conference then recommended that testing HDL and LDL levels would be more effective in determining coronary artery disease risk.

Remember that cholesterol is insoluble in the blood. In order to circulate back and forth through the bloodstream from areas of production (mostly the liver but also the intestines, adrenals, and sex glands) to areas of need, it needs something that will carry it through the blood. Lipoprotein is such a carrier because it is both water and fat-soluble. This polarity picks up the fatty cholesterol with the lipoprotein's fat-soluble core and then circulates the cholesterol through the watery bloodstream through the lipoprotein's water-soluble exterior. In this way the lipoprotein acts like a taxicab shuttling the cholesterol around the body. Because different kinds of lipoproteins carry cholesterol in different, even opposite, directions, they give a more accurate reading of what cholesterol is doing in the body than simple total serum cholesterol. More specifically, the Yin and Yang polarity of these lipoproteins determines their "density." The high-density lipoproteins (HDL) move inward in a centripetal direction and carry cholesterol from the body to the liver where it can be changed to bile, excreted into the intestine through the bile duct of the gallbladder, and discarded from the body through the stool. This is the reason

---

[a] Singman, H.S., et al. "The Anti-Coronary Club: 1957 to 1972." In *American Journal of Clinical Nutrition* 33:1183-91 1980.

[b] Hjermians, Ingram. "A randomized primary prevention trial in coronary artery disease: The Oslo study." In *Preventive Medicine* 12:181-84 1983.

[c] Keyes, Ancel. *Seven Countries: A Multivariate Analysis of Death and Coronary Heart Disease*, Cambridge, Mass.: Harvard University Press, 1980.

why organizations such as the AHA recommend high HDL levels. For example, "HDL (high-density lipoprotein) cholesterol is the 'good' cholesterol. A high level of HDL (60 mg/dL and above) *lowers* your risk of heart disease and heart attack. *HDL* cholesterol tends to carry excess cholesterol back to the liver where it is removed from the body."[25] Low-density lipoproteins (LDL) move outward in the opposite centrifugal direction and carry cholesterol out from the liver to the body according to areas in need. One should understand that the "cholesterol" in HDL and LDL is exactly the same! Cholesterol is neither "good" nor "bad." The only real difference is the lipoprotein taxicab—the HDL and LDL—because they indicate which way the cholesterol is moving in the body, inwards or outwards.

LDL was originally thought to be indicative of cholesterol attaching itself to arterial plaque simply because it was moving out into the bloodstream. The theory is that the more LDL is in the blood, the more cholesterol is available to attach to the arterial walls. This idea is based on an overly-mechanical interpretation of cholesterol where less is better and more is worse. According to this theory, HDL is called "good" cholesterol because it "appears" to lower cholesterol by sending it back to the liver where it can be rid from the body, and LDL is called "bad" cholesterol because it "appears" to raise cholesterol levels by circulating it into the body. The actual relationship between *elevated* cholesterol and arterial plaque is just a conjecture and has never been scientifically proven. In addition, HDL contains more protein than fat and cholesterol, while LDL contains two times more cholesterol than fat and protein. In reality, HDL and LDL work together like a seesaw. Increases of HDL are accompanied by decreases of LDL and vice versa.

Further findings in the mid 1980s reveal the existence of three different kinds of LDL cholesterol: (1) the reduced form found in fresh, natural foods; (2) the oxidized form found in rancid fats and oils, especially the more fragile polyunsaturated varieties; and (3) lipoprotein (a) [Lp(a)]. The reduced form of LDL is only a weak risk factor for coronary artery disease. However, the oxidized and Lp(a) forms show a much stronger risk correlation. *Only the oxidized form of LDL can damage the arteries and lead to atherosclerosis* in tissues where AO levels have become depleted due to the over consumption of refined and industrially processed foods.

Lp(a) resembles LDL with the addition of an adhesive repair protein called apo(a) made in the liver. The apo(a) goes through the bloodstream to the arteries to repair them by combining with other repair proteins such as fibrin and fibrinogen. While Lp(a) may be a strong risk factor for heart disease, it is no more the cause than cholesterol itself. Both Lp(a) and apo(a) are normal and necessary in the body. High blood cholesterol does not always develop into coronary artery disease. *Coronary artery disease frequently develops when cholesterol levels are normal or even low.*

To understand the underlying cause of coronary artery disease, the reason for high levels of Lp(a) should be known. Again, these have to do with AO deficiencies in the body including Vitamin C and E. High levels of Lp(a) are accompanied by decreases in Vitamin C, while increases of Vitamin C lower blood levels of Lp(a). Omega 3 essential fatty acids also lower the blood levels of apo(a) as well as the levels of fibrin and fibrinogen.

On the other hand, while cholesterol-lowering drugs have been unable to lower levels of Lp(a) as of 2006,[a] lower levels of cholesterol achieved through cholesterol-lowering diets and especially drugs are statistically associated with increased cancer. One explanation is that LDL also carries fat-soluble AOs, which prevent cancer, to the cells along with cholesterol and fats. When there is a decrease of LDL, less of these AOs are able to get to our cells, which then become cancerous. On the energetic level, any arbitrary or mechanical manipulation of cholesterol that emphasizes HDL over LDL will automatically suppress Liver Qi function[b] and result in the patterns of Stagnant Liver Qi and Congealed Liver Blood, both of which can lead to psycho-emotional disorders, violence, and cancer.

The Cholesterol Controversy

Cholesterol is NOT the cause of coronary artery disease and is also NOT a reliable indicator because of the following five factors:

1) Cholesterol consumption does not match the death rate for coronary artery disease
2) Cholesterol lowering drugs are not effective in preventing or treating coronary artery disease and can cause extremely undesirable side-effects
3) Major studies fail to prove the connection between cholesterol and coronary artery disease
4) Political maneuvering interferes with true scientific research
5) Sound nutritional practice creates a simple, effective, and safe cure available to all at a minute fraction of the cost of cholesterol-lowering drugs

CAD Is Unrelated to Cholesterol Levels

The death rate for coronary artery disease is unrelated to cholesterol consumption because coronary artery disease has skyrocketed in the last 100 years while cholesterol consumption has remained about the same. Many individuals, as well as many groups of traditional people, consume diets very high in saturated fats with no heart disease. Most notably are the Inuit Eskimos of Greenland, the South Pacific Islanders, and the Masai people of Africa. The Inuit consume large amounts of saturated fat from cold-water marine animals and fish; the South Pacific Islanders consume large amounts of saturated fat from Coconut oil; and the Masai eat nothing but milk, blood, and meat and yet have one of the lowest cholesterol levels in the world measuring about *fifty*

---

[a] As of 2006, no international standards for determining Lp(a) levels or commercial sources of testing for Lp(a) levels exist.[www.MedicineNet.com]
[b] Healthy Liver Qi is characterized primarily by its ability to expand.

percent lower than most Americans.[a] Furthermore, many people who succumb to coronary artery disease have normal or even low cholesterol. Autopsies reveal that people with low cholesterol have some of the most severely diseased arteries.[26] In seventy percent of the population, cholesterol levels are not raised significantly by dietary increases of cholesterol because the liver, where 80 percent of the blood cholesterol is made, naturally regulates cholesterol levels according to the relation between dietary intake and physiological need. For this reason cholesterol levels are not easily affected in the general population by food.[b] Even the effects of eating high cholesterol foods like two or three eggs per day over a long period can hardly be measured. Furthermore, the methods devised by the AHA to lower cholesterol have neither lowered cholesterol levels through diet effectively nor have they decreased the incidence of coronary artery disease.

According to Dr. Uffe Ravnskov in his thoroughly researched book on cholesterol and global cholesterol policy, *The Cholesterol Myths*, most scientific studies also show that cholesterol is not an important factor in coronary artery disease. He describes how in more than thirty studies of over 150,000 people with previous heart attacks it has been shown that the amount of saturated fat these people have eaten is irrelevant to coronary artery disease. **Whereas the current doctrine teaches that *high* levels of LDL-cholesterol and *low* levels of HDL-cholesterol are supposed to increase the risk of coronary artery disease, many studies contradict this approach.** For example, in Russia the increase of coronary artery disease is found to be more often associated with *low* levels of LDL-cholesterol.[c] In addition, a 1986 report of 7000 middle-aged men in England, led by Dr. Stuart Pocock and his team, concluded that low HDL-cholesterol is not a major risk factor for coronary artery disease. When, in 1989, Dr. David Gordon and nine American scientists at the NHLBI challenged these results in their analysis of over 15,000 men and women, they were forced to conclude that HDL-cholesterol is only of marginal value in the intervention and screening for coronary artery disease risk.[d] In one of the longest follow-up studies of HDL-cholesterol (twenty-four years), the Finnish group of the Seven Countries Study[e] showed that more than twice the number of men died from

---

[a] Shaper, A.G. "Cardiovascular studies in the Samburu tribe of northern Kenya." In *American Heart Journal* 63, 437-442, 1962.

[b] That is, from the SAD.

[c] Shestov, D.B. "Increased risk of coronary heart disease death in men with low total and low-density-lipoprotein cholesterol in the Russian Lipid Research Clinics prevalence follow-up study." In *Circulation* 88, 846-853, 1993.

[d] Gordon, D.J., and others. "High-density lipoprotein cholesterol and cardiovascular disease. Four prospective American studies." In *Circulation* 79, 8-15, 1989.

[e] The Seven Countries Study was one of the first to claim that low cholesterol levels led to less coronary artery disease.

heart attacks in areas where the HDL-cholesterol was HIGH than in other areas where it was the lowest.[a]

Moreover, about one fifth of patients who have died from heart attacks show no evidence of atherosclerosis. Oddly, a coronary artery can be totally obstructed without any symptoms or damage to the heart. **In women, most studies have found that high cholesterol is not a risk factor at all.** In fact, the death rate for women is five times greater with low cholesterol.[b] Children exhibit great differences in cholesterol levels, but according to Dr. William Weidman of the Mayo Clinic in Rochester, Minnesota, and investigators in the Bogalusa Heart study of New Orleans, no connection exists between these levels and the amount of animal fat they ate.[c]

Undesirable Side-Effects

Cholesterol is a normal and necessary lipid in the body. Artificial attempts to regulate cholesterol can create significant physiological harm. Cholesterol-lowering drugs are associated with serious side effects including a high rate of cataract formation and liver damage.[d] They are so dangerous that tests actually need to be done every month for the first year and a quarter and then periodically forever. The newest group of cholesterol-lowering drugs, called statins, including Zocor®, Mevacor®, Pravachol®, Lescol®, Lipitor®,[e] and Lovastatin®, inhibit the body's production of a precursor to cholesterol called mevalonate. Mevalonate is also a precursor to other important biological substances whose functions relate to the activation of smooth muscle cells and the clotting of blood.[f] These functions are also related to the Liver in acupuncture theory, which controls the tension/flexibility of the muscles. Imbalances of the Liver also inhibit the function of the Spleen-Pancreas, which is noted in acupuncture theory for its ability to "keep the blood vessels in their place," and is thus related to blood clot formation. When cholesterol is artificially lowered or mevalonate is inhibited, these functions as well as other important Liver functions, especially its psycho-emotional function, are suppressed.

---

[a] Keys, A., and others. "HDL serum cholesterol and 24-year mortality of men in Finland." In *International Journal of Epidemiology* 13, 428-435.

[b] Those who agree with this conclusion include Dr. Bernard Forette and a team of French researchers from Paris as well as the NHLBI itself.

[c] Weidman, W.H., and others. "Nutrient intake and serum cholesterol level in normal children 6 to 16 years of age." In *Pediatrics* 61, 354-359, 1978.

[d] Cataract formation is seen as a simple extension of Liver Qi damage in acupuncture as is cancer.

[e] Lipitor®, a cholesterol-lowering drug, works by inhibiting an enzyme (3-hydroxy-3-methylglutaryl-coenzyme A (HMG-CoA) reductase) that produces cholesterol in the liver. It also facilitates LDL catabolism, or breakdown, by increasing the uptake of LDL in the liver, and by decreasing LDL production.

[f] The platelets produce less of the substance necessary for blood clotting, thromboxane.

OTHER "SIDE-EFFECTS" OF CHOLESTEROL-LOWERING DRUGS INCLUDE A TWENTY PERCENT INCREASE OF DEATH RATES DUE TO CANCER, HOMICIDE, AND SUICIDE. *ALL* of the statins produce cancer in rodents.[a] The only reason the FDA approved them is that the rat doses were much higher than the recommended clinical dose. Nevertheless, the blood levels of statins causing the cancer in the rodents are similar to that taken normally by heart-risk patients. Because it takes more than twenty years for clinical cancer to develop in humans after exposure to a carcinogen, and because no controlled trials of this duration have taken place, we have absolutely no way of ascertaining whether the millions of healthy people being treated with statins will develop cancer in the future. One of the Liver-related cancers associated with the statins is breast cancer.[b] Dr. Frank Sacks in the CARE study of 1996 found *twelve times more breast cancer* in the treatment group than in the control, a highly relevant statistical finding.

According to Matthew Muldoon, assistant professor of the Department of Medicine at the University of Pittsburgh, Pennsylvania, artificially lowered cholesterol levels have also been found to be related to alcohol abuse, poorly internalized social norms, low self-control, aggression, violence, homicide, and suicide.[c] Dr. Beatrice Golomb at the University of California at Los Angeles meticulously analyzed all studies published relating to low or lowered cholesterol levels and violence since 1965 and concluded that this association is definitely causal.[d] While never researched in any of the cholesterol-lowering trials, these patterns can be expected to increase as the general population is exposed to these drugs. These symptoms could include not only more death but also more rampant social aggression in the workplace and the home in the form of physical and psychological abuse, as well as the general inability to realize one's dreams and the unhappiness resulting from this dysfunction. As these are all Liver Qi functions in acupuncture, the problems associated with them become greater when the concentration of cholesterol is lowered below the individual's normal level by artificial, pharmacological means.

Homicide and suicide are two expressions of Liver imbalance in acupuncture relating to what is called Stagnant Liver Qi. Homicide results when the stagnant Liver Yang explodes outward, while suicide results when the same stagnant Yang can find no significant outlet and so implodes. The inability of an individual to regulate these inward and outward movements of energy in a

---

[a] Newman, T.B., and Hulley, S.B. "Carcinogenicity of lipid-lowering drugs." In *Journal of the American Medical Association* 27, 55-60, 1996.

[b] See the chapter on Breast Cancer later in the author's book *Natural Healing With Essential Oils* for a detailed discussion of how breast cancer is related to the Liver.

[c] Muldoon, M.F; Manuck, S.B.; and Matthews, K.A. "Lowering cholesterol concentrations and mortality: a quantitative review of primary prevention trials." In *New England Journal of Medicine* 323, 439-435, 1990.

[d] Golumb, B.A. "Cholesterol and violence: is there a connection?" In *Annals of Internal Medicine* 128, 478-487, 1998.

positive manner is related to depression in acupuncture theory. Violent behavior and psycho-emotional problems can be exacerbated with cholesterol-lowering drugs because they suppress the very Liver functions that regulate the ability to express frustration appropriately through creative and positive channels. Dr. Golomb recommends that these psychological conditions should be taken into consideration before cholesterol-lowering medications are prescribed. Cholesterol-lowering medications can also interfere with patients attempting to wean themselves from psycho-pharmaceutical drugs because they interfere with these normal Liver psycho-emotional functions. The symptoms resulting from the suppression of these functions by cholesterol-lowering drugs can easily be confused with a relapse of the depressed condition, and the patient and their doctor may erroneously conclude that they may never be able to live without medication. The best strategy for these people should first be to create a foundation to responsibly and naturally protect the heart and then begin a systematic lowering of the psychoactive drugs.[a]

Failure to Prove the Cholesterol Connection

The first mammoth trial to lower blood cholesterol with drugs, the Coronary Drug Project, was conducted in 1967 by the NHLBI. This trial tested the cholesterol-lowering effects of nicotinic acid (Vitamin B_3, or niacin), clofibrate (Atromidin®), thyroid hormone, and estrogen (the female sex hormone) on more than 8000 middle-aged men who already had at least one heart attack. Estrogen and thyroid hormone were discontinued before the end of the trial because of their unfavorable results. The patients receiving clofibrate and nicotinic acid suffered numerous and severe side effects from treatment, and those treated exclusively with clofibrate died with the same frequency as those in the control group.[b]

In 1973 Dr. Charles Bemis at the Peter Bent Brigham Hospital in Boston was one of the first to study the inside of coronary vessels. He found that atherosclerosis was 33 percent *more prevalent* in those whose cholesterol went *down* than in those whose cholesterol went *up*.[c] Dr. Demetrios Kimbris and his group confirmed these results the following year in Philadelphia where the coronary arteries of seventeen out of twenty-five patients with high cholesterol worsened (68 percent) in contrast to seven out of ten patients with

---

[a] See the work of Peter Breggin, M.D. for protocols on how to realistically accomplish this goal.

[b] The Coronary Drug Project Research Group. "The coronary drug project: findings leading to further modifications of its protocol with respect to dextrothyroxine." In *Journal of the American Medical Association* 231, 360-381, 1975.

[c] Bemis, C.E., and others. "Progression of coronary artery disease. A clinical arteriographic study." In *Circulation* 47, 455-464, 1973.

low cholesterol (70 percent).[a] Dr. Clarence Shub and his colleagues of the Mayo Clinic observed similar results when coronary atherosclerosis *increased* for *all* patients whose cholesterol had *decreased* by more than 60 mg/dl, the normally acceptable reduction.[b] According to Dr. Ravnskov's research, "Study after study has confirmed the startling finding of Bemis and his colleagues."[27]

In 1985, Dr. Lars Solberg and his co-workers from Oslo, Norway, in co-operation with researchers at Louisiana State University, made a weak claim correlating atherosclerosis with high blood cholesterol. But many of those he studied who had normal coronary vessels had the same cholesterol levels as those where all three coronary vessels were constricted. Even more contradictory was the finding that those with two narrowed coronary vessels had a lower cholesterol average than those with just one narrowed vessel.[c]

Only 22 studies of the several hundred that Dr. Ravnskov examined recorded changes of both the coronary artery system and changes in the total or LDL-cholesterol. Seventeen of these were angiographic trials and five were observational studies. Only one of these studies found evidence for *any* connection between blood cholesterol levels and coronary artery disease. This was the LDL-Apheresis Atherosclerosis Regression Study (LAARS) conducted by Dr. Abraham A. Kroop and his co-workers from various institutions in the Netherlands. This group used a combination of cholesterol-lowering methods, including the statin Zocor® and a technique called LDL-apheresis, which circulates the patient's blood plasma through a machine that takes away most of the LDL with chemicals. While Dr. Kroop achieved a record lowering of cholesterol of 47 and 63 percent (from 303 to 115 mg/dl), *no correlation was attained either between the amount of cholesterol lowered and the angiographic changes, or the condition of individual patients, which was unrelated to the amount of cholesterol lowered.* **The patients worsened or improved no matter how much cholesterol was lowered.**[d]

Even when *all* the randomized and controlled trials that lowered cholesterol were put together in what is called a meta-analysis, Ravnskov found *no relationship* between the degree of cholesterol reduction and coronary artery disease. If anything, he found the following:

1. Heart attack *deaths were equal* in both the treatment and the control groups

---

[a] Kimbiris, D., and others. "Devolutionary pattern of coronary atherosclerosis in patients with angina pectoris. Coronary arteriographic studies." In *American Journal of Cardiology* 33, 7-11, 1974.

[b] Shub, C., and others. "The unpredictable progression of symptomatic coronary artery disease." In *Mayo Clinic Proceedings* 56, 155-160, 1981.

[c] Solgerg, L.A., and others. "Stenoses in the coronary arteries. The Oslo study." In *Laboratory Investigation* 53, 648-655, 1985.

[d] Kroop, A.A., and others. "LDL-apheresis atherosclerosis regression study (LAARS). Effect of aggressive versus conventional lipid lowering treatment on coronary atherosclerosis." In *Circulation* 93, 1826-1835, 1996.

2. The *total* number of deaths was greater in the *treatment* groups
3. No trial demonstrated any statistically acceptable coronary mortality
4. Coronary mortality, including that found in the treatment groups, was *higher* the longer the trials continued

Politics Betrays Science

Major organizations like the NHLBI and the AHA, with significant ties to the food and pharmaceutical industries, administer more than 90 percent of all cardiovascular research grants. A tremendous amount of money is spent to conduct a study on coronary artery disease. Investors are highly motivated by the financial return they expect to receive. The studies they fund determine not only which products they will produce, but also provide valuable information as to how they will influence the medical community and the general public to buy these products. Television ads now inundate the consumer with new drugs and are accompanied by seductive images to convince the public to goad their doctors into prescribing them. Doctors are pressured by the media into prescribing these drugs, sometimes against their better judgment. If they do not acquiesce, the patients will go to another doctor who will prescribe them. Doctors are also deluged by young and sexy pharmaceutical sales reps that badger doctors into prescribing these drugs to keep up their regional quotas. Inexpensive and natural remedies like brown rice and leafy greens, which can not be patented, will never receive funding because the profit is not there to be made. Any researcher with personal ideas, especially if they differ from the agendas of these major organizations, will have little or no chance of finding financial support.

The history of research into coronary artery disease reveals how this funding imbalance can distort true scientific findings. Many of these quasi-scientific reports on the correlation between blood cholesterol and atherosclerosis are funded with federal tax monies awarded by the NHLBI. Those reports done by American coronary angiography specialists, for example, use what look like form letters to support their conclusions and offer nothing but extremely weak correlation coefficients (*0.36 percent or even smaller*). These specialists give no individual figures and never mention other studies that disagree with their supposed findings, a tactic never used in honest traditional scientific or academic research. The 1968 "Dietary Goals for the United States," the first of its kind and researched and written by the Senate Select Committee on Nutrition and Human Needs chaired by Senator George McGovern, used this tactic to force government agencies to conform to their cholesterol-lowering agenda. The maneuvers of this committee were described by the internationally famous science journalist, Gary Taubes, in his article called "The Soft Science of Dietary Fat," published in the prestigious *Science Magazine*. Apparently, the senators had already organized the press and public opinion before the scientific facts were established. Robert Levy, director of the NHLBI, described his position: "The good senators came out with the guidelines and then called us in to get advice" on how to substantiate their position.[a]

Doctors, Professors, and Nutritionists Speak Out

In spite of how well entrenched the cholesterol/heart doctrine is established in the eyes of the general public, the field of medicine, and governmental policy, many well-informed and highly regarded doctors, professors, and nutritionists are highly critical of this approach. Among them are:

- Mary Enig has her Ph.D. in Nutritional Sciences and is president of the Maryland Nutritionist's Association. Dr. Enig is currently a consultant to individuals, industry, and government on nutrition and has served as Editor and Contributing Editor for several professional journals on nutrition. Dr. Enig has spoken out against the hazards of *trans*-fatty acids and has defended the SaFAs against the economic and political agendas that have maligned them.
- Michael Gurr is an associate professor of biochemistry at the School of Biological and Molecular Sciences in Oxford, editor-in-chief of a nutritional review, and editor of several other scientific journals. Dr. Gurr has spoken out against the weak correspondence between animals and man in vascular pathology, the flaws and biases in epidemiological research, the lack of correspondence between fat consumption and coronary mortality, the weak predictability of measuring blood cholesterol, and the lack of improvement from artificially lowering cholesterol through drugs.[b]
- George Mann is a retired professor of medicine and biochemistry at Vanderbilt University. As early as 1977, he spoke out against the lack of relationship between diet and cholesterol, fat consumption and death rate, and the unfavorable outcomes of the cholesterol trials. In 1985, he called these ideas the "greatest scientific deception of our times." He was especially critical of the LRC directors whom he accused of manipulating data and delaying a solution to coronary artery disease for fear of losing their soft money funding.[c] The LRC is the study that established cholesterol as *the* direct cause of coronary artery disease.
- Michael F. Oliver is former professor and director of the Wynn Institute for Metabolic Research in London. He was one of the first critics against the campaign to lower cholesterol in the general

---

[a] Taubes G. "Nutrition: The soft science of dietary fat." *Science Magazine* 292, 2536-2545, 2001.
[b] Gurr, M.I. "Dietary lipids and coronary heart disease: old evidence, new perspective." In *Progress of Lipid Research* 31:195-243, 1992.
[c] Mann, G.V. "Coronary heart disease: doing the wrong things." In *Nutrition Today* July/August, 12-14, 1985.

population, especially "when the accumulated evidence is that total mortality is unchanged or possibly even increased." He was particularly cautious about the unforeseen, dangerous, and possibly carcinogenic long-term effects of cholesterol-lowering drugs.[a]

- Edward R. Pinckney, former co-editor of the *Journal of the American Medical Association* and editor of four other medical journals, published his book *The Cholesterol Controversy* in 1973. In commenting on this book, Uffe Ravnskov suggests, "It seems impossible that any sensible and honest doctor who has read this book could continue to teach his patients about the dangers of cholesterol."[28] Pinckney himself declares that cholesterol gives only a "rough indication" of disease, particularly stress, and that any artificial attempts to change it through diet or cholesterol-lowering drugs "may well cause more trouble than it could relieve." He also cites the complicity of the dairy industry for their failure to respond to attacks because of their alliance with the polyunsaturated fat industry, whose products they distribute at an even greater profit. Pinckney also accuses the passivity of the dairy industry because of their government subsidies, which give them a bigger profit than they could make on the open market. Overall, he criticizes that consumers "have been taken in by certain commercial interests and health groups who are more interested in...money than...life."[b]

- Raymond Reiser is a former professor of biochemistry at Texas A & M University. As early as 1973 he criticized recommendations for lowering cholesterol through diet because they were based on a "practice of referring to secondary or tertiary sources, each taking the last on faith, which has led to the matter-of-fact acceptance of a phenomenon that may not exist." He also analyzed the references used by the AHA for their dietary recommendations and concluded that they were based on "unsupportive and contradictory studies." He dismissed their "rationale as not a logical explanation...but an assemblage of obsolete and misquoted references."[c]

- Dr. Paul Rosch is especially vitriolic in his criticism of the cholesterol campaign, which he says "comes from speculation, rather that any solid proof." He accuses the public of being "brainwashed" about the benefits of lowering cholesterol while "nothing could be further from the truth." Professor Rosch offers

---

[a] Oliver, M.F. "Dietary fat and coronary heart disease." In *British Heart Journal* 58:423-428, 1987.

[b] Pinckney, E.R., and Pinckney, C. *The Cholesterol Controversy.* Los Angeles: Sherbourne Press, 1973.

[c] Reiser, R. "A commentary on the rationale of the diet-heart statement of the American Heart Association." In *American Journal of Clinical Nutrition* 40:654-658, 1984.

the explanation that the promotional campaign waged by drug companies, the food industry, and medical supply houses gives them a huge financial incentive with which to infiltrate the medical and governmental agencies who should protect us from "such unsubstantiated dogma." [a]   Dr. Rosch is particularly well credentialed to make these criticisms. He is Clinical Professor of Medicine and Psychiatry at New York Medical College, President of the American Institute of Stress, Honorary Vice President of the International Stress Management Association, and Chairman of its US branch. He has also been the editor or sub-editor of several well-known medical journals as well as the President of the New York State Society of Internal Medicine, Chairman of the International Foundation for Biopsychosocial Development and Human Health, and Expert Consultant on Stress to the United States Centers for Disease Control. In addition, he has appeared on numerous television programs such as *The Today Show*, *Good Morning America*, *60 Minutes*, *Nova*, and on other network presentations on CBS, NBC, PBS, and BBC. He is published in every major medical journal and is quoted in major American newspapers and magazines.

- Dr. Ray Rosenman is retired Director of Cardiovascular Research in the Health and Sciences Program and SRI International in Menlo Park, California, and Associate Chief of Medicine at Mt. Zion Hospital and Medical Center in San Francisco. He has published four books, many chapters for textbooks, and many journal articles on heart disease. He concludes that dietary lipids can not explain the variables of mortality in coronary artery disease and that "clinical trials...fail to provide adequate evidence that lowering cholesterol...is associated with a significant reduction of mortality or...longevity [and that] the preventive effects of dietary and drug treatments have been exaggerated by a tendency...to...inflate supportive results, while suppressing discordant data."[b]

- The late Dr. Russell Smith, an experimental psychologist and statistician, studied the cholesterol issue thoroughly in cooperation with Edward Pinckney and published their findings in two large and highly regarded scientific reviews as well as in a popular book. Dr. Smith is probably the most outspoken critic of the cholesterol campaign. He charges that "much of the epidemiological research...has been conducted...by individuals with no formal

---

[a] Rosch. P. In *Health and Stress. The Newsletter of the American Institute of Stress*. 1995, number 1; 1998, number 1; 1999, number 8; 2001, numbers 2, 4, 7.

[b] Friedman, M; Rosenman, R.H.; and Byers, S. O. "Deranged cholesterol metabolism and its possible relationship to human atherosclerosis: a review." In *Journal of Gerontology* 10:60-85, 1955.

education and little...training in the scientific method. Consequently, studies are often poorly designed and data are often inappropriately analyzed and interpreted. Moreover, biases are so commonplace; they appear to be the rule, rather than the exception.... Many researchers routinely manipulate and/or interpret their data to fit preconceived hypotheses.... Much of the literature, therefore, is nothing less than an affront to the discipline of science. [In addition] the current campaign [to lower cholesterol through diet and drugs] is based on fabrications, erroneous interpretations and/or gross exaggerations of findings and...the ignoring of massive amounts of unsupportive data.... It does not seem possible that objective scientists could ever interpret the literature as supportive." [a] Dr. Smith also considers the work of leading scientists from the NHLBI and the AHA as "incompetent and sloppy" as well as being unscientific:

The political and financial power of the NHLBI and AHA...alliance...[is] able to use its power and prestige to suppress a great body of unsupportive evidence and even defy...logic.[29]

Reviewing the Cholesterol Trials

Dr. Uffe Ravinskov reviews all the cholesterol-lowering studies and discusses not only their findings but also their strong and weak points. He describes the methods by which they reached their conclusions and provides a thorough and responsible criticism for each. The following paragraphs in this section summarize his perspective on twelve of these trials, most of which are single trials involving only one study. A few, however, are studies of larger groups of studies representing many trials together. The following are major reasons why Ravnskov's criticisms show that these studies provide invalid conclusions concerning the relationship between coronary artery disease and the lowering of blood cholesterol:

1. Weakening of trials due to a pre-formulated agenda
2. Weak statistical correlation
3. Failure to provide actual figures
4. Failure to discuss or even mention studies with contradictory findings as well as exclusion of any statement contradicting the cholesterol-lowering hypothesis, even those made by prominent groups and concluded by other major studies
5. Failure to achieve scientific consensus BEFORE the agendas are fed to the press
6. Biased control groups that were picked specifically to give the results the trials were seeking

---

[a] Smith, R.L. *Diet, blood, cholesterol and coronary heart disease: a critical review of the literature.* Vector Enterprises. Vol. 1, 1989; Vol. 2, 1991.

7. Conclusions reached that were contrary to the findings
8. Gross exaggeration of figures describing the benefits of cholesterol-lowering drugs
9. Over-generalization of benefits for isolated risk-groups that were presented to the public at large

Pre-Formulated Agenda

As mentioned previously, the very first cholesterol studies were completed in Russia and published in 1911 independently by Anitschkov and Ignatowski. When they fed *vegetarian* rabbits *animal* food the rabbit's arteries plugged up with a fatty/fibrous material sticking to the lining of their arterial walls. The results of these findings were then projected onto humans in spite of the fact that human arterial plaque is different because it grows within the arterial wall instead of on it like it does in rabbits. Even the curious anomaly of feeding vegetarian rabbits a highly carnivorous diet never fazed the researchers in making their projection. While we can not possibly know whether these results occurred because of the unnatural diet these rabbits were fed or the stress induced by force-feeding them, these "scientists" rashly concluded that the cause of the arterial plugging in the rabbits was the food they were fed and not the "way" the food was fed to them. Follow-up studies over the next several decades produced similar results with vegetarian animals but failed totally with carnivorous dogs. Carnivores and omnivores, like humans, are obviously able to digest animal fat better than vegetarian rabbits. The reason researchers even attempted such a silly study and then ignored this finding and moved forward with cholesterol research can only be explained by the common, yet egregious, desire to prove an already formulated agenda.

Biased Control Groups

In a cholesterol-lowering trial in the early 1970s, the Upjohn Company tested its new drug colestipol (Lestid®) on more than 2,000 men and women with high cholesterol. The apparently amazing results in lowering the number of heart attacks compared to the control group were slanted because patients were not randomly assigned to treatment and control groups. Instead, the control group was stacked with a disproportionate number of individuals with familial hypercholesterolemia, those whose cholesterol metabolism makes them statistically more vulnerable than others for heart attacks. No such results have ever been achieved in any trial before or since.[a]

Another so-called "blinded" study was the Cholesterol-Lowering Atherosclerosis Study (CLAS) directed in 1987 by Dr. David Blankenhorn and his group from the University of Southern California medical department with the support of the NHLBI and the Upjohn pharmaceutical company. This was

---

[a] Dorr, A.E. and others. "Colestipol hydrochloride in hypercholesterolemic patients—effects on serum cholesterol and mortality." In *Journal of Chronic Disease*, 31, 5-14, 1978.

the study that historically established the national guidelines to lower cholesterol to 185 mg/dL. A blinded study is one in which neither the patients, the researchers, nor the doctors know which group is the treatment group and which is the control. In this study, however, the treatment group received "marker" drugs that made it easy to tell which group was which. In addition to the cholesterol-lowering drug they were testing, colestipol, patients in the treatment group were also given nicotinic acid. The side effects of nicotinic acid are extremely obvious and include severe flushing and itching of the skin. One can not imagine that these patients were not aware of this discomfort and did not relay it to each other and their doctors. In short, EVERYONE in this "blinded" trial knew which group was which. The CLAS was not a blind study at all! In addition, the researchers skewed the results by having those in the treatment group take the drugs for a period of three months *before* the trial so that those whose cholesterol did not go down could be excluded. If these overt manipulations were not enough, they were considered statistically significant only because the researchers used a well-known unreliable test.

A "one-tailed t-test" is not as reliable as a two-tailed t-test, the criteria of which is more difficult to satisfy. A one-tailed t-test is not reliable enough to use when the results of a study can go either way, which is why scientists have agreed not to use it except when the results are only expected to go in one way. Such an expectation was certainly not the case in the CLAS, and the director even promised before the study began not to use it. Nevertheless, the NHLBI and the AHA then adopted Dr. Blankenhorn's claims as well as his suggestions to lower blood cholesterol guidelines down to an even lower level of 185 mg/dl as the new national policy, which would affect around 40 million healthy Americans.[a] What is important to realize here is that this study was used to establish national guidelines for such a low level in spite of the fact that the only way they could get results to prove their agenda was by (1) claiming that the test was "blind" when it obviously was not; (2) making sure that the treatment group would respond the way they wanted them to BEFORE the trial began; and (3) using an inaccurate and slanted statistical method to prove their results.

Conclusions Contrary to Findings

At the same time, the World Health Organization tested clofibrate in 10,000 middle-aged men with the highest blood cholesterol levels. While after five years the treatment group was 25 percent more successful in preventing nonfatal heart attacks than the control group, the number of those who had *died* from heart attacks was equal; while 68 percent *more* patients in the clofibrate group died from other diseases;[b] and only four to five years after the trial, the

---

[a] Blankenhorn, D.H., and others. "Beneficial effects of combined colestipol-niacin therapy on coronary atherosclerosis and coronary venous bypass grafts." In *Journal of the American Medical Association* 257, 3233-3240, 1987.
[b] 128 or 0.0256 percent as opposed to 87 or 0.0174 percent.

number of heart attack deaths was *larger* in the clofibrate group. Nevertheless, clofibrate is still recommended as a useful drug in many countries.[a]

Another trial conducted in 1985 by Dr. Tatu Miettinen in Finland tested about 1,200 middle-aged, overweight, and hypertensive business executives with high blood cholesterol and found that, while diet and cholesterol-lowering drugs were effective in lowering blood cholesterol by 6.3 percent and blood pressure by about 5 percent, and while lowering tobacco consumption was able to lower cholesterol by about 13 percent, these improved risk factors did NOT yield favorable results with coronary artery disease. In fact, TWICE as many heart attacks were experienced in the treatment group as in the control group due to the use of the clofibrate drugs[b] as the investigators reasonably concluded.

While the results of the Miettinen trial implicated clofibrate as a potential "cause" of coronary artery disease, they were glossed over during the next four years in favor of the LRC trial, which was cited 612 times in medical journals compared to the mere 15 times for the Miettinen trial. During this period, clofibrate was being used as a cure for coronary artery disease by millions of people. Think of what recalling such a drug would do to the popularly entrenched BELIEF in the so-called scientific medical system! Most likely, the sponsors of clofibrate realized that the more sensible approach was to wait for a newer drug to replace clofibrate. Then they would not have to be held accountable.

Exaggerated Figures

In 1979, the NHLBI, led by Dr. Manning Feinleib and a team of co-workers studying the coronary vessels of those who had died, reached the very low correlation coefficient of only 0.36 percent and then went ahead anyway to conclude that blood cholesterol levels best predicted atherosclerosis. The official write-up of this study never explained this dubious conclusion and used no diagrams or data, nor did they discuss or even comment on the low correlation coefficient.[c] Apparently, they can say whatever they want.

In 1982, the MRFIT Trial of 12,866 American men especially prone to heart attack was used to claim the "proven" benefit of lowering blood cholesterol. The treatment group was given cholesterol-lowering drugs and was taught about the rationale behind the trial, how to read food labels, how to use low-fat polyunsaturated foods from the grocery store, and was counseled by doctors, nutritionists, psychologists, nurses, and other health professionals as to nonsmoking and other benefits. The control group received nothing and

---

[a] See *British Heart Journal* 40, 1069-1118, 1978; and *The Lancet 2*, 379-385, 1980.

[b] Miettinen, T.A., and others. "Multifactorial primary prevention of cardiovascular diseases in middle-aged men with dyslipidemia." In *New England Journal of Medicine* 317, 1237-1245, 1987.

[c] Feinleib, M and others. "The relation of antemortem characteristics to cardiovascular findings at necropsy." In *The Framingham Study. Atherosclerosis* 34, 145-157, 1979.

continued eating the SAD. This was the most ambitious medical study ever conducted. Seven years and $150,000,000 later, no statistical difference was found in either the deaths from heart attacks (115 in the treatment group as opposed to 124 in the control) or the number of total deaths from all causes (265 in the treatment group as opposed to 260 in the control).[a] Four years after the end of the trial, no statistical difference in the deaths from heart attacks between the two groups was reached. The slight improvement in the treatment group was more than cancelled by the higher death rate in the control group due to cancer. Ironically, the most significant feature of the trial was that blood cholesterol differences were trivial even though the drastic dietary changes undergone by the treatment group included a 50 percent lowering of cholesterol intake, and a 25 percent lowering of saturated fat intake.[b]

Only the favorable results, however, were publicized.[30] For example, it was promoted that the risk of dying from a heart attack with cholesterol above 265 mg/dl was 413 percent greater than with cholesterol below 170. However, when comparing the risk groups within this study, 1.3 percent of those with the highest cholesterol value died of a heart attack compared to the 0.3 percent of those with the lowest values, a difference of only one percent! Dr. Ravnskov points out that, while this meager one percent does not have the same alarming effect, "both figures are [technically] correct because 1.3 is 413 percent of 0.3."[31] In other words, while the statistical differences were only one percent between those with high as opposed to those with low cholesterol, the results of the cholesterol-lowering drugs were falsely promoted as being 413 percent better!

Another grossly mismanaged and misrepresentative trial was the Lipid Research Clinics Coronary Primary Prevention Trial (LRC) put on by the NHLBI in 1984 to test the effectiveness of cholestrymine in 4,000 individuals with high cholesterol, 40 mg/dl higher than those in MRFIT. After seven to eight years the results were analyzed. While the summary of the paper claimed a 19 percent lowering of nonfatal coronary heart attacks and a 30 percent lowering of fatal heart attacks, three flaws can be found with this exaggerated conclusion:

1. By ignoring the total number of men involved, the true figures were obscured. Only 10 percent, or 190 men, experienced a nonfatal heart attack after taking the cholestrymine as opposed to 11.1 percent, or 212, of the controls, a difference of only 1.1 percentage points; while 1.7 and 2.3 percent experienced fatal heart attacks, a difference of only 0.6 percentage points, or 12 individuals

2. Only by *including* uncertain cases of individuals who may or may not have died from a heart attack were they able to reach their 30 percent figure, and only by *excluding* uncertain cases were they able to reach their 19 percent figure

---

[a] *Journal of the American Medical Association* 248, 1465-1477, 1982.
[b] *Journal of the American Medical Association* 86, 744-758, 1986.

3. The fact that almost as many as three times more men died violently from homicide, suicide, or trauma from the treatment group was totally ignored[a]

While these unfortunate deaths negated overall improvement from the drug treatment group, the false positive side of this study continues to be emphasized today. Even the new disease called *hypercholesterolemia* was invented just to support this bias. What is ignored in this study, and cholesterol-lowering studies, in general, is that by artificially lowering cholesterol the function of the Liver Qi is suppressed, an action that directly leads to these well known and serious consequences.

Only two hundred lives would be saved per year in the US in men with blood cholesterol as high as in the LRC study, provided of course that the result of the study was not merely due to chance, which the study never proved. Nevertheless, Dr. Daniel Steinberg, chairman of the conference that started the publicly funded National Cholesterol Education Campaign, declared in a 1990 letter to the editors of the *Atlantic Monthly* that 100,000 lives could be saved each year.[b] Much closer to the truth, however, the director of the LRC study himself, Dr. Basil Rifkind, admitted in a medical journal just a few months later that deaths from coronary artery disease had NOT been reduced by such scientific trials and that "further gains in life expectancy are unlikely." [c] Furthermore, while the LRC study focused exclusively on only the upper 0.8 percent of the blood cholesterol levels (which is one percent of mankind), LRC trial directors had no reservations in recommending cholestrymine for other age groups, for those with close to normal cholesterol, and also for women, regardless of the fact that the LRC trial had not studied women and that high cholesterol is not considered a risk factor in women nor is such treatment of any use.

In addition, while both groups in the study received dietary instruction, and thus no reasonable conclusions about diet could be drawn, the directors still advocated that lowering cholesterol with the AHA's diet is beneficial. Conventional treatment for high cholesterol involves putting patients on the AHA's diet and then, when that fails as it usually does, cholesterol-lowering drugs. While the diets recommended by the AHA, as of 2003, do mention whole grains to their credit, most of the strategy is centered on lowering cholesterol through fat reduction diets as well as increasing physical activity and dietary fiber. The AHA also recommends reducing *trans*-fatty acids to reduce

---

[a] The Lipid Research Clinic's coronary primary prevention trial results. 1. Reduction in incidence of coronary heart disease." In *Journal of the American Medical Association* 251, 351-64, 1984.

[b] *The Atlantic Monthly*, January 1990.

[c] *British Medical Journal* 310, 815, 1990.

LDL, not because it poses any threat to health on its own.[a] These conventional dietary methods, however, fail to predict, prevent, or cure coronary artery disease. Placing people on conventional diets to prevent heart disease is just an excuse to promote drugs by default since the diet-promoters know by now that standard AHA diets do not work. Such a strategy only gives the public the illusion of choice so that their natural resistance for taking drugs is lowered while their inclination toward natural healing methods is undermined! Meanwhile, the connection between these highly refined diets and heart disease is overlooked.

Scientific misrepresentation in cholesterol-lowering trials has escalated even further with the trials of the statin drugs. The statins are the biggest selling category of prescription drugs and net $12.5 billion in the US each year. Twelve million Americans currently take statin drugs and the industry hopes that number will soon TRIPLE. When the absolute figures for statins are compared instead of the relative figures used by doctors and drug companies in their ads, there is only an approximate two to three percent better chance of surviving a heart attack by taking them over a four-to six-year period (95 percent compared to 92), and even less for healthy individuals.[b] According to one trial (the 4S trial), 235 high cholesterol individuals and 826 normal cholesterol individuals would have to consume a statin drug for four to five years in order to prevent one fatal heart attack at a cost of $150,000 per saved life.[32] Most of mankind would have to be medicated (97.6 percent, in fact) by this approach just to save the lives of a few.

Paradoxically, however, while the drug companies manufacturing the statins claim to lower cholesterol by 30-40 percent or more, the trials used to provide these statistics reveal that lowering cholesterol levels has little or no bearing on the outcome of coronary artery disease. For example, the Expanded Clinical Evaluation of Lovastatin trial (EXCEL),[c] which studied the effect of Lovastatin® on more than 8,000 high-cholesterol individuals, found that the death rate for coronary artery disease was only 0.3 percent better in the treatment group than in the control.[d] These meager results did not stop at least twenty reports from being published in various medical journals touting how effective and how well people tolerate Lovastatin®. If these results are really so obvious, why has the final outcome of the trial not been published after more than ten years since it began? The use of pseudo-science to promote the

---

[a] 1990 studies in Holland and the Harvard School of Public Health were verified in 1992 by USDA studies that coronary artery disease as well as breast and prostate cancer is related to excessive *trans*-fatty acid intake.

[b] 98.8 percent compared to 98.4 percent in the WOSCOPS trial and 99.67 percent compared to 99.55 percent in the AFCAPS/TexCAPS trial.

[c] Bradford, R.H., and others. "Expanded clinical evaluation of lovastatin (EXCEL) study results." In *Archives of Internal Medicine* 151, 43-49, 1991.

[d] 0.5 percent or 32-33 individuals out of a group of about 6,600 for the Lovastatin® group and 0.2 percent or 3 or 4 individuals out of 1,650 for the control group receiving the placebo.

economic agendas of the pharmaceutical and food industries instead of using their financial power to promote science is the glaring but all-too-obvious answer!

Ignoring Contradictory Studies

And yet, huge sums of money are poured down the drain in support of cholesterol research and medication. Cholesterol-lowering medication runs $2,000 per year, per person, forever. Current sales of the most popular drug runs over $1 billion per year and are soon expected to double. The cholesterol industry itself, involving screening tests and cholesterol-lowering drugs, nets $20 billion-plus per year. In this blind race for medical power and control, the FDA and the physicians who follow their lead ignore important studies indicating that the cholesterol approach does not really work.

In 1992, an article in the *British Medical Journal* evaluating twenty-two different studies concluded that, "Lowering serum (blood) cholesterol concentrations does not reduce mortality (or death) and is unlikely to prevent coronary artery disease. Claims of the opposite are based upon preferential citation of supportive trials." In 1992, even Dr. William P. Castelli, the director of the famous Framingham Study was forced to admit:

> The more saturated fat one [eats], the more cholesterol one [eats], the more calories one [eats], the LOWER the person's serum cholesterol.[33]

In the Framingham Study, a *decrease* of cholesterol was more strongly associated with death than an *increase* of cholesterol. According to the report: **"For each 1 percent mg/dl drop of cholesterol there was an 11 percent *increase* in coronary and total mortality."** [34] The Framingham report, however, was misquoted and turned head over heels by the NHLBI and the AHA in a joint statement published in their review called *The Cholesterol Facts*:

> The results of the Framingham study indicate that a 1 percent reduction...of cholesterol [corresponds to a] 2 percent reduction in CHD [Coronary Heart Disease] risk.[a]

This statement blatantly contradicts the original Framingham report, which explicitly states that *mortality increases by 11 percent for each 1 mg/dl reduction in blood cholesterol*. In fact, thirty years after the first cholesterol measurements in Framingham, lowering cholesterol levels have made no difference in preventing coronary artery disease in most men.[b]

---

[a] Gotto, A.M.; LaRosa, J.C.; Hunninghake, D.; and others. "The cholesterol facts. A summary of the evidence relating dietary fats, serum cholesterol and coronary heart disease. A joint statement by the American Heart Association and the National Heart, Lung and Blood Institute." In *Circulation* 81, 1721-33, 1990.

[b] Those above the age of 47.

In 1993, *Circulation*, the "medical journal" of the AHA, summarized nineteen worldwide studies of nearly 650,000 men and women. This AHA report found *no* predictive value for cholesterol levels in women at any age, *no* predictive value in men with cholesterol levels between 160 and 240, while men with cholesterol levels under 160 were 17 percent more likely to die from *anything* than men with moderate levels (between 160 and 190). In other words, the information in all of these worldwide studies and the massive cholesterol-screening program is of no value.[35] Nevertheless, the AHA still insists that eating fat and cholesterol causes heart attacks.

AHA fundraisers, dependent as they are upon public donations, use the cholesterol theory to claim progress in fighting the disease after going for so many years without plausible explanation. The education they provide to the general public concerning the benefits of a low fat/low cholesterol diet influences the medical profession as well. Most doctors are too busy to read the medical literature on which the cholesterol theory is based and tend to follow the policies of organizations such as the AHA, the NHLBI, and pharmaceutical companies. Together, these organizations play a strong role in determining the direction of research and healthcare.

Promotion Before Consensus

One of the key steps in the cholesterol campaign was to establish dietary recommendations for the entire US. To this end, the NHLBI convened a three-day development conference in 1984 in Bethesda, Maryland, called the Consensus Development Conference. With top researchers in the field in place, the report fed to the press *looks* like it was the result of a general consensus, but nothing was further from the truth. Printed copies of the ensuing "national cholesterol education program" were prepared weeks before the meeting even took place and were distributed without discussion when the program was announced to the public at a press conference. This announcement was made in spite of objections among the researchers that the problems with the cholesterol studies made it unwise to rush such unfounded guidelines into place, especially when they were to be enacted on such a massive level. Nevertheless, the chairperson heartlessly forced the shocking conclusion on the second day by stating, "It has been established beyond a reasonable doubt that lowering elevated blood cholesterol levels will reduce the risk of heart attack deaths due to coronary heart disease."[a]

In the twenty studies discussed by the researchers at the conference, the only one showing *any* relation between cholesterol and coronary artery disease showed no more correlation than would be made by chance. As H. Ahrens of Rockefeller University pointed out, if the scientific method had been applied, the unusual study would be discounted, not the nineteen that were consistent.[36] Overnight, Americans were led to believe that twenty-five percent of them were sick with the new hypercholesterolemia disease, and that increasing

---

[a] Winslow, C.M. In *Journal of the American Medical Association* 260:505-509 1988.

polyunsaturated fatty acids and decreasing animal fats would reduce the incidence of coronary artery disease. Margarine and vegetable oil companies profit immensely from these studies while continuing to fill the public with the toxic effect of refined vegetable oils and *trans*-fatty acids through their products. These companies deceive people with the cholesterol-free "advantages" of their products through their advertisements while as blood cholesterol levels *fall*, the general health of the public *gets worse*, and death rates from heart attack *increase*.[37]

In fact, many people with high cholesterol live the longest. Among the elderly, the population where 90 percent of all cardiovascular disease takes place (in those over 60), high cholesterol is not a risk factor. In fact, twice as many of the elderly die with low cholesterol than with high cholesterol. Of the remaining 10 percent, half are women who are not at risk from high cholesterol at all. Therefore, **only 5 percent of those who die from a heart attack are at risk from high cholesterol!** As Ravnskov suggests: "How is it possible that high cholesterol is harmful to the artery walls and causes fatal coronary heart disease, the most common cause of death, if those whose cholesterol is the highest, live longer than those whose cholesterol is low?"[a]

To the contrary, much evidence suggests that high cholesterol prevents illness and death while low cholesterol is associated with higher mortality. For example, low cholesterol is associated with increased mortality from gastrointestinal and respiratory diseases because low cholesterol predisposes people to infectious disease. One example is that those with low cholesterol have double the risk of testing positive for HIV compared with those with the highest cholesterol. In the $150,000,000 MRFIT study mentioned earlier, where manipulated summaries proclaimed that cholesterol-lowering drugs would lower the incidence of heart attack, **the risk for people with low cholesterol was actually four times as great** (see page 85).

In studies done at several German and British university hospitals, researchers found that the risk of dying of chronic heart failure was strongly associated with low serum cholesterol and low LDL. The largest study, led by Dr. Tamara Horwich and performed by Professor Gregg C. Fonorow and his team at the UCLA Department of Medicine and Cardiomyopathy Center in Los Angeles (including over a thousand patients with severe heart failure), found after five years that twice as many patients with low cholesterol died than those with high cholesterol. As high cholesterol has been shown to protect against bacterial infections, the ability of LDL to inactivate dangerous bacterial toxins is among its other important health benefits.

---

[a] "The Benefits of High Cholesterol," Uffe Ravnskov, MD, PhD in *The Benefits of High Cholesterol* sponsored by the Weston A. Price Foundatation.

Historical Landmarks in the Cholesterol Campaign

In all, the cholesterol campaign is one in which a modicum of science has been used to give the pretense of respectability to the overriding interest of industrial profit. When viewed in a historical perspective these motives become clear. Mary Enig, Ph.D. and Sally Fallon present this perspective in their 1999 article called "The Oiling of America," first published in *Nexus Magazine*. A summary of this perspective is given below.

1950

By 1950, coronary heart disease was the highest cause of death in the United States, affecting more than one of every three people. The nutritional background was that butter consumption at this time dropped almost 50 percent while margarine consumption quadrupled and vegetable oil consumption more than tripled.[a]

1954

In 1954 David Kritchevsky published a paper describing the effects of ridiculous Russian experiments on the feeding of oxidized cholesterol from animal fats to vegetarian rabbits.[b] Kritchevsky's articles were then used to support the theory that saturated fat and cholesterol from animal food raises cholesterol levels in the blood and forms plaque in the arteries.

1956

In 1956, an AHA fund-raiser aired on all three major television networks and presented the new lipid hypothesis as the cause of the new epidemic of heart disease and prescribed the Prudent Diet in which corn oil, margarine, chicken and cold refined cereal replaced butter, lard, beef, and eggs.

1957

In 1957, the Nutrition Bureau of the New York Health Department initiated the Anti-Coronary Club Trial, in which a group of businessmen were placed on the Prudent Diet. That same year, the food industry began to advertise the health benefits of low-fat vegetable oils.

1961

In 1961 the AHA published its first dietary guidelines in which authors Irving Page, Ancel Keys, Jeremiah Stamler, and Frederick Stare recommended the

---

[a] Enig, M. In *Trans Fatty Acids in the Food Supply: A Comprehensive Report Covering 60 Years of Research*, 2nd Edition, Enig Associates, Inc., Silver Spring, MD, 4-8, 1995.
[b] Kritchevsky, D. et al, "Effect of Cholesterol Vehicle in Experimental Atherosclerosis." In *American Journal of Physiology*, July-September, 178:30-32, 1954.

substitution of polyunsaturated vegetable oil for saturated fat.[a] Stamler later published his views in a 1966 publication sponsored by the Mazola oil company, manufacturers of Corn oil and margarine, called *Your Heart Has Nine Lives* in spite of having to wait for "definitive proof." Stamler was responsible for many of the low-fat dietary practices began at this time such as the substitution of skim milk and low-fat cheeses for cream, butter, and whole cheeses as well as the reduction of eggs and the de-fatting of red meats.

1964

Doctors like Dr. William Castelli, Director of the Framingham Study, and Dr. Antonio Gotto, Jr., former AHA president, began to endorse the Prudent Diet. Dr. Gotto even sent a letter printed on the Baylor College of Medicine De Blakey Heart Center letterhead promoting this diet to practicing physicians.[b]

1966

In 1966 the results of the 1957 Anti-Coronary Club Trial, published in the *Journal of the American Medical Association,*[c] revealed that those on the Prudent Diet achieved a only moderate lowering of cholesterol (220 compared to 250) while eight people died of heart disease from the Prudent Diet in contrast to none in the control group who ate meat three times a day. Ironically, the director of the study himself, Dr. Jolliffe, succumbed in 1961 from vascular thrombosis. Promoters of the lipid hypothesis speculated that the poor results of the Anti-Coronary Club Trial were due to the small numbers of participants in the trial. In response, Dr. Irving Page urged a National Diet Heart Study of one million men organized by the National Heart Lung and Blood Institute in six major cities. However, when the pilot study of 2,000 men resulted in exactly the same number of deaths in both the Prudent Diet and the control group, the Diet Heart Study was abandoned "for reasons of cost" while Dr. Page himself died of a heart attack.

1968

In 1968 the AHA first warned of *trans*-fats in their diet heart statement: "Partial hydrogenation of polyunsaturated fats results in the formation of *trans* forms which are less effective than *cis, cis* forms in lowering cholesterol concentrations. It should be noted that many currently available shortening and margarines are partially hydrogenated and may contain little polyunsaturated fat of the natural *cis, cis* form." Because the shortening industry strongly objected to this statement and its potential indictment of the presence of *trans*-fats in the

---

[a] Keys, Ancel. "Diet and Development of Coronary Heart Disease." In *Journal of Chronic Disease*, October, 4 (4):364-380, 1956.

[b] Smith, R. L. and E. R. Pinckney. In *The Cholesterol Conspiracy*, Warren H. Green, Inc. St. Louis, MO. 125, 1991.

[c] Cristakis, G. "Effect of the Anti-Coronary Club Program on Coronary Heart Disease Risk-Factor Status." In *Journal of the American Medical Association*, 198 (6):129-35, November 7, 1966.

food supply, a researcher from Procter and Gamble convinced the medical director of the AHA to remove it. The result was that the 150,000 copies of the printed statement were never distributed.[a] The recommendations that did reach the public were restricted to the three main points of cholesterol dogma—restrict calories, substitute polyunsaturated vegetable oils for saturated animal fat, and reduce cholesterol in the diet.

1970

By the early 1970's the National Heart Lung and Blood Institute, the AMA, the American Dietetic Association, and the National Academy of Science all endorsed the lipid hypotheses and the avoidance of animal fats for those Americans in the "at risk" category.

1970

After the Second World War, partial hydrogenation was introduced that enabled the Omega 3 EFAs in Soy and Canola oils to be "selectively hydrogenated" and made into margarines and shortenings that replaced the previously used Cottonseed oil. As a result, Soybean production rose from virtually zero in 1900 to 70 million tons in 1970. By the twenty first century Soybean oil was used in almost eighty percent of all hydrogenated oils. Soybean shortenings contain about 40 percent *trans*-fats while Canola oil shortening contains about 50 percent. Refined Canola oil itself contains as much as 4.6 percent-unlabelled *trans*-fats.[b]

1973

In 1973 the FDA changed the Food, Drug and Cosmetic Act of 1938 so that junk food would no longer have to be labeled as the imitation everyone knew it to be. The older law specified that new industrially made "foods" had to be labeled "imitation," a term that obviously defined them as inferior. The new law created a loophole so that industrially made imitation foods no longer had to be labeled as such as long as they added artificial vitamins to bring the levels of essential nutrients up to the same amounts found in real food. As a result, fake industrial foods like coffee creamers, imitation egg mixes, processed cheeses, and imitation whipped cream with souped-up artificial vitamin additives could then be sold as real and healthy foods. The new labels then popped up touting the health benefits of these "foods" that were now low in cholesterol and rich in polyunsaturates. These new regulations, adopted without the consent of Congress, tremendously magnified the lobbying clout of the edible oil industry and totally obscured the literal "definition" of food for the general public who was left in a defenseless position that allowed them to be easily manipulated in regard to matters of nutrition and health from that point on.

---

[a] Staff of the Select Committee on Nutrition and Human Needs, United States Senate. "Dietary Goals for the United States—Supplemental Views." Government Printing Office, Washington, DC 139-140, November 1977.
[b] O'Keefe, S. and others. In *Journal of Food Lipids* 1:165-176, 1994.

1973 to 1977

Congress sided with the food industry during the years 1973 to 1977 when the Senate Select Committee on Nutrition and Human Needs, chaired by George McGovern, actively promoted the use of industrial made vegetable oils through their "Dietary Goals for the United States," which buried all opposing testimony and laid down the law about human nutrition and disease by stating categorically that "the over consumption of fat, generally, and saturated fat in particular...has been related to six of the ten leading causes of death" in the United States. Meanwhile, animal fat consumption had declined while vegetable fat intake, especially from liquid vegetable oils and margarine, had increased threefold since 1909. These figures were available at the time in the *Journal of American Oil Chemists*—a report that the McGovern Committee never used.[a]

1976

The FDA established GRAS (Generally Recognized as Safe) status in 1976 for hydrogenated Soybean oil.

1980

In 1980 the Seven Countries Study promoted that diets high in SaFAs are bad for the heart in spite of the fact that several countries studied with high cholesterol and saturated fat intake had less problems with heart disease than countries with low cholesterol and saturated fat. This discrepancy was simply ignored.

1982

In 1982 the enormously expensive Multiple Risk Factor Integration Trial (MRFIT) first differentiated between LDL and HDL as risk factors in CAD in spite of the fact that it found no statistical difference in either the deaths from heart attacks or the number of total deaths from all causes.

1983

Mary Enig's nutritional compilation on the fatty acid composition of foods was finally published in 1983 in the *Journal of the American Oil Chemists Society*.[b] Her analysis enabled researchers to confirm that the American public was consuming twice as much of the potentially dangerous *trans*-fat (12 grams as opposed to the 6 to 8) as was asserted by the mainstream Institute of Shortening and Edible Oils (ISEO).

---

[a] Rizek, R. L. et al. "Fat in Today's Food Supply—Level of Use and Sources." In *Journal of the American Oil Chemists Society*, 51:244, 1974.

[b] Enig, M. G. et al. "Fatty Acid Composition of Fat in Selected Food Items with Emphasis on Trans Components." In *Journal of the American Oil Chemists Society*, 60 (10):1788-1795, 1983.

85

Coronary Artery Disease and Cholesterol

1983

The Framingham Heart Study contended that high serum cholesterol is *a* risk factor in coronary artery disease while the next director of the study, Dr. William P. Castelli, admitted that the more saturated fat and cholesterol one eats, the LOWER the person's serum cholesterol becomes.

1984

The Lipid Research Clinics Conference (organized by the NHLBI to spotlight almost 40 years of research on lipids, cholesterol, and heart disease) claimed that results from the Framingham Study showed that "total plasma cholesterol is a powerful predictor of death related to CHD." The study itself, however, showed virtually no difference in coronary heart disease *events* for individuals with cholesterol levels between 205 mg/dL and 294 mg/dL or even extremely high cholesterol levels—up to almost 1200 mg/dL.[a]

1984

The Lipid Research Clinics Coronary Primary Prevention Trial (LRC) made three important, but unfounded, claims: (1) that high serum cholesterol is *the* cause of coronary heart disease; (2) LDL creates arterial plaque; and (3) diets high in SaFAs are bad for the heart. However, the only real difference between treatment and control groups concerning nonfatal heart attack in this study was trivial compared to the amount claimed (1.1 percentage points instead of 19 percent). The fact that three times more men died violently in the treatment group was totally ignored.

1984

The 1984 Cholesterol Consensus Conference defined everyone with cholesterol levels above 200 mg/dL as "at risk" and then called for mass cholesterol screening while suggesting the avoidance of saturated fat and cholesterol for all "at risk" Americans along with the replacement of butter with margarine. This conference also launched the nationwide National Cholesterol Education Program (NCEP), whose goal was to convince the otherwise skeptical medical profession to come on board in the cholesterol campaign. Members serving on the coordinating committee of the NCEP (who were also representatives of the American Pharmaceutical Association) helped compile a "Physicians Kit" teaching the importance of cholesterol screening, the advantages of cholesterol-lowering drugs, and the benefits of the Prudent Diet that was sent to every doctor in the country.

1986

In November of 1986, The *Journal of the American Medical Association* published a series on the Lipid Research Clinics trials including one called

---

[a] Smith, R. and E. R. Pinckney. *Diet, Blood Cholesterol and Coronary Heart Disease: A Critical Review of the Literature*, Vol 2, Vector Enterprises, Sherman Oaks, CA, 1991.

"Cholesterol and Coronary Heart Disease: A New Era" by the longtime American Heart Association member Scott Grundy, MD, PhD.[a] In the same article, Grundy contradicted himself saying "The recent consensus conference on cholesterol…implied that levels between 200 and 240…carry at least a mild increase in risk" as well as an earlier statement that "Evidence relating plasma cholesterol levels to atherosclerosis and CHD has become so strong as to leave little doubt of the etiologic connection." Grundy advocated that by calling for "the simple step of measuring the plasma cholesterol level in all adults…an enormous number of patients will be included." Grundy realized that "Many physicians will see the advantages of using drugs for cholesterol lowering" even though "a positive benefit/risk ratio for cholesterol-lowering drugs will be difficult to prove." While even today this positive risk/benefit ratio has never been established, the massive cholesterol program of screening and cholesterol-lowering drugs nevertheless nets sixty billion dollars per year in the US alone.

1987
In 1987 the Cholesterol-Lowering Atherosclerosis Study (CLAS) established national guidelines to lower cholesterol to 185 mg/dL in spite of serious flaws in the study. Directors claimed that this test was "blind" when it was obviously not; the treatment group was selected to respond the way directors wanted BEFORE the trial began; and results were proved only by using an inaccurate and slanted statistical method.

1993
By the nineties, butter, lard, and tallow consumption decreased 60 percent while *trans*-fat consumption tripled and liquid vegetable oil consumption increased *fifteen times* since the early 1900s when heart disease was virtually unheard of.

2000
The cholesterol campaign has escalated to the point where almost the entire population is actively encouraged to take cholesterol-lowering drugs while the amount of *trans*-fats on labels is hidden and almost impossible to discern.

Stress and the Spirit of the Heart

To understand how the stress of modern life can affect the heart we should first examine the psycho-spiritual functions of the Heart in acupuncture theory, which is associated with Fire in the Five Phases. To begin, the word for Heart in Chinese also means "mind" or "consciousness." A better rendering would be "Heart/Mind." Heart functions, therefore, have to do with specific Fire-related aspects of consciousness. In particular, these characteristics include natural spontaneity, openness, clarity, a balanced sense of control, appropriateness, and happiness. The so-called "openings" of the Heart in

---

[a] Grundy, S. M. "Cholesterol and Coronary Heart Disease: A New Era." In *Journal of the American Medical Association*, 256 (20):2849-2858, November 28, 1986.

acupuncture theory allow one to be open and present to the natural and social world without prejudice or preconception. A person who is "open" is as able to know and be comfortable with one's self as he or she is with others. Such a person can then achieve the clarity necessary to be appropriate in different kinds of social interactions and, therefore, preserve what is essential to social hierarchies without losing the fundamental openness that keeps these relations vital. According to this perspective, even the cohesion and Spirit of society as a whole is dependent upon this awareness, which can be summarized as the ability of its members to be conscious of the fundamental unity-within-difference of All Things.

The ability of the Heart to be open to this unity allows it to bear witness to the magical inter-connection of All Things that is most essential to life. Paradoxically, it is this bearing witness, or simple conscious awareness, that gives each person the necessary control of his or her individual role within the greater scheme of the whole. Each person honors this most fundamental unity through the simple presence of his or her being and is, thus, empowered by the greater connection they make to the whole. This function bears a certain responsibility to respond appropriately to the questions that such a direct approach to life brings. By respecting these questions, listening to the appropriate answers from within, and then responding to those answers, each person honors the life they choose to live. The ability to follow through with this function, that is, the ability to be clear and self-aware, appropriately gives people the capacity to be in control of their lives. When a person loses this fundamental openness and fails to resolve the questions that life presents to them, they will ultimately lose this control and, thus, the control over the physical health of their heart as well. When people abdicate this control, either to another person or to organizations, then the Spirit of their Heart can be lost. Eventually, others will take advantage of this situation by taking more than what they need. The excess they accumulate will eventually cloud over their own clarity so that the truth of their fundamental self, or True Nature, will be lost. Both parties can end up deficient in the Spirit that fulfills their lives while the debris of accumulated excess will cloud what ability is left to be clear in their Heart/Mind. At this point, the Fire of meaningless, competitive, and stress-inducing activity will take the place of happiness and fulfillment. Sound familiar?

According to the ancient Chinese text *Daodejing*, or "Book of the Way and its Power," the loss of clarity that results from the abdication of the Heart Spirit along with the accompanying exploitation by others is the source of all the evil in the world.[a] This situation sets the stage for the divide-and-conquer mentality that pits each individual against the other and creates the stress of the dog-eat-dog extreme we know so well in our modern way of life. This mentality is so insidious that it can penetrate all aspects of life—from the food choices we

---

[a] See the author's forthcoming work entitled *The Restoration of Humanity in the Daodejing*, for a complete discussion of this topic. See also the author's work entitled *The Twelve Spirit Points of Acupuncture.*

make, to the leaders we choose, and all the way to the policies they make, which we then have to live by and accept. The cholesterol controversy is one of the manifestations of this situation and serves to amplify this loss of control on the social level where the simple and basic knowledge of what constitutes healthy food has been lost and is now left to government agencies to control. Individual health and happiness is now mostly relegated to science, industry, the corporate world, and government agencies, which then try to provide answers that are not theirs to give. Such a force-fed solution is doomed to corruption from the start.

Given the degree of degenerative disease in modern society, it only stands to reason that the contributing factors are so obvious they are hidden from view. Modern people cannot see them because they are blinded by their own worldview, which they take for granted simply because it is so commonplace. They even defend it for this very reason. What this mentality reveals is the inability to question the basic foundations of life. Only by questioning these foundations can we develop an intimate relationship with them, and only when they are an intimate part of us can we be certain *we* are in appropriate control. When one questions the food choices available in the modern world, eventually one realizes that food and the mentality that produces it are two sides of the same coin. Whole and natural food produces healthy and happy lives while healthy and happy lives crave whole and natural food. In contrast, refined and industrial-quality food produces fragmented, stressful, and artificial lives, while fragmented, stressful, and artificial lives crave refined and industrial-quality food in order to perpetuate the illusion of happiness. Such a person is on the verge of losing their Heart Spirit as well as their physical heart and life itself.

Problems with Saturated Fat

SaFAs and Cholesterol

To further untangle the cholesterol controversy, we must follow several twists and turns involving the limitations of the exclusive focus on cholesterol as the "cause" of coronary artery disease, and especially the confusion between cholesterol and SaFAs and the role SaFAs are left to play in our understanding of this disease. The thread running through this confusion is summarized below.

Cholesterol is known to be a component of atherosclerotic plaque and so the conventional approach reasons that it should be removed to prevent coronary artery disease. Conventional methods use drugs to lower cholesterol. Removing cholesterol artificially, however, ignores more important reasons for *why* it builds up in atherosclerotic plaque. The artificial lowering of cholesterol also leads to a toxic, dysfunctional condition of the Liver Qi, which then leads to other serious disorders. SaFAs theoretically raise blood cholesterol levels because, while they do not contain any cholesterol per se, they do replace the cholesterol in membranes, which is then free to circulate in the bloodstream. Therefore, the conventional approach recommends that SaFAs should also be lowered. Conventional methods use diet to lower SaFAs by restricting animal fats.

However, people are led to believe that reducing the amounts of SaFAs in their diet will also lower their blood cholesterol levels. This approach does not work very well because reducing or even eliminating SaFAs from the diet will have little or no practical effect on cholesterol levels. The amount of cholesterol that can be spared from the membranes by reducing SaFAs is simply not enough to lower blood cholesterol levels effectively. The amount of cholesterol in animal food associated with SaFAs is not enough to lower cholesterol effectively either. More than thirty studies of more than 150,000 individuals have shown that people who eat more saturated fat and less polyunsaturated oil than other people have not had *any* more heart attacks than those who eat less saturated fat and more polyunsaturated oil.[38] Atherotic blockages are actually 74 percent UNSATURATED. In fact, according to Mary Enig, the false idea that saturated fat leads to heart disease is nothing more than a marketing scheme concocted by the margarine and polyunsaturated oil companies and only became current dogma, not through science, but through incessant repetition.[39] When hydrogenation was introduced into the US as early as 1910, margarine was primarily (90 percent) made from Coconut oil, animal tallow, or lard. However, this 90 percent was replaced with hydrogenated and refined vegetable oils by the 1940s. In response to the charge made by researcher Ancel Keys in the late 1950s stating that coronary artery disease is caused by hydrogenated vegetable fats, the industry mounted a public relations campaign that promoted the belief that only the SaFA part of the hydrogenated oils was causing the problem while the refined polyunsaturated part was good.[40]

The more prevalent reason people think reducing SaFAs will lower blood cholesterol is because of the confusion between cholesterol and SaFAs, which people have been led to equate. While both of these substances do occur together in animal quality foods, and cholesterol can only be found in animal foods, cholesterol and SaFAs are not the same. Both are lipids but they belong to entirely different groups. Cholesterol belongs to the sterol group and SaFAs belongs to the triglyceride group. In regard to coronary artery disease, cholesterol is a component of atherosclerotic plaque while SaFAs are not. SaFAs can, however, accumulate as fat deposits that line blood vessel walls when they are eaten to excess.[a41]

In addition, the SAD does not usually work to lower SaFAs because people on the SAD still consume large amounts of refined sugar and refined carbohydrates, both of which turn into SaFAs when these foods are eaten to their typical excess. When the attempt to lower SaFAs through the SAD fails to lower cholesterol, people are then led to think they have no choice but to take cholesterol-lowering drugs.

According to Mary Enig, eating 400 mg of cholesterol per day will only increase serum cholesterol levels 3-4 mg/dL.[42] This means that for every 100 mg of cholesterol consumed the serum cholesterol will only go up 1 mg/dL.

---

[a] The only exception is the medium-chain SaFAs in tropical oils, like Coconut oil, which are quickly burned as an energy source and do not accumulate as fat deposits.

Since the daily amount of dietary cholesterol recommended by the AHA is 300 mg/dL, a person eating that amount could quadruple their intake of dietary cholesterol to 1200 mg/day and their serum cholesterol would only go up 9 mg/dL, an insignificant amount.[a] An individual could eat cholesterol-containing animal food all day long and their serum cholesterol would still be insignificant as the serum cholesterol levels of the Masai prove.[b] Conversely, one could eliminate cholesterol from the diet at the same rate. If a person consuming the recommended daily amount of cholesterol eliminated all cholesterol from their diet and became a total vegetarian, they would theoretically lower their serum cholesterol 3 mg/dL.[c] However, eliminating dietary cholesterol altogether will only lower serum cholesterol to a certain point. Total vegetarians do not have zero serum cholesterol and total meat-eaters like the Masai do not have extremely high serum cholesterol. The reason is because the liver regulates serum cholesterol levels. When healthy people with low cholesterol eat cholesterol-containing food, their cholesterol will go up, but in those people with very high levels of cholesterol (hypercholesterolemics), eating cholesterol-containing food will lower their total cholesterol levels in compensation.[43]

The conventional dietary strategy is then to replace SaFAs in the diet with refined PUFAs, which is one of the biggest reasons why cholesterol binds to the coronary arteries in the first place.[d] PUFAs soften membranes, which then demand more cholesterol to make them harder. The more industrially refined, modified, and damaged the PUFAs are, the more harm they will do to the membranes and arteries.

A Relative Perspective

Animal foods contain the highest concentrations of long-chain SaFAs, those that are more associated with the build-up of fat deposits in the body. Any standard textbook on gross pathology will show pictures of these deposits on the coronary and other arteries. While these deposits may in fact be there, current studies can not statistically prove that they are implicated in coronary artery disease. How can this be? One answer is that different types of people react differently to these foods in different circumstances. An excess of animal fats may create coronary artery disease in some individuals but not in others. In addition, the amount constituting excess will not be the same in different individuals. The problem is to find out why this is so and how to tell the difference. Because these types have inadvertently been thrown together into the same study groups, few studies to this date have examined the relation between SaFA deposits in the arteries, dietary intake, and physical activity.

---

[a] 1200 minus 300 equals 900, which divided by 9 equals 9 mg/dL.

[b] One could eat animal foods at breakfast, lunch, and dinner, like many do on the SAD, and the dietary intake of cholesterol would only be about 1100 mg.

[c] 300 divided by 100 equals 3 mg/dL.

[d] The consumption of refined PUFAs has increased much more than SaFAs since the increase of coronary artery disease in the twentieth century. See the Chapter on "Dietary Fats and Oils" for a further explanation.

Reasons for why these differences may occur include individual constitution, condition, and activity. For example, wild animals like walruses that eat a diet consisting of large amounts of fatty food (fish) have atherosclerosis but no coronary artery disease.[a] In addition, primitive people like the Masai consume a diet consisting of 100 percent animal foods and also exhibit a great deal of atherosclerosis but do not have coronary artery disease. What differentiates the coronary arteries of animals like walruses and traditional people like the Masai from most Western people is that the size of their arteries is much wider as a result of their activity. Walruses are constantly swimming about in the cold ocean waters. They need the extra fat to keep warm and to sustain the immense amount of energy they need to stay alive and thrive in this harsh environment. They also stay active enough to counterbalance the fat deposits in their arteries. The Masai are also very active. They run to get from place to place instead of driving cars, as modern people are apt to do. They need animal fats to give them the energy to cover such distances in their daily life while their extremely active lifestyle counterbalances their fat deposits. If these subjects are taken out of their environmental context, but allowed to continue eating the same foods, their previous good health will change. The stress from walruses living in concrete pools and African tribes people living in high-rise apartment buildings will make their health worse unless their diets change.

One of the reasons why excessive amounts of animal foods in the diet can be associated with heart attacks is because of their high percentage of PGE_2. PGE_2 is the prostaglandin responsible for stimulating tension and clotting and is associated with high blood pressure. PGE_2 is also produced in the body from the essential fatty acid, LA. But, while the PGE_2 converted from vegetable quality LA is converted slowly with other prostaglandins that balance its constricting effects, the PGE_2 in animal food is entirely constricting. This means that eating animal foods presupposes one to a constricted condition including constriction of the arterial muscles. If either psycho-emotional or psychosocial tension builds up and/or the person exhibits fatty arterial buildup from excess SaFAs or atherosclerotic plaque from oxidized cholesterol, he or she will fulfill all the conditions necessary for a heart attack. Conversely, the less animal food a person eats, the less of this constriction and the more likely it will be that the person will be able to prevent or survive a heart attack if he or she suffers from acute or chronic psycho-emotional or psychosocial stress.

In addition to the psycho-spiritual aspects of coronary artery disease, modern science fails to consider individual differences based on inherited constitution, the conditions individuals have developed through the course of their lives, and the lifestyle they lead in determining the factors leading to coronary artery disease. These factors are different than simple causal connections, which are difficult, if not impossible, to pin down in such a complicated and multifaceted disorder. These differences, however, can be determined through acupuncture theory and can account for why some people will get coronary artery disease from fat deposits or atherosclerotic plaque in

---

[a] Other animals in this category include seabirds, penguins, seals, and sea lions.

their arteries and why others may not. In general, the causes for coronary artery disease can be summarized as follows:

1. Atherosclerotic plaque due to the consumption of refined food and leading to the acupuncture patterns of Deficient Liver and Kidney Yin and Deficient Heart Yin
2. Fat deposits in the arteries due to the excess consumption of refined PUFAs,[a] long-chain animal quality SaFAs, refined sugar, refined carbohydrates, and excesses of fats and oils in general. These conditions lead to the acupuncture patterns of Deficient Heart Yang and Turbid Mucous Obstructing the Heart
3. Stress due to psycho-emotional imbalance, abdication of the Heart Spirit, and constriction in the muscular walls of the arteries. These conditions can be caused or exacerbated by the consumption of refined food, refined salt leading to hypertension, as well as stimulants and drugs including cigarettes, alcohol, and coffee. These conditions can lead to the acupuncture patterns of Deficient Heart Yang; Deficient Liver, Kidney, and Heart Yin; Stagnant Liver Qi; and Congealed Heart Blood[b]

Nutritional Causes of CAD

Free Radicals and Oxidation

Cholesterol, LDL, TGs, and free radicals damage arteries only when they are oxidized. Free radicals are oxidized in the body when they are not supported by AO nutrients. When lipids (fats) go rancid, they oxidize and become the most dangerous dietary substances to the heart and arteries. The natural oxidation of AOs prevents the production of the damaging by-products of cholesterol and fatty acids. When AO support (especially Vitamin C, E, carotene, selenium, and sulfur) is weak, the arteries are damaged by free radicals. When the arteries are damaged, repair mechanisms including apo(a) synthesis are stimulated, which increases cell proliferation. The arteries then thicken and narrow.

Free radicals and AOs form two parts of an organic whole, which supports health and well being naturally. When the body becomes nutritionally deficient through the intake of refined foods, it becomes AO deficient as well. The binding force, therefore, between the AOs and free radicals is gone so the free radicals are left unchecked. Instead of performing useful functions, the free radicals are now free to destroy whatever they can. Free radicals are also

---

[a] The rise of coronary artery disease in the twentieth century was accompanied by the massive consumption of refined PUFAs, foods that had never been exposed to mankind previously.

[b] For a thorough discussion of these and other acupuncture patterns and their treatment, see the author's *Natural Healing With Essential Oils.*

93

formed when synthetic pollutants, heavy metals, chlorine, drugs, pesticides, or tobacco smoke introduced from outside the body break the AO/free radical bond.

All of the Four Whites deplete AOs. Fats and oils that are stored too long or are not refrigerated are probably rancid. These include hidden lipids in packaged food. Eat fresh, homemade foods to avoid this problem, especially when trying to heal disease and treat the valuable yet fragile unrefined, unsaturated vegetable oils (especially the EFAs) with care and respect. Coconut oil is probably the least resistant of vegetable oils to free radical attack because its stability prevents it from being so easily oxidized. The presence of Coconut oil also helps prevent the oxidation of other oils.

Chronic Infection

Besides AO depletion and free radical proliferation, other injuries to the arterial wall that initiate plaque formation include high blood pressure, diabetes, and chronic infection. Some organisms like herpes, for example, once the acute infectious stage has passed, live indefinitely in the body causing a chronic, low-grade infection that may only be noticed as a decrease of well-being. When the immune system is weak and unable to control the infection, these microorganisms are free to colonize the arteries and damage the arterial wall. LDL then circulates cholesterol and protein that combines with coagulated blood platelets to precipitate the growth of atherosclerosis and heart disease.

Infections can also cause heart disease. We know this because heart disease can sometimes be treated with antibiotics. Reliance of antibiotics, however, weakens the immune system over time. In fact, the weakening of the immune system caused by over-reliance on antibiotics may be a significant factor in allowing these opportunistic microorganisms into the coronary arteries.

A higher rate of heart disease and stroke is associated with the bacteria involved in the development of dental cavities and gum disease as well as chlamydia, which has been found to measurably thicken arterial walls. While the arteries became more normal in size after being given antibiotics, Coconut oil will kill these organisms naturally, as well as other organisms associated with atherosclerosis such as Helicobacter pylori and cytomegalovirus (CMV), without putting the immune system more at risk, as antibiotics tend to do. The relation between dental cavities, gum disease, and Helicobacter pylori to atherosclerosis can also be addressed with Krill oil. Krill oil contains the super powerful AO astaxanthin, which effectively prevents and reverses these problems.

Vitamin C

Linus Pauling, the Nobel laureate and discoverer of Vitamin C, has proposed that Vitamin C is a cause and cure for coronary artery disease. The connection between Vitamin C and cardiac disease was discovered through complications resulting in the termination of a study on Vitamin C and scurvy when some of the volunteers developed cardiac emergencies after consuming a Vitamin C deficient diet for several months. Vitamin C protects against oxidized lipoproteins by recharging other AOs and forming collagen and elastin, the proteins that make strong and flexible arteries. Vitamin C deficiency weakens the arteries and causes arterial bleeding so that it becomes necessary for LDL to deposit the repair proteins (apo(a)) and fibrinogen/fibrin in the arteries that eventually builds up into plaque. These thickened arteries protect us from Vitamin C deficiency in the short term, but thicken and block the arteries over time. An optimum and continuous intake of Vitamin C will prevent and reverse atherosclerosis. The only reason it is not used in mainstream medicine is because it is too cheap to profit from and it cannot be controlled or patented by drug companies.[a] Other nutrients that support Vitamin C therapy for peripheral arterial disease include niacin and the sulfur-containing N-acetyl cysteine, carnitine, lysine, and proline.

Diet

The late Dr. Roger Williams, professor of chemistry at the University of Texas, founder of the Clayton Foundation (where many vitamins were discovered), member of the board that set the first minimum daily allowances, discoverer of panothenic acid (Vitamin B_5), and the person who named folic acid (Vitamin B_9), believed that serum cholesterol will take care of itself if people consume a wide assortment of wholesome foods containing adequate amounts of all of the essential nutrients. Refined food lacks all of these beneficial qualities including vitamins, minerals, EFAs, fiber, enzymes, and AOs. Indeed, the addition of these nutrients through the consumption of whole foods in the diet can lower cholesterol and TG levels in the blood and prevent degenerative disease.

Organic farming, the mainstay of the whole foods industry, was replaced with chemical fertilizers and pesticides developed in the nineteenth century in the aftermath of World War I. Home refrigeration prepared the way for the replacement of fresh garden produce with prepackaged frozen foods during the 1920s. These two "advances" made it possible for the refined food industry to dominate the palates and health of consumers. Refined food creates more profit in part because there are more "things" to sell once a given source is taken apart. Even the vitamin industry uses this tactic to sell nutrients removed from refining whole foods like grain back to the consumer. The nutritional needs of people have been marginalized by this move. Infant "formula" has replaced breast milk since the late 1920s by eighty-five percent of American women. Processed cow's milk is one of the primary factors leading to nutritional imbalance.

An adequate supply of vitamins and minerals in addition to Omega 3 and Omega 6 essential fatty acids are needed to prevent and treat coronary artery disease. While Vitamin C may be one of the key factors, others include Vitamin B_3 (niacin), the sulfur-containing amino acids carnitine and lysine, active forms

---

[a] Vitamin C is found in nearly all fruits and vegetables especially cabbage, bell peppers, broccoli, sprouts, and parsley.

of cysteine (N-acetyl cysteine), proline, as well as magnesium, coenzyme Q_{10}, and others.[a]

Sugar

One of the most prominent features of the Standard American Diet is refined sugar, which accounts for 50 percent of carbohydrate intake. Not only is refined sugar void of nutritional value, it robs the body of vitamins and minerals in order to be metabolized. Over time, refined sugar consumption puts the body in a chronic state of nutrient debt. The same is true for refined grain and refined oil. Refined sugar is also converted into triglycerides to protect the body from its toxic effects. According to Erasmus, "Sugar also increases oxidation damage, cross-links proteins, inhibits immune functions, and interferes with the transport of Vitamin C.... When sugar is cut from their diet, rats live almost twice as long as when their diet contains it."[b][44]

For these reasons, refined sugar is more often associated with coronary artery disease than is cholesterol or fats. In addition, the increase of coronary artery disease since 1900 parallels the increase of refined sugar in the diet, not cholesterol consumption, which has remained constant. According to Michio Kushi, the triglycerides formed from excess sugar consumption are first stored in the periphery of the body (buttocks, thighs, and midsection) where it is the primary cause of overweight and obesity. As these areas fill up, the excess fat collects in the deeper, more central regions of the internal organs causing the blood vessels within and around them to lose their elasticity.

Vitamins and Minerals

Vitamin deficiency from refined food plays a crucial role in developing physical degeneration such as coronary artery disease. Many vitamins, especially Vitamin C, play AO roles in the body by preventing free radicals from damaging the cells and tissues. Unlike most animals that can make Vitamin C from glucose, human beings need to obtain it from foods. Under extreme stress, even the Vitamin C a person can obtain from food is insufficient.

Vitamin A (beta-carotene) is an efficient AO and can be converted in the body according to need. The 1990 issue of *Circulation* published a study by Harvard Medical School of 22,000 physicians who experienced a 50 percent reduction in all major cardiovascular events, including heart attacks, strokes, bypass surgery, and cardiovascular death, simply by taking Vitamin A. Beta-carotene is abundant in yellow-orange vegetables like carrots, and especially in chlorophyll-rich foods like the leafy greens—kale, collards, and watercress as well as cereal grasses and micro-algae.

---

[a] Natural food sources for these nutrients include: for niacin—whole wheat, wheat germ, peanuts, nutritional yeast, and meat; for lysine—amaranth; for N-acetyl cysteine—garlic, onions, broccoli, cauliflower, avocados, and eggs; for proline—wheat germ, dairy products, eggs, and meats; for magnesium—legumes, green vegetables, and most whole grains and seeds; for coenzyme Q_{10}—peanuts, spinach, mackerel, salmon, sardines, and beef.
[b] Lifespan can be increased another 33 percent in this case by the addition of chromium.

Dr. Roger Williams speculated that coronary artery patients have higher than average Vitamin B_6 requirements. Studies have shown that monkeys deficient in Vitamin B_6 rapidly develop atherosclerosis.[a] Vitamin E deficiency was shown in a study done by the World Health Organization to be the best predictor of heart attack risk. Vitamin E, another powerful AO in the body, is plentiful in whole wheat and Wheat Germ oil as well as Grape Seed oil and Krill oil.

Mineral deficiencies related to coronary artery disease include magnesium, selenium, and zinc as well as calcium, copper, and chromium. Magnesium is normally the most prevalent trace mineral in the body. Yet, magnesium deficiency has been linked to coronary artery disease in many studies. Magnesium inhibits platelet stickiness, plays a pivotal role in energy metabolism, and is the catalyst for hundreds of intra-cellular enzymes. People who have died of arterial spasm show 15 to 30 percent lower levels of magnesium than those dying of other causes. A direct correlation exists between the decrease of magnesium and the amount of coronary artery spasm because of the connection between magnesium and the Liver. Magnesium is found most abundantly in chlorophyll-rich foods whose green color is healing to the Liver. A well-regulated Liver determines the flexibility or rigidity of the muscles, including the muscles in the coronary arteries. Sometimes magnesium deficiency can be so low that the body cannot build up adequate stores orally and must temporarily be given intra-muscular shots until the person regains their balance. Red cell magnesium tests, though more difficult to perform, are ten times more accurate than serum magnesium tests.

Magnesium deficiency has increased sixty-six percent over the past fifty years. Reasons for this increase include soft water with low mineral content, refined grain, packaged food, lack of chlorophyll-rich foods, and overcooking. Eighteen percent of the magnesium of whole wheat or brown rice is lost when they are refined to white flour and white rice. Fifty percent of the minerals are leached out in the soaking water of factories. Another twenty-five percent is lost when the cooking water for the food is discarded. All of these loses and more typically occur with commercially canned and frozen vegetables.

Selenium[b] also protects from oxidation and free radicals. Zinc[c] inhibits atherosclerotic plaque. Lower than normal levels of zinc are found in the plasma and arteries of heart attack patients, while marked improvements are seen when high zinc supplements are given to severe atherosclerosis patients.

The importance of sufficient vitamins and minerals in treating and preventing coronary artery disease increases with the amount of animal food

---

[a] Natural food sources for Vitamin B_6 include wheat germ, peas, lentils, beans, carrots, cabbage, broccoli, spinach, potatoes, tomatoes, walnuts, bananas, watermelon, eggs, tuna, chicken, turkey, liver, and kidney.

[b] The best natural food source of Selenium is whole wheat.

[c] Natural food sources for zinc include whole grains, legumes, pumpkin seeds, sunflower seeds, mushrooms, spinach, eggs, dairy products, fish, poultry, and meat.

present in the diet. Vegetarians need nutrients to protect their heart as well. While strict vegetarians have a twenty-five percent lower risk of death from coronary artery disease than meat eaters, this risk may only be slightly lower when eggs and dairy products are included in their diets if they do not take nutritional supplements[45] or include greater proportions of cereal grasses and micro-algae in the diet.

Fats and Oils

Total fat intake is not as important as the quality of fat. Women with a total fat intake of 46 percent of calories have no greater risk of heart attack than those with a total fat intake of 29 percent of calories.[46] The most dangerous fats and oils are the unsaturated vegetable oils that have been hydrogenated, partially hydrogenated, or refined. Many of these are hidden by food processors in cakes, candy, cookies, chips, pies, pastry, powdered milk, powdered eggs, margarines, artificial creamers and spreads, salad dressings, and mayonnaise including soy mayonnaise. Refined vegetable oil can even be found concealed in dried fruit (currants and blueberries) or granola sold in the bulk section of major natural foods stores in the US. Because the polyunsaturated fatty acids originally derived from vegetable oils in these industrially produced foods are refined and extremely unnatural, they accelerate tumor development more than saturated fats and oils. Refined polyunsaturated fatty acids are also three times more prevalent in atherosclerosis than saturated fatty acids and they increase cholesterol production. The exception, of course, is when these polyunsaturated oils are in their natural, unrefined, or essential fatty acid state, in which case they can lower high cholesterol levels by up to 25 percent.

Table 7: Products with Dangerous Hidden Oils and Fats

1)	Candy	6)	Powdered eggs
2)	Cakes	7)	Margarines
3)	Cookies, Pies	8)	Artificial creamers and spreads
4)	Chips	9)	Salad dressings
5)	Pastry, Powdered milk	10)	Mayonnaise

Dietary Regimes

Many different dietary regimens attempt to prevent and reverse heart disease. Some are successful, while some are not. Those regimens that are not successful include the diets proposed by the Standard American Diet and the US Dietary Goals of the American Heart Association. The nutritional comparisons between these two diets and the Standard Macrobiotic Diet, which *has* been proven successful by Harvard medical researchers, are summarized in the table below. Diets proving successful for heart disease, in addition to the macrobiotic diet, include the traditional diet of Hainan, China (still in practice today), the Pritikin Diet, and the Ornish Diet (both in the US).

Table 8: Nutritional Comparison of Different Diets

Diet	Fat	SaFAs	MUFAs	PUFAs	Protein	R. Carbs	C. Carbs
SAD	42 %	16 %	19 %	7 %	12 %	18 %	28 %
USDG	30 %	10 %	10 %	10 %	12 %	10 %	48 %
SMD	15 %	2 %	8 %	5 %	12 %	0 %	73 %

SAD = Standard American Diet   SMD = Standard Macrobiotic Diet
USDG = US Dietary Goals of the AHA
R. Carbs = Refined Carbohydrates
C. Carbs = Complex Carbohydrates

Over 90 percent of people in Hainan live on farms. The rest of China ignored economic development there so it was left in its traditional pre-modern state. Agriculture in Hainan is still organic, the food is extremely fresh (supermarkets do not exist), and the grain they eat is mostly unrefined brown rice. The people that live there currently have the best health in the world. While death from coronary artery disease is generally rare in China (.05 percent) and fat consumption is low (20 percent), the death rate is even lower in Hainan where coronary artery disease is even more rare. Infant death rate in Hainan is comparable to the US (13 versus 9 per 1,000 live births), and the average life expectancy from birth (87) is ten years longer than anywhere else in the world.

The Pritikin, Ornish, and Macrobiotic diets were all based on the cholesterol theory and worked by lowering dietary fat much below the 30 percent AHA recommendations (down to 10 percent), in addition to raising the intake of complex carbohydrates and fresh vegetables and drastically reducing the consumption of sugar and commercially canned or frozen food. These practices alone increase the amount of vitamins, minerals, and AOs four to six times and is in stark contrast to the nutrient-deficient diet recommended by the AHA. Whether the 30 percent fat recommendation of the AHA is sufficiently low or not, the junk food and refined carbohydrates alone people eat on this diet are enough to feed the coronary artery disease process by itself!

Nathan Pritikin opened his successful Pritikin Longevity Center in Santa Barbara, California during the mid 1970s when he practiced and taught a vegetarian diet of 10 percent fat. Pritikin started this diet in 1958 after being diagnosed with coronary artery disease. By the time of his death in 1985, his condition was completely reversed as revealed by his autopsy where his coronary arteries were described as being as clean as those of a newborn baby's.

Dean Ornish was an MD affiliated with the University of California Medical School in San Francisco. He created a lifestyle program to reverse heart disease that included a 10 percent fat vegetarian diet, non-smoking, exercise, meditation, and group therapy. He did a study comparing this group to those following the standard AHA diet and receiving routine medical care and presented the findings in what he called *The Lifestyle Heart Trial* to the medical profession in 1990 through the medical journal *Lancet* and his book *Eat More,*

Weigh Less, and to the general public through the CBS-TV program, *60 Minutes,* as well as an hour-long episode on the Public Television *NOVA* series.

Ornish's program worked in 85 percent of patients and was able to improve blood flow in the arteries by 200 percent, while people eating the AHA diet worsened.[47] Conventional medical approaches using cholesterol-lowering drugs have only been able to achieve from 16-39 percent success in opening up arterial obstructions and are associated with serious liver-damaging side effects, whereas those in the Ornish program experienced none. Experts complimenting Ornish's work, nevertheless, complained that his program was too much of a change for most Americans to undertake.

The macrobiotic diet, however, imposes none of the lifestyle changes of the Ornish program (non-smoking, exercise, meditation, and group therapy) and works with dietary changes alone.[a] Three macrobiotic studies were undertaken in Boston by Harvard medical researchers between the years 1972 and 1981 consisting of hundreds of mostly ordinary middle-class Americans from many different racial and ethnic backgrounds who grew up on the Standard American Diet and then switched their way of eating.

One of the ways heart researchers measure cholesterol is to compare total cholesterol with HDL, which gives a ratio. Heart attack victims have ratios from 4.6 to 5.7. Marathon runners, who tend to exemplify good hearts because of their cardiovascular fitness, have ratios of 3.4. Dr. Castelli, who ran the Framingham Studies, noted that macrobiotic vegetarians had even lower ratios of 2.5, a level "at which we rarely, if ever, see coronary heart disease."[48]

Cholesterol levels in the macrobiotic group were also significantly lower than the general public; 32 percent lower, in fact, than any group *ever* recorded for modern industrial society (126 mg dl). Blood pressure was also very low with an average of 105.3/59.5 mm Hg in the first study, lasting less than two years, and 108/63 in the second study, which lasted about three years.

The third study added modest amounts (250 grams) of beef to the diet during the middle period of the experiment to evaluate the effects of meat consumption on the macrobiotic diet in relation to coronary artery disease. During the time when the beef was added to the diet, cholesterol levels went up an average of 19 percent and the systolic blood pressure went up significantly (about 3 mm Hg). Both returned to previous levels when meat was discontinued. The report, published in the 1981 *Journal of the American Medical Association,* stated that these levels are "characteristic of persons of low risk...for myocardial infarctions (heart attacks)."[49]

In spite of the overwhelming success of the macrobiotic diet in treating degenerative disease, such as coronary artery disease, the macrobiotic perspective on fats and oils never addresses the importance of essential fatty

---

[a] The macrobiotic diet emphasizes whole grains, beans, fresh organic vegetables, sea vegetables, seeds, nuts, fruits, small quantities of unrefined polyunsaturated vegetable oils, unrefined and trace mineral-rich sea salt, fermented foods such as miso, tamari, and naturally pickled vegetables such as nuka (bran) pickles, sauerkraut, and kimchee as well as fish as an occasional option.

acids. In addition, it can unintentionally advocate the use of refined oils due to the labeling scams by the oil industry, which confuse refined polyunsaturated oils with expeller-pressed oils through the misuse of the term "cold-pressed."

Early macrobiotic teachings also followed the cholesterol theory as can be found in *The Cancer Prevention Diet*, p. 233: "Mobile shellfish such as shrimp and lobsters are to be avoided because of their high cholesterol content." Macrobiotic leaders, then, have inferred that heart attack is caused by cholesterol:

> Accumulation may also occur both in and around the arteries. These fatty deposits, including cholesterol...reduce the heart's ability to function properly and hamper the smooth passage of blood through the arteries. The end result is often a heart attack. The major causes of this problem are foods containing large amounts of hard, saturated fat [that is, cholesterol].[a50]

In staying true to its principle of eating whole foods, the Standard Macrobiotic Diet obtains its supply of essential fatty acids from whole grains, beans, and seeds. There is, however, a lack of appreciation of the importance of essential fatty acids, especially Omega 3 fatty acids, and there is little or no historical effort made to correct deficiencies of these elements. Flaxseed oil and Hempseed oil are not currently being recommended. Instead "white-meat fish or low-fat seafood" is being recommended "a few times a week on average" either "for those in good health who desire animal food," or for "individuals suffering from circulatory disorders" to replenish their stores of eicosapentaenoic acid (EPA).[51] However, white-meat fish and seafood do not contain *any* appreciable amounts of EPA, which is found instead in cold-water fish such as trout, salmon, mackerel, sardines, and tuna.[b] These early recommendations need to be updated to reflect this understanding to benefit essential fatty acid deficiencies in the macrobiotic and general population.

---

[a] This typical association here between cholesterol and hard saturated fat is misleading. Cholesterol belongs to the "sterol" family of lipids, not the "triglycerides" family, which contains both the saturated and unsaturated fats. While excess animal food may cause fat deposits, these are not connected to cholesterol deposits *per se*.

[b] The death rate in the Netherlands was 50 percent lower for fish-eaters consuming at least 30 grams of fish per day than for those who did not eat fish.

Figure 24: Combined EPA/DHA Content if Fish

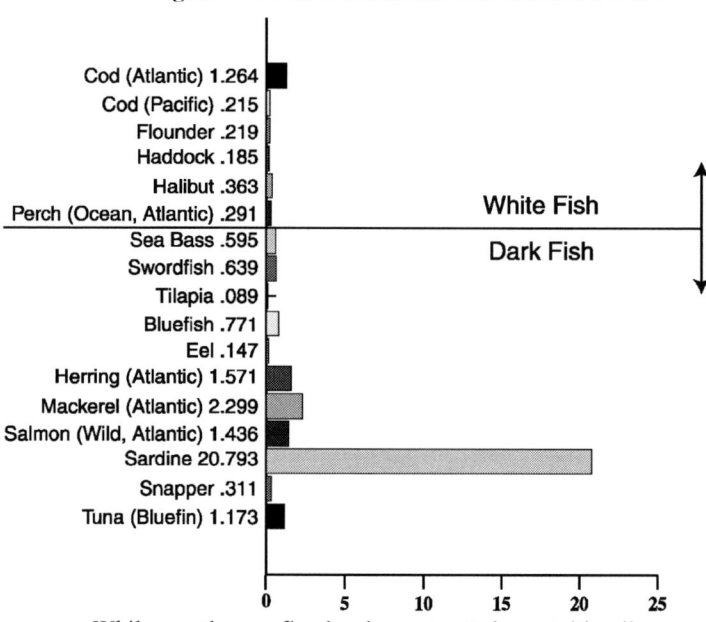

While mostly unrefined polyunsaturated vegetable oils are used in the macrobiotic diet in small to moderate quantities on occasion, one exception is the use of dark Sesame Seed oil, which in the book *Diet For a Strong Heart* is said to "retain the Vitamin E and other nutrients that make it a balanced food product."[52] Probably because it was unknown to the authors, dark Sesame Seed oil is often fully refined and has lost its vitamin and mineral content by definition. In the same book, the source of this confusion is stated:

> Unrefined oils (often labeled "cold-pressed" to indicate processing at low temperatures) are extracted from raw seeds by non-chemical methods.... Macrobiotic cooking makes use of unrefined vegetable oils, *such as dark sesame oil*.... Refined vegetable oils, and hydrogenated products such as soy margarine are minimized or avoided.[53]

We should be very clear about one thing regarding the so-called "cold-pressed" vegetable oils. The term "cold-pressed" does not, in any way, shape, or form, mean that extensive heat was not applied to it before bottling! Oils that are labeled "cold-pressed" are very typically refined oils that have been subjected to enormous temperatures. Consumers as well as macrobiotic leaders have been tricked into thinking there was no heat applied because there was no "extra" heat applied during pressing, while there is tremendous heat applied to these "cold-pressed" oils AFTER they have been pressed in the refining process.

While the therapeutic macrobiotic diet still works exceptionally well in reversing and preventing coronary artery disease, this small but significant error shows up with more impact when the diet is expanded for healthy individuals. Because the dangers of refined polyunsaturated oils have not yet been stringently enough defined in macrobiotics, this single error is overlooked in practice for healthy people with serious consequences. Like the rest of the population, macrobiotic people can be lulled into complacency by the oil industry. They do not understand the full meaning of labels and so consume refined oils all too frequently, justifying it to themselves as fulfilling their sensory and sentimental appetites. Cookies, chips, and tempura (deep-fried vegetables) are their downfall and several wonderful people and macrobiotic teachers of mine have died from coronary artery disease and cancer as a result.

Natural Remedies

Among the useful natural remedies for coronary artery disease used to regulate the detrimental effects of bad quality fats and oils are saunas,[a] onions, miso, shiitake mushrooms, and sea vegetables. Garlic and onions increase HDL, and help neutralize the negative qualities of oils in sautéing. Miso is a fermented soy paste, similar to tamari soy sauce and is primarily used to make a simple but delicious soup stock. In Japan, the National Cancer Research Center reported that eating miso soup every day lowers the risk of dying from cancer, heart disease, and other major illnesses by an overwhelming 43 percent. According to Michio Kushi, "Those who abstained from miso also had 29 percent more fatal strokes, three-and-a-half times more deaths resulting from high blood pressure, 33 percent more stomach cancer, and 19 percent more cancer at all other sites in the body."[54]

Another natural vegetable product used to dissolve excessive animal fat and protein in the body, lower cholesterol, and to protect against both heart disease and cancer is the shiitake mushroom. Shiitake mushrooms used in Japan have resulted in almost complete regression of soft-tissue tumors. You can find shiitake mushrooms in mail order catalogues and natural food stores. The best deal is to find them in your local Chinatown once you know what to look for. The medicinal ingredient is found in the spores of the mushrooms. Therefore, look for dried mushrooms with closed caps. Once the caps open, the spores disperse and the medicinal ingredients are gone.

In addition to protecting against nuclear radiation,[b] sea vegetables like kombu, wakame, nori, hiziki, and others, improve fat metabolism; reduce blood levels of cholesterol in high blood pressure; reduce arteriosclerosis; and generally strengthen the blood, heart, and circulatory system. Several varieties also contain a natural blood thinner often used to prevent clotting through intravenous injection.

---

[a] Saunas are able to help reduce the level of chemicals in the fat.

[b] Medical researchers at McGill University in Canada reported that sea vegetables help eliminate radioactive strontium from the body.

Oil Production

The Extraction and Pressing Process

Cold Pressed

The term "cold-pressed" has become a meaningless term used by the oil industry to mislead uninformed consumers into thinking that they are getting something they are not. While "cold-pressed" does assure the consumer that additional heat was not applied to the oil during "pressing" and that the oil was not extracted with chemical solvents, it hides the fact that the temperatures reached during "unheated" pressing can reach up to 185-203°F. More importantly, the oil may also be refined after the pressing, in which case the temperature reaches 160-200°C (320-392°F) or more. In this case the consumer is led to believe that the oil never reached a temperature much above body temperature (98.6°F) because of the common sense meaning of the term "cold-pressed." No one in their right mind would stick their finger into oil this hot and call it COLD!

The confusion resides between the educated consumer's desire to get an oil processed with minimal heat and the spin that the fat and oil industry puts on this desire by obscuring the two parts of fat and oil processing: pressing and refining. Manufacturers typically label oils "cold-pressed" and then heat the life out of them in the refining process. Because manufacturers are not required to label oils that are refined (or solvent extracted either), the consumer is deliberately misled into thinking that the "cold-pressed" oils they buy at a higher price at the natural foods store are unheated. In reality, these oils are probably not as cold as you think.

When pressing vegetable oils for health, the lower the heat used in pressing, the better the quality and the healthier the oil. Light and oxygen destroy the health benefits of oils and create adverse chemical reactions faster in the presence of heat. These reactions more than double with every 10°C (18°F) of heat applied to the oil causing UFAs to eventually twist into unhealthy facsimiles of their original shape. The valuable but fragile EFAs are also damaged in most commercial operations because the pressing temperature is too high and sufficient precautions are not used to exclude light and air. Even more destructive than the heat at this beginning stage is the exposure of the oil to air, which makes it turn rancid, a problem that needs to be "fixed" by the oil industry through further "refining" (aka boiling) of the oils at extremely high temperatures.

The term "cold-pressed," in traditional societies, refers to oils that are not heated at all prior to pressing. In modern times, however, oils are *sometimes* heated prior to pressing to increase the yield of the final product. In this case the oils can be boiled for up to two hours at temperatures up to 120°C (248°F). Normally, however, oils are not heated *prior* to pressing. While some oils, like the Flora brand Flaxseed oil, do not exceed 97°F in the pressing, the general pressing temperature for small presses is about 50°C (122°F)[a] or higher while medium-sized press temperatures reach 65-85°C (150-180°F). The inside of large-sized presses heats up to 54-72°C (130-160°F) with overall temperatures reaching up to boiling (100°C or 212°F) just from the enormous pressure involved. The modern pressing of oils in giant presses takes only a few minutes at temperatures of approximately 185°to 203°F. Nowadays even these boiled oils can be labeled "cold-pressed" because the boiling temperature is the result of pressure and not heat externally applied to the seed cake. Nevertheless, even the relatively "low temperature" reached in the large-sized presses is high enough to cause the oils to react with oxygen 100 times faster than at room temperature.

This degree of heat is not nearly as problematic as the temperature reached during refining or even cooking. Problematic temperatures during cooking begin at about 160°C (320°F) and start to become serious above 200°C (392°F). Refining temperatures are considerably higher and continue over much longer periods of time. To the uneducated consumer the oils appear the same, but in reality they are converted into unnatural *trans*-configurations or cross-linked, oxidized, dimerized, or polymerized fatty acids whose insidiously changed shape makes them toxic to life, a problem that is then passed on to the medical profession to "fix."

One way the manufacturers of refined oils get around the labeling issue is through the unsanctioned use of the term "cold-pressed," which signifies that *no* "additional" heat was used in the pressing of the oil and implies that no heat was involved in the production of the oil *period*. Nevertheless, it is typical for manufacturers to use the term "cold-pressed" even if the oil is refined, a process they do not have to state on the label. Manufacturers get away with using this term only because it is mechanically and legally correct. This gross misuse of the labeling laws allows manufacturers to take advantage of the consumer who erroneously thinks they are getting an oil processed with no heat when, in fact, the refining process heats the oils severely for a long and protracted period.

There are the two ways to extract or expel the oil from its source. "Solvent extraction" is an industrial method of extraction that involves soaking the oil source in gasoline (hexane or white gas, to be technically correct). They do this because the yield is greater than when the oils are mechanically pressed. Who would buy these oils if they were labeled honestly regardless of all the studies their paid researchers make that claim to justify this process? If asked, manufacturer representatives respond by saying that no gasoline is left in the oil once it reaches the consumer. Usually, however, they do not say anything and you can only tell the difference if the words "expeller pressed" are explicitly stated on the label. The only commercial exception to these legalized

---

[a] This is the temperature that is defined as "cold-pressed" in Switzerland.

infringements on the term "cold-pressed" are the extra virgin Olive oils[a] and some brands of Peanut oil made by expeller pressed peanuts.

Neither do manufacturers have to label their oils refined, although some of the better companies will. Since it is not mandatory to label fats and oils as degummed, refined, bleached, deodorized, or even partially hydrogenated, they don't. The only way to know if a particular oil is unrefined is that ONLY *unrefined* fats and oils are allowed by the FDA to say so on the label. **If a bottle of oil does not say *unrefined* then it is *refined* by default. Again, the only exception is for Olive oil,** which usually uses the term "extra virgin" in place of "unrefined." **If the term "extra virgin" is not on the label, it is *always* "refined."** Even then, most extra-virgin Olive oil is refined as well.

The only protection for the consumer in such an age of misinformation is to know how to read labels properly. Ignore the term "cold-pressed" other than to register that the company who uses it is either ignorant of the issues or may be trying to mislead you. The bottom line is that if the label does not state the oil is "expeller-pressed" or "unrefined," it *is* heat extracted, solvent extracted, and/or refined by default. **Stay away from all oils that do not say "expeller-pressed" and "unrefined" explicitly on the label with the exception of some "extra virgin Olive oil!"** Choose small batch-pressed oils whenever possible.

Solvent Extraction

Solvent extraction increases production yields by heating and agitating finely ground seed meal at temperatures from 131° to 149°F in white gasoline,[b] chemically called hexane or heptane. Sometimes, solvent extraction is applied to the remaining seed cake after being mechanically pressed. The solvent is then evaporated from the oil-solvent mixture by boiling it at a temperature of about 302°F so the solvent can be reused. Solvent-extracted oils contain traces of these chemical solvents, which can seriously affect one's health. These solvents are lung irritants and nerve depressants and can have detrimental effects on health even in very tiny doses. Expeller-pressed oils are sometimes mixed with solvent-extracted oils and sold as "unrefined." Most solvent-extracted oils, however, are *refined.* Pesticide residues contaminating edible oils can also undermine health by interfering with nerve functions and oxidation processes. **In order to avoid this contamination, always use organic oils for nutritional purposes!**

---

[a] You can not rely on Olive oils labeled "extra virgin" either. The only way to know for sure if Olive oil is expeller-pressed without additional heat and/or refined is to call the manufacturer and ask. Even then, use discretion. Always trust small presses more than large corporations. See the section on "Olive Oil Processing" at the end of this chapter for more specific recommendations.

[b] Oil factories actually blow up occasionally since the solvents used for extraction are so highly inflammable.

The Refining Process

Refining

The market for industrial quality edible oils doubled between 1975 and 1992 when 80 million tons of the oil were sold for over 80 billion dollars. The great majority of these fats and oils are extremely injurious to health. Added to this amount is the profit made by the fast food industry, the snack food industry, and restaurants that use these oils, as well as the medical profession whose services are sought to symptomatically treat the problems these foods create without ever bothering to address the cause. The realization that such a large part of the modern economy is based on such a wanton destruction of health is ironic, if not shocking and disheartening.

Refined oil, or "white oil," like its industrial cousins white flour, white sugar, and white salt, has most of its nutrients (especially vitamins, AOs, and minerals) removed to achieve a longer shelf life. Longer shelf life assures that greater quantities can be made at one time and seasonal variations do not have to be taken into account. The greater the amount of oil that can be made at one time, the greater the profit that can be made for the manufacturer. Unfortunately, this profit is all at the expense of the consumer because the resulting food is not only empty and without nutritional value, but also laden with harmful chemicals that are detrimental to health.

The oil refining process, for example, uses Drano (chemically called sodium hydroxide), sometimes mixed with sodium carbonate to separate chemically "impure," but nutritionally valuable, materials from the oil usually at a temperature of 167°F. Refining removes free fatty acids (which turn to soap), phospholipids, protein-like substances, and minerals from the oils and leaves some red or yellow pigments behind.

Refining produces many unnatural breakdown products by uncontrollable random processes, which are different from batch to batch. Many of these products are still unknown. Others include toxic substances such as *trans*-fatty acids, polymers, cyclic compounds, aldehydes, ketones, epoxides, and hydroperoxides. Unnatural AOs are added to refined oils to take the place of those removed to further improve shelf life.[a] However, since these unnatural AOs do not match the requirements of the molecular architecture of enzyme systems and membranes, they may contribute to premature aging, poor general health, immune suppression, and degenerative disease over time. Consumption of refined polyunsaturated oil creates a greater risk for developing cancer than SaFAs, which actually protect against it.

Bleaching

Bleaching gets rid of the pigment and remaining soap left after the refining process by boiling the refined oil in acid-treated activated clays for 15

---

[a] For a partial list of these unnatural AOs, please refer to the "Enriching" stage of oil refining below.

to 30 minutes at temperatures up to 230°F. Some of the pigments removed in bleaching contain valuable vitamins such as beta-carotene and chlorophyll as well as natural aromatic substances. Whatever twisted EFAs are left in the oil after refining are then turned into toxic peroxides and conjugated fatty acids during bleaching.

Degumming

The manhandling of the oil during refining and bleaching makes it unpalatably thick. Degumming makes oil pour better from the bottle and is carried out by placing the refined and bleached oil in a combination of phosphoric acid and water at a temperature of about 140°F. Degumming not only removes the valuable phospholipids and lecithin, which are then sold separately as supplements, but also any remaining chlorophyll, calcium, magnesium, iron, and copper. All of these minerals are vital for maintaining a healthy heart and arteries. Imagine if your employer took all the green ink out of the paper money he paid you with and you were left with only worthless blank paper!

Deodorizing

Deodorization removes all tastes and odors from free fatty acids and aromatic oils created by the refining, bleaching, and degumming stages of oil refinement as well as the peroxides produced during refining and bleaching. Deodorization involves distilling the remaining oil under pressure, steam, and exclusion of air at the destructively high temperature of 464° to 518°F for up to an hour. This process removes all remaining Vitamin E and phytosterols. The high temperatures reached in the deodorizing and hydrogenating aspects of oil refining are the most destructive in the entire refining process. UFAs become mutagenic and capable of damaging human genes as well as the offspring of those who consume them when oil is heated to temperatures above 302°F. *Trans*-fatty acids begin to form above 320°F, form in substantial quantities above 392°F, and increase exponentially above 220°C (428°F).

Deodorization destroys all remaining nutritive value in the oils and replaces them with toxic *trans*-fatty acids; unnatural isomers of UFAs; cyclic compounds created when straight-chain fatty acid chains turn into a ring; rubbery, plastic materials formed from the cross-linking of fatty acids into dimers and polymers; and other altered breakdown products. When introduced through diet, these substances interfere with normal body functions. The process of the weakened and unbalanced body attempting to discharge them produces degenerative disease.

One should realize that the important Omega 3s are transformed into *trans*-fats during the deodorization process. This means that refined oil products advertised as high in Omega 3s will not have the health benefit expected and may instead actually contribute to heart disease.

Table 9: The Four Stages of Refining Vegetable Oils

Stage	Purpose	Heat	Time	Agents	Result
Refining	Maintains longer shelf-life	116°F		Drano	Removes nutrients
Bleaching	Cleans left-over soap & pigment from the refining stage	230°F	15-30 minutes	Acid treated activated clays	Removes chlorophyll & beta-carotene and transforms the EFAs into toxic peroxides & conjugated fatty acids
Degumming	Pours more easily	140°F		Phosphoric acid	Removes phospholipids, lecithin, & remaining minerals
Deodorizing	Removes bad tastes & odors from the previous three stages	518°F	1 hour under pressure		Removes all remaining nutrients & replaces them with toxic & deadly compounds

Enriching

Synthetic AOs added to refined oils not for health but solely to prolong shelf life include butlated hydroxytoluene (BHT), butlated hydroxyanisole (BHA),[a] propyl gallate, tertiary butyhydroquinone (TBHQ), citric acid, and methlysilicone. Finally, a defoamer is added and the oil is ready for market.

Fractionation and Transesterification

Fractionation and transesterification are further refining processes used to impart unnatural characteristics, make them easier to work with, or replace good quality natural oils that have been given a bad reputation (i.e. Coconut oil). Fractionation and transesterification have nothing to do with adding nutritional value to the oil. These processes begin with fully refined oils since any natural ingredients (i.e. nutrients) would interfere.

Fractionation involves untying the three fatty acid molecules of a given triglyceride and then recombining them in different "designer" ways. This

---

[a] BHT and BHA are suspected mutagens and carcinogens and have been banned in many countries including Japan, Romania, Sweden, and Australia.

process results in a different quality than the original oil but does not add any harmful ingredients other than those made through refining. Nevertheless, the body just has to figure out how to use them since it has never encountered them in its previous 3.2 billion years of evolution. Coconut oil is typical of oils that are fractionated as it can be turned into three or more different types, each with its own melting point. Coconut oil can be fractionated into a harder, more saturated version with a higher melting point or a softer, more unsaturated version with a lower melting point, or anywhere between. Fractionated Coconut oil with a lower melting point is often used as a carrier oil in essential oil therapy because it is easier to get out of the bottle. Otherwise, in cold weather, the Coconut oil would not pour or drip out. Alternative methods to using refined and fractionated Coconut oil for a carrier oil would be to mix the essential oils with natural centrifuged Coconut oil in its liquid state and then place the mixture in a large-mouthed jar for easy application.

Transesterification goes a step beyond fractionation by reattaching the single fatty acid chains randomly to the glycerol molecules so that fatty acids from different oils can be combined to form "hybrid" triglycerides unlike the oils from which they were derived. While these "synthetic" oils may have properties valuable to the food industry, their questionable effect on health is improbable, untested, and unknown.

Hydrogenation and the *Trans*-Fatty Acids

Hydrogenation was patented in 1903 and introduced into the US in 1910. By 1911, the first commercial hydrogenated product, Crisco, went on sale. These foods were originally touted as heart-friendly just because they were not saturated. They were, however, riddled with deadly TFAs.[55] By the 1930s, Corn, Peanut, and Cottonseed oil were commonly hydrogenated; and by the 1940s, margarines made from 90 percent vegetable oil replaced the Coconut oil and animal fat combinations available before World War II. Today, hydrogenated or partially hydrogenated oil comprises one-third of all the edible oil produced. In the US alone, 42,000 foods contain TFAs! They are in all processed foods, especially margarine, which accounts for up to 30 percent of all TFAs consumed. **While only 2-3 grams of TFAs per day (slightly less than that found in a doughnut) increases health risks (TFA intake in women doubles the chances of heart disease), TFA consumption in the SAD can be conservatively estimated to reach at least 40 grams per day.**[56]

Hydrogenation products keep so long they never spoil. They compete with butter in spread-ability, are cheaper, and have higher melting points than animal or tropical oils (111°F for hydrogenated oils as opposed to 55°F for UFAs in their natural *cis*-configuration). Their solidity gives body, consistency, and texture to oil products. These useful qualities are offset by the altered substances they contain, especially, but not exclusively, the *trans*-fatty acids and **the toxic metal catalysts used to produce them,** which **account for twice as many food additives in the SAD as all other additives from all food sources combined.**

Oil Production

The hydrogenation process inserts extra hydrogen atoms into the double bonds of UFAs at a temperature of 250°C (482°F) in the presence of a metal catalyst (50 percent nickel and 50 percent aluminum)[a] over a period of twelve hours in a partial vacuum to turn the liquid UFAs into synthetic mirror images of natural semi-solid or solid SaFAs. People are led to believe that because hydrogenated (or refined) oil can be heated without further damage, they will not damage it by cooking with it at high temperatures, especially those temperatures that occur through deep-frying. While this may be technically true, the more honest reason why *consumers* will not damage hydrogenated (or refined) oil is because the *manufacturer* has already damaged it for them.

Natural *trans*-fatty acids found in the fats of ruminant animals (antelope, buffalo, cow, deer, goat, and sheep) occur in only very minor amounts (less than 2 percent to 5 percent) and differ substantially from those found in synthetic hydrogenated and partially hydrogenated oils due to the placement of their double bonds. Synthetic *trans*-fatty acids, however, comprise more than 60 percent of margarines and shortenings and have actually been banned by the Dutch government. In the US they are just re-labeled so we can not tell that they are there. As early as 1958, researchers questioning the safety of *trans*-fatty acids in relation to cancer and heart disease were squelched by the edible oil industry. The main tactic by this industry was to shift the emphasis by mounting an unwarranted attack on the "saturated" fat hydrogenated products were meant to replace as well as meat, dairy fats, and (yes, you guessed it) cholesterol.

The process of hydrogenation twists the double bonds of LA and LNA in the unsaturated EFAs and destroys them to create unnatural SaFAs or *trans*-fatty acids. Hydrogenation takes the natural fatty acid bond apart, flips it over 180°, and then reconnects it forming an unnatural *trans*- bond (or straight) out of what was previously a natural *cis*- bond (or bent).[b] Therefore, hydrogenated oil consumption demands a higher content of LA consumption to compensate for the resulting inhibition of LA functions. EFA function is also involved with energy and electron exchange reactions on the molecular level. These functions are impaired by TFAs because, instead of taking part in these vital reactions, they interfere. Their molecules are altered from their natural state, a background that sets the stage for the future development of degenerative disease.[c] Cell membrane permeability is also interfered with by TFAs so that needed nutrients can not get in and harmful toxins can not get out and are stuck inside the cells where they do further damage. This condition causes a diminishing of cellular

---

[a] Traces of each of these metals remain in the final product. Aluminum in the human body is associated with mental senility, osteoporosis, and cancer. According to Erasmus in *Fats That Heal, Fats That Kill*, p. 100, "Aluminum is also present in processed cheese, canned soft drinks, acidic liquids in aluminum cans, antacids, underarm deodorants, flow agents in table salt, and some water supplies."
[b] See Figure 5: "*Cis*- and *Trans*- Configurations" on page 8.
[c] Omega 3s are known to inhibit some cancers.

vitality and may lead to allergic reactions and impaired immune function. Consumption of *trans*-fatty acids creates cellular destruction, which continues until entire tissues and organs are also destroyed and chronic, degenerative disease is established.

Trans-fatty acids are mirror images of the natural *cis*-configurations. They fit into enzyme and membrane structures, taking up space and blocking the *cis*- forms without performing the necessary functions of the *cis*- forms. Enzymes have the ability to recognize the difference in shape between TFAs and *cis*-fatty acids and refuse to use TFAs when they do not fit the functions for which the natural *cis*-configurations were intended. Enzymes break down TFAs more slowly than *cis*-configurated fatty acids. In times of increased activity, stress, or crisis, TFAs prevent fatty acids, normal fuel for the heart, from being available and create a risk for fatal cardiovascular consequences.

Trans-fatty acids also interfere with the production of PGs. Prostaglandins regulate the tone of muscle in the walls of arteries so that blood pressure can be appropriately regulated. PGs also regulate the stickiness of platelets, the clotting of blood, kidney function, inflammation response, and the integrity of the immune system. *Trans*-fatty acids can rapidly increase blood cholesterol levels up to two to three times more than SaFAs, and can also increase blood fat (up to 47 percent), atherosclerotic plaque, and LDL.

The negative impact of *trans*-fatty acids on human health can be summarized as follows:

Negative Impact of *Trans*-Fatty Acids On Human Health

1. Alter fatty acid composition
2. Interfere with EFAs and increase the effects of EFA deficiency
3. Increase LDL cholesterol and lower HDL cholesterol (the greater the consumption of TFAs, the greater the imbalance between HDL and LDL)
4. Raise lipoprotein (a) [Lp(a)] in contrast to the SaFAs, which lower it
5. Raise total serum cholesterol
6. Alter membrane transport function
7. Decrease immune function
8. Precipitate childhood asthma
9. Lower the quality of breast milk[a]
10. Increase insulin levels and place diabetics at greater risk
11. Decrease the ability of red blood cells to respond to insulin
12. Decrease testosterone in males, create abnormal sperm, and interfere with gestation in females

---

[a] Infants fed *trans*-fatty acids through formulas as opposed to being fed natural breast milk have decreased visual acuity. The more *trans*-fatty acids are consumed, the greater the decrease in visual acuity will be.

13. Block the formation of PGE$_1$ and PGE$_2$ by interfering with enzyme function
14. Block enzymes responsible for ridding the body of carcinogens and drug medications
15. Increase the formation of free radicals[57]

Identifying *trans*-fatty acids in commercial food products follows the same rule of thumb as reading labels on fats and oils. Unless the label explicitly states "expeller-pressed" and "unrefined," the oil is refined and contains *trans*-fats by default. Hydrogenated or partially hydrogenated oils contain TFAs by definition even though the labels may claim that hydrogenated or partially hydrogenated products contain ZERO *trans*-fats. Products containing *trans*-fatty acids are less easy to identify. However, **almost all prepared food sold commercially that requires fat or oil will contain refined, hydrogenated and partially hydrogenated oils, and therefore the *trans*-fatty acids**, because they are cheaper and will last indefinitely. Conventionally processed liquid vegetable oils contain 15-19 percent *trans*-fatty acids, while shortening and margarine contain about 35-48 percent.

The reason that margarine contains more *trans*-fats than refined vegetable oil is because margarine is made from hydrogenated fat, which deliberately creates *trans*-fats in order to create texture. In contrast, refined vegetable oil only creates *trans*-fats secondarily due to the extreme heat in the deodorizing stage of the refining process. Beware that the new law requiring *trans*-fat to be labeled will only apply to the *trans*-fats deliberately made from hydrogenation. Because the *trans*-fats in refined vegetable oil are not created intentionally, they may not have to be labeled as such, even if they are still there in significant quantities. If you really want to avoid *trans*-fats, ignore label scams that say the product does not contain *trans*-fats and look for oils that are labeled "unrefined" instead.

According to the Department of Health and Human Services of the FDA, "food manufacturers have until Jan. 1, 2006, to list *trans*-fat on the nutrition label. The FDA estimates that by three years after that date, *trans*-fat labeling will have prevented from 600 to 1,200 cases of coronary heart disease and 250 to 500 deaths each year." This rule declares that any product containing .5 grams or more *trans*-fat per serving size must state the amount of the *trans*-fat contained in the product on the label. Manufacturers will then divide the product into the total number of serving sizes, figure the amount of *trans*-fat contained in each serving size and then add these amounts up again to get the total amount of *trans*-fat in addition to the amount of *trans*-fat per serving size.

The loophole in this stipulation is that the serving sizes may be small enough so that the amount of *trans*-fat per serving size is less than .5 g. If the amount of *trans*-fat per serving size is less than .5 g, the manufacturers will not be required to list it and will be able to state that the amount of *trans*-fat per serving size is 0 g. When all the serving sizes in the product are then added up, they will be able to state that the total amount of *trans*-fat is 0 g. even though it may contain almost 50 percent. In fact, in this way even products with the most *trans*-fat will be able to state they their products contain none. The public will then assume that the risk of getting heart disease from such a product is greatly reduced because *trans*-fats have been eliminated. Nevertheless, by the magic date of 2009, heart disease will remain the same or even increase because the public, believing these products are safe from TFAs, will eat more.

One possible trick to figuring out the TFA content of packaged food is to check the Nutrition Facts box on the label. If it lists the amounts of saturated fat, polyunsaturated fat, and monounsaturated fat, simply add the amount of grams for these three categories and subtract the total from the total grams of fat listed. The remainder is the amount of TFAs the product contains.[58]

Excess use of heat in cooking with even good quality unrefined monounsaturated and polyunsaturated oils can also form *trans*-fatty acids and can destroy the valuable EFAs, especially the Omega 3s.[a] Cooking with these oils can defeat the purpose of using them. Only certain unsaturated oils can be safely used in cooking (especially Avocado, Grape Seed, and Macadamia) and these only if precautions are taken not to overheat them. Even small amounts of overheated unsaturated oils can destroy health, especially if they are eaten frequently or over time. Why go to the trouble of buying good quality oils at the natural food store and then go home and burn them up on the kitchen stove? While cooking with oils is not the most nutritionally sound way to use them, the "safest" oil to cook with is a stable saturated oil like centrifuged Coconut oil.

Partial Hydrogenation

The hydrogenation process is so random that it cannot be controlled chemically and can only be stopped once the desired degree of "hardening" has been achieved. If this process is not brought to completion, a staggering amount of totally unregulated intermediate compounds are created. Very little is known about the effects of these substances on the human body. Also created are large quantities of *trans*-fatty acids and other altered fat substances. **Some partially hydrogenated fats sold commercially in the US have *trans*-fatty acid contents of more than 50 percent**. Common products produced by partial hydrogenation turn cheap oils into margarines, shortenings, shortening oils, and partially hydrogenated vegetable oils. Partial hydrogenation creates oils with short-lived sensory and sentimental pleasures such as spreadability, mouth feel, and texture as well as the mechanical convenience of longer shelf life. The long-term payment for these short-lived pleasures is the loss of health and the development of degenerative disease. These oils are frequently used in baking. Cookies, chips, and donuts are filled with them. Oils for deep-frying are frequently stabilized by partial hydrogenation to "prevent" oxygenation, polymerization, or heat damage, processes that are really just hidden from the consumer.

---

[a] The types of TFAs formed in cooking and in the Deodorizing stage of refining vegetable oils are different from the delta-6, 7, 8, 9 et cetera *trans*-fats formed through hydrogenation but are *trans*-fats nontheless.

Hydrogenation Politics

The FDA plans to mandate the labeling of hydrogenated and partial hydrogenated products by 2006, almost one hundred years after their first commercial appearance in 1911. This time period constitutes three generations of exposure to a mutagenic product. How long will it take for this labeling to positively affect the general public provided that the presence of TFAs in products is not just obscured? If the cigarette industry is any standard to go by, another hundred years and six generations could go by before hydrogenated and partially hydrogenated products have disappeared. The effect of this experiment on the gene pool of the human race is frightening. The *trans*-fats contained in hydrogenated and partially hydrogenated products are just SOME of the toxic compounds created by the modern refining of fats and oils. Will it take another two hundred years to clear THEM from the diet? According to the American justice system, the food-processing industry is innocent until proven guilty. Who has the time and financial backing to question their practices in a court of law? The government will never do it. You can not expect the fox to guard the sheep.

In response to the new labeling law, food-processing companies will respond by creating new "margarines" and related products. They are doing so already. I spoke with representatives of one of the major companies that target the natural foods market. When asked why they use refined oils in their so-called healthy oils, I was told that "it would have such a horrible taste that it would be next to impossible to consume." Apparently, this representative and her company have never tasted a bona fide, expeller-pressed, unrefined vegetable oil in their lives. These good quality, natural oils are among the most delicious of all foods. While, to their credit, they do use organic, expeller-pressed, and non-GMO oils, the oils this company uses are all fully refined. The representative was even proud of this fact and told me "all oils are inedible unless they are refined" and that their oils are "fully refined, bleached, and deodorized." While we may not have the power to prove such products harmful in court, we certainly do not have to buy them!

By-Products Creating Disease and Degeneration

Free Radicals

Refining processes of the Four Whites, including the refinement of dietary fats and oils, separate valuable nutrients from the original, natural whole. Individual particles from this refinement are no longer connected with one another so they contribute to the formation of extreme physiological reactions. Some particles are discarded so the body becomes deficient in these substances, while others that are left interact with normal physiology by throwing it out of balance. These two aspects can be thought of as Yin and Yang aspects of one original whole that has been fractured by synthetic interference with the natural, organic whole. In modern nutrition these aspects are called antioxidants (AOs) and free radicals. AOs are usually related to nutrients that are lost, discarded, or used elsewhere in the chemical industry (the rape of natural food for industrial profit), while the free radicals are left to create undisciplined damage to health and well-being. AOs are related to the Yin that nourishes, while the free radicals are related to the Yang of physiological activity. When these two function together, as they do in whole foods, there is health. When the free radicals stimulate physiological activity without the natural control of the AOs originally contained in the foods they are derived from, they become destructive. In acupuncture theory, free radical destruction can be thought of as "false fire" brought about by the deficiency of Yin, in this case the AOs.

Free radicals contain unpaired electrons. They are constantly looking for a partner, are very active, and will draw electrons from other molecules whenever they can. These free radicals represent extreme Yang and are impossible to catch or pin down. They can even can change from a particle to a wave and back again in a fraction of a second. Free radicals normally serve vital, normal functions and are involved in thousands of chemical reactions necessary for energy production and activity. The body uses the AO nutrients to confine the activity of free radicals to useful purposes. When AOs are deficient, free radicals escape uncontrollably to damage molecules in our cells and tissues. Chain reactions can occur where 30,000 cycles of free radical destruction rampage through the body breaking chemical bonds and creating totally different molecules than were originally present, molecules that serve only to destroy health.

Other practices that break the organic whole and create free radical proliferation include the exposure of UFAs to light and oxygen (oil turns rancid in the light 1000 times faster than in the dark), mineral imbalance (especially an excess of iron and copper in the body,[a] and food irradiation, which destroys nutrients, produces unnatural toxic chemicals in foods, and produces billions of unnatural free radicals.[b]

The free radical theory is part of the explanation for aging and degenerative disease such as cancer and coronary artery disease. Free radicals are derived mostly from nutritional deficiency stemming from refined foods— the Four Whites. Other contributing factors to the creation of free radicals include the widespread deficiency of Omega 3 fatty acids resulting in the imbalance between Omega 3s and Omega 6s, and the presence of toxic industrial substances in the environment and in the food supply. This second category includes heavy metals, pesticides, additives, preservatives, colors, flavors, drugs, medications, and *trans*-fatty acids. When people consume

---

[a] Modern people are often deficient in iron and copper and take mineral supplements as a symptomatic remedy while the root of the problem is ignored. One of these roots is the imbalance between pathogenic and healthy flora in the intestines. Pathogenic bacteria in the intestines can block iron absorption. The result is that the excess iron taken into the body through supplementation only serves to stimulate free radical proliferation.

[b] The food industry whitewashes research on the destructive effects of irradiation in an attempt to market their products.

natural foods in harmonious Yin-Yang balance with one another, free radicals are not much of a health concern. While valuable in alerting us to abuses in the food industry, the free radical theory is subject to large-scale marketing abuse by manufacturers wishing to capitalize on the enormous potential for profit that such a fear-based theory can conjure. These are the brothers and sisters to the companies that separated AOs from free radicals in the first place. The profusion of disease they cause provides the rationale for the profusion of antidotes they make for sale.

Another example of the imbalance created by the oil-refining industry concerns Vitamin E. Vitamin E is one of the more expensive vitamins and is collected from the sludge of oil refinement and sold back to the consumer at a profit. Many unaware consumers are left to consume the Vitamin E-deficient oils the industry refines and develop signs of fatty degeneration, which produce brown spots on the skin over time, especially on the head, face, and back of the hands in the elderly.

Antioxidants

Free radicals are only dangerous when they are out of control. The more Yin AOs keep the Yang free radicals in check. The balance between them creates health. Powerfully known AOs include Vitamin C, B_3, and E, carotene, cysteine, selenium, bioflavonoids, and coenzyme Q_{10}. Also important are enzymes containing zinc, manganese, and copper. Hundreds of natural AOs are produced by almost every kind of plant, for example, potatoes, cabbage, broccoli, cauliflower, Brussels sprouts, bananas, and red grapes, as well as an AO called sesamol found in Sesame Seed oil. Many common spices, herbs, and essential oils, including celery, sage, oregano, cumin, cloves, myrrh, and frankincense, also contain AOs in abundance. EFAs from fresh dietary oils also contain rich supplies of AOs, which protect the oils as much as they protect those who consume them. These oils are very fragile, however, and can turn rancid within a few hours or days if not refrigerated.

Olive Oil Processing

Most edible oils are derived from seeds. Because olives are one of the few sources of edible oils derived from fruits, they require special consideration in their processing. Subtle differences that influence the outcome of the Olive oil include variety, climate, growing conditions, soil conditions, age of the olive tree, and even the influence of the packer or producer.

Olive fruits are also very delicate and can easily be damaged if they are picked when overly ripe, decayed after being attacked by pests, bruised after falling from trees, or abraded from being packed too densely or deeply in containers prior to pressing. Any of the above factors can easily damage the ripe fruit causing it to break down, ferment, and become defective. Prolonged storage of the fruit also encourages oxidation and fermentation, which leads to defects in quality and flavor of the oil. The olives also need to be protected from excess temperature arising during pressing. The best quality oils should be handled and pressed below 86°F. They should also be handled in clean work environments to prevent fermentation and rancidity arising from the contamination of waste products.

The Olive oil industry has developed five different levels of processing to handle poor-quality fruit from these factors, and each level represents degeneration in quality from the original oil simply pressed from the pure fruit. These levels are distinguished by the way the fruit is handled prior to pressing, the care given during pressing, the acidity of the oils after pressing, and the degree of refinement after pressing.

Old style terms like "cold-pressed," "first-pressed," and "second-pressed" were used in pre-modern times but often have little meaning today. Traditionally, only about 40 percent of the oil from olives could be extracted during pressing. Later, the remainder was pressed a second time with the addition of heat in order to increase the yield. This practice originated the terms "cold-pressed" and "first-pressed" to distinguish good quality extraction from the lesser quality that arises from the additional heat of the second press. Today, modern facilities exert even greater pressure and heat during the "first-press" so that up to 90 percent of the oil can be obtained from the olives during the first pressing, which is no longer "cold" even though it is often termed "cold-pressed."[a] The remaining 10 percent is then extracted in refineries that use more heat and/or chemicals to remove the oil.

Grades
Premium Select

The highest grade of Olive oil is sometimes called Premium Select and is made from handpicked olives and pressed under huge stone wheels within 24 hours after harvest with little pressure and no heat and then slowly left to filter before bottling. The care in producing Premium Select (as well as most Extra Virgin) Olive oil results in oils with flavors that range from the very sweet and mild to the very bitter and pungent. Because of the delicacy during its handling, Premium Select Olive oil has an acidity rate lower than 1 percent with some as low as .1 to .225 percent.[b] This most nutritionally sound process is expensive and is usually only available from small estates.

Premium Select Olive oil, as well as good quality Extra Virgin Olive oil, contains an extraordinarily high polyphenol count. Polyphenols are the AOs in Olive oil that account for its important heart-protecting and anti-cancerous functions. A healthy Olive oil should have a polyphenol count of between 100 and 250 milligrams per liter. The addition of heat during processing or even during cooking destroys these important AOs.

---

[a] See the section called "Cold Pressed" at the beginning of this chapter to find out how HOT these "cold-pressed" oils can be.

[b] The lower the natural acidity the better the oil.

119

Extra Virgin

The second highest grade of Olive oil is called Extra Virgin and is also made from handpicked olives within 2-3 days of their harvest. This extra time causes some degeneration in the quality of the fruit. The olives are then pressed under metal crushers that do produce some heat that further alters the quality and taste. While Extra Virgin Olive oils must have an acidity rate of no more than 1 percent, many of them only qualify according to this limiting chemical requirement to meet mass-produced standards and do not have the quality and taste of what the public expects from true Extra Virgin Olive oil. In fact, low quality oils are often refined to bring the acidity down to "qualify" (chemically at least) as "Extra Virgin."

Furthermore, "Extra Virgin" Olive oil is often systematically diluted with cheaper non-olive oils, especially by the biggest Olive oil brands from Italy. In spite of strict European regulations to the contrary that even lead to international arrest warrants for this illegal practice, at least ten thousand tons of Hazelnut oil is routinely added to Olive oil and then labeled as "Extra Virgin." As much as 20 percent of "Extra Virgin" Olive oil can be comprised of the cheaper Hazelnut oil and is undetectable to the consumer. These deceitful practices can even be worse in California where there are no regulations and where there are not even enough olives grown to account for the Olive oil it produces.

Unfortunately, the label "Extra Virgin" does not guarantee high quality oil whose nutritional value has not been compromised through processing as the term implies. In fact, because the U.S. is not a member of the International Olive Oil Council, the term "Extra Virgin" has no official meaning and should only be used by consumers as a guideline. The best quality "Extra Virgin" Olive oil companies will describe why their brand deserves the label it receives. Look for descriptions that state that the Olive oil is organic, processed on family estates (often for hundreds of years), hand-harvested, estate bottled and pressed, pressed on the same day as harvested, first-pressed, low in *natural* acidity, unfiltered, and stored in dark glass or even stoneware bottles.

Virgin

Virgin Olive oil is a more cost-effective process because it is made from machine-harvested olives, which are more over-ripe than the olives that are made into Premium Select or Extra Virgin Olive oil. These olives are often picked up from the ground along with their leaves and twigs. Some of these olives are bruised and will then become rancid before pressing. The harvest is often shipped in poorly ventilated containers where it becomes moldy before it is pressed. Since extraction takes place in a centrifuge with hot water used to help separate the oil, the AO-rich, water soluble, polyphenols are then lost so that the shelf life and nutritional quality is lowered. Virgin Olive oil only has a shelf life of a few months in contrast to Premium Select or good quality Extra Virgin Olive oil, which can last for up to three years. Virgin Olive oil is also filtered so it looks clear as opposed to Premium Select or Extra Virgin Olive oil, which looks cloudy. Virgin Olive oil is slightly more acid (1½ to 2 percent) and is generally milder. Lesser quality Virgin Olive oil can have an acidity of up to 3.3 percent.

Pure

Pure Olive oil, often simply called Olive oil, is commercial grade oil that comes from the second pressing and is solvent-extracted from the olive pulp, skins, and pits before it is refined. This Olive oil is only called "pure" because no other oils than olive are added. Pure Olive oil is light in color and bland.

Refined

Refined Olive oil is obtained from defective Virgin Olive oil with a natural acidity above 3.3 percent and then sent to a refinery to reduce the acidity and remove any other impurities or objectionable characteristics. Refined Olive oil comes in two varieties: Refined Olive Pomace and Olive Pomace. Refined Olive Pomace is obtained by treating olive pomace with solvents after which it is then refined. Olive Pomace is a combination of Refined Olive Pomace and Virgin Olive oil that is added to cover up the tastelessness and unpleasant smell of Refined Olive Pomace. Some Refined Olive oil is called Light and Extra Light. All refined oils originate from materials that are so bad they cannot be consumed without refining.

Oil Production

Food and Cooking

Nutrients

Students of nutrition are taught that RDA levels should be reached but not exceeded. Such an emphasis aims at controlling only the obvious nutritional deficiencies in famine areas or poverty situations. Connections between sub-optimal intake of nutrients and degenerative disease are ignored. Otherwise, the industry would have to change radically. Such a misreading of nutritional requirements leads to an average American diet with very little vitamin or mineral content. Seventy-three percent of the SAD consists of refined fats and oils, sugar, and white flour products that have been stripped of their nutritional content by the same "edible" food industry that supplies nutritionists with grant money for their research. No wonder that the researchers found what their employers were looking for—justification for the ongoing exploitation of food and human reserves. The nutrient level of the SAD is only sufficient to prevent the most obvious deficiency diseases. Not until a person's nutrient intake falls below 70 percent of the RDA level do the standard diseases of malnutrition develop.

Commercially canned or frozen vegetables, for example, have lost 50 percent of their minerals and 80 percent of their Vitamin B_6. When whole-wheat flour is refined into white flour, the losses are 8 percent of the protein, 40-87 percent of the chromium, 85-91 percent of the manganese, 56-88 percent of the cobalt, 67-85 percent of the copper, 66-77 percent of the zinc, 43-48 percent of the molybdenum, 86 percent of the Vitamin E, 71-98 percent of the pyridoxine (B_6), 64 percent of the pantothenic acid (B_5), 46 percent of the folic acid (B_9), 60 percent of the calcium, 70 percent of the biotin (B_7), and 77 percent of the potassium. One should realize that almost all of the wheat products sold in the US are refined, including those labeled "whole wheat," which contain just enough real whole wheat added back into the refined white flour to qualify as "whole wheat" for the label. In the US, grain can legally be labeled "whole" even if it contains only 65 percent!

Partially hydrogenated vegetable fats as well as rancid or overheated fats and oils contain breakdown products that range from immediately to chronically toxic. These fats are dangerous to consume and should never be purchased. If you find them in your kitchen, throw them away immediately! Tropical oils, such as centrifuged Coconut oil are the safest for frying because they contain mostly stable SaFAs and only small quantities of the easily perishable EFAs. Unrefined and un-hydrogenated tropical oils are known to decrease cholesterol levels and are rich sources of Vitamin E, which protects arteries and helps to prevent coronary artery disease. Other vegetable oils that are "relatively" safe for sautéing if proper care is used are Avocado oil, Grape Seed oil, and Macadamia oil especially, but also Sesame Seed oil, Peanut oil, and Olive oil. These oils contain little or none of the fragile Omega 3s.

123

Cooking Methods

The best way to use vegetable oil in the diet for nutritional reasons is to take it raw on top of foods during meals. This method is preferred in treating disease conditions (when more than two tablespoons of oil per day are needed) due to essential fatty acid deficiency or to benefit from the secondary attributes of oils, like those found in extra virgin Olive oil or Coconut oil. In normal, healthy situations good quality, un-salted and slightly roasted seeds can be more reliable than bottled oils. The best way to roast seeds and nuts is to buy them raw and then place them in the oven at 180°F for two hours. Roast them in small batches and store them in lidded, lightproof containers.

The historical use of fats and oils in cooking is primarily based on the use of stable saturated animal fats, which were better able to withstand the destructive temperatures involved in sautéing and deep-frying. Vegetable quality oils, with the exception of Olive oil, have only been commercially available on a large scale since the twentieth century with the advent of large presses. Because of their fragility, they were used raw in earlier times, while food was primarily cooked with animal fat. The refining process placed greater quantities of vegetable oils on the market at the same time that the saturated fatty acids in animal fats were erroneously labeled as causing disease. Now most people use refined vegetable oils to cook with because they are cheaper and because they are unaware of the health risks these oils can cause. Most people who have become aware of these risks have switched to using better quality vegetable oils to cook with and go to the trouble of using expeller-pressed, unrefined vegetable oils without realizing the damage that cooking temperature can do to these oils.

Before we discuss the possibilities of "safe" frying, let us first review the temperatures at which the *trans*-fatty acids are produced.

Table 10: Temperatures in *Trans*-Fatty Acid Formation

+ 302°F	Mutagenic
+ 320°F	TFAs Begin to Form
+ 392°F	TFAs Form in Large Quantities
+ 428°F	TFAs Increase Exponentially

To avoid the mutagenic effects caused by exposing UFAs to high temperatures as well as the creation of *trans*-fatty acids, one should **avoid deep-fried foods** and tempura (the Japanese equivalent) **altogether** as the temperature required reaches between 350-400°F, a temperature well within the range of *trans*-fatty acid production. Light sautéing in medium heat-resistant oils like Sesame, Peanut, and Olive oils (140-180°F) is "possible" because this temperature is well below the range of *trans*-fatty acid formation and closer to the temperatures used for expeller pressing by medium size presses (150-180°F).

And yet, the smoke point of some oils is only 180-200°F, approximately the same temperature reached by the giant modern expeller presses (185-203°F). The smoke point, which is well below the temperatures reached in bleaching (230°F for 15-30 minutes), deodorization (464-518°F for up to an hour), or hydrogenation (482°F for over twelve hours), nevertheless registers the point at which some of the more important nutrients in the unrefined oils are destroyed. These are the more fragile materials removed during the refining process. Other, even more fragile and, as yet, unidentifiable materials are most likely destroyed in cooking between the temperatures of 140-180°F.

If you want to find out for yourself what a difference heating these oils makes, try the taste test with your friends and family. Start with a bottle each of good quality expeller-pressed, unrefined Sesame, Peanut, Olive, and Flaxseed oil. Heat about two to three tablespoons of each of the oils separately in a small pan and pour them into small wine glasses or labeled paper cups to cool. Place the glasses on squares of paper with the name of the oil on them so you will not forget which is which. Then taste about a quarter of a teaspoon of one of the raw oils followed by a comparison taste of the cooked oil. Go through each of the four oil pairs one by one and notice the difference. The raw oils contain many different wild and pleasant flavors that disappear when they are cooked. Tasting the cooked oils at first seems pleasant enough, but after a few moments one is shocked at how bland this pleasant taste really is. The aftertaste reveals the burned flavor from the residue of the fatty acids and other important materials you may have "smoked" even before the standard Smoke Point is reached.

Frying and deep-frying rapidly oxidize AOs in the oil and create free radicals that continue to destroy natural molecules in the oil. Frying and deep-frying can also create *trans*-fatty acids. Oxidation products are far more toxic than TFAs and include materials from unnatural chemical breakdown as well as dimer and polymer products with unknown effects on health. These altered and toxic products accumulate in the cells over decades because the cells have not evolved the ways and means to detoxify themselves of these agents. Prolonged toxification from these unnatural materials eventually produces degenerative disease as the cells and organs produce their own toxic chemicals trying to get rid of them.

The "safest" way to fry or sauté is to generally use the more heat and oxygen resistant SaFAs and MUFAS in place of UFAs, especially the EFAs, which should be totally avoided in cooking. In general, MUFAs are better than PUFAs for cooking because they do not turn rancid as easily. The double bonds in the PUFAs make them chemically unstable and more prone to rancidity, oxidation, and attack by free radicals. However, some PUFAs contain high amounts of AOs that help to stabilize these oils in cooking. You have a choice on how to use these AOs responsibly. You can either use them up to protect the oils in cooking or you can use the oils raw so the AOs can be reserved to protect and heal your skin, membranes, and arteries. Standard recommendations of oils for cooking include centrifuged Coconut oil followed by Macadamia oil,

125

Avocado oil, Grape Seed oil, Sesame oil,[a] Peanut oil, Olive oil, or butter.[b] Avoid high oleic Sunflower and Safflower oils, which, while they may be more stable, are created through genetic engineering. Do not use any oil for frying and deep-frying if you are attempting to reverse disease, or if you are trying to achieve optimum health. Never use shortenings and margarines for frying because they are already over laden with altered substances. The use of garlic and onions for frying will minimize free radical damage because of their sulfur content.[c] The safety of using UFAs in baking lays half way between safe boiling and unsafe frying. While the inside of the bread is steamed at an acceptable temperature even for sensitive oils, the outside temperature of the crust gets too high. Use butter or centrifuged Coconut oil to brush the top of the bread or to line the pan instead.

The best way to gage which oils can be used safely is by their Smoke Point. A complete list of oils and their Smoke Points is given in Table 10: "Smoke Points of Edible Oils." The four categories of Smoke Points include (1) No Heat oils, (2) Low Smoke Point oils, (3) Medium Smoke Point oils, and (4) High Smoke Point oils.

No Smoke Point oils include Black Currant Seed oil, Borage oil, and Evening Primrose oil. These oils are high in EFA derivatives and should NEVER be used for cooking!

Low Smoke Point oils are those with Smoke Points below 300°F and include Flaxseed oil, Hempseed oil, Pumpkinseed oil, and Wheat Germ oil (all containing significant amounts of the fragile Omega 3s), as well as Peanut oil and Sesame oil. Because of their Omega 3 content, these oils (with the exception of Peanut oil and Sesame oil) should also NEVER be used for cooking either. Sesame oil contains the natural preservatives sesamol and sesamin that helps stabilize the oil for low temperature cooking. In spite of their relatively low Smoke Points, Sesame oil and Peanut oil are often recommended for cooking, especially in Europe, usually in combination with Olive oil, a Medium Smoke Point oil.

Medium Smoke Point oils are those with Smoke Points below 320°F and include Olive oil, Soybean oil, Sunflower Seed oil, and Walnut oil. These

---

[a] Macrobiotic recipes often call for the use of "dark sesame oil" (e.g. Kushi, *Diet For a Strong Heart*-373, 394). While the use of dark sesame oil is minimal (1 tablespoon) and restricted to "healthy" individuals, "dark sesame oil" should be avoided if it is refined.

[b] The disadvantages of butter are that it concentrates pesticides about 5-10 times more than any vegetable oil, interferes with EFA metabolism, contains antibiotic residues from both cattle feed and injections that can encourage the growth of candida, contains up to 6 percent *trans*-fatty acids, and lacks the nutrients required for its own metabolism.

[c] One of my Japanese cooking teachers, Cornelia Aihara, always recommended sautéing onions over low heat over a long period until they became translucent. This way the onions are fully cooked instead of burned (browned) while the healing integrity of the oil is protected.

oils are still too fragile to cook with reliably. Cook with them at your own risk. In spite of their higher Smoke Point, Soybean and Walnut oils are also high in Omega 3s and should NOT be used in cooking for this reason. Olive oil has many delicate plant compounds that are nutrients to the body and can easily be destroyed through cooking.

High Smoke Point oils are those with Smoke Points above 400°F and include Almond oil, Avocado oil, Coconut oil, Grape Seed oil, Hazelnut oil, Macadamia oil, and Rice Bran oil. These oils are the safest for most baking, sautéing, and stir-frying from the Smoke Point perspective. Beware of oils that claim they are good for various high-heat cooking purposes as they have most likely been refined. If you find the word "refined" on the label, leave the oil on the grocery store shelf where it belongs.

Table 11: Smoke Points of Edible Oils

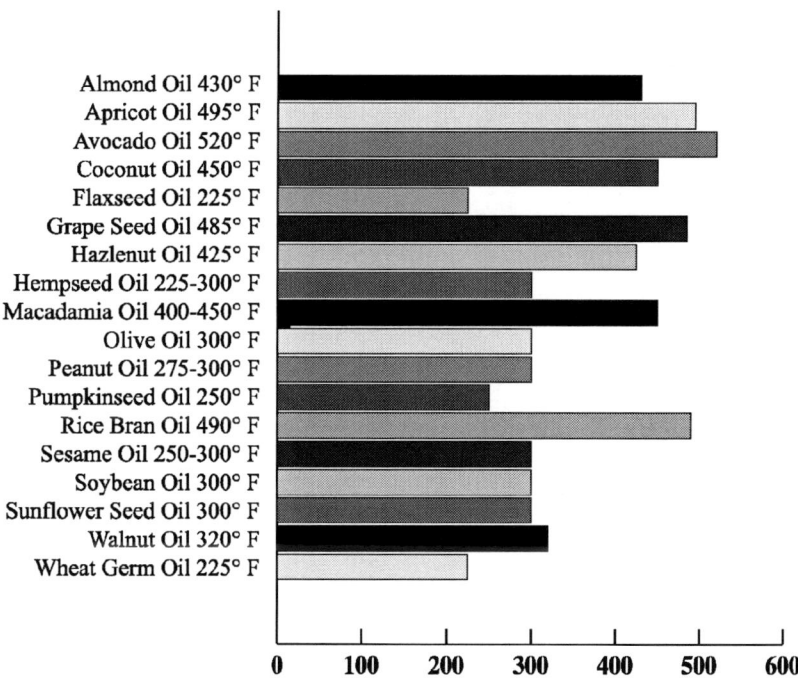

The Sixty Second Interval

The smoke-point of unsaturated, unrefined vegetable oils on medium to high heat on a gas stove in a heavy cast iron skillet takes a minute and a half (180 seconds) to reach, and much less time in a thinner metal pan or on an electric stove. Measured in terms of easily detectable variables during cooking, this distance can be divided into three separate intervals and marked by two important points we will call the Kissing Point and Scream Point of oils. The

Food and Cooking

Kissing Point is the interval reached when raw food placed in the oil will begin to gently sizzle (approximately 140°F). The Scream Point is the interval reached when raw food placed in the oil will begin to crackle violently (approximately 180°F). The Kissing Point is when the food begins to cook in the oil and is the lowest possible temperature in which food can be safely sautéed. The Scream Point is the point at which the oil starts to rapidly self-destruct.

To cook as safely as possible with unsaturated, unrefined vegetable oils, you must keep the oil temperature near the Kissing Point. This means that care must be taken to get the food in the pan before the temperature reaches more than 140°F. This only takes 60 seconds on a medium to high flame. Do not risk putting the oil in the pan on the flame before all the food you are going to put in is already chopped and ready. If the doorbell, phone, or a family member interrupts you, take the pan off the burner or turn the heat off until you are paying attention again. **If the oil smokes, throw it away, wash the pan, and start over!** An even better way is to use medium-low heat so neither the Scream Point or Smoke Point will be reached before the food is placed in the pan. **The best way is to place a small amount of the uncooked food together with the oil in the pan BEFORE you turn on the heat.** Place the rest of the food in the pan once the Kissing Point is reached. This way the Kissing Point will be reached accurately without further risk to the oil.

Table 12: The Kissing and Scream Points of Oils

Melting Point	⇐ 180 Seconds ⇒					Smoke Point
	60 Seconds ❶	Kissing Point (140°F)	60 Seconds ❷	Scream Point (180°F)	60 Seconds ❸	

Special Oils

Yang Within Yin: Medium-Chain SaFAs

Coconut Oil
History

Coconut oil is one of the first oils in history to be used for food and medicine. Its health and cosmetic uses are recorded in Ayurvedic literature, the health system of ancient India. Half the world's population, the Asian community, uses Coconut oil. Pacific Islanders have traditionally used Coconut oil as a dietary staple for thousands of years. These Islanders gained a reputation from 16th and 17th century European explorers for their beauty, physical endowment, and good health, qualities imbued with the fabled search for the fountain of youth.

Coconut oil contributes up to 60 percent of the total caloric intake in Polynesian diets. Almost all of that (90 percent) contains vegetable-quality saturated fat, a different type of saturated fat than that found in animal products. In contrast, the American Heart Association recommends that no more than 30 percent of our total calories should come from fat while saturated fat should be limited to no more than 10 percent. Nevertheless, while Tokelauan Polynesians derive almost 60 percent of their energy from the saturated fat obtained from coconuts, they are relatively free from degenerative disease, they are generally lean and healthy, and their blood cholesterol levels are 70-80 mg lower than populations eating modern diets.

In the 1930s, Weston Price, a nutritional researcher and dentist, carried out a series of epidemiological studies on the health of Pacific island populations where coconut was a dietary staple and found them to be almost entirely free from tooth decay in spite of the fact that they never brushed their teeth, flossed, used mouthwash, or visited dentists.[a] The traditional Islanders were also free from diabetes, coronary artery disease, and cancer. So much for the dietary recommendations of the AHA!

Contents

The saturated fatty acids in Coconut oil are different from those referred to by the AHA because of their chain-length. Normal animal-quality SaFAs are long-chain fatty acids, whereas most of the saturated fatty acids in Coconut oil are medium-chain. Coconut oil is the richest source of medium-chain fatty acids (MCFAs) at 64 percent.

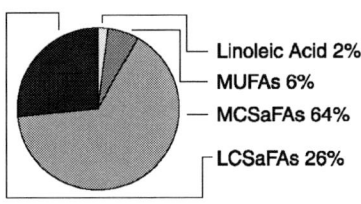

- Linoleic Acid 2%
- MUFAs 6%
- MCSaFAs 64%
- LCSaFAs 26%

---

[a] The study found 0.3 percent tooth decay among those who ate traditional foods compared to 30 percent for Islanders eating westernized diets.

Other sources are Palm Kernel oil (58 percent) and butter (6 percent). Pancreatic enzymes break long-chain fatty acids down into smaller lipoproteins and circulate them through the blood to the rest of the body. Eventually, they are picked up by the liver and either used to produce energy or repackaged into other lipoproteins or triglycerides. MCFAs bypass the trek through the body and go straight to the liver to be converted directly into energy. They are not stored as body fat. MCFAs do not need enzymes to break them apart and easily permeate the mitochondria to provide the cell with a source of energy.

Traditional diets comprised of Coconut oil always include other oils from vegetables and fish to make them more balanced. These combinations supplement the EFAs, which are not contained in Coconut oil. In turn, Coconut oil works synergistically with EFAs, doubling their efficiency and providing AO protection for them. These factors make the MCFAs in Coconut oil "conditionally essential" because they are just as important under certain conditions.

Three different types of MCFAs are found in Coconut oil: lauric acid (48 percent), caprylic acid (8 percent), and capric acid (7 percent). Lauric acid has twelve carbons in its chain; capric acid has ten; and caprylic acid has eight. Lauric acid is the most important of the three. Being first identified in the Mediterranean fruit and seed of the bay laurel tree, lauric acid imparts tremendous antimicrobial properties to Coconut oil. Other vegetable oils are completely deficient in lauric acid, while Coconut and Palm Kernel oils are its richest natural source.

Function

The MCFAs in Coconut oil increase energy and metabolism so that the body functions more efficiently to speed healing and protect against illness. The lauric acid in Coconut oil is highly antimicrobial. In fact, researchers discovered in the 1980s that lauric and capric acids in Coconut oil effectively kill HIV in lab cultures and reduce the HIV load as well as kill other opportunistic, harmful organisms. Some viral loads have been lowered to non-detectable levels after only a few weeks of eating coconut. The current yearly cost for HIV medications runs over $15,000 per person. If the price of Coconut oil were not so cheap, pharmaceutical companies might be more motivated to fund more research into its usefulness for this condition.

Treatable Conditions

Coconut oil has been traditionally used in folk remedies to treat a wide variety of ailments, including:

Debility, cachexia (a state of ill-health, malnutrition, and wasting in chronic disease), swelling, tumors; abscesses, rash, erysipelas (an acute feverish disorder with inflammation and swelling of the skin), burns, bruises, wounds, scabies, alopecia; colds, flu, fever, typhoid; blenorrhagia (catarrhal conjunctivitis), earache, gingivitis, sore throat, toothache; cough, asthma, bronchitis, hematemesis, hemoptysis, tuberculosis; nausea, constipation, dysentery, dropsy, jaundice, scurvy;

calculus; amenorrhea, dysmenorrhea, menorrhagia, gonorrhea, and syphilis.[59]

Coconut oil has also been recognized by modern research and study for treating a wide variety of disorders, including:

- HIV
- Skin and Hair Problems
- Osteoporosis
- Epilepsy
- Breast Feeding
- Coronary Artery Disease
- Digestive Problems
- Obesity
- Diabetes
- Crohn's Disease
- Gallbladder Disease
- Liver Disease
- Hepatitis C
- Genital Herpes
- Candida

- Skin and Hair
  Polynesian women have been using Coconut oil for soft cancer-free skin and smooth hair for thousands of years in spite of their constant exposure to the hot, tropical sun and wind with very little clothing. What makes smooth, elastic, and supple skin is the strength of its connective fibers. As the number of AOs in our tissues dwindle due to the amount of refined foods in our diet, the subsequent free radicals that are formed not only attack the internal organs, they attack the skin. This damage can be gauged by the liver spots on the skin, which indicate the amount of free radical damage to the internal organs. Other sources of free radical damage are cigarette smoke and pollution from radiation or ultra-violet light. Coconut oil prevents free-radical formation and protects against them.

  Lotions and creams containing chemical additives also increase free-radical activity. These substances bring temporary improvement to the skin but accelerate aging over the long run and can even promote skin cancer. Centrifuged Coconut oil is free of these additives and provides a safe and natural remedy for dry, rough, and wrinkled skin and chapped lips, bringing not only quick relief but also healing and repairing the skin tissue with repeated use over time. Coconut oil removes dead cells on the surface of the skin while strengthening the underlying tissues without leaving any greasy residue. The antiseptic properties of the lauric acid in Coconut oil also help to prevent fungi and bacteria from infecting the skin. Coconut oil can also be used to protect the skin from sunburn, which allows it to gradually adapt to greater amounts of exposure.

- Osteoporosis

    Populations that use coconuts as a major part of their diet rarely get osteoporosis. Coconut oil enhances the absorption and retention of calcium and magnesium and is used to treat children with rickets, a disease similar to osteoporosis in adults. Oxidized vegetable oils interfere with bone formation and contribute to osteoporosis through the free radicals they produce. Coconut oil acts like an AO to protect bones from free radical destruction.

    Coconut oil also contains a substance called pregnelone used to make progesterone. When women get older, their progesterone and estrogen tend to become imbalanced due to the dilution of natural progesterone by environmental estrogens from meat, milk, and pesticides. Since pregnelone is converted in the body to progesterone, it may have the same bone-building effect as progesterone. If so, the pregnelone in Coconut oil may also prevent osteoporosis.

- Breast Feeding

    MCFAs have reduced epileptic seizures in two-thirds of children by more than 50 percent during a ten-week treatment period. Coconut oil contains the same nutrients as human breast milk and is, therefore, a major component of baby formula. Breastfed children are generally healthier and brighter than those who are not breast-fed. According to Bruce Fife, ND, Ph.D., breastfed children

    > Receive antibodies and other substances necessary to protect them against childhood illnesses.... They have better teeth and jaw formation, they are less prone to allergies, have better digestive function, and are better able to fight off infectious disease.[60]

    Coconut oil in the diet can help nursing mothers increase the quality of their breast milk, while low-birth weight babies can gain weight with Coconut oil supplementation, because the MCFAs in Coconut oil are easily digested without the need of pancreatic enzymes. In addition, the proportion of lauric acid to other MCFAs in Coconut oil is similar to that of mother's milk. Mothers with sub-normal lauric acid in their milk can increase it from 3.9 percent to 9.6 percent after only fourteen hours of taking Coconut oil. The MCFA content will be even greater if the nursing mother consumes Coconut oil every day. The normal amount of lauric acid in mother's milk helps to protect the child from infectious disease. The MCFA content of mother's milk, or in Coconut oil supplementation for underweight babies, helps them gain weight more quickly and prevent nutritional deficiency.

- Coronary Artery Disease

Coconut oil can also reduce the risk of heart attack. Seventy-five percent of the plaque that collects in arterial walls is comprised of unsaturated fats and cholesterol because poly- and monounsaturated fat is fragile and easily oxidized. Only when over-processing and heating oxidize vegetable oils do they create arterial plaque. Saturated fat, in general, does not collect in the arteries because it does not oxidize so easily. The medium-chain saturated fat in Coconut oil is even less of a problem because it is metabolized quickly and does not accumulate in the body at all. The two dietary oils that create no risk of platelet stickiness are found in the two Yang categories of oils—the Omega 3s (Yang within Yang) and the MCFAs in Coconut oil (Yang within Yin).

- Digestive Problems

Coconut oil is also good for serious digestive problems. MCFAs require less energy and fewer enzymes to digest. The need for pancreatic fat-digesting enzymes is not required so there is less strain on the pancreas and digestive system. More physical energy, then, can be devoted to healing. Coconut oil or its derivatives are used in hospitals intravenously or through a tube in the throat to nourish people with digestive problems. Coconut oil has been used to feed the very young, the critically ill, and those with emergency conditions. Coconut oil can also be used to treat stomach ulcers, 90 percent of which are caused by helicobacter, a lipid-coated bacteria that is killed by lauric acid without endangering friendly intestinal bacteria.

- Obesity

Fifty-five percent of affluent, western populations are overweight and twenty-five percent of these are obese. Twenty-five percent of obese people are teenagers. No wonder dieting has become a way of life! However, according to the Mayo Clinic, 95 percent of dieters regain all or more of their weight within five years. The reason is that the basal metabolic rate (BMR) is slower in overweight people than others. Therefore, overweight people burn up fewer calories with the same amount of physical exercise than skinny people. Dieting only decreases the BMR more so that a lower calorie meal on a diet will have the same effect as the higher calorie meal eaten before the diet. The net effect is that dieting only makes overweight people worse. The trick to losing weight is not to manipulate calories but to increase metabolism through exercise, Coconut oil, whole foods, acupuncture, herbs, and essential oils. Regular exercise increases metabolism even during the periods when a person is not exercising. Low-fat diets increase the risk of nutrient deficiency, especially of the fat-soluble vitamins, and degenerative disease. Coconut oil promotes general health and has fewer calories than other fats, no more in fact than protein or carbohydrate. Using Coconut oil in place of other oils lowers caloric intake because it is digested and processed more efficiently than other fats. MCFAs can increase metabolic rate by 50 percent in less than a week! Using Coconut oil instead of long-chain SaFAs or vegetable oil will help promote weight loss as long as the caloric intake of the rest of the diet remains the same. In contrast, *refined* polyunsaturated vegetable oils depress thyroid activity and lower metabolic rate.

- Diabetes

Diabetes is the sixth leading cause of death in the US with 45 percent of the population at risk and puts those people who have it at high risk for kidney disease, high blood pressure, stroke, cataracts, nerve damage, hearing loss, and blindness. Diabetics lack energy because their cells are not able to get the glucose that is necessary to produce the energy they need. Diabetics need to become more Yang by increasing their metabolic rate. They will them be more able to control their blood sugar by increasing insulin production and glucose absorption into the cells.

There are two kinds of diabetes: Type I and Type II. The level of glucose in the blood is elevated in both types of diabetes while cells are deprived. In Type I diabetes the pancreas does not produce enough insulin to transport glucose to the cells so insulin injections need to be taken. In Type II diabetes the cells are unable to absorb the glucose in spite of the fact that insulin levels may be normal.

While fat restriction diets tend to help diabetics, the biggest fat problem is refined vegetable oil. Polyunsaturated oil is important in building and regulating cellular membranes where glucose is absorbed. When polyunsaturated oils are refined, they oxidize easily and reduce the ability of the cell membranes to allow hormones, glucose, and other substances to flow in and out of the cell, especially in Type II. Coconut oil raises metabolic rate, improves insulin secretion, and supplies energy directly to the cells without the need of insulin, thus helping in both types of diabetes. Increased metabolic rate stimulates insulin production and increases glucose absorption into the cells.

According to *The Healing Miracles of Coconut Oil* by Bruce Fife, N.D., Coconut oil is useful in treating diabetes. Not only does Coconut oil not contribute to diabetes like refined or oxidized vegetable oils do, it helps regulate blood sugar so that diabetic symptoms are minimized. The Nauru people, for example, never contracted diabetes until they abandoned their traditional diet, which included large amounts of Coconut oil. Coconut oil improves both insulin secretion and the utilization of blood glucose. In India, Type II diabetes increased when the population discarded Coconut oil in favor of the so-called "heart-friendly" polyunsaturated vegetable oils. Fife recommends Coconut oil for diabetics and borderline diabetics because it helps to stabilize blood glucose levels while reducing excess body weight. He claims, "It is probably the only oil a diabetic should eat." Other Yang categories of oils, the Yang within Yang Omega 3s, for example, also need to be considered.

- Crohn's Disease

Crohn's disease is characterized by chronic inflammation of the intestines accompanied by diarrhea, abdominal pain, bloody stools, anemia, and weight loss. Coconut oil soothes the inflammation and, even better, kills the microorganisms that cause the inflammation in the first place.

- Gallbladder Disease

Bile is produced in the liver and drains into the gallbladder where it breaks fats down into small particles so they can be absorbed. The MCFAs in Coconut oil place fewer demands on the gallbladder because they do not need the gallbladder for the fats to be broken down. Surgical removal of the gallbladder not only hinders fat digestion, it leads to serious deficiencies of the fat-soluble Vitamins A, D, E, K, and beta-carotene. Because Coconut oil is more easily digested, it can promote the absorption of these fat-soluble vitamins.

- Liver Disease

The liver is responsible for metabolizing fats, producing bile, storing vitamins and minerals, secreting hormones, and detoxifying the body. Alcohol, drugs, viruses, and bacteria can produce a chronic inflammation of the liver known as hepatitis. There are three types of hepatitis: hepatitis A, B, and C. The hepatitis A virus is transmitted by poor sanitation and hygiene. Forty percent of young adults in the US have been exposed to hepatitis A. Twenty percent of the African and Asian populations are infected by hepatitis B, whereas the US rate is only 1 percent. Hepatitis B and C are passed by sexual contact, needle-sharing among drug abusers, or by inadvertent needle sticks in medical situations. Hepatitis C is the most severe type of hepatitis because it often leads to liver cirrhosis, which is characterized by scarring and massive tissue destruction.

The MCFAs in Coconut oil inactivate the hepatitis virus so that the immune system can fight off the infections. The fatty acids in Coconut oil protect the liver from free-radical damage and tissue death and can even rejuvenate dead tissue.

- Candida

Candida albacans is a common fungus of the intestinal tract and mucous membranes. Normally, Candida is kept in check by beneficial intestinal flora, but when it gets out of control, it causes oral thrush and diaper rash in babies and vaginal yeast infections in women. When the immunity is weakened from taking steroids or immunosuppressive drugs, or when the beneficial flora are killed by antibiotics, systemic candida infections can grow out of control and affect the entire body. Recurring infections are a sign of systemic yeast infection, especially when accompanied by a white discharge. When vaginal infections are treated as if they were localized in only one area of the body, even a single course of antibiotics can lead to a systemic candida infection. Birth control pills can also place women at risk. However, the caprylic acid in Coconut oil is as effective as the most popular antifungal prescription drug (nystatin) without any of the side effects.

Dosage

Relatively few of even the most allergy-prone individuals have allergic reactions to Coconut oil because it is so non-toxic. One could consume more than 3½ tablespoons a day (the proportion of MCFAs a nursing baby receives and the amount HIV-infected individuals are recommended to consume) of

Coconut oil without worry. Polynesian Islanders consume as much as 10 tablespoons a day and have excellent health. Where 1 tablespoon a day is beneficial and significant enough to reduce the viral load in HIV patients, for most adults 2-4 tablespoons daily is a reasonable amount. One could take up to 4-8 tablespoons a day temporarily during sickness. If nausea and vomiting prevent oral intake, then Coconut oil can be massaged into the skin where it will be readily absorbed. In this case, massage 2-4 tablespoons of oil two or three times a day over the entire body.

Offshoots: Medium-Chain Triglycerides

Medium-Chain Triglycerides (MCTs) can also be created industrially by fractionation and transesterification. Medium- and long-chain fatty acids are separated from their glycerol molecule (the molecule that holds fatty acid chains together) and then only the MCFAs are reconnected to the glycerol. This process results in an oil that is a 100 percent MCFA. While this synthetic product has stability as well as therapeutic benefits, MCTs suffer from the loss of minor components, especially the most important MCFA, lauric acid. MCTs may also contain harmful breakdown products from the refining process as all fractionated and transesterified oils are made from oils that have been previously refined.

MCTs are easily metabolized and easily absorbed. They pass easily through membranes and are not stored as fat deposits. MCTs are useful for the malabsorption of fat, weight loss, impairment of the liver, athletic workouts, and for intravenous formulas used in hospitals. Negative effects of excessive use of MCTs, however, can lead to ketosis or the inhibition of Vitamin E, amino acids, and other substances due to the tying up of albumin protein, which transports them in the blood. Because of these negative effects, and because of the availability of good quality, natural coconut oil, MCTs should be avoided.

Production Methods

Coconut oil is often thought of as coconut butter since Coconut oil becomes solid at room temperature (76°F). The oil is expressed through one of four methods: (1) Direct Micro Expeller, (2) Cold Pressed, (3) Hand-Pressed, and (4) Centrifuged.

Direct Micro Expeller Coconut oil (DME) is extracted from freshly grated coconut meat after it has been dried and pressed. The resulting mixture of about 90 percent oil and 10 percent water is then allowed to stand, usually with the application of heat, to separate the pure oil from the water. The water must be removed since moisture content of 0.1 percent or less is needed to prevent the oil from becoming rancid. Cold-pressed Coconut oil, as usual, is a misnomer because, while it may be initially pressed from unheated oil, it will have to be heated afterwards to remove the water content.

Hand-pressed Coconut oil is the traditional homemade method in which the fresh coconut meat is grated and pressed into coconut milk that is then allowed to ferment for approximately 48 hours to separate the oil from the solids and water. The remaining oil is then heated to reduce the moisture content. Because the temperature and length of heating varies from one batch to another, considerable variations exist between different batches.

Centrifuged Coconut oil is the only method that is done without heat. Fresh coconut milk is centrifuged to separate the mixture into three layers: (1) the solid components, (2) the water, and (3) the oil. Since no heat is applied in this method, it retains all of the flavor and scent of fresh coconut and is available in the USA under the trade name Coconut Oil Supreme™ (www.coconutoil-online.com or 800-922-1744).

Fractionated Coconut Oil

Fractionated Coconut oil is generally used as a carrier oil for essential oils since they are completely soluble in it. Fractionated Coconut oil is obtained by heating Coconut oil so that the top liquid fraction is removed. Fractionated Coconut oil is clear, odorless, tasteless, and liquid at room temperature. This very fine oil is capable of penetrating the skin easily and is non-staining. Because of the molecular structure of its fatty acids, it has an indefinite shelf life, a property that helps to extend the life of the oils it is used with. Nevertheless, it does not contain all the healing properties of natural coconut oil, which should be used instead if therapeutic results from the Coconut oil are to be obtained.

Yang Within Yang: Principal Omega 3 Sources

Krill Oil
What is Krill?

Krill are tiny ⅜ to 2⅜ inch long shrimp-like crustaceans, or plankton, found in the cold, deep waters of the Antarctic and the North Pacific Oceans. While the biomass of krill exceeds 500 million tons and is the most abundant on the planet, less than one half of 0.1%

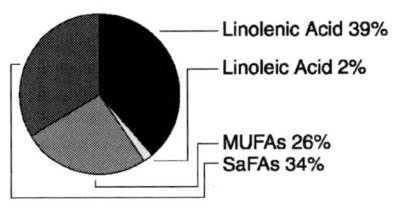

Linolenic Acid 39%
Linoleic Acid 2%
MUFAs 26%
SaFAs 34%

of the existing resources is harvested every year. While krill are normally used for food by whales and fish, they have also been used as a traditional food for the Japanese. Almost 43 percent of Japanese krill is used for human consumption in the form of boiled and frozen krill as well as peeled tail meat and krill paste.

Krill have adapted to these cold waters through their high content of Omega 3 derivatives—EPA and DHA—most of which are linked to phospholipids instead of the more common link to the triglycerides.[a] Krill oil can contain up to 40 percent phospholipids as well as high amounts of the powerful AO astaxanthin. This unique combination of high Omega 3 content (especially in the form of the EPA and DHA derivatives), phospholipids, and the AO astaxanthin makes Krill oil very useful in nourishing the brain as well as in preventing and treating inflammatory disorders related to the following:

---

[a] "Krill Omega-3 Oil: Nutraceutical Synergy on the Cutting Edge," by Parris M. Kidd, Ph.D., in *Total Health* 25:4.

137

- Unregulated cholesterol levels
- Cardiovascular disease
- Menstrual problems including PMS and painful menstruation
- Gastric disorders due to infection by the helicobacter pylori bacterium
- Elevated blood sugar
- General skin health including the prevention and treatment of skin cancer

The important phospholipid content of Krill oil, however, is dependent upon the krill being processed in the absence of heat, light, and oxygen. To date, Neptune Krill Oil (NKO™) is the only company using these extraction methods and is the only company to make krill oil with a high phospholipid content.[a]

Nutritional Factors in Krill Oil

Phospholipids are important lipids for nourishing the brain and maintaining the integrity of cell membranes. Phospholipids work synergistically in NKO™ with Omega 3 EFAs and the super-antioxidant astaxanthin like they do naturally in the cell membranes of the body. The phospholipids enhance absorption while the super-antioxidant astaxanthin protects against FA breakdown and cellular inflammation. This combination makes the EPA and DHA in NKO™ safer and more effective than that found in Fish oil even though the amount is less (24 percent, compared to 30 to 50 percent for most fish oils).[61]

Krill are simpler forms of Omega 3 than that found in Fish oil and are easier to digest and assimilate. In fact, fish do not make their Omega 3s, but get it from the plankton they eat.[62] In turn, the plankton gets their Omega 3s from micro-algae. Fish oils are an economical way to obtain Omega 3 derivatives, but taking phospholipid-rich Krill oil is more ideal.[63] In addition, Krill oil does not cause any of the stomach reflux or regurgitation associated with Fish oil (64 percent of the subjects in one study).[64]

Krill oil is also much more stable than Fish oil and resists oxidation for more than 50 hours at 208°F while Fish oil will go rancid in one-sixth the time at much less temperature (only 8 hours at 176°F). Fish oil is notoriously prone to rancidity and is the most rancid-prone of all polyunsaturated fatty acids, a main drawback to their use.[65] Krill oil also contains the AOs Vitamin E and A as well as a bioflavonoid. These multiple super-antioxidants in Krill oil, not the phospholipids or Omega 3s, account for its stability, a feature that not only protects the oil but also protects the body against free radical attacks.[66] While the super-antioxidant astaxanthin itself is over 40 times more powerful than Vitamins A and E and more than 4 times more powerful than enzyme CoQ_{10}, the

---

[a] Tina Sampalis, M.D., Ph.D., private conversation, 06-09-06.

combined AO power of NKO™ is over 7 times more powerful than astaxanthin and 48 times more powerful than Fish oil![a67]

Most Krill oil is harvested with sustainable practices under International Treaty regulation. Because krill are at the bottom of the food chain, in contrast to the large fish that are the primary sources of Fish oil, they are (unlike fish) free of mercury, PCBs, dioxins, heavy metals, and other toxins.

Krill Oil in Chronic Inflammatory Disorders

While tissue inflammation can be useful in acute disorders after bodily injury where it is a normal part of the body's immune response, chronic inflammation is associated with serious health problems including pathologically elevated cholesterol, cardiovascular disease, arthritis, PMS, and certain forms of skin disease. One of the main factors associated with chronic inflammation is C-Reactive Protein (CRP), which is found in elevated levels in the body during high levels of alcohol consumption; low levels of physical activity or physical exertion, chronic fatigue, sleep disturbance; depression; hormone replacement therapy; cancer; systemic lupus erythematosus; rheumatoid arthritis; acute bacterial, viral, and other infections; pulmonary tuberculosis; heart attacks, hypertension; obesity, diabetes, inflammatory bowel disease; and uremia.[b] The presence of CRP also links dental infections and other chronic low-grade infections to heart disease.[c]

Research has indicated that astaxanthin reduces inflammation in humans[d] and rats, reduces the injury by CRP to rabbit hearts,[68] and decreases the effect of joint pain and stiffness associated with osteoarthritis in humans.[e] An osteoarthritis study observed nearly a 31 percent drop in CRP levels in those participants taking NKO™ compared to a rise in CRP levels among those in the placebo group. After 30 days the treatment group experienced 162 percent less joint pain and stiffness than the placebo group, which remained virtually unchanged. In addition, functional impairment lessened significantly compared to the placebo group, which only experienced slight improvement after the 30 days.[69] The overall positive response from the NKO™ is most likely due, not only to the presence of its strong anti-inflammatory AOs, but also its high level

---

[a] According to a USDA-developed test determining antioxidant capacity.

[b] Kushner I. "C-Reactive Protein and the Acute Phase Response." In *Hospital Practice.* 1990 March 30; 13-28; and Deodhar S.D. "C-Reactive Protein: The best laboratory indicator available for monitoring disease activity." *Cleveland Clinic Journal of Medicine.* 1989 56 (2):126-129.

[c] Mattila KJ, Pussinen PJ, Paju S. "Dental Infections and Cardiovascular Diseases: A Review." In *Journal Periodontol.* 2005 Nov. 76 (11-s):2085-2088.

[d] Suzuki Y, Ohgami K, Shiratori K, Jin XH, Ilieva I, Koyama Y, Yazawa K, Yoshida K, Kase S, and Ohno S. "Suppressive effects of astaxanthin against rat endotoxin-induced uveitis by inhibiting the NF-kappaB signaling pathway." In *Experimental Eye Research.* 2006 February 82:2, 275-281.

[e] Sampalis T. "Evaluation of the Effect of NKO on Biomarkers of Chronic Inflammation In Vivo." June 9, 2004. Unpublished research.

of Omega 3 derivatives—EPA and DHA, which are also known for their strong anti-inflammatory effect.

Natural Cholesterol Regulation with Krill Oil

NKO™ is even more effective in regulating cholesterol levels than Fish oil [a] because of its high levels of anti-inflammatory super-antioxidants in combination with the phospholipids and Omega 3s. After 12 weeks of treatment in patients receiving 1 or 1.5 grams of Neptune Krill Oil, serum cholesterol levels dropped up to 13.7 percent and fell 32 points from 231 mg/dL to 199 mg/dL. In patients taking up to 2 to 3 grams, serum cholesterol levels dropped up to 18 percent and fell 55 points from 251 mg/dL to 206 mg/dL. In contrast, patients taking Fish oil experienced only a 5.9 percent reduction as their levels fell only 13 points from an average of 231 mg/dL to 218 mg/dL. The placebo group experienced a 9.1 percent INCREASE that rose from an average of 222 mg/dL to 242 mg/dL.[70]

Table 13: Serum Cholesterol Levels of Krill and Fish Oils

	Percent	Points	mg/dL
1 or 1.5 g NKO™	-13.7%	-32	231 mg/dL to 199 mg/dL
2 to 3 g NKO™	-18%	-55	251 mg/dL to 206 mg/dL
Fish Oil	-5.9%	-13	231 mg/dL to 218 mg/dL
Placebo	+9.1%	+20	222 mg/dL to 242 mg/dL

LDL levels were also lowered significantly with Neptune Krill Oil. Given a daily dose of 1 gram, LDL levels dropped 54 points and 32 percent from an average of 168 mg/dL to 114 mg/dL; with a daily dose of 1.5 grams, LDL levels dropped 59 points and 36 percent from 165 mg/dL to 106 mg/dL; with a daily dose of 2 grams, LDL levels dropped 69 points and 37 percent from 183 mg/dL to 114 mg/dL; and with a daily dose of 3 grams, LDL levels dropped 68 points from 173 mg/dL to 105 mg/dL. **In contrast, patients treated with Fish oil achieved no significant LDL reduction.[71]**

Table 14: LDL Levels of Krill and Fish Oils

	Percent	Points	mg/dL
1 g NKO™	-32%	-54	168 mg/dL to 114 mg/dL
1.5 g NKO™	-36%	-59	165 mg/dL to 106 mg/dL
2 g NKO™	-37%	-69	183 mg/dL to 114 mg/dL
3 g NKO™	-39%	-68	173 mg/dL to 105 mg/dL
Fish Oil	0%	0	

In the same experiment, HDL levels also rose significantly with Neptune Krill Oil—44 percent from 57.2 mg/dL to 82.4 mg/dL at 1 gram daily;

---

[a] Bunea R., El Farrah K., and Deutsch L. "Evaluation of the Effects of Neptune Krill Oil on the Clinical Course of Hyperlipidemia." In *Alternative Medicine Review*. 2004; 9 (4):420-8.

43 percent from 58.8 mg/dL to 83.9 mg/dL at 1.5 grams daily; 55 percent from 51 mg/dL to 79.3 mg/dL at 2 grams daily; and an impressive 59 percent from 64.2 mg/dL to 102.5 mg/dL at 3 grams daily. In contrast, the HDL levels of those participants taking Fish oil rose only an insignificant degree—a 4.2 percent increase from 56.6 mg/dL to 59.03 mg/dL. HDL levels of the placebo group were relatively unchanged.

Table 15: HDL Levels of Krill and Fish Oils

	Percent	mg/dL
1 g NKO™	+44%	57.2 mg/dL to 82.4 mg/dL
1.5 g NKO™	+43%	58.8 mg/dL to 83.9 mg/dL
2 g NKO™	+55%	51 mg/dL to 79.3 mg/dL
3 g NKO™	+59%	64.2 mg/dL to 102.5 mg/dL
Fish Oil	+4.2%	56.6 mg/dL to 59.03 mg/dL

Triglyceride levels also dropped significantly as the dosage of Neptune Krill Oil increased. A 27 to 28 percent reduction of triglycerides occurred with doses from 2 to 3 grams daily as opposed to an insignificant reduction for those participants taking Fish oil.[72]

Table 16: Triglyceride Levels of Krill and Fish Oils

	Percent	mg/dL
2 g NKO™	-27%	160.4 mg/dL to 116.1 mg/dL
3 g NKO™	-28%	152.8 mg/dL to 112.3 mg/dL
Fish Oil	-3.2%	

Patients followed up after the study was completed over a period of another 12 weeks at daily maintenance dosages of 500 mg showed even greater changes in cholesterol regulation, especially in regard to serum cholesterol, LDL, and triglyceride levels. Serum cholesterol declined 19 percent from the baseline; LDL declined 44 percent from the baseline; and triglyceride levels dropped from the 12 percent reduction at the end of the study to 25 percent on the maintenance dose.[73]

Menstrual Disorders and Krill Oil

According to current statistics, 85 to 97 percent of women will have premenstrual symptoms sometime during the course of their lives. Roughly one-third of them will have conditions so severe they will have to seek medical attention. The lives of 3 to 5 percent of them will also be notably disrupted[74] and a full 10 percent of them will be so incapacitated during their periods that their social activities, relationships, school, and work will be disrupted. In fact, 140,000,000 work hours are lost every year from this condition.

Physical symptoms include insomnia, excessive sleeping, fatigue, joint or muscle pain, bloating, difficult concentration, headache, dizziness, fainting, collapse, breast tenderness or swelling, food cravings, overeating, nausea, vomiting, diarrhea, low back pain, painful menstruation, and cramping.[75]

Psycho-emotional symptoms occur between ovulation and the onset of menstruation and include anxiety, tension, edginess, irritability, anger, sadness, and decreased interest in work or hobbies.

Physical causes of both these physical and psycho-emotional problems are related to lipid imbalance including a deficiency of phospholipids and Omega 3 EFAs, enzyme deficiencies disrupting the conversion of EFAs to their respective prostaglandins, an imbalance between Omega 3 and Omega 6 EFAs, and AO deficiency leading to an exaggerated chronic inflammatory response and the proliferation of free radicals.

The synergistic combination of the phospholipids and high amount of Omega 3 derivatives in Neptune Krill Oil can be very effective in alleviating these conditions—more effectively, in fact, than Fish oil because the process used to create fish oil can damage phospholipids.[76] Both phospholipids and Omega 3s have a positive effect on the brain and most likely account for the relief provided by Neptune Krill Oil for the psycho-emotional and nervous system-related symptoms in PMS.

Omega-3s in Krill oil also produce the anti-inflammatory PGE_3s, which help to alleviate much of the tenderness, pain, and anxiety. The EPA and DHA derivatives of Omega 3 are also very relaxing and help decrease the constriction in the muscles and blood vessels of the uterus that causes the pain. They also balance the constriction and inflammation caused by the over-abundance of Omega 6s that typically occur in the SAD. Omega 6s convert to both the anti-inflammatory and relaxing PGE_1 AND the inflammatory and constricting arachidonic acid (AA) . AA buildup in the cellular membranes can trigger the production of the pro-inflammatory PGE_2s, which are directly linked to menstrual pain. Women with PMS have significantly higher levels of Omega 6 in their blood than normal, while their GLA levels are typically low.[a] In addition, AA is released in the body prior to menstruation as progesterone levels drop. This onslaught of AA then produces an overabundance of PGE_2 as well as other inflammatory metabolites such as leukotrienes and cyclooxygenase. Cyclooxygenase is an enzyme involved in arthritis pain that also causes vasoconstriction and contraction of the uterus and, hence, pain.[77]

The Yang prostaglandins from Omega 3 (PGE_3) and 6 (PGE_1) have an expanding nature and stimulate metabolism. They balance the Yin constricting nature of PGE_2, which is produced from AA via Omega 6. When these two Yang prostaglandins slightly outweigh the Yin prostaglandin, a good balance is established that can help control the cravings for food and sweets that sometimes occurs before menstruation. If PGE_1 is deficient, too much insulin can be secreted to counteract the preponderance of the constricting PGE_2, which leads to an attack of acute hypoglycemia with the resulting increase of appetite and cravings for sweets. PGE_1 insufficiency can be caused by either inadequate intake of essential fatty acids or conversion disorders where GLA can not be

---

[a] Brush, M.G. "Evening primrose oil in treatment of premenstrual syndrome." In Clinical *Uses of Essential Fatty Acids*, Horrobin D.F., editor, Eden Press: Montreal, Quebec, 1982:155-162.

converted from Omega 6 and so PGE_1 can not be made.[78] The EPA and DHA Omega 3 derivatives in Fish oil or Krill oil can help control these cravings until the conversion problem is addressed.

The EPA and DHA derivatives of Omega 3 in Krill oil can supplement PGE_3 deficiency and help correct the joint or muscle pain, headache, dizziness and fainting, collapse, and breast tenderness or swelling. The super-antioxidants in Krill oil can help alleviate the insomnia, joint or muscle pain, headache, dizziness, and fainting. The FA deficiencies with their corresponding symptoms in menstrual disorders are summarized below:

- **Phospholipid Deficiency**
  Excessive sleeping, insomnia, fatigue, difficult concentration, headache, dizziness and fainting, collapse, anxiety, tension, edginess, anger, sadness, decreased interest in work or hobbies
- **EPA/DHA Deficiency**
  Joint or muscle pain, headache, dizziness and fainting, collapse, breast tenderness or swelling
- **AO Deficiency**
  Insomnia, joint or muscle pain, headache, dizziness, fainting
- **EFA Imbalance/Omega 6 Conversion Disruption**
  Bloating, joint or muscle pain, dizziness and fainting, collapse, breast tenderness or swelling

In a double blind study of PMS women, half received Neptune Krill Oil and the other half received Fish oil every day during the first month and just before and after menstruation for the following two months.[a] Each group experienced equal results in reducing weight gain, abdominal pain, bloating, and swelling. However, the group taking Neptune Krill Oil also experienced a significant reduction of other physical as well as psycho-emotional symptoms including breast tenderness, joint pain, the feeling of being overwhelmed and stressed, irritability, and depression; and were able to reduce analgesic medication up to 40 percent after the first menstrual cycle and up to 50 percent by the end of the three-month study. In addition, none of the women in the Neptune Krill Oil group experienced any gastric reflux as opposed to 64 percent of the women in the group taking Fish oil.[79]

Blood Sugar Regulation with Krill Oil

Studies have also shown that Neptune Krill Oil can also lower blood sugar by up to 6.3 percent in those participants taking 1 to 1.5 grams per day, and by 5.6 percent in those taking 2 to 3 grams per day. Blood sugar continued to decrease for those continuing to take a maintenance dose of 500 mg per day. In contrast, those participants taking 3 grams of Fish oil per day lowered their

---

[a] Sampalis F., Bunea R., Pelland M.F., Kowalski O., Duguet N., Dupuis S. "Evaluation of the effects of Neptune Krill Oil on the management of premenstrual syndrome and dysmenorrhea." In *Alternative Medicine Review*. 2003 8 (2):171-79.

blood sugar by 3.3 percent while the placebo group showed only a slight decrease.[80]

Treating Stomach Disorders with Krill Oil

Normal inflammation caused by blood cells such as the T-lymphocytes in the process of bolstering immunity sometimes damages the gastric mucosal lining, which then becomes prone to the invasion of bacteria. One of the most pervasive of these bacteria in our society, affecting about half of the world population, is Helicobacter pylori. Helicobacter pylori are associated with chronic type B gastritis, increased risk of peptic ulcers, and gastric cancer.[81]

When the body is low in AOs, such as carotenoids and vitamin C, it may become more vulnerable to Helicobacter pylori infections. In animal studies, for example, antioxidant levels are used to predict the bacterial load of Helicobacter pylori as well as the likelihood of contracting Helicobacter pylori infection. Mice treated with astaxanthin from algae or Neptune Krill Oil showed significantly lower levels of Helicobacter pylori infection than those of untreated animals.[a] Therefore, Krill oil is a good oil for preventing and treating these kinds of stomach disorders.

Krill Oil and the Skin

In addition to a greater sense of well being and happiness, the combination of phospholipids, Omega 3 derivatives, and AOs in Neptune Krill Oil also exhibits a positive effect on the skin, hair, and nails. One study showed a 58 percent reduction in wrinkling, redness, and other skin conditions.[b] In an animal study, mice taking NKO were 20.8 percent less likely than the placebo-fed mice to develop skin cancer under high UVB exposure and 13.4 percent less likely under normal exposure. They were also 14.6 percent more likely to be normal under high UVB exposure and 26.8 percent more likely under normal exposure.[82] These numbers are illustrated in the following table.

---

[a] Bennedsen M., Wang X., Willen R., Wadstrom T., Andersen L.P. "Treatment of H. pylori infected mice with antioxidant astaxanthin reduces gastric inflammation, bacterial load and modulates cytokine release by splenocytes." In *Immunology Letters.* 1999 Dec 1;70 (3):185-9.

[b] Sampalis T. Unpublished research, in print.

Table 17: Skin Cancer in Mice

High UVB Exposure

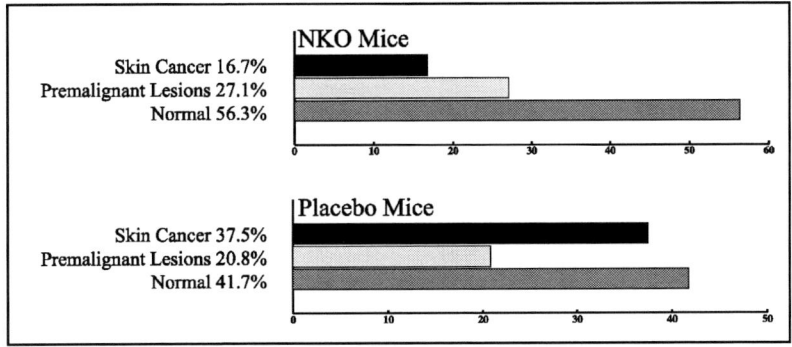

Normal UVB Exposure

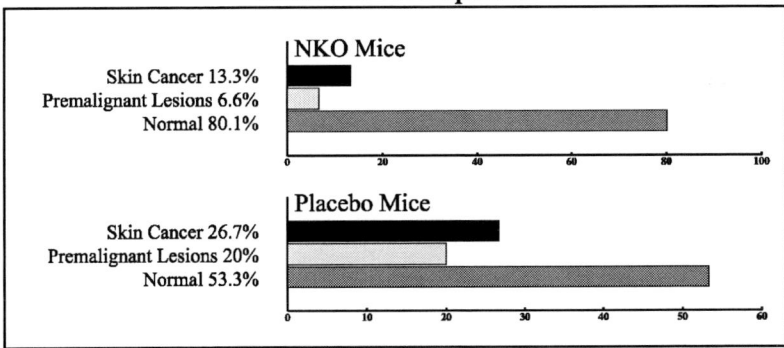

Dosage

The general principal for taking Krill oil is to begin with a fairly high daily intake for the first two months and then reduce it to a maintenance level. For example, take 1 to 2 grams of NKO daily for one to two months followed by a daily maintenance dose of 0.5 to 1 gram depending on health issues and body size.[83] To benefit the menstrual cycle, take 1 gram daily for the first 1 to 2 months followed by a maintenance dose of 500 mg. For cardiovascular benefits, generally start with a minimum of 1500 mg per day followed by a maintenance dose of 1 gram per day after the blood lipid levels have altered, a period of up to four months. Up to 3 grams per day should be used for achieving a quicker result for those wishing to manage serious heart disease medically rather than surgically. Doses of up to 6 grams per day should pose no appreciable risk.[a]

---

[a] Kidd, Parris M. Ph.D. "Krill Omega-3 Oil: Nutraceutical Synergy on the Cutting Edge," In *Total Health* 25:4.

Use Krill oil with caution or after suitable allergy testing in those with seafood allergies. People who bleed easily or are taking anticoagulant medication should only use Krill oil with medical supervision.[84]

Fish Oil

The main benefit from Fish oil is that some kinds of it, especially cold-water fish, contain good amounts of the important Omega 3 essential fatty acid derivatives—EPA and DHA. A high consumption of these EFA derivatives, or even simple consumption of as little as one meal per week of fatty fish,[85] can

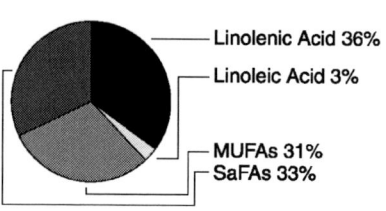

Linolenic Acid 36%
Linoleic Acid 3%
MUFAs 31%
SaFAs 33%

decrease mortality by 30 percent and decrease the risk of heart attack by 45 percent.[86] Oils from fish such as herring and cod liver oil, however, are probably not as good because of the cetoleic acid and capelin oils found in them (up to 12 and 20 percent).[a] In order to get EPA and DHA from fish, it needs to be taken in capsule form or obtained from fresh fish, preferably raw, at least every two weeks. The richest sources of Omega 3s come from trout, salmon, mackerel, sardines, tuna, and eel, while less important sources can be obtained from scallop, clam, oyster and squid.

Brown and red algae such as kelp, kombu, wakame, and dulse are also good sources of EPA and DHA. The body can normally make EPA (the starting material for making Prostaglandins 3s) without fish from the Omega 3s found in LNA. Two tablespoons of flax oil are equivalent to two large capsules of fish oil. The advantage of using Flaxseed oil is that the EPA made from it in the body will be fresher (EPA and DHA are more easily destroyed by light, air, and heat than LNA), more stable, and less likely to contain toxins like PCBs (polychlorinated biphenyls) or heavy metals like mercury absorbed from the environment by fish.

For those few people that are nutritionally or genetically unable to make this conversion, Fish oil or Black Currant Seed oil[b] are required. For those unable to convert EPA from LNA, saturated and monounsaturated fat, *trans*-fatty acids, and cholesterol should be reduced while Vitamins B_3, B_6, C, magnesium, and zinc, or the whole foods that contain them,[c] should be taken to speed up and increase EPA conversion.

---

[a] Cetoleic acid may be toxic to heart tissue.

[b] Black Currant Seed oil contains SDA, which can convert in the body under normal conditions into, first EPA, and then PGE_3 and DHA.

[c] Vitamin B_3 is found naturally in whole wheat, wheat germ, peanuts, nutritional yeast, nori (a sea vegetable), and meat. Vitamin B_6 is found naturally in wheat germ, peas, lentils, beans, carrots, cabbage, broccoli, spinach, potatoes, tomatoes, walnuts, bananas, watermelon, eggs, tuna, chicken, turkey, liver, and kidney. Magnesium is found naturally in most whole grains and seeds, legumes, and green vegetables. Zinc is found naturally in whole grains, legumes,

Historically, the most common way of balancing EFAs was through the addition of fish to the diet. Many fish, especially cold-water fish, supply more than reasonable amounts of EFAs and their important derivatives. Throughout European history the international trade in fish in conjunction with the all-important salt trade was a major event. In fact, as early as 130-200 AD, the Greek physician Galen praised such Omega 3-rich fish as the sardine and mackerel for the important roles they played in this trade. Salted cod was the staple of the North Atlantic fishing trade for centuries.[87] These fish and others are very high in Omega 3 EFAs and their important derivatives, EPA and DHA.

The main problem with using these sources in times before modern refrigeration was preservation for which curing with salt was the most important means. One of the ways in which this was done from the early Greek period to the fall of the Roman Empire was through fermenting fish in salt brine—a process that was undertaken on a massive scale and similar to the traditional method of obtaining Coconut oil or Grape Seed oil. In those days, fermented salted fish was called *garum*. The best *garum* was reserved for the wealthy elite while lesser qualities were also produced for the masses. Good quality *Garum* could also be easily made at home. The trick was to ferment the fish by using the correct amount of salt so the fish would not spoil. When done properly, the *garum* was considered "medicinal." According to Mark Kurlansky in *Salt: A World History*, "Physicians saw in *garum* all of the health benefits of salted fish contained in a bottle. It was prescribed as a medicine or, more commonly, mixed with other ingredients to make a medicine, usually for digestive disorders, and for such problems as sores....But it was also prescribed for other ailments including sciatica, tuberculosis, and migraine headaches."[88] *Garum* was also used in Asia, where it may have originated. In fact, the ancient Chinese fermented fish, especially herrings and sardines, with their soy sauce and used it as a condiment with other dishes. Most likely, *garum* was an ancient method of supplementing Omega 3s, which are known for their ability to heal skin problems, musculo-skeletal problems, and to alleviate tension in general, problems similar to those with *garum* in earlier times..

---

pumpkin seeds, sunflower seeds, mushrooms, spinach, eggs, dairy products, fish, poultry, and meat.

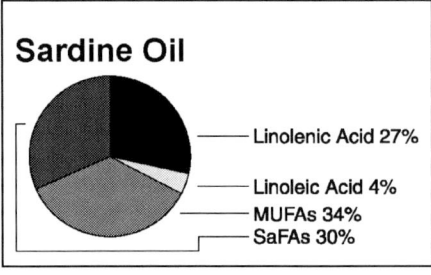

Omega 3 derivatives of sardine oil include SDA (3 percent of the oil), EPA (10 percent), DPA (2 percent), and DHA (11 percent).

Sardine Oil

- MUFAs: Palmitoleic Acid (8%), Oleic Acid (15%), Gadoleic Acid (6%), Erucic Acid (6%)
- SaFAs: Lauric Acid (.1%), Myristic Acid (7%), Palmitic Acid (17%), Stearic Acid (4%)

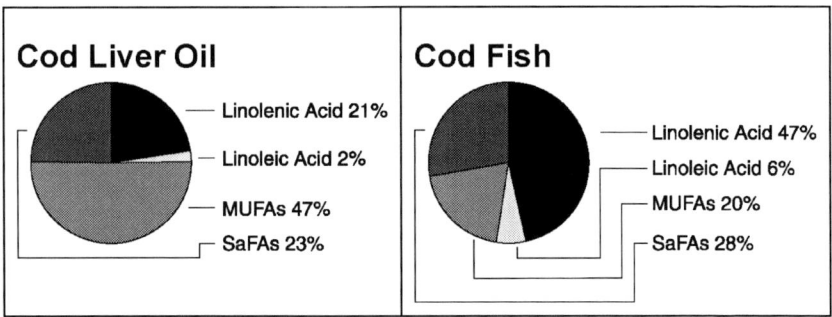

Cod liver oil contains many Omega 3 derivatives including SDA (3 percent), EPA (10 percent), DPA (2 percent), and DHA (11 percent). Most of its MUFAs are Oleic Acid (15 percent), and most of its SaFAs are comprised of Palmitic Acid (11 percent). The large w3:w6 ratio of cod liver oil (11:1) makes it useful for rehabilitating Omega 3 deficiencies. However, care should be used because fish livers absorb more of the ocean's hazardous wastes than any other tissue.

Cod Liver Oil

- MUFAs: Palmitoleic Acid (8%), Oleic Acid (21%), Gadoleic Acid (10%), Erucic Acid (7%)
- SaFAs: Myristic Acid (4%), Palmitic Acid (11%), Stearic Acid (3%)

Cod Fish

- MUFAs: Palmitoleic Acid (3%), Oleic Acid (13%), Gadoleic Acid (3%), Erucic Acid (.6%)
- SaFAs: Myristic Acid (2%), Palmitic Acid (19%), Stearic Acid (6%)

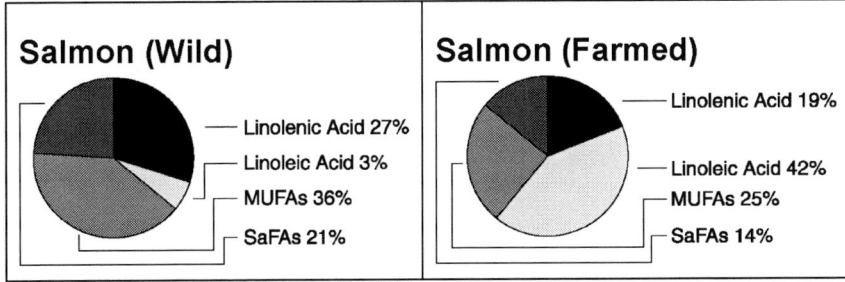

Wild salmon has slightly more of the Omega 3 derivative DHA and DPA, than farmed salmon. Farmed salmon has no DPA. Wild salmon also has a much higher w3:w6 ratio (7:1) than farmed salmon (1:2) and can, therefore, be used for rehabilitating Omega 3 deficiency whereas the farmed salmon can not.

Table 18: EFA Derivatives of Salmon

	Wild Salmon	**Farmed Salmon**
SDA	1 Percent	1 Percent
AA	4 Percent	11 Percent
EPA	5 Percent	6 Percent
DPA	5 Percent	0 Percent
DHA	18 Percent	12 Percent

Salmon (Wild)
- MUFAs: Palmitoleic Acid (10%), Oleic Acid (23%), Gadoleic Acid (5%), Erucic Acid (3%)
- SaFAs: Myristic Acid (5%), Palmitic Acid (14%), Stearic Acid (4%)

Salmon (Farmed)
- MUFAs: Palmitoleic Acid (4%), Oleic Acid (11%), Gadoleic Acid (8%)
- SaFAs: Myristic Acid (3%), Palmitic Acid (8%), Stearic Acid (2%)

Flaxseed Oil

Flax has been grown for its seeds and fiber for linen cloth since antiquity. Its earliest uses can be traced to the Babylonians in 5000 BC, Swiss archaeological sites from 3000 to 4000 BC, and Egyptian burial chambers from 3000 BC. To this day Ethiopians use flaxseed in stews,

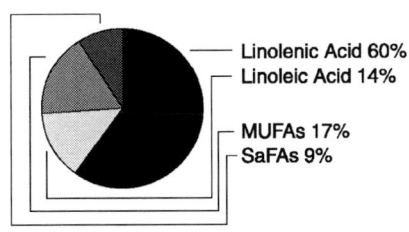

porridges, and drinks; present day Abyssinians eat it roasted; and people from the Middle East cook it in a traditional dish called Ful Medames with fava beans, garlic, lemon juice, olive oil, and salt.

Grown for centuries in India as a food grain, flaxseed in the diet has even been strongly advocated by Mahatma Gandhi for better general health. Udo Erasmus cites ancient East Indian scriptures, which state, "In order to reach the highest state of contentment and joy, a yogi must eat flax daily."[89] Known as *Yamazi*, flaxseed has also been part of the Chinese herbal pharmacopoeia for centuries. One of the first records of flaxseeds used as food comes from ancient Greece where they combined it with corn. In the fifth century BC, Hippocrates, often called the "Father of Medicine," used flaxseeds for relieving intestinal disorders. The Greeks passed it on the Romans who praised it for its health benefits throughout their civilization. The Romans also found flaxseed already widely cultivated in their invasions of Gaul in 57 BCE.

While the use of flaxseed as food declined after the fall of the Roman Empire, by the eighth century AD, Charlemagne, the King of France, restored the culinary and medicinal use of flaxseeds to prominence throughout Europe. He even *ordered* his subjects to consume flaxseeds for disease prevention! By the sixteenth century AD, flaxseeds were advocated by the great alchemist Paracelsus and were used commonly as a food source throughout Europe. The Germans used them in a variety of whole-grain breads, and continue to do so today. During and after medieval Russia, flaxseeds were commonly combined with flaxseed oil, hemp seeds, and peas during religious fasts. By the 17th century, dishes with flaxseed oil were even prepared for the Tsar. In nineteenth century England, flaxseed oil was important enough to merit union monitoring so that adulteration could be prevented. These practices were passed on to the early North American colonists who were the first to plant flaxseed in the United States.

Flaxseed and its oil has the capacity to treat many disorders, including coronary artery disease, high triglycerides, cancer, diabetes, obesity, inflammatory conditions, bowel obstruction, colon cancer, depression, juvenile delinquency, schizophrenia, visual impairment, and mental debility among the elderly. Flaxseed stimulates energy production and creates heat deep inside the body to enhance all life processes.

Because of its high percentage of LNA (60 percent), Flaxseed oil is the best oil to correct fatty degeneration from Omega 3 deficiencies. Flaxseed contains all the amino acids necessary for human health but, like most vegetable proteins, is low in lysine, methionine, and cysteine (needed by premature infants). Flaxseed is also high in lignans,[a] which have important anti-bacterial, anti-viral, anti-fungal, and anti-cancer properties. While flaxseed contains 100 times as many lignans as wheat bran, the next best source, only two percent of lignans end up in the Flaxseed oil. The best way to consume lignans is from the fresh, ground seeds. These more Yang properties of Flaxseed oil make the Omega 3s more suitable for Stagnant Liver Qi conditions than the more Yin Omega 6s, which are generally better for Liver inflammatory conditions instead.

Flaxseed needs to be ground in a small grinder because the tough seed coat renders the nutrients thoroughly indigestible. Passed seeds could be planted

---

[a] Lignans should not to be confused with lignins, an insoluble fiber.

and still grow. One tablespoon of Flaxseed oil equals three tablespoons of flaxseed. **During the important six-month Omega 3 recovery period, a person needs to take one tablespoon of Flaxseed oil per each fifty pounds of body weight per day.** A one hundred-fifty-pound male, for example, will need to consume three tablespoons of Flaxseed oil per day. This amount is the equivalent of nine tablespoons of flaxseed. The daily maximum of flaxseed is six to eight tablespoons because the seeds absorb five times their volume of water and, at this amount, will dry up the intestines. However, people with degenerative disease should consume even more. The amount some people need to take prohibits the consumption of flaxseed so they need to take the oil instead; or take the oil and fresh-ground seed together in the same day to reduce this unacceptable quantity of straight flaxseed. Taking flaxseed during this period is still useful to receive the benefit of the lignans even if it is used in smaller amounts. **For every three tablespoons of flaxseed taken, you can take one tablespoon less of the flaxseed oil.**[90] Ground flaxseed can be mixed into smoothies or into cooked oats, barley, wheat, or corn for a good breakfast cereal. Flaxseed that is already ground and sold in stores should be avoided because it is usually rancid.

Hempseed Oil
Nutrition

Hempseed oil has an agreeable taste something like Sunflower Seed oil. It contains a large amount of both Omega 3 and Omega 6 EFAs in a very good 1:3 ratio of Omega 3s (19 percent) to Omega 6s (59 percent) and is therefore the best EFA oil for regular consumption.

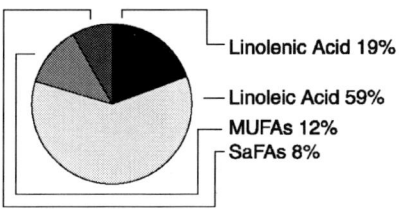

- Linolenic Acid 19%
- Linoleic Acid 59%
- MUFAs 12%
- SaFAs 8%

Hempseed oil also contains 1.7 percent GLA and 2-4 percent SDA[91] and so can also be used to help address EFA conversion problems even before the supplementation stage has taken place. Flaxseed oil, Fish oil, or Krill oil when taken exclusively for too long (over two years in some cases with Flaxseed oil), will result in Omega 6 deficiency. The balanced profile of Hempseed oil prevents this imbalance from occurring and is the best EFA oil to take once the initial Omega 3 deficiency is corrected, *especially* for vegetarians would otherwise never get enough Omega 3. Shelled hempseed also contains the phospholipid lecithin and other important nutrients derived from lecithin including choline, inositol, and phytosterols. Choline regulates the Liver and Gall Bladder as well as nerve impulses from the brain and nervous system. One of the derivatives of choline, acetylcholine, is crucial for short-term memory and is lacking in Alzheimer's patients.[92]

Hemp seeds and Hempseed oil are also high in other "essential" nutrients including magnesium-rich chlorophyll, calcium, iron, potassium, phosphorus, sulfur, ascorbic acid, beta-carotene, riboflavin, niacin, thiamin, fiber, histidine, and enzymes. In fact, enzymes were first discovered in hempseed.[93] Hemp seeds are so rich in these "essential" nutrients that they comprise almost two-thirds of the entire seed![94]

Shelled hempseed also contains more than 30 percent high-quality, easily digestible protein,[95] more, in fact, than meat (chicken contains 23.5 percent protein) or fish[96] and only slightly less than soybeans (35 percent protein).[97] All ten essential amino acids, the building blocks of protein, are contained in shelled hempseed including high amounts of cysteine and methione, the amino acids often lacking in a vegetarian diet.[98] Three most important types of protein found in hempseed are edestin protein (65 percent), albumin protein (35 percent), and glutamic acid. Edestin and albumin proteins have been intensively studied since the early twentieth century and are the most potent and easily digested vegetarian sources of protein.[99] Edestin protein is also used to manufacture antibodies and so is crucial to the development of a healthy immune response. Albumin protein is made in the liver and supports liver and kidney health. One distinct advantage of hempseed protein over soy protein is that hempseed protein lacks the enzyme inhibitors found in soy protein that block the uptake of important enzymes such as trypsin that are necessary for protein digestion. Unless used properly through traditional fermentation, the high levels of enzyme inhibitors in soybeans can result in chronic amino acid and protein deficiencies. The use of shelled hempseed as a protein source avoids this problem.

History

Hemp is a very sturdy and extremely fast-growing plant that can reach a height of ten feet or more in a year with deep roots capable of drawing a wealth of minerals to the surface to enrich the hemp plant as well as the soil. Hemp has been recommended for slowing down and reversing the "greenhouse effect" and can be grown without pesticides or as a companion to other more vulnerable plants to prevent their infestation. Both hemp and flax were historically cultivated for their fiber and seeds. Linen comes from flax while canvas and rope come from hemp. Because Hempseed oil burns cleanly with no smoke and therefore does not irritate the eyes, it has been used to light lamps for ages before electricity was introduced.[100] Hempseed has been used throughout world history for food, feed, fuel, and fiber and is named in almost every language.[101] The Hebrew word *Tsli'q* means "roasted hempseed" and refers to a meal of roasted hempseed popular in medieval times.[102]

Many places are named after hemp where its use was important historically, including Bangladesh, Hampshire, and Hampton.[103] Cultivation of hemp goes back five to twelve thousand years in China where it originated. In many parts of Asia where other vegetable oils were unavailable or too expensive, Hempseed oil was the only source of vegetable oil.[104] In India, where Hempseed oil has also been pressed since ancient times, it is traditionally mixed with rice or amaranth to make *mura*, the nutritious staple of the poor.[105] Samurai warriors in feudal Japan made rice balls with hempseed to keep them strong in battle.[106] The Nepalese still grow and press Hempseed oil as was observed by a National Geographic expedition documenting village life there during the 1970s.

Early Chinese references to hemp can be found in the *Book of History (Shijing)* from the eleventh century BC and the *Book of Rites (Liji)* from the second century BC.[107] Hemp is twice as old as soybeans, which also originated in China and, with Rapeseed oil, is one of the earliest crops cultivated for vegetable oil.[108] According to Richard Rose in the *HempNut Cookbook*, "The consumption of raw or toasted hempseed is very common in China [even today]"[109] where it is used as a food, a long-term longevity tonic to prevent old age,[110] and for medicine. The *Ben Cao Gang Mu* pharmacopoeia of the Ming dynasty (1368-1644) devotes a large section to hempseed where it is classified as strengthening to the digestive system and noted for healing menstrual irregularities, prolapsed uterus, childbirth, postpartum recovery, fever reduction, severe vomiting, Blood Deficiency (Blood is made from the transformation of food in the digestive system, according to Chinese Medicine), dysentery, constipation due to internal dryness from Blood insufficiency, and wound healing, including ulcerations, sores, burns, hair loss, and dry throat.[111]

In the West, Pliny the Elder, Emperor Nero's physician, used hempseed as early as the first-century Rome.[112] By the fifteenth century hempseed was an abundant food among European peasants whose health was better and more resistant to disease than the nobility's.[113] European monks of that time ate hempseed three times a day in porridge, gruel, or soup. The British herbalist Nicholas Culpepper used hempseed medicinally in 1794 for venereal disease and cough.[114]

In America, the founding fathers of the United States thought hemp was so important they required all farmers to grow it under penalty of fine and even grew it themselves.[115] Prior to the Civil War, the US produced thirty thousand tons of hemp fiber and during World War II farmers were encouraged to grow hemp for fiber needed for parachute rigging.[116]

False Drug Allegations

At this time, food-grade hemp is illegal to grow in the US because of its false association with marijuana. Even though hemp was still used for birdseed, thousands of tons of hempseed had to be imported every year by the US since 1980.[117] The five hundred thousand acres of hemp now growing wild throughout the US make it the second largest crop in the world next to China's even though it is illegal to grow and often destroyed by the DEA. In fact, this wild, non-drug related hemp accounts for over 95 percent of the DEA's ridiculous "marijuana" seizures.[118] While these drug busts should have been aimed at cannabis with a high-THC count, the chemical responsible for marijuana highs, the wild, industrial, and food-grade hemp does not have this drug-like affect because it has a low-THC count.[119] Nevertheless, because of this association, edible hempseed and Hempseed oil can not be legally grown in the US and must be imported and rendered incapable of germination either through heat or radiation sterilization, which destroys the nutrient capacity, or by shelling.[120] While strains of hemp containing very little THC have always been available, its controversial (yet erroneous) drug associations with marijuana make it impossible to produce in the US. These rules are certain to be changed in the near future as both government and the public realize the tremendous nutrient value of hempseed and its oil as well as the significant economic opportunities as importing hempseed drives the price to the consumer up. Once these laws are changed, hempseed and Hempseed oil will undoubtedly take their place as the most nutritious, most balanced, and most affordable oil for mass consumption. For now, though, it must be imported and strict organic guidelines are more difficult to achieve. One good source, though, is "Living Harvest Hemp Oil," available at www.livingharvest.com (1-888-690-3958).

Use

Hempseed oil is hard on machinery and therefore more difficult to make than Flaxseed oil but the yield of the oil is high. Only five pounds of hempseed can make one pound of hempseed oil.[121] The daily dose of Hempseed oil is between one to three tablespoons for adults and half that amount for children.[122] One teaspoon of Hempseed oil equals two teaspoons of shelled hempseed so the daily dose of hempseed is between 2 to 6 tablespoons for adults.[123] The EFA properties of Hempseed oil make it fragile so, like Flaxseed oil, it must be protected from heat, light, and oxygen by refrigeration to prevent rancidity. Nevertheless, some sources claim that it can withstand cooking temperatures of up to 475°F for short periods—no longer than thirty minutes.[124] Other heat-resistant oils (like Avocado oil), when used together with Hempseed oil, will increase these heat resistant qualities. Nevertheless, for healing purposes, do not cook with Hempseed oil because of the significant amounts of fragile EFAs it contains.

Treatable Conditions

Because of its abundant amount and ideal ratio of EFAs, many conditions can be helped with shelled hempseed and Hempseed oil including:

- Osteoporosis

EFA supplementation with shelled hempseed and Hempseed oil can improve calcium absorption and strengthen the bones, especially in the elderly, where bone loss is often associated with calcification of the kidneys and arteries.[125]

- Earache

Hempseed oil can be dropped into the ear to loosen earwax, reduce pain, and fight infection.[126]

- Diabetes

Because shelled hempseed and Hempseed oil are rich in nutrients that regulate blood sugar and are low in carbohydrates, diabetics can use them advantageously to lower their glycemic index.[127]

- Psycho-Emotional Problems

EFAs, such as those found in such optimal balance in Hempseed oil, regulate and balance the Yin-Yang functions of the Liver to help people feel calmer, manage stress better, stabilize nerve and brain functions, and increase the electric currents across the cell membranes of the brain. According to Nobel prize nominee Dr. Johanna Budwig, these properties have helped treat people with addictions to alcohol, cigarettes, drugs, and sex/violence patterns.[128] Omega 3 EFAs have also been found to be useful in regulating other over- and under-active mental problems such as aggression, dementia, hyperactivity, ADHD, bipolar disorder, depression, dyslexia, learning disabilities, and schizophrenia.[129] The human brain is comprised of 60 percent lipids generally and up to 80 percent in the dendrites and synapses.[130] Therefore, EFAs are one of the most essential nutrients to regulate the brain. Children require a balance of Omega 6 and Omega 3 EFAs for the brain to mature properly. Learning disabilities can easily occur from deficiencies in Omega 3. The proper balance of Omega 3 and Omega 6 EFAs is also important in treating attention deficit disorder, depression, and schizophrenia. Depression has been observed to be 90 percent less in countries where the Omega 3 content is sufficient.[131]

- Tuberculosis

Hempseed has been used in Czechoslovakia for thirty years to successfully treat tuberculosis.[132]

Oils For Conversion Deficiencies

Black Currant Seed Oil

Black Currant Seed oil contains Omega 6 and Omega 3 as well as their first derivatives, GLA (15 percent) for Omega 6 and SDA (2 percent) for Omega 3. Black Currant Seed oil is, therefore, ideal for the 20 percent of the population unable to synthesize Omega 3s and 6s into their

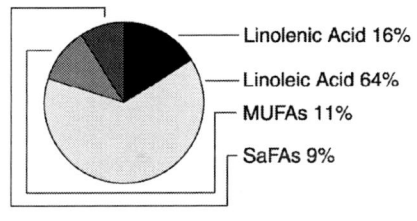

Linolenic Acid 16%
Linoleic Acid 64%
MUFAs 11%
SaFAs 9%

respective prostaglandins. The main drawbacks of using Black Currant Seed oil are that it is more expensive than other EFA-rich oils and that it is only available at this time in capsule form. Nevertheless, Black Currant Seed oil represents an important source of both EFAs in the almost perfect ratio of 1:4, especially since anyone deficient in GLA will be automatically deficient in SDA, a problem that simply taking GLA-rich oils like EPO or Borage oil will not solve.

Borage Oil

Borage oil is the highest and most cost-effective natural source of GLA (24 percent, which is 2½ times that found in Evening Primrose oil. Borage oil is an important oil to correct GLA deficiencies in those unable to make the conversion from

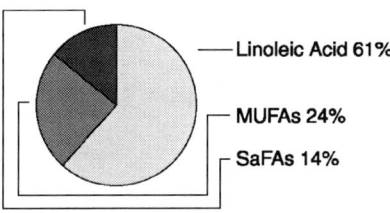

Linoleic Acid 61%
MUFAs 24%
SaFAs 14%

Special Oils

Omega 6. The Omega Nutrition label makes a god quality, organic, unrefined Borage oil. However, Borage oil contains no Omega 3, which must be taken to compliment Borage oil's effectiveness. While the effects of GLA in Evening Primrose oil have been studied more than those in Borage oil, Borage oil can generally be used in place of Evening Primrose oil because of its greater GLA content.

Evening Primrose Oil

Evening Primrose oil comes from the oil-rich seeds (12 percent oil content) of the Evening Primrose flower, a common ornamental perennial in many English and Eastern American gardens. Originating in North America, where it was used by the American Indians to heal bruises,

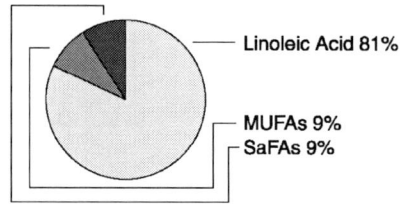

skin problems, and asthma, the Evening Primrose eventually stowed away with cotton in cargo ships and made its way to Britain, where it escaped and is now found growing wild along roadsides and sandy waste sites. Evening Primrose became known as the "King's Cure All" in Europe because of its almost magical properties. In 1919, scientists discovered its active principle, a new fatty acid called gammalinolenic acid (GLA). By 1960, scientific investigations began to find other possible health uses. Today, Evening Primrose oil is useful in a wide variety of ailments, including:

- Improved blood flow
- Wound healing
- Healthy heart function, blood pressure, cholesterol levels
- Asthma
- Allergies
- Healthy hair, skin and nails
- Psoriasis, eczema, dermatitis and dry skin
- Joint inflammation and swelling associated with arthritis including rheumatoid arthritis
- Multiple sclerosis
- Breast pain, premenstrual and menopause syndrome symptoms
- Weight loss without dieting
- Hyperactive children
- Withdrawal symptoms in recovering alcoholics
- Schizophrenia
- Cancer

What all of these problems have in common with Evening Primrose oil (EPO) is its ability to regulate the Liver. In acupuncture theory, the Liver is responsible for the storage of Blood and the circulation of Qi. The Yin-Yang spectrum of Liver imbalance in acupuncture includes deficiencies of both Yin and Blood, stagnation in the circulation of Qi and Blood, low-grade inflammatory conditions throughout the body, and excessive circulation of the Qi and Blood, which rushes up to and agitates the upper body, especially the head. Psycho-emotionally, these conditions result from anger that is either repressed or uncontrolled. Physically, they result from Blood deficiencies (Deficient Liver Blood); toxic conditions of the Blood, which heats up and tries to escape through the skin or head (Blazing Liver Fire); a blockage created by industrial quality fats and oils (Stagnant Liver Qi); or deficiencies in good quality essential fatty acids (Deficient Liver Yin).

Physiologically, the Liver is responsible for storing the products and regulating the actions of metabolism. The Liver stores carbohydrate, fat, protein, the fat-soluble Vitamins A, D, E, K, B_{12}, minerals, and toxins, especially alcohol toxins, and converts these to bile while detoxifying the overall system. Part of the conversion process involves the breakdown of fats, the reciprocal conversion between glycogen and glucose, fat and protein to glucose, and glucose to fat. In acupuncture, breakdowns in these conversion processes are classified as Wind Disorders because they register in symptoms that change from one state to another, migrate around the body, or rise into the upper body causing pain, agitation, and disruptions of consciousness such as dizziness and stroke.

The Liver Meridian, in acupuncture, also corresponds to the two-hour time period of the day centered around midnight and is said to flourish in the nails and flower in the eyes. The Liver Meridian flows through both the genital region and the breast and is a significant factor in their well-being. Stagnant Liver Qi and Deficient Liver Blood, especially, block the harmonious flow of menstruation and lead to all sorts of problems, including PMS, heart and arterial constriction, asthma, multiple sclerosis, and arthritis. Deficient Liver Yin contributes to allergies, joint inflammation, rheumatoid arthritis, menopausal problems, and hyperactive children. Deficient Liver Blood leads to problems in wound healing and loss of menstrual periods. Blazing Liver Fire can lead to inflammatory skin conditions, alcoholism, and schizophrenia.

Among these Liver patterns, three, in particular, stand out in relation to EPO: (1) the Liver circulates predominantly at night; (2) it regulates change from one state to another; and (3) it regulates fat metabolism. In turn, these three patterns relate closely to three aspects of the EPO plant: (1) its yellow flowers open only in the evening and fade quickly in bright sunlight; (2) its peculiar genetic behavior; and (3) the presence of its most active ingredient, GLA.

The genetic behavior of EPO is significantly different than other plants. When ordinary plants are cross-pollinated, the first generation offspring are identical while the second generation forms a mixture between the two parents. New varieties are produced with each successive generation. With evening primrose, however, the first generation is mixed in a way that does not resemble either of the two parents or each other, while succeeding generations breed true to the original parents for many generations without variation in spite of the existence of at least a thousand varieties. What this means on the archetypal level of the Pattern/Templates[a] is that EPO has the capacity to normalize the regulatory capacities of the Liver through its GLA by bringing Liver imbalances (the unrecognizable new varieties) back into balance (the original parents).

Evening Primrose oil contains 9 percent GLA, 72 percent Omega 6 essential fatty acids (linoleic acid), and 9 percent MUFAs. Essential fatty acids, in general, promote the circulation of blood, especially on the capillary and cell membrane levels. The cell membranes are the more expanded physical structure of the cell and are, therefore, regulated by the Liver, which controls expansion and contraction at this level. If there are enough EFAs, the cell membrane is fluid; if there is not enough, it is too rigid (Liver Stagnation, Deficiency, or Excess).

Table 19: Correlation Between Liver Function and EPO

	Liver	Evening Primrose Oil
1	**Circulates at night**	**Blooms at night**
2	Regulates change	Genetic stability
3	Regulates fat metabolism on the global as well as the cellular levels	GLA regulates membrane fluidity

Heart Disease

The GLA in Evening Primrose oil is 163 times more powerful than linoleic acid in reducing cholesterol in the blood. After about three months of using Evening Primrose oil, the maximum effect in lowering cholesterol will be reached. Heart attack victims have blood that is 4½ times stickier than in normal people. The platelets in this sticky blood stick to each other and to the walls of the arteries and bind with cholesterol deposits to form clots, which block the flow of blood and cause thromboses and stroke. The Prostaglandin 1 (PGE_1) converted from the GLA of EPO stops blood platelets from clumping together, lowers cholesterol levels, and lowers high blood pressure.

Allergies (eczema, asthma, cystic fibrosis)

Many atopic allergic reactions result from a defect in the liver enzyme delta-6-desaturase, which converts linoleic acid to GLA.[b] PGE_1 also stimulates the T-lymphocytes, which play a key role in the immune system. Atopy is characterized by itching that flares up on occasion, asthma that comes and goes, hay fever, allergies (house dust), and migraines, all syndromes of Liver Wind in

---

[a] The Pattern/Templates are a category of Yin-Yang archetypes (universal templates) from which individual things of the world are patterned. Examples include the Five Phases and the Doctrine of Signatures, which can be used to define the function of therapeutic substances like food, herbs, and essential oils.

[b] This enzyme is deficient or inhibited in diabetes, obesity, elderly people, and in the presence of insulin, coffee, TFAs, or alcohol. Native American, Irish, Celtic, Scottish, and Scandinavian populations often have a greater than average deficiencies of this enzyme. Other enzymes involved in prostaglandin conversion are delta-4 and 5-desaturase.

acupuncture theory. Other problems of atopy, which can also be related to these Liver syndromes, include ulcerative colitis, Crohn's disease, ear problems, nasal polyps, and some obstetric problems.

Skin, Hair, Mouth and Nails

Many types of acne, eczema, poor hair quality, painful dryness of the eyes and mouth, and brittle nails are associated with deficiencies of EFAs in the diet. Signs are often symptoms of Liver deficiency and can be corrected by the GLA in EPO, which helps to clear skin blemishes and wrinkles due to dryness. Omega 3 fatty acids work even better.

Rheumatoid Arthritis and Inflammatory Disorders

Rheumatoid arthritis, often classified as an autoimmune disease where the body mistakenly attacks itself, is a systemic disease affecting the whole body, especially in women. Rheumatoid arthritis is also associated with the constricting prostaglandins, the PGE_2s, which also come from arachidonic acid in foods like meat and dairy products. Other reasons for this imbalance of prostaglandins could be that people are not eating enough *cis*-linoleic foods, blocking agents are getting in the way of the crucial delta-6-desaturase enzyme, or a shortage may exist of some of the co-factors, Vitamin C, B_6, zinc, and magnesium. In any case, once the PGE_1 is restored again through EPO, the normal balance of prostaglandins is restored as well.

Raynaud's syndrome, where the patient suffers from sudden attacks of pallor and extreme coldness in the extremities due to spasms in the arteries reducing blood flow (lack of Liver Qi circulation in acupuncture), can also be stopped in its course by infusions of PGE_1 within four to twelve weeks. Non-steroidal anti-inflammatories like aspirin and indomethacin block the conversion of arachidonic acid to prostaglandins, while the anti-inflammatory steroid drugs simply block the release of arachidonic acid. Both of these drugs also block the release of dihomo-gammalinolenic acid (DGLA) and its conversion to PGE_1. DGLA produces both PGE_1 and PGE_2. Arachidonic acid produces the detrimental prostaglandins like PGE_2. If the person is taking even very small doses of these drugs, GLA, the active ingredient of EPO, does not work. In these cases, it is advisable to give EPO for six weeks or so to build up stores of GLA and DGLA, and then cautiously tapered off the non-steroidal and steroidal drugs.

Multiple Sclerosis

Multiple Sclerosis (MS) is related to the use of saturated animal fat and industrial quality oils and is much more common in countries where these types of food are eaten than where they are not. EPO has been more widely used for MS than for any other condition. The symptoms of MS often come and go in a typical Liver Wind pattern. People suffering from MS have trouble with walking and hand movement as well as eyesight and speech. While the linoleic acid form of Sunflower Seed oil is known to reduce the frequency and severity of relapses, GLA is much better in correcting the major defects. Surveys have recorded 65-72 percent improvement with the best results occurring in people who took EPO for at least 2-3 years. Unrefined Sunflower Seed oil in combination with Omega 3s have been used with equal effectiveness.

PMS

Forty percent of women get PMS symptoms and ten percent get them very badly. Up to sixty-one percent of women have experienced complete relief of PMS symptoms by taking EPO, while an additional twenty-three percent have experienced partial relief. EPO plus vitamins and minerals has an almost ninety percent success rate (Omega 3 usage only reaches a fifty percent success rate). Most women take EPO a few days before their periods while others take it all through their menstrual cycle. Women with PMS are low in EFAs, a shortage that can lead to an apparent excess of the female hormone prolactin. In this case the EFAs resemble Liver Yin, while the prolactin resembles the false Fire, which aggravates fluid metabolism and changes in mood. PGE_1 helps to smooth out the actions of the rapidly changing hormone levels in the second half of a woman's menstrual cycle. This type of regulation, again, is consistent with Liver imbalances in acupuncture. Vitamin B_6 is also helpful for many women who suffer from PMS.

Benign Breast Disease

The most successful results with EPO are for benign breast disease, especially when the symptoms worsen just before a period begins. Benign breast disease is generally a classic Stagnant Liver Qi syndrome. A shortage of EFAs in the diet definitely leads to excessive amounts of fibrous tissue. Liver stimulants such as coffee, tea, and cola drinks make benign breast disease worse while ridding them from the diet makes it better. Breast tenderness and lumpiness has been significantly reduced after only three months of EPO. Symptoms get better gradually and women using EPO for nine to twelve months often completely eradicate their symptoms. An interesting side effect is that EPO tends to make women's breasts larger, sometimes going up several cup sizes without putting on weight anywhere else. This phenomenon occurs more predominantly in women who have been taking EPO for more than six months or even years.

Obesity

For those beyond ten percent of their ideal body weight, EPO has also been effective in helping people lose weight. The prostaglandins resulting from EPO metabolism are thought to accelerate the mitochondrial activity in the brown fat. These mitochondria are the energy producing (fat-burning) substances used to create body heat. Brown fat both stabilizes weight and helps the adaptation to cold weather. When this process is disrupted, normally active calories are laid down as fat. Sodium-potassium ATPase is an essential enzyme needed for this transfer of energy and is responsible for more than twenty percent of the total energy used by the body. Under-activity of Sodium-potassium ATPase is a major cause of obesity but can be reactivated with Evening Primrose oil, which activates this enzyme when it is low.

Hyperactive Children

In acupuncture, hyperactive children are overly Yang stemming most frequently from the Liver imbalances of excess Fire from Deficient Liver Yin[a] or Blazing Liver Fire. Some hyperactive children are very sensitive to wheat and milk, which are Liver triggering foods. Hyperactive children also get very thirsty, which is a symptom of excess Yang. Hyperactivity is more common in boys (Yang) than girls (Yin) possibly because males need three times the quantity of EFAs as females (Yang needs Yin to make balance). In addition, many of the foods and food additives regularly given to children are the same substances that cause blockages in the conversion process of EFAs. These dietary and metabolic deficiencies can be corrected with the addition of correct EFAs in the diet, such as EPO. Two-thirds of these children respond favorably to EPO. In some children, asthma, allergies, and eczema also cleared up with the hyperactivity.

Alcoholism

The effect that alcohol has on the regulation of PGE_1 also points to its involvement with the Liver in acupuncture. Low levels of alcohol consumption have a beneficial effect on the production of PGE_1 while excessive amounts rob the body of it. PGE_1 levels fall far below normal when alcohol is withdrawn probably accounting for the hangovers, withdrawal symptoms, and depression that go with heavy drinking. Benefits of EPOs include the following:

1) Improve liver function
2) Lessen the effects of heavy drinking
3) Prevent hangovers
4) Make alcohol withdrawal easier
5) Improve brain function
6) Relieve post-drinking depression
7) Reduce the demand for tranquilizers
8) Lower the incidence of hallucinations during the period of alcohol withdrawal

Giving EPO could also prevent alcohol tolerance, a major factor in addiction as well as fetal alcohol syndrome.

Schizophrenia

Schizophrenics exhibit low levels of PGE_1 and high levels of PGE_2. They also have virtually no DGLA and very little linoleic acid while containing three times the normal amounts of arachidonc acid. EPO has been effective in treating some chronic schizophrenia.[b] Cutting out Liver related foods such as hybridized wheat and milk and the arachidonic acid-containing foods such as

---

[a] The acupuncture texts say that there is not enough Yin to love the Yang which then floats away to aggravate other areas of the body and other organ systems.

[b] Either alone or in combination with zinc therapy since some schizophrenics seem to be zinc-deficient.

meat, dairy, and peanuts has also been beneficial in some patients. Omega 3s give equal or better results.

Cancer

Cancer cells produce large amounts of PGE_2 and cannot make PGE_1. GLA is toxic to malignant cells, but has no effect on normal cells. GLA taken from EPO is known to have reduced cancer cell growth by up to seventy percent. In practice, Omega 3s inhibit cancer cells more effectively and should always be given with EPO since Omega 3 deficiency is more problematic in cancer but also because the PGE_2s in Omega 6s generally enhance tumors, while the PGE_3s Omega 3s inhibit them.

Side Effects and Cautions

Caution with EPO is warranted for those taking blood thinners, medications for epilepsy and schizophrenia, during pregnancy, or while breast-feeding. EPO is generally regarded as safe in normal doses, while excessive use can cause headaches and gastro-intestinal upset such as nausea. These reactions can usually be avoided by taking the capsules with food or when the oil is rubbed into the skin. Rashes can sometimes appear on very delicate skin when EPO is rubbed into the abdomen but can be avoided by rubbing the oil into the thighs or inside of the forearms. EPO should always be rubbed into the skin for children less than 2-5 years of age but can also be taken orally in older children. The oil is easily absorbed, as it is very fine.

Due to its reaction with some orthodox drugs, probably the highly toxic neuroleptics, there have been three reported cases of seizure in schizophrenics taking Evening Primrose oil. Nevertheless, Evening Primrose oil has been used safely through centuries of documented folk use. The Evening Primrose is, after all, an edible plant, and no ill effects have ever been recorded when the plant has been used on its own.

The biggest drawback of EPO is that it only addresses half of the EFA conversion problem. The same enzyme deficiency that blocks the conversion of Omega 6, Linoleic Acid (LA), to GLA also blocks the conversion of Omega 3, Linolenic Acid (LNA) to Stearidonic Acid (SDA). Omega 3 deficiency is more problematic in our society than conversion block. The wiser approach is to first balance Omega 3 and Omega 6 intake, and then add EFA derivatives in a balanced ratio of Omega 3s to Omega 6s. Black Currant Seed and Hempseed oil can address the conversion of Omega 3s and 6s because they contain both GLA and SDA. SDA helps create PGE_3 without needing the enzymes necessary to convert it directly from LNA in the same way that GLA creates PGE_1 without needing the enzymes necessary to convert it directly from LA. Otherwise, the EPO should be combined with an Omega 3 derivative such as Flaxseed oil, which can sometimes help by itself because it addresses the more prevalent Omega 3 deficiency.

EPO is often refined and often solvent-extracted, although expeller-pressed unrefined options are now available. One good brand is "Health from the Sun." Some people experience a worsening of symptoms with EPO either from the solvent residues in the oil or from an underlying Omega 3 deficiency only made worse by the addition of more Omega 6s. Organic, fresh, mechanically pressed, and unrefined Borage Oil, an even greater source of GLA, is also now available.

Special Oils

Other Edible Oil Sources

Fats and Oils in Vegetables

Almond Oil

The related sweet almond, apricot, and prune oils are primarily monounsaturated oils (61 percent). Almond oil contains 30 percent linoleic acid and Vitamin E, and is very flavorful as well as soft, scentless, and moisturizing to the skin. These secondary properties plus its stability as

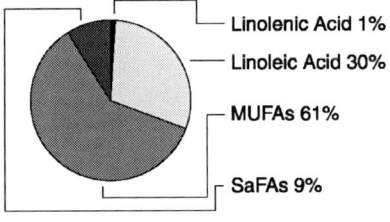

Linolenic Acid 1%
Linoleic Acid 30%
MUFAs 61%
SaFAs 9%

a MUFA make it a good massage oil and a carrier oil for dry and inflamed skin conditions, especially for babies. While EFA-rich oils are better for the skin, they can become rancid too quickly for easy external application. For good skin, use EFA-rich oils internally and almond, apricot, or prune externally, or as a carrier oil for essential oils.

Apricot Kernel Oil

Very rich in MUFAs but also containing a moderate portion of linoleic acid, apricot kernel oil spreads easily and is useful to nourish, revitalize, moisturize, and restructure the skin.

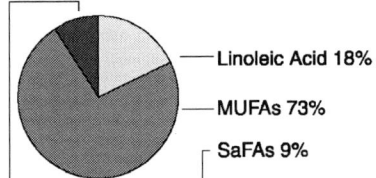

Linoleic Acid 18%
MUFAs 73%
SaFAs 9%

Calendula Oil

Calendula oil is an infusion of calendula flowers in another food grade oil, usually an organic, extra virgin Olive oil. By itself, Calendula oil's diaphoretic and anti-bacterial actions make it useful for breaking fevers and skin eruptions through sweating. This oil is widely used as a topical application for rashes, abrasions, and acne and was even used during the Civil War to draw out infection and speed the healing of wounds. Calendula oil is a tonic, soothing, and restorative oil for any type of skin condition, especially dry skin and has been traditionally used in ancient Egypt and the entire Mediterranean region to help preserve skin freshness, protect the skin from over-drying, and reduce wrinkles from aging during summer time from over-exposure to the sun. Use Calendula oil for wounds, scars, badly healing abscesses, light burns, and sunburn. Used internally, Calendula oil helps circulate and cleanse the blood, and has been used traditionally for gastric and menstrual discomfort.

To make your own traditional Calendula oil, crush the fresh or dried flowers and place them in a glass jar. Fill the jar with good quality Olive oil, cover and store. Shake the jar every day for two weeks and then strain the oil through cheesecloth into a clean glass jar or bottle. You could also use Hazelnut oil or Macadamia oil in place of the Olive oil. Add Vitamin E as a preservative.

Canola Oil

Canola oil is widely touted as the healthiest salad and cooking oil available because of its low saturated (5 percent) and high monounsaturated fatty (57 percent) acid content. Canola oil also contains 23 percent Omega 6 and 10-

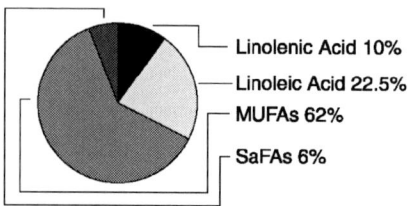

Linolenic Acid 10%
Linoleic Acid 22.5%
MUFAs 62%
SaFAs 6%

15 percent Omega 3 in the ideal ratio of 1:2. While these qualities have made Canola oil fashionable since its inception in the late 1970s, Canola oil is more of a high-tech designer oil than it is a natural food. In fact, the name "canola," unlike other oil names, which are derived from the actual names of the source, is made up of the words "Canada" and "oil." Thus, the name "canola oil" means "Canadian oil" to avoid the negative association with the word "rapeseed" and also because, like its name, the oil is fabricated by hybridization from the rapeseed plant (a type of mustard). According to Mary Enig, early varieties were genetically modified by selection mutation breeding while later varieties were genetically engineered through recombinant DNA technology.[a] These earlier varieties were genetically hybridized to lower the high erucic acid content of the rapeseed. Canola has now become one of the most genetically engineered crops (55% of the North American crop in the year 2000). Nowadays, farmers complain that these later genetically modified varieties have spread of their own accord through the entire gene pool.[b] The export of Canola oil represents a large part of the Canadian economy and is therefore subsidized by the Canadian government to industries involved in food processing. According to rumor, the Canola oil industry in conjunction with the Canadian government paid the US Food and Drug Administration (FDA) $50 million to have Canola oil placed on the GRAS List (Generally Recognized As Safe) before any studies on humans were made. Studies using Canola oil with animals, however, showed fatty degeneration of the heart, kidney, adrenals, and thyroid gland. These organs developed scar tissue that remained after the Canola oil was removed from their diets.

In April 1997, Monsanto recalled 60,000 bags of genetically engineered canola seed (enough to plant more than 700,000 acres, or half the size of the state of Delaware) because an unapproved gene slipped into the batch by mistake. Monsanto creates these genetic manipulations so that the plants will be able to resist the herbicide toxicity of Roundup, their top moneymaking product. Like hybridized wheat and the allergic response it causes in humans, these

---

[a] Enig 120.

[b] See http://www.percyschmeiser.com for a firsthand account of one farmer's struggle against the invasion of genetically modified organisms by high tech seed companies.

manipulations have nothing to do with human nutritional needs. Indeed, the genes in the recalled seed have never been approved for human consumption. One of Monsanto's spokesmen said, "We may never know how this happened." If they do not know now, they obviously will not be able to prevent it from happening again in the future! Even if they did know and did take the necessary precautions to prevent it from happening again, how could we trust that the same problem would not happen again with a different gene? Then again, we are lucky that we even found out about this one! With all the money at stake, why would such a large and powerful company even bother to tell us if they could get away with keeping it to themselves?[a]

Rapeseed and mustard oil have been used in India and China for centuries without apparent damage to health, especially when used in the traditional context with accompanying SaFAs such as from ghee, Hempseed oil, Coconut oil, or lard. Nevertheless, the Canadian government made the claim that the 40 percent erucic acid[b] contained in these plants causes fibrotic heart lesions in humans so they should be removed from the US market and replaced with genetically modified Canola oil. According to the Canadian government, Canola oil was originally modified to remove certain glycosides (goitrogenic compounds that produce sugars on hydrolysis) found in rapeseed as well as the so-called toxic erucic acid thereby creating a new Low Erucic Acid Rapeseed or LEAR.

---

[a] Even the essential oil industry hides their mistakes from their customers to protect their products. One notably large and influential "therapeutic grade" essential oil company followed these tactics with one of their peppermint oil crops. The company invested millions of dollars the year of the 911 World Trade Center attack in a showcase crop of peppermint. Unfortunately, when it came time to harvest the crop all the migrant workers were deported because of the terrorist scare. Since the company had to scramble to get the crop picked, they took a shortcut. They harvested all the weeds together with the peppermint in order to save time. Who knows what "medicinal" or toxic properties these weeds contained? Nevertheless, they were distilled together with the peppermint in the same batch. The workers even labeled it "pepper-weed" as a joke. When the head of the company came to inspect the final product, he took a smell and turned his back to the workers while they waited for his instructions. The oil didn't smell quite right. Then he turned around to the workers and said, "Put it in the blends." Obviously, the three million dollars he would have lost was more important than his integrity or the health and well-being of the customers depending on his judgment. If someone like this in the natural healing industry would deliberately deceive the public in such a matter, why wouldn't bigger industries like the Canola Oil industry, or any genetic-engineering company with many times more of an investment at stake, cover their tracks in the same way when they need to?
[b] Erucic acid is a long-chain (22-carbon) MUFA also found in small quantities in Macadamia Nuts and butter.

This move created a huge cash crop for the Canadians. During the 1980s, the American Heart Association in collusion with government agencies, and university nutrition departments promoted industrialized PUFAs as a healthy alternative to what they described as the "artery-clogging" saturated fats. Nutritional information coming out at this time, however, implicated refined PUFAs as the cause of numerous health problems including cancer.[a] These findings caught the food industry in a bind. It could not continue to make positive claims about refined PUFAs because of the danger to health associated with them; nor could it go back to the promotion of SaFAs because of their previous stand against them. The only way out was to embrace the use of monounsaturated oils, such as Olive oil. This solution led to the popularization by Ancel Keys and others of the virtues of the Mediterranean diet. However, because the supply of Olive oil was not sufficient to meet the world's demands, its price went up and became prohibitive for industrial use in processed foods. Canola oil, in containing almost as much MUFAs as Olive oil (60 percent compared to 70 percent), provided a cheaper alternative. Plus, it contains a healthy portion of the EFAs in their ideal ratio of 1:2. Cutting edge health books then began to extol the virtues of Olive oil while substituting Canola oil in their recipes. By the 1990s, Canola oil achieved worldwide status and became the oil of choice in gourmet and health food markets.[b]

Nevertheless, dangers associated with Canola oil include easy rancidity because of its high sulfur content, Vitamin E depletion, growth retardation because of its high content of hemagglutinins (it is not allowed in infant formulas),[c] decrease in platelet count, increase in platelet size, high blood pressure, and stroke.[d] Unofficial allergic responses to Canola oil include tremors, shaking, palsy, lack of coordination, numbness and tingling in the extremities, slurred speech, memory problems, blurred vision, heart arrhythmias, and urinary problems. All of these symptoms cleared up once Canola oil was discontinued. When Canola oil was removed from animal feed after the Mad Cow episode in England and Europe between 1986 and 1991, the disease disappeared. While some of these reports may be exaggerated, mainstream claims that Canola oil is not harmful to humans can only be made in light of the fact that no long-term studies on humans have been conducted.

The most common modern source of Omega 3 available in conventional markets is Canola oil, which was genetically modified and then genetically engineered to produce an inexpensive oil that could be easily grown

---

[a] Mary Enig and Sally Fallon. In "The Oiling of America." At www.westonaprice.org/oiling.htm.

[b] Sally Fallon and Mary G. Enig. "The Great Con-ola." In *Nexus Magazine*, Aug/September 2002.

[c] According to Mary Enig, "Canola oil [is] not appropriate...for growing children [and] is not allowed in infant formula in the US or Canada." Enig 111.

[d] WMN Ratnayake and others. "Influence of Sources of Dietary Oils on the Life Span of Stroke-Prone Spontaneously Hypertensive Rats." In *Lipids* 35(4):409-420.

in the northern hemisphere. Canola oil has the perfect 1:2 EFA ratio; it is low in SaFAs, and is high in MUFAs, the balanced FAs that have been known to naturally regulate healthy cholesterol levels. The biggest problem with Canola oil is that its health risks are questionable because of its genetic manipulation. We know that the modern hybridization of other important crops like corn and wheat have been genetically modified to make them suitable for chemical insecticides, herbicides, and fertilizers. This tinkering has led to a major problem with food allergies from these products and many people are now seriously allergic to them. Imagine how the immune systems of these plants are revved into super over-drive before being fed to humans. The immunity of those who eat these foods then charges into biochemical overdrive as well—an overdrive manifesting through the serious food allergies to these foods we must now face! Canola oil has only been used since the late 1970s. We have no way of knowing that it is safe or even of finding out. Therefore, in spite of some of the good sociological intentions accompanying the rise of Canola oil into the world market, we are forced to eliminate it from our selection for these important health and environmental reasons and use the old reliable standby—Hempseed oil instead!

Cottonseed Oil

Although popular in the US during the nineteenth century, cottonseed oil should not be used for human consumption because of its toxic effects on the liver and gallbladder from both toxic natural ingredients as well as the enormous amount of pesticide residues it absorbs during the growing season.[a] Cottonseed oil also delays sexual maturity, interferes with EFA functions, and multiplies the power of fungus-produced aflatoxins to cause cancer.

Foraha Oil

Foraha (Calophyllum Inophyllum), also known as Tamanu, is a valuable cold pressed, fixed oil that is excellent as a carrier oil for diluting essential oil formulations. Foraha contains terpenic essences, benzoic acid, oxibenzoic acid, Vitamin F, lipids, glycerides, saturated fatty acids, calophylloilide acid, calophyllic acid, coumarin derivatives, and phophor-amino acids. Foraha oil has many uses and is rich and thick with a spicy nutlike smell. Foraha oil has been known to stimulate cell regeneration thus assisting wounds to heal as well as to soothe inflammation, relieve pain, and assist broken capillaries to repair. Foraha oil has also been used for many conditions such as eczema, burns, rashes, ulcers, and insect bites.

Some of the properties of Foraha are analgesic, antibiotic, anti-microbial, anti-rheumatic, antiseptic, and vulnerary. Using this oil along with the essential oil of Helichrysum italicum in a 50/50 mixture has been successful in healing and fading old scars and in smoothing wrinkles. Foraha mixed with an equal amount of the essential oil of Ravintsara has "produced dramatic

---

[a] Cotton is one of the most heavily sprayed plants on the face of the earth.

improvement and complete remission of shingles within seven days!"[133] Foraha can also be used to help the following body systems:

Nervous/Brain/Mind: Neuritis due to leprosy.

Immune: Increases cellular immunity.

Skin, Hair, and Nails: Ulcers, atonic wounds, zona lesions, eczema, physical and chemical burns, radio dermatitis, fissure of post-surgical wounds. Use on scalp to stimulate hair growth.

Muscular/Skeletal: Sciatica, rheumatism. Helps children who are slow in learning to walk.

Cardio-Vascular/Lymphatic: Increases oxygen circulation to capillaries; aids capillary detoxification.

Digestive: Hemorrhoids.

Genito-Urinary: Aids detoxification and moves toxins to the urinary system for excretion.[134]

Grape Seed Oil

Grape Seed oil is extracted from grape seeds after being pressed for wine. One ton of grapes are needed to make one 8 ounce bottle of Grapeseed oil. Cold-pressed Grape Seed oils are rare and hard to find because the seeds are very hard and difficult to press without heat and solvents. One

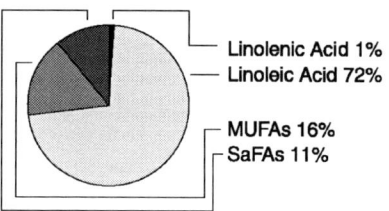

- Linolenic Acid 1%
- Linoleic Acid 72%
- MUFAs 16%
- SaFAs 11%

exception is the *Salute Santé* brand,[a] which is pressed at temperatures that never exceed the outdoor temperature at the time it is pressed (around 100°F). This unique and high quality brand is packaged in UV protective dark glass bottles or stainless steel, not the usual plastic, penny-pinching bottles that allow UV light into the oil so that it quickly degrades. The *Salute Santé* brand of Grape Seed oil wins this authors award for best tasting of all edible oils.

Grape Seed oil has been used for centuries in Europe where, in 1569, Emperor Maximilian II of Italy granted a monopoly for the pressing of Grape Seed oil. In those days, the grape seeds were placed in giant vats, mixed with water, and covered. During the following winter, they were pounded every few days until they finally yielded a mash. This mash was then gently heated to separate the oil from the water much in the same way that traditional hand-pressed coconut oil is made today.

Growth patterns in the grape plant exhibit interesting Yin-Yang properties that help explain the health functions of Grape Seed oil. Grape is a fast-growing climbing vine that uses other structures (stakes or trees) to support its rapid ascending growth. Rapid growth and climbing high are examples of

---

[a] *Salute Santé* can be reached at www.grapeseedoil.com or 707-251-3900.

extreme Yang functions. Wild grape will grow as high as the surrounding trees that hold it up. This extreme Yang in the grape plant needs extreme Yin for balance and can be found in the seed, the most condensed (Yin) part of the plant. This extreme Yin takes the form of highly potent AOs in the grape seed and in Grape Seed oil. In fact, grape seed extract is one of the most potent forms of AOs found in nature. These AOs give Grape Seed oil further Yin attributes such as the ability resist heat as well as to lower LDL and increase HDL.

Grape Seed oil is very high in Vitamin E, a probable factor in its especially high resistance to heat. This quality potentially makes it as good for baking and sautéing as it is for salad dressing.

Table 20: Smoke Points of Unsaturated Oils

Source	Temperature
Grape Seed Oil	485°F
Olive Oil	250°F
Peanut Oil	450°F
Sesame Oil	410°F
Soybean Oil	450°F
Sunflower Seed Oil	392°F

As one of the fat-soluble vitamins, Vitamin E is dependent upon FAs for its circulation throughout the body. Only plants can synthesize Vitamin E; animals can not make it. Whatever small quantities of Vitamin E animal food might contain is only due to the animals eating it from plants.

The chemical name for Vitamin E is "tocopherol," which combines the Greek words "ol" (meaning "alcohol") with "phero" ("to bring forth") and "tos" meaning "childbirth." Accordingly, Vitamin E was first used as an essential nutrient for the normal development of the fetus. Now it is used for female reproductive problems and for male impotence. There are five kinds of tocopherols. They are named according to the first four letters of the Greek alphabet—alpha, beta, gamma, delta—and simply represent four different chemical variations of Vitamin E. The third tocopherol, gamma-tocopherol, is the most potent form for preventing breast cancer.[a]

High dietary levels of Vitamin E are known to protect against abnormal blood clotting, heart attacks, strokes, and cancer,[b] which arise from the abnormal oxidation of cholesterol and fatty acids.[135] This type of fatty degeneration from oxidized cholesterol and FAs can also be observed externally in the brown spots seen on the exposed skin of the elderly.[136] **The Helsinki and Framingham Heart Studies claim that using Grape Seed oil reduced the risk of cardiac events by 41 to 55 percent!** According to the *Journal of Arteriosclerosis* (1990; 10:5), **Grape Seed oil added to the diet also created a 13-14 percent increase in HDL in only two weeks.**

---

[a] Kline, K. In *Journal of Nutrition* 134:345S-346S, 2004.
[b] Wagner, KH. In *Annals of Nutrition & Metabolism* 48:169-188, 2004.

Vitamin E is a potent AO that prevents the oxidation of LDL cholesterol by free radicals.[a] Vitamin E is also a natural preservative in polyunsaturated vegetable oils and keeps them from going rancid on the shelf as well as in our bodies.[137] Other kinds of AOs are also readily available from the grape plant. For example, the red pigments in grapes and wines, called bioflavonoids, are also excellent AOs known for their ability to protect the liver and arteries.[138] An even stronger AO (30-50 times more powerful than Vitamin E) and contained in large amounts in the *Salute Santé* brand of Grape Seed oil) is called proanthocyinidins (OPC). These three strong AOs present in Grape Seed oil account for much of its ability to heal those diseases associated with oxidation and free radical damage and also account for its heat-resistant capacity.

Grape Seed oil is one of the richest natural sources of Vitamin E, especially among the edible oils. Other oils rich in Vitamin E include Wheat Germ oil (223mg), Grape Seed oil (100mg), Sunflower Seed oil (54mg), Hazelnut oil (47mg), and Rice Bran oil (32mg). Two of these, Sunflower Seed oil and Rice Bran oil, are also well known for their heat-resistant qualities. Since MUFAs are also heat-resistant, oils that are higher in Vitamin E content often have a lesser proportion of MUFAs.

Table 21: High Vitamin E Oils and their Omega 6/MUFA Proportions

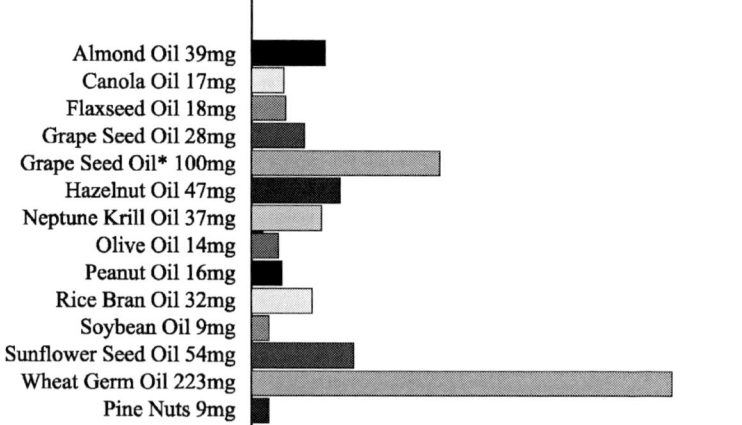

Salute Sante Brand

Grape Seed oil is, therefore, a very good choice for rehabilitating a body ravaged by free radical damage and also for general Vitamin E depletion. Both of these conditions are rampant in the general population, twenty to forty

---

[a] de Nigris, F. In *Biochemical Pharmacology* 59:1477-1487, 2000; and Dutta, A. In *Journal of the American College of Nutrition* 22 (4):258-268, 2003.

percent of which is Vitamin E deficient. There are several reasons for this deficiency. Eighty-six percent of Vitamin E is lost through typical food processing![139] Much of it is also used up in frying and deep-frying where it helps protect polyunsaturated oils.[a140] The refining process of vegetable oils also removes Vitamin E altogether and replaces it with BHT, an artificial preservative[141] associated with an increased risk for cancer. Cancer rates go up by themselves when Vitamin E is removed from polyunsaturated oils.[142] This rate only increases more when these artificial preservatives are added. Also, the form of Vitamin E predominant in the SAD (gamma-tocopherol) does not get to the body as easily as alpha-tocopherol, which is preferentially loaded onto the LDL for circulation.

Grape Seed oil is also known to raise HDL and lower LDL in humans. Raising HDL levels is also correlated with the reversal of both hypertension and impotence. These results are more likely due to the high AO content in Grape Seed oil than its high, unrefined Omega 6 content (72-76 percent), although both can raise HDL levels in people used to eating refined, hydrogenated, or partially hydrogenated vegetable oils. [b] The Vitamin E forms part of the plasma lipoprotein carrier vehicles necessary for transporting cholesterol from the liver to the body.[143] In fact, increased cancer from cholesterol-lowering drugs may result in part from the suppression of Vitamin E distribution through these carrier vehicles. Vitamin E delivery to the cells decreases in direct proportion to the decrease in carrier vehicles for cholesterol as occurs through artificial cholesterol lowering with drugs.[144]

Conversely, as the Vitamin E and other AOs increase through the addition of Grape Seed oil in the diet, the LDL and HDL protein carrier vehicles pick up cholesterol more easily. Once these AOs reach the Peripheral Tissues (PTs) of the body, they are then able to displace the oxidized cholesterol found there into the bloodstream where HDL can pick up the cholesterol so that HDL is increased and the cholesterol can be returned to the liver. In the following table, we can see the Vitamin E quotient in edible oils measured in mg per 100g of sample. While Grape Seed oil is one of the better oils for cooking, it should be used raw when using it to reverse free radical damage in the arteries, skin, and elsewhere. Do waste the wonderful AOs in Grape Seed oil when you are trying to heal disease and only use it for cooking once your health is firmly established. Because the Omega 6 level of Grape Seed is so high (72-76%), an additional source of Omega 3 such as Fish oil, Flaxseed oil (4:1), or Chia Seeds (3:1) should be taken in compensation.

---

[a] One tablespoon of Omega 6 per day requires almost the entire RDA (less than 30 International Units) of Vitamin E for AO protection. The *Salute Santé* brand of Grape Seed oil contains 100mg per 100g of Vitamin E, which at 14 IU, is 47 percent of the RDA.
[b] According to Erasmus, other foods, herbs, and supplements known to increase HDL include garlic, onions, brewer's yeast, ginseng, fish, lecithin, chromium, and Vitamin C. [Erasmus-336]

Table 22: Vitamin E Quotient in Edible Oils

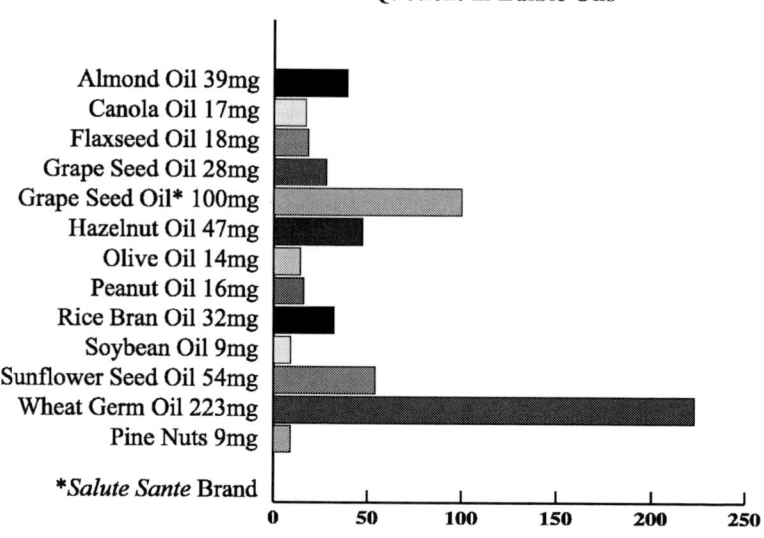

Almond Oil 39mg	
Canola Oil 17mg	
Flaxseed Oil 18mg	
Grape Seed Oil 28mg	
Grape Seed Oil* 100mg	
Hazelnut Oil 47mg	
Olive Oil 14mg	
Peanut Oil 16mg	
Rice Bran Oil 32mg	
Soybean Oil 9mg	
Sunflower Seed Oil 54mg	
Wheat Germ Oil 223mg	
Pine Nuts 9mg	

*Salute Sante Brand

Jojoba Oil

Jojoba oil is odorless, easily absorbed, and well known for its moisturizing, non-irritating properties. Jojoba oil is frequently used for dry, flaky skin and facial wrinkles to create an ageless looking skin; it does NOT block pores, cause blackheads, or promote acne; and DOES, however, rejuvenate the skin, promote new cell growth, and stop the production of sebum especially in those with oily skins. Jojoba oil is non-greasy and leaves no oily after-feel. Jojoba oil can increase the suppleness of the skin by 45 percent. Repeated use of Jojoba oil has been known to reduce superficial facial lines by up to 26 percent and is non-allergenic. University studies have concluded that five of the most common skin bacteria and fungi, including *staphylococcus aureus* and *pseudomonas aeruginosus* as well as the fungus *candida albicans*, cannot survive in Jojoba oil and have been completely destroyed in 1 hour and 15 minutes. Jojoba oil has also been found to relieve the symptoms of psoriasis.

Macadamia Oil

Sixty percent of the MUFAs in Macadamia oil are comprised of Oleic Acid. Macadamia oil contains the largest percentage of MUFAs of any known food. A very good quality unrefined, expeller-pressed Macadamia Nut oil is now available from Australia. It has a balanced, though

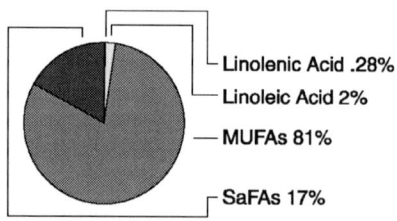

- Linolenic Acid .28%
- Linoleic Acid 2%
- MUFAs 81%
- SaFAs 17%

neglible, FA content, a factor that makes it a popular oil in healthy weight-loss diets that strive to eliminate bad quality EFAs, especially the common Omega 6s that are mostly refined, over-heated, and allowed to become rancid in modern society. Because of its high Smoke Point (400-450°F), Macadamia oil is also good for cooking. This quality in combination with its negligible, yet balanced (1:1), EFA content makes Macadamia oil especially valuable as a cooking oil. You can use it for cooking without creating an EFA imbalance! It must, however, be supplemented with EFAs.

FA content of MUFAs: Palmitoleic Acid (18%), Oleic Acid (60%), Gadoleic Acid (3%), Erucic Acid (.32%), Nervonic Acid (.02%). FA content of SaFAs: Lauric Acid (.1%), Myristic Acid (.9%), Palmitic Acid (8%), Stearic Acid (3%), Arachidic Acid (3%), Behenic Acid (.85%), Lignoceric Acid (.39%).

Olive Oil

Olive trees used for Olive oil production grow in Italy, Greece, Turkey, Morocco, Tunisia, Spain, Portugal, France, California, and Australia. The average Italian uses fifteen quarts of Olive oil per year (an average of 3½ tablespoons per day).

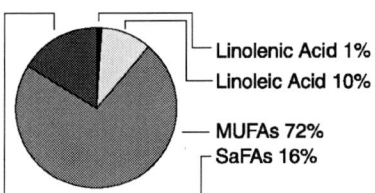

Linolenic Acid 1%
Linoleic Acid 10%
MUFAs 72%
SaFAs 16%

Researcher Ancel Keys observed that in the 1950s healthy traditional people from the Greek island of Crete consumed as much as ½ cup of olive oil per day per person and even drank it by the wineglass for breakfast![145] Olive oil is pressed from the fruit of trees 100 to 500 years old and is predominantly a monounsaturated fatty acid (approximately 72 percent) including 63-83 percent oleic acid and .5-3 percent palmitoleic acid, which accounts for its stability and keeping qualities. Olive oil is often touted as an Omega 9 in order to insinuate that it has EFA characteristics, which it does not. Olive oil is a poor source of EFAs containing 8-10 percent LA and only about 1 percent LNA.

While not technically an EFA, MUFAs do have the advantage of their balance and stability in terms of keeping properties, cooking, and cholesterol regulation. Neither the low percentages of EFAs nor the relatively high percentage of MUFAs in Olive oil can account for its known positive effect on health or popularity. There are also contradictions in the function of Olive oil that can only be explained by its minor ingredients, some of which are unique to olives. For example, while MUFAs raise blood triglycerides when taken excessively, Olive oil lowers the risk of coronary artery disease; and while the palmitic acid (7.5-18 percent in Olive oil) is thought to raise blood cholesterol, Olive oil protects the arteries.

While these minor components only constitute about 2 percent of the profile, this meager 2 percent is comprised of over one hundred different volatile compounds, some of which have never been studied. More common compounds include phytosterols, chlorophyll, magnesium, Vitamin E, beta-carotene (pro-vitamin A), and polyphenols. Phytosterols protect the heart and lower cholesterol. Chlorophyll also protects the heart and arteries and also contains magnesium, which is usually deficient in people with cardiovascular problems; beta-carotene and Vitamin E are AOs, which protect against free radical destruction. Polyphenols also contain AOs and helps to lower blood pressure.

Extra-virgin Olive oil helps to regulate membranes as well as cell formation and differentiation; reduce the risk of diabetes; promote bone formation in children; reduce osteoporosis; strengthen the brain; regulate cholesterol (it lowers LDL and raises HDL); reduce gallstone production; improve fat digestion; detoxify the liver;[a] and lower the incidence of cancer including breast and prostate cancer. Extra-virgin Olive oil also protects against the mutagenic effect of toxic chemicals, destructive rays, and refined UFAs.

Extra Virgin Olive oil is the only unrefined oil available in the mass markets although most Olive oil labeled "extra-virgin" is refined.[b] To retain the function of its protective fatty acids (80 percent of its content), health experts recommend that Olive oil be consumed in its raw state and not in cooking. Traditional Mediterranean dietary practices used butter and lard for cooking and used Olive oil raw on top of prepared food and whole wheat bread. A common practice is to place a container of it on the dinner table as one would a fine wine. When heated above 150°C (302°F) through cooking, Olive oil's protective qualities are not only destroyed, they become mutagenic. Even the lower temperatures achieved in sautéing can destroy the "minor" ingredients in Olive oil.

---

[a] Combined with 1/3 cup of fresh lemon juice, 2/3 cup of raw olive oil is commonly and historically used as a flush to rid toxins from the liver and stones from the gallbladder. This procedure begins by fasting on green apples during the day and then taking the lemon/olive oil mixture before bed. EFA-rich oils, however, are even more effective.

[b] See the section on Olive Oil processing in the Oil Production chapter for general guidelines on selecting a good quality Olive oil. Recommended labels include: *Bionaturae* (organic, first cold-pressed, small farm, hand harvested, pressed on the day of harvest, stored in dark green glass bottles); *Columela* (Spain, estate bottled, first cold-pressed); *Badia a Coltibuono* (Italy, extra virgin, green glass bottle, first cold press, free of heat or chemicals, lowest natural acidity 0.21%, pressed on day of harvest); *Olio Verde* (Italy, unfiltered, mechanically pressed, prized olives, family tradition); *Ravida* (Italy, estate bottled since 1773, no pesticides or fertilizers, three Sicilian olive varieties; *Catillo* (Andulasia, estate bottled and pressed since 1780, unfiltered; *DaMorgada* (Portugal, organic, first cold-press); *Nunez de Prado* (Spain, organic, first cold-pressed, unfiltered, family estate); *Douro Carm* (Portugal, organic, first cold-press, hand-picked, low acidity 0.1%, cold extraction, unfiltered); *A L'Olivier* (France, since 1822, clay bottle); *L'Estornell* (Spain, organic, first press, Arbequina olives).

Peanut Oil

Peanut oil is a stable, highly monounsaturated oil (47 percent Omega 9). Chinese foods are usually fried in peanut oil. Peanut oil is very good when it is obtained as a batch-pressed unrefined oil. The problem is that, because they grow underground, peanuts

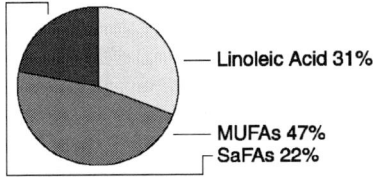

— Linoleic Acid 31%

— MUFAs 47%
— SaFAs 22%

are susceptible to an extremely rare but carcinogenic fungus that grows if the peanuts get damp. If this mold is present and if the peanuts are ingested over a long period of time, the alfatoxins produced by this mold may cause liver cancer. If the peanuts are fungus-free, the oil is fine. Nevertheless, peanuts are a common source of food allergies (second only to seafood). The immune system of some people creates antibodies in reaction to the protein in peanuts. The antibodies, then, create allergic reactions ranging from a mild tingling to death from anaphylactic shock. This reaction is much greater in Canada, the US, and the UK (countries more reliant on hyper-cleanliness and vaccinations) than in Asia and Africa where peanut allergies are almost non-existent. One theory suggests that the natural immune systems of people living in developed countries has weakened due to this reliance and that peanut allergies are symptomatic of this much deeper concern.

Pumpkinseed Oil

Pumpkinseeds and Pumpkinseed oil, along with Walnuts and Walnut oil, are the top two Secondary Omega 3 nutritional oils.[a] Pumpkinseed oil is a good source of Omega 6 (43-60 percent) and Omega 3 (0-15 percent) EFAs as well as Omega 9 FAs. The EFA ratio of

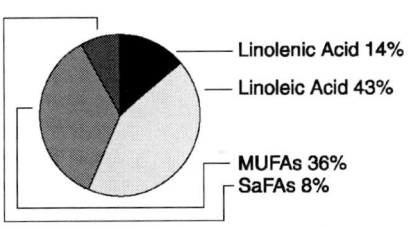

— Linolenic Acid 14%
— Linoleic Acid 43%

— MUFAs 36%
— SaFAs 8%

Pumpkinseed oil is 1:7, a ratio high enough for regular use, but too low to make Pumpkinseed oil a Primary Source of Omega 3s. Several other components in Pumpkinseed oil account for its beneficial effect on the genitourinary system for both males and females, especially the prostate in males. These components include selenium, zinc, and potassium, which strengthen the bladder muscles, soothe irritation, benefit the flow of urine, drain the tissues and diminish swelling; cartinoides, which are successful in treating malfunctions of the bladder and the urinary passages; Vitamin E, which prevents premature births and menopausal problems; and Vitamin B.

Christopher Columbus originally discovered the seed oil Pumpkin in December 1492 from Native Americans while exploring the New World.

---

[a] These oils are high in Omega 3s but low in their EFA ratio.

Leonard Fuchs described it in his 1543 *New Herb Book* as Ocean-cucumber (*Cucurbita pepo*) without reference to any of its culinary or healing properties. In Europe, the earliest use of pumpkin was probably as animal feed and diet for the poor. In the early 1700s, field workers in Austria's Steiermark region rediscovered a unique pumpkin seed that possessed a pleasant tasting membrane over the seeds instead of the more usual hard shell. The first documented reference to the pressing of these seeds for medicinal oil was on February 26, 1735. In March 1773, the Styrian State Government asserted some control over the pumpkin growing in order to focus its use away from cooking and onto medicinal use. Today, the Steiermark pumpkin fields cover more than five times more than their well-known vineyards. Thirty-three square yards of farmland yield thirty-three pumpkins, which produce one liter of oil. While the seeds need to be heated to approximately 58° to 65°C (136° to 149°F), they nevertheless retain the advantages of a cold-pressed oil.

Pumpkinseed oil alleviates problems in the ovaries, prostate, and bladder; improves potency and general sexual health; helps bladder control; increases energy; maintains optimum brain function; and creates smooth skin. When raw pumpkinseeds are lightly toasted in the home oven at 180°F for two hours, they can reduce the need to take the oil.

Rapeseed Oil

Rapeseed oil has been used for many centuries in India and China. It contains a very long-chain monounsaturated fatty acid, erucic acid (40-50 percent), which has been removed from Western markets to promote the new genetically modified Canola oil created by the Canadian government. These new varieties replace the erucic acid with high levels of oleic acid.

Rice Bran Oil

Rice Bran oil is a stable monounsaturated oil that contains a moderate portion of Omega 6s but little Omega 3s. While it is a good source of the AOs gamma-oryzanlol and cycloartenol as well as Vitamin E, Rice Bran oil should not be used for frying because of its high content of 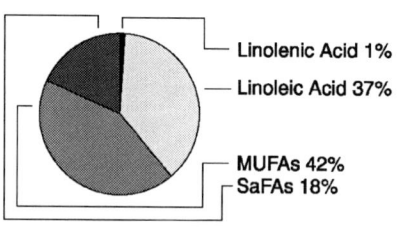 Omega 6 EFAs (35 percent) and AOs. A possible exception is when it is combined with the more stable Sunflower Seed oil. The stability of the Sunflower Seed oil is thought to protect the AOs in the Rice Bran oil, which in turn protects the more fragile but minor amount of Omega 3 (1 percent) EFAs in the Sunflower Seed oil. Better yet, use it raw for the Vitamin E. While not always "refined," Rice Bran oil is, nevertheless, produced from refined grain and should only be used on occasion for some of its medicinal qualities.

Linolenic Acid 1%

Linoleic Acid 37%

MUFAs 42%

SaFAs 18%

Safflower Oil

Safflower oil, a thistle relative, has been used for thousands of years. It was especially popular during the 1970s in the heyday of refined PUFAs because of its extremely high percentage of Omega 6. There are two varieties of safflower oil. One is a high linoleic (one of the richest sources of the Omega 6s at 75 percent) and the other is high oleic.

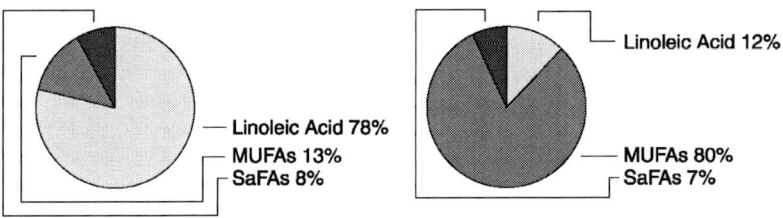

Figure 25: High Linoleic   Figure 26: High Oleic

Sesame Oil

At 43 percent, Sesame Seed oil is one of the moderately rich sources of the Omega 6s (Sunflower Seed oil is 64 percent) and is easy to press without heat and should be unrefined and generally un-toasted. [a] Sesame oil lacks the fragile Omega 3s

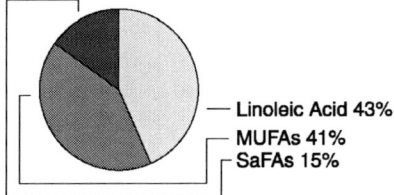

and contains the natural preservatives sesamol and sesamin, which help to stabilize the oil for low temperature cooking and shelf life. These oxidative properties are conferred to other oils when cooking. One recommended combination for cooking is to use Sesame, Peanut, and Olive oil together.

Soybean Oil

Fresh, unrefined soybean oil is both high quality and tasty. Soybean oil contains 53 percent Omega 6 and 8 percent Omega 3 as well as lecithin and phytosterols. According to Erasmus, "It also contains other natural factors that inhibit some kinds of

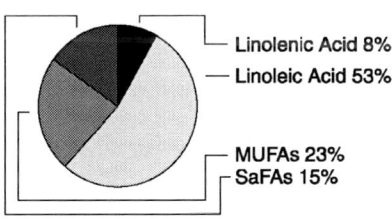

---

[a] Good quality, delicious, toasted Sesame oil can be obtained from the Natural Import Company at www.naturalimport.com (1-828-277-8892), as well as the Goldmine Natural Food Company at www.goldminenaturalfood.com (1-800-475-3663).

cancers."[146] Soybean oil also has a reasonably good EFA ratio of 1:8, which makes it one of the better Secondary Sources of balanced EFAs. Seventy percent of the refined food grade oil used in the US is soybean oil.

In Asia, where soybeans originated, only fermented soybeans have been used as food in such traditional products as miso, tamari, or tempeh. Modern nutrition compliments traditional wisdom and tells us that soybeans contain substances in their hulls that interfere with metabolism, suppress growth, and upset the balance of the endocrine system. For example, hemagglutinin makes red blood cells clump together so that oxygen cannot be properly absorbed; trypsin inhibitors suppress growth; isoflavones reduce hormones needed for proper thyroid function, raise estrogen levels, and may be implicated in breast cancer, brain function in men, and developmental abnormalities in infants; and phytic acid may block the absorption of certain minerals, including magnesium, calcium, iron and zinc. The modern processing of soybeans sometimes involves the spray drying of soy curds at temperatures high enough to produce carcinogenic nitrites.

It is not likely, however, that any of these substances are found in expeller-pressed, unrefined, organic soybean oil because they are confined to the hull, which is not contained in soybean oil. Since soybeans are the single most genetically modified crop, make sure that the soybean oil you use is not genetically engineered (Non-GMO) and that it says so on the label.

Sunflower Seed Oil

Sunflower Seed oil varies in its Omega 6 content according to different temperate zones. Omega 6 content is higher in the north (Canada) and lower in the south (Florida). Because of its low Omega 3 content, Sunflower Seed oil is now being promoted in Europe as a stable frying

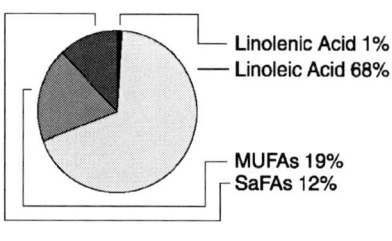

Linolenic Acid 1%
Linoleic Acid 68%
MUFAs 19%
SaFAs 12%

oil in combination with the two AO-rich oils Sesame Seed and Rice Bran.

Walnut Oil

Walnut oil is a very flavorful and delicate oil primarily used for salad dressings. While natural walnut oil should be carefully stored because of its high levels of EFAs (12 percent Omega 3 and 68 percent Omega 6 in an EFA ratio of 1:5.6), most of what is commercially obtainable is refined.

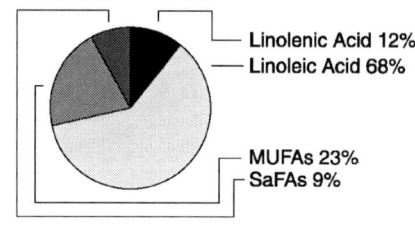

Linolenic Acid 12%
Linoleic Acid 68%
MUFAs 23%
SaFAs 9%

Wheat Germ Oil

Wheat germ oil is the overridingly richest natural source of Vitamin E of all edible oils, contains some Omega 3 (5 percent), and is a rich source of a 28-carbon fatty alcohol, which, according to Erasmus, protects heart function and may help nerve regeneration. While the fresh,

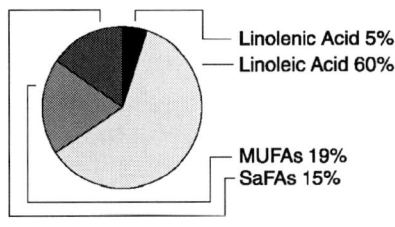

Linolenic Acid 5%
Linoleic Acid 60%

MUFAs 19%
SaFAs 15%

unrefined wheat germ oil has a nice taste, most commercially available wheat germ oil tastes awful because it is old and rancid. Like Rice Bran oil, Wheat Germ oil is produced from refined grain and should only be used on occasion for some of its medicinal qualities.

Oils in Nuts, Seeds, and Fruits

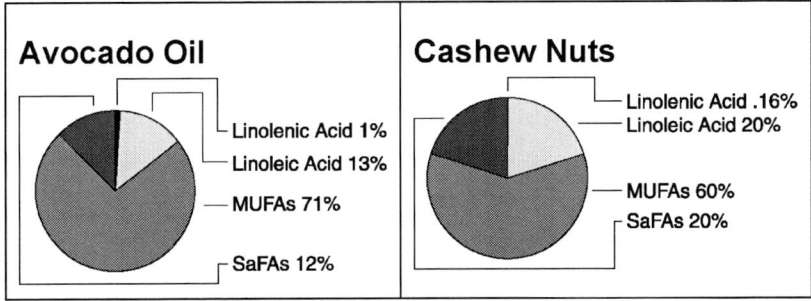

Avocado Oil

Linolenic Acid 1%
Linoleic Acid 13%
MUFAs 71%
SaFAs 12%

Cashew Nuts

Linolenic Acid .16%
Linoleic Acid 20%
MUFAs 60%
SaFAs 20%

Most of Avocado oil's MUFAs are Oleic Acid (68 percent of the whole) and its SaFAs are comprised of mostly Palmitic Acid (11 percent of the whole). Most of the MUFAs in Cashew Nuts are Oleic Acid as well (60%), while its highest SaFa content is comprised of Palmitic (10%) and Stearic Acid (8%). The low Omega 3 content (1 percent) and high MUFA content (71 percent) in Avocado oil makes it one of the top heat-resistant oils for cooking. Avocado oil has the highest Smoke Point of all oils at 520°F.

Avocado Oil
- MUFAs: Palmitoleic Acid (3%), Oleic Acid (68%)
- SaFAs: Palmitic Acid (11%), Stearic Acid (1%)

Cashew Nuts
- MUFAs: Palmitoleic Acid (.3%), Oleic Acid (60%), Gadoleic Acid (.14%)
- SaFAs: Caprylic Acid (.04%), Capric Acid (.04%), Lauric Acid (.04%), Myristic Acid (.04%), Palmitic Acid (10%), Stearic Acid (8%), Arachidic Acid (.67%), Behenic Acid (.44%), Lignoceric Acid (.26%)

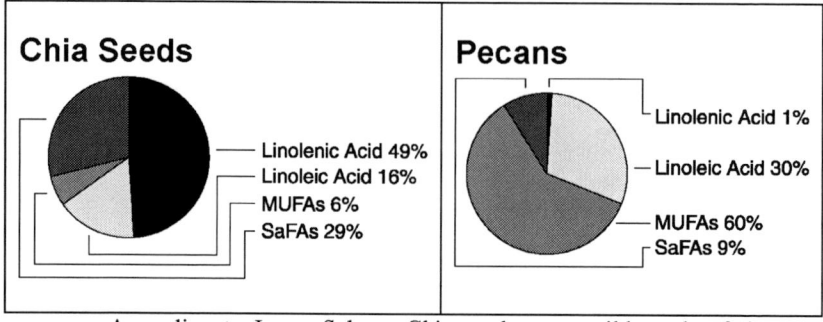

Chia Seeds
- Linolenic Acid 49%
- Linoleic Acid 16%
- MUFAs 6%
- SaFAs 29%

Pecans
- Linolenic Acid 1%
- Linoleic Acid 30%
- MUFAs 60%
- SaFAs 9%

According to James Scheer, Chia seed was a wild staple of the pre-Columbian Aztecs and Mayas and is a perfect food. Chia seed is as high in Omega 3s as flaxseed and has an EFA ratio of 3.5:1, a factor that makes it a Primary Source in rehabilitating Omega 3 deficiency. Chia seed also contains all of the Vitamin B complex, five times as much calcium as milk, and sufficient amounts of the commonly deficient, osteoporosis-preventing, and menopausal-regulating mineral boron. Boron helps calcium retention in the bones and teeth and also improves mental alertness, thinking, memory, and attention span. Chia seeds also contain protease inhibitors, unusually potent AOs that block the development of cancer.[a] Dissolve 3-4 tablespoons in water, or grind like flaxseed, and spread on cooked whole oats for breakfast.

Most of Pecan's MUFAs are Oleic Acid (60 percent of the whole).

Chia Seeds
- MUFAs: Palmitoleic Acid (.1%), Oleic Acid (6%), Gadoleic Acid (.13%)
- SaFAs: Myristic Acid (.1%), Palmitic Acid (6%), Stearic Acid (3%), Arachidic Acid (.3%), Behenic Acid (.03%)

Pecans
- MUFAs: Oleic Acid (60%), Gadoleic Acid (.3%)
- SaFAs: Palmitic Acid (6%), Stearic Acid (3%), Arachidic Acid (.1%)

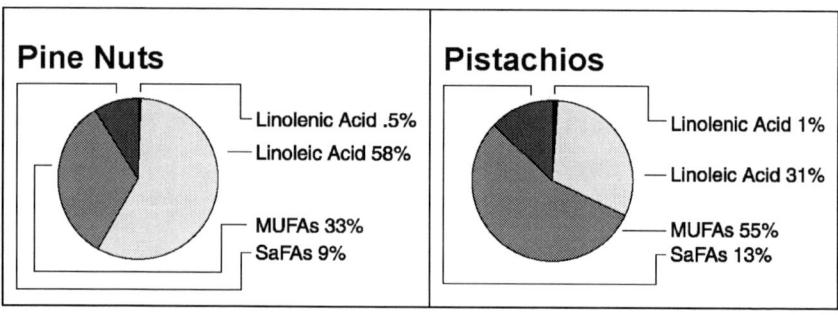

Pine Nuts
- Linolenic Acid .5%
- Linoleic Acid 58%
- MUFAs 33%
- SaFAs 9%

Pistachios
- Linolenic Acid 1%
- Linoleic Acid 31%
- MUFAs 55%
- SaFAs 13%

---

[a] Brown rice and legumes also contain high concentrations of protease inhibitors.

Most of the SaFAs in Pistachios are comprised of Palmitic Acid (12 percent of the whole). Pine Nuts contain a large portion of Oleic Acid (31 percent).

Pine Nuts
- MUFAs: Palmitoleic Acid (.03%), Oleic Acid (31%), Gadoleic Acid (1%)
- SaFAs: Palmitic Acid (6%), Stearic Acid (2%), Arachidic Acid (.4%), Behenic Acid (.1%)

Pistachios
- MUFAs: Palmitoleic Acid (1%), Oleic Acid (54%), Gadoleic Acid (.17%)
- SaFAs: Palmitic Acid (12%), Stearic Acid (1%), Arachidic Acid (.1%), Behenic Acid (.1%)

Fats and Oils in Animals

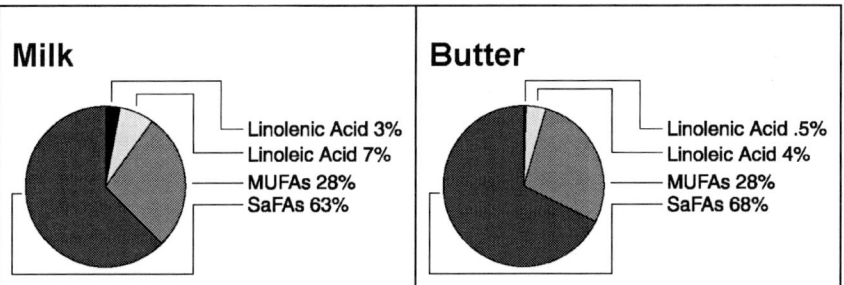

All of the MUFAs in milk are comprised of Oleic Acid and 26 percent of its FAs are comprised of the SaFA, Palmitic Acid. Twenty-five percent of the FAs in Butter are comprised of the MUFA, Oleic Acid and 27 percent are comprised of the SaFA, Palmitic Acid.

Milk
- MUFAs: Oleic Acid (28%)
- SaFAs: Butyric Acid (3%), Caproic Acid (3%), Caprylic Acid (3%), Capric Acid (3%), Lauric Acid (3%), Myristic Acid (10%), Palmitic Acid (28%), Stearic Acid (12%)

Butter
- MUFAs: Palmitoleic Acid (1%), Oleic Acid (27%), Gadoleic Acid (.13%)
- SaFAs: Butyric Acid (4%), Caproic Acid (3%), Caprylic Acid (2%), Capric Acid (3%), Lauric Acid (3%), Myristic Acid (10%), Palmitic Acid (29%), Stearic Acid (13%), Arachidic Acid (.18%)

Other Edible Oil Sources

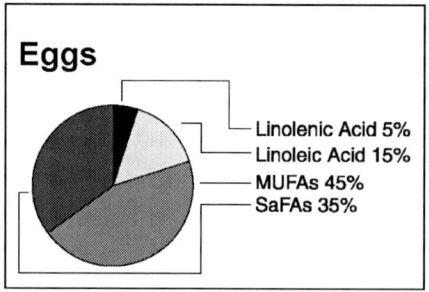

Eggs

- Linolenic Acid 5%
- Linoleic Acid 15%
- MUFAs 45%
- SaFAs 35%

Forty-one percent of the FAs in eggs are comprised of the MUFA, Oleic Acid and 26 percent of its FAs are comprised of the SaFA, Palmitic Acid. Egg whites do not contain lipids.

Eggs
- MUFAs: Palmitoleic Acid (3%), Oleic Acid (41%), Gadoleic Acid (.33%), Erucic Acid (.04%)
- SaFAs: Caprylic Acid (.04%), Capric Acid (.04%), Lauric Acid (.04%), Myristic Acid (.4%), Palmitic Acid (26%), Stearic Acid (9%), Arachidic Acid (.1%), Behenic Acid (.1%), Lignoceric Acid (.04%)

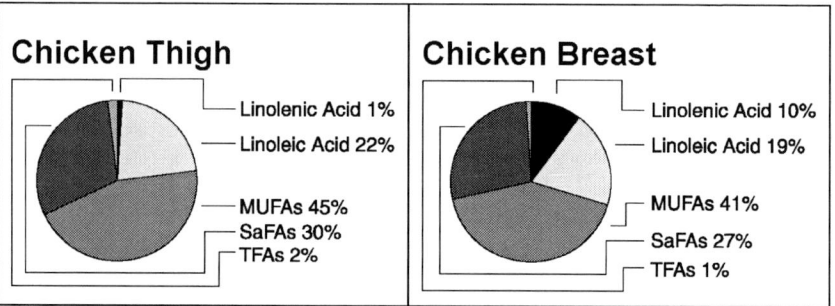

Chicken Thigh

- Linolenic Acid 1%
- Linoleic Acid 22%
- MUFAs 45%
- SaFAs 30%
- TFAs 2%

Chicken Breast

- Linolenic Acid 10%
- Linoleic Acid 19%
- MUFAs 41%
- SaFAs 27%
- TFAs 1%

The FA content in chicken thigh and chicken breast is mostly the same. Most of the MUFAs are Oleic Acid. The total percentage is greater in the thigh (38 percent) than the breast (34 percent).

Chicken Thigh
- MUFAs: Palmitoleic Acid (6%), Oleic Acid (38%), Gadoleic Acid (1%)
- SaFAs: Lauric Acid (.17%), Myristic Acid (.88%), Palmitic Acid (23%), Stearic Acid (6%)
- TFAs (natural): 1.5%

Chicken Breast
- MUFAs: Palmitoleic Acid (5%), Oleic Acid (34%), Gadoleic Acid (.1%)
- SaFAs: Lauric Acid (.11%), Myristic Acid (.86%), Palmitic Acid (21%), Stearic Acid (6%)
- TFAs (natural): 1%

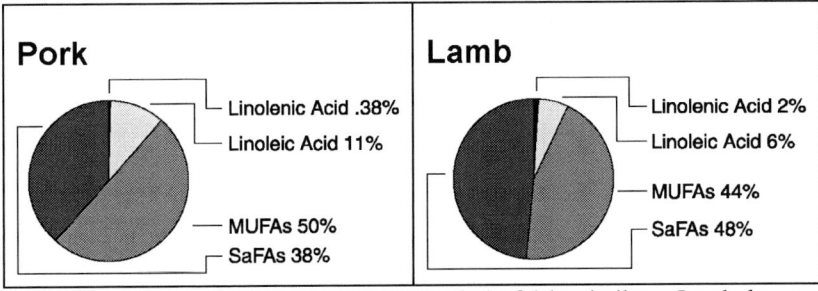

The FA content of pork and lamb is fairly similar. Lamb has an additional 10 percent more SaFAs. Most of the MUFAs in each are Oleic Acid, 46 percent of the total FAs in pork and 39 percent in lamb.

Pork

- MUFAs: Palmitoleic Acid (4%), Oleic Acid (46%), Gadoleic Acid (.76%)
- SaFAs: Capric Acid (.19%), Lauric Acid (.19%), Myristic Acid (1%), Palmitic Acid (24%), Stearic Acid (12%)

Lamb

- MUFAs: Palmitoleic Acid (3%), Oleic Acid (39%)
- SaFAs: Capric Acid (.3%), Lauric Acid (.5%), Myristic Acid (5%), Palmitic Acid (24%), Stearic Acid (15%)

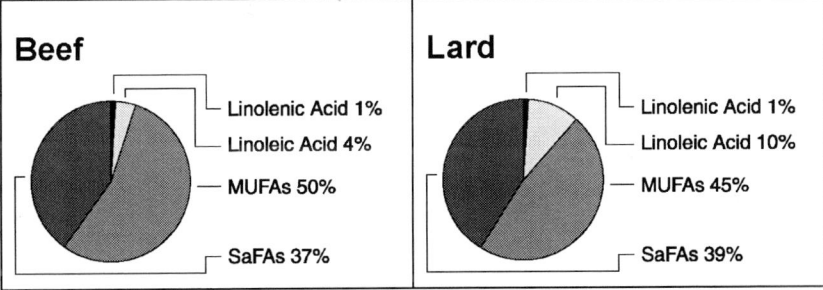

The FA content in beef and lard is practically the same. Fifty percent of the MUFAs in beef and 41 percent in lard of the total FAs are Oleic Acid.

Beef

- MUFAs: Palmitoleic Acid (4%), Oleic Acid (50%), Gadoleic Acid (.03%)
- SaFAs: Capric Acid (.09%), Lauric Acid (.06%), Myristic Acid (3%), Palmitic Acid (25%), Stearic Acid (12%)

Lard

- MUFAs: Palmitoleic Acid (3%), Oleic Acid (41%), Gadoleic Acid (1%)

Other Edible Oil Sources

- SaFAs: Capric Acid (.1%), Lauric Acid (.2%), Myristic Acid (1%), Palmitic Acid (24%), Stearic Acid (14%)

Good Oils, Bad Oils: What to Use, What to Avoid

General Principles

The Seven Categories

The seven categories of edible oils that we need to understand to secure our health and longevity and prevent tragic and unnecessary disease are:

1) **Necessary and Vital**
   These are the essential fatty acids (Omega 3s especially, but also the more common Omega 6s).
   Primary Omega 3s are those that have both a high EFA ratio and also a predominance of Omega 3s. These are most useful in restoring Omega 3 deficiencies and include Krill oil, Fish oil, Flaxseed oil, Black Currant Seed oil, and Chia Seeds. Because of its balanced EFA ratio, Hempseed oil is the very best oil for Regular consumption. Generally speaking, you do not have to worry about throwing your EFA ratio out of balance when taking Hempseed oil as you do with most other oils— Coconut oil and Macadamia oil being the two exceptions. The only concern is that this ratio should vary somewhat for different individuals, for different sexes, and for different times and activities.
   Take these oils internally, preferably raw as a "dressing" on top of food. Whole seeds are a great way to take them, but use the oils as well.

2) **Especially Important for Enzyme Deficiencies**
   • Use Evening Primrose or Borage oil for those deficient in the enzymes necessary to convert GLA and PGE_1 from Omega 6. Take in capsules or by the spoonful like medicine.
   • Use Black Currant Seed oil especially for those deficient in the enzymes necessary to convert SDA and, therefore, EPA, DHA, and PGE_3 from Omega 3s. In addition, Black Currant Seed oil contains more GLA than EPO and therefore can be used as a Primary Oil for correcting both Omega 3 and 6 enzyme deficiencies.
   • Hempseed oil also contains both GLA and SDA and so can be used to correct EFA enzyme deficiencies as well. Hempseed oil contains as much or more SDA (2 to 4 percent) as Black Currant Seed oil (2 percent) but less GLA (1.7 percent) than EPO (9 percent). The EFA ratio of these derivatives is also in good proportion (1:1 to 2:1) in Hempseed oil. The only conceivable drawback is the relatively low GLA content compared with EPO or Borage oil (24 percent). While the presence of these derivatives in Hempseed oil does enable it to be used to correct EFA deficiencies over a longer period, the presence of

so much more GLA in EPO and Borage oil gives the additional option to use them for an initial period with a Primary Omega 3 source and then follow up latter with either Black Currant Seed oil or Hempseed oil to correct the Omega 3 deficiency. A third option would be to take EPO or Borage oil with either Black Currant Seed oil or Hempseed oil plus a Primary Omega 3 source for the initial period (6 months to 2-3 years) and then use other strategies for regular maintenance.

3) **Good for Energy, General Nutrition, Immune Disorders, and Lack of Breast Feeding**
   - Use Coconut Oil raw on top of foods or as a spread for whole-wheat, non-yeasted bread.

4) **Medicinal Uses**
   - Use raw Pumpkinseed oil taken internally or as a rectal implant[a] for prostate problems.
   - Use Olive oil raw for its hundreds of minor ingredients known to be beneficial to health.
   - Use Grape Seed oil for its high AO levels to clean the arteries and regulate cholesterol. Make sure you balance its EFA ratio by taking the appropriate amount of Primary Omega 3s.

5) **Cooking Purposes**
   - Use centrifuged Coconut oil and Macadamia oil for cooking because, in addition to being heat-resistant, they also contain low levels of the fragile EFAs and those they do have are in the acceptable ratio so you do not have to worry about upsetting your EFA ratio. Use them regularly with Hempseed oil as your Regular EFA source.
   - Use Avocado oil for high temperature cooking or Grape Seed oil as a more locally sustainable source in temperate or moderate climate zones.
   - Use Sesame Seed, Sunflower Seed, Peanut, Rice Bran, and/or Olive oil for low temperature cooking. Be sure to adhere to the Kissing Point principle.

6) **External Use for Treating the Skin**
   - Use Almond, Apricot Kernel, Foraha, Hazelnut, and especially Calendula and Jojoba oil.
   - Foraha used externally on the skin is also great for draining toxins from the skin, joints, lymph nodes, digestive system (used for hemorrhoids), and urine.

7) **Avoid**
   - All hydrogenated fats including Olestra, Earth Balance, margarine, vegetable shortening, partially hydrogenated vegetable oil,

---

[a] Use a dropper bottle to insert a dropper full into the rectum once per day, preferably with three drops each of the therapeutic grade essential oils of Yarrow, Juniper Berry, Carrot Seed, and Cypress added to the Pumpkinseed Oil (see www.willmountain.com for these and other therapeutic grade essential oils).

deep-fried chips (corn chips). Do not believe labels that claim to contain no *trans*-fats, especially if they are hydrogenated or partially hydrogenated and always check your source.

• Most commercial baked goods including cookies, donuts, fast foods, breakfast cereal, and energy bars.

• Nondairy creamers, flavored coffees, whipped toppings, bean dips, gravy mixes, and salad dressings.

• Pre-packaged foods such as Ramen noodles, soup cups, and Frozen Food.[a]

• Canola oil—a highly genetically modified substance.

• Do not use plastic containers because the chemicals in the plastic leach out easily into the oil and interfere with healthy processes. Because the chemistry of the plastic and oil are similar, the taste of the plastic is less easily detectable than with other products. Glass bottles are much better, especially amber, brown, or green ones that can block the UV light.

---

[a] See http://www.bantransfats.com.

Blends/Combinations

Type	Oil	Company	Expeller Pressed	Unrefined	Organic	Bottling	Oil or Capsules	Rating
W3	Flaxseed	Flora	Yes 97°F	Yes	Yes	BG	Oil	5+
		Omega Nutrition	Yes	Yes	Yes	PB	Both	4
		Spectrum	Yes	Yes	Yes	PB	Both	4
		Barleans	Yes	Yes	Yes	PB	Yes	4
		Health from Sun	Yes	Yes	Yes	PB	Both	4
SDA	B Currant Seed	Health from Sun	Yes	Yes	No	PB	Caps	2
W6	Sunflower	Flora	Yes 113°F	Yes	Yes	BG	Oil	5+
	Sesame	Eden	Yes	Yes	Yes	BG	Oil	5
		Omega Nutrition	Yes	Yes	Yes	PB	Oil	4
		Spectrum	Yes	Yes	No	CG	Oil	3 ½
GLA	EPO	Health from Sun	Yes	Yes	Yes	PB	Both	4
		Spectrum	Yes	Yes	Yes	PB	Caps	3
		Barleans	Yes	Yes	Yes	PB	Caps	3
	Borage	Omega Nutrition	Yes	Yes	Yes	PB	Oil	4
		Spectrum	Yes	Yes	No	PB	Caps	2
		Barleans	Yes 110°F	Yes	No-Pest	PB	Both	3 ½
W3 & W6	Pumpkinseed	Flora	Yes	Yes	Yes	BG	Oil	5
		Omega Nutrition	Yes	Yes		PB	Oil	3
		Spectrum	Yes	Yes		PB	Oil	3
	Hempseed	Living Harvest	Yes	Yes	Yes	BG	Oil	5
SDA & GLA	B Currant Seed	Health from Sun	Yes	Yes	Yes	PB	Both	4
Vitamin E	Wheat Germ	Spectrum	EP	Yes	No	PB	Oil	3
	Almond	Flora	EP	Yes	Yes	BG	Oil	5
Lecithin	Soybean Non-GMO	Eden		Yes	Yes	BG	Oil	6
MCFA	Coconut Oil	Coconut Oil Supreme	Centrifuged	Yes	Yes	PB	Oil	4 ½
Other	Olive Oil		Extra Virgin	Extra Virgin				

- Codes: BG = Brown Glass; CG = Clear Glass; EP = Expeller Pressed; PB = Plastic Bottle
- Stabilizer: Rosemary Essential Oil

Daily Practice

Correction Stage

Because of the over-reliance on refined oils from the food industry during the twentieth century as well as the marginalization of Omega 3-rich traditional foods, the majority of the US population is now EFA deficient, especially in the Omega 3s. This Omega 3 deficiency creates a chronic pattern of Liver disharmony along with disharmonies in other related organs dependent upon the health and balance of Liver Qi. Therefore, the first concern of anyone interested in securing their health through the consumption of good quality edible oils needs to be the functional restoration of these internal organs, especially the Liver, skin, and cells. This process will take at least six months to eighteen months of diligent practice to complete and should be maintained regularly thereafter. The cells will recuperate within the first six-month period, while the Liver will take an additional year at least. One of the ultimate goals of this stage is to produce the necessary amount of Prostaglandin 3s for good health.

Unless there are enzyme deficiencies that prevent the conversion of Omega 3s, the primary oil during the Correction Stage should be Flaxseed oil because it contains the greatest amount of Omega 3. Flaxseeds and Chia seeds can also be used. The recommended daily portion is 1 tablespoon of oil per fifty pounds of body weight per day. For an average 150-pound person, this will be 3 tablespoons per day of Flaxseed oil. While the whole flaxseed is a vital food of itself and important for its important lignans, it is not possible to get enough Omega 3 EFAs from it alone during this stage. A person would need to take 9 tablespoons of flaxseed per day to meet the requirement of the 150-pound person mentioned above. Regular (weekly) consumption of a variety of sea vegetables and micro-algae will also supply partial requirement for the vital Omega 3s. Since sea vegetables are one of the most mineral-rich foods available, they will also supply much of the nutrition needed to correct the enzyme deficiencies that block prostaglandin conversion from EFAs in general.

Conversion Deficiencies

As stated earlier, 20 percent of the population in unable to convert PGE_3 from Omega 3 because of the liver enzyme deficiencies of delta-4,5,6-desaturase. These enzymes convert Omega 3 into SDA, which then goes on to produce EPA, DHA, and Prostaglandin 3 (LNA $\rightarrow$ SDA $\rightarrow$ EPA $\rightarrow$ DHA and PGE_3) . The enzyme delta-6-desaturase is also responsible for converting Omega 6 into GLA, which then goes on to produce DGLA and Prostaglandin 1 (LA $\rightarrow$ GLA $\rightarrow$ DGLA $\rightarrow$ PGE_1) . This enzyme deficiency has been linked to excess consumption of saturated fatty acids, *trans*-fatty acid and alcohol consumption; an over-abundance of serum cholesterol; the presence of chronic viral infections; anti-inflammatories (both steroidal and non-steroidal); a history of cancer and radiation; lack of insulin; and nutrient deficiency.[a] All of these factors are related to Liver dysfunction in acupuncture theory. While the correct use of fats and oils will significantly help to heal the Liver, one can also use acupuncture and Chinese herbs to reach the causal level of this problem, especially when the roots are on the psycho-emotional level.

Meanwhile, prostaglandin insufficiency can be treated symptomatically by taking specific oils and/or their supplements, which bypass steps in the conversion process so that the prostaglandins can be created more directly. If you are in one of these risk groups or have a Liver syndrome according to acupuncture, you should take these oils and/or their supplements until the underlying cause is corrected. In general, different oils are needed to address the different LNA (Omega 3) and LA (Omega 6) problems. For PGE_3 (and Omega 3) deficiency, take Black Currant Seed oil, Fish oil, or Krill oil because they supply the SDA or EPA that converts more easily to PGE_3. Krill oil is especially useful because its Omega 3 FAs are attached to phospholipids so that the Omega 3s in Krill oil are more readily absorbed. Krill oil is especially useful when the Omega 3 deficiency symptoms are more psycho-emotionally involved. For PGE_1 (and Omega 6) deficiency, take Borage oil and/or Evening Primrose oil because they supply the GLA that converts more easily to PGE_1. Black Currant Seed oil has the advantage of correcting the deficiencies for both PGE_1 and PGE_3. It has the same amount of GLA as EPO, but less than Borage oil. Hempseed oil is also a good alternative.

- Omega 3 Deficiency: Black Currant Seed oil and/or Fish or Krill oils
- Omega 6 Deficiency: Borage oil and/or Evening Primrose oil
- Both Omega 3 and Omega 6 Deficiency: Black Currant Seed oil and/or Hempseed oil

EFA Maintenance

For long-term usage beyond the initial correction stage, one must consume an acceptable ratio between Omega 3 and Omega 6 EFAs. Historically, this ratio was around 1:2. Today, most authorities generally widen the range from 1:1 to 1:5.[b] However, because of the over-reliance on PUFAs during the twentieth century, most Americans have an extremely unbalanced and unhealthy ratio of between 1:20 and 1:50. This imbalance leads to a severe Omega 3 deficiency that fosters the development of many chronic diseases, all of which depend on increasing the Omega 3:Omega 6 ratio for their reversal.

---

[a] Deficient nutrients related to the inability to convert prostaglandins from EFAs include: vitamins B_3, B_6, C, and E, zinc and magnesium. These nutrients are stripped from whole foods during food processing and are all contained in more than adequate amounts in a Natural Foods diet of unrefined grains, legumes, vegetables, nuts, seeds, fruits, and sea vegetables. The SAD, with its reliance on refined and industrialized food, is largely responsible for these EFA conversion problems.
[b] Hempseed oil contains the ideal ratio of 1:3.

For example, a higher Omega 3 ratio is generally associated with reducing the risk of breast cancer. While a 1:2.5 ratio has been known to reduce cell proliferation in patients with colorectal cancer the lower Omega 3 ratio of 1:4 had no effect. Furthermore, a 1:2 or 1:3 ratio is known to reduce inflammation in rheumatoid arthritis and a 1:4 ratio is associated with a 70 percent reduction of total mortality in cardiovascular disease. Finally, a 1:5 ratio is beneficial for asthma sufferers while a 1:10 ratio has adverse consequences. As you can see, the optimal ratio varies from condition to condition as well as from person to person. Because this ratio was so imbalanced during the last century, some researchers recommend reversing the generally accepted optimal ratio from 1:2 to 2:1 until the Omega 3 deficiency is corrected (a period of roughly six months).

In addition, other oils should be regularly consumed for their Vitamin E, lecithin, AOs and MUFAs, MCFAs and anti-infectious fatty acids, and other phyto-nutrients. Examples for these categories include:

- Omega 6-rich Oils: Grape Seed, Sunflower Seed and Sesame Seed oils
- Balance between the Omega 3s and 6s: Hempseed oil and Black Currant Seed oil
- Vitamin E: Almond oil, Grape Seed oil, Wheat Germ oil, and Krill oil
- Lecithin and Phospholipids: Soybean oil as well as Flaxseed oil, Hempseed oil, and Rice Bran oil, but especially Krill oil
- AOs and Omega 9s: Olive oil, Macadamia oil
- MCFAs and anti-infectious fatty acids: Coconut oil

Several companies make good blends of these oils to make it easier to obtain such a variety in a smaller overall quantity on a regular basis without becoming rancid by sitting on the shelf too long. The advantage in using these blends is that you can purchase a needed balance of all the oils in an amount small enough that can be used up before the oils go rancid, usually a period of about six weeks. The disadvantage is that different people need different amounts and proportions of these oils for different activities and at different times of their life. One constant blend will provide an arbitrary "ball park" balance but will not be able to account for these personal needs and important differences. Therefore, one should supplement the blend with other different oils over the course of time as reason dictates or intuition calls. Start out by purchasing small 8-ounce bottles of two to three of these different oils and rotate through the list as you finish them. Remember to use the EFA ratio guidelines given below.

Strategies in Choosing Oils for Long-Term Use
General Criteria

In choosing edible fats and oils for long-term use, we need to consider the following eight criteria:

1. The FA balance between SaFAs, MUFAs, and PUFAs
2. The balance between vegetarian and carnivorous food in the diet
3. The EFA balance between the Omega 3s and Omega 6s
4. The care with which the EFAs are produced and handled
5. Whether the fat or oil source is natural or man-made
6. Whether the fat or oil source is ecologically sustainable
7. Whether the fat or oil source has an acknowledged and verifiable history
8. The ability of the natural, unrefined oil to withstand the heat produced in cooking

The FA balance between SaFAs, MUFAs, and PUFAs has to do with individual activity, physical location, and type of diet, that is, whether the diet is vegetarian or carnivorous. The more Yin animal foods you eat and the greater the SaFAs in your diet, the more Yang physical activity you need to balance the strong Yin embodied in these foods. People living in tropical or subtropical climates where the weather is mild and relatively unchanging should consume relatively more MUFAs. In contrast, people living in temperate climate zones where the weather changes more dramatically from one season to the next, should have a greater consumption of SaFAs and PUFAs.

In modern society, carnivorous diets that include fish tend to have a greater portion of natural EFAs than vegetarian diets. While vegetarians can find sources for these EFAs, they will not be as commonly found because the traditional sources have become marginalized, as in the case of Flaxseed oil and Hempseed oil. More special attention will have to be given for vegetarians in order to supply these EFA needs. At this time, these oils are NOT available in restaurants so you need to carry them with you as you would a nutritional supplement when traveling. Don't forget! Take them regularly like medicine so you will stay out of trouble.

The balance between Omega 3 and Omega 6 EFAs involves both quantity and proportion. People need to get enough EFAs directly through diet because they can not make them in the body like they can SaFAs and MUFAs. We need these EFAs because of the three different prostaglandins they produce—PGE_1 and PGE_2 from Omega 6 and PGE_3 from Omega 3. PGE_1 and PGE_3 are relaxing and expanding in function (Yang) while PGE_2 is tightening and constricting (Yin). We need both in a proportion where the Yang slightly outweighs the Yin. To achieve this balance, the Omega 3 ratio needs to be high—close to 1:1, 1:2, or even 1:3. When the Omega 3 ratio gets too low, the amount of Yin (constriction and structuralization) becomes too great for the Yang (organic function) to sustain. When this imbalance occurs, the stage is set for the Yin to overcome the Yang, a condition that increases the risk for degenerative disease. In contrast, the higher the Omega 3 proportion gets, the greater the Yang. More Yin diseases like cancer and heart disease generally need more Yang oils and therefore higher than balanced ratios.

The quality of EFAs also needs to be good. EFAs are especially prone to destruction by food refining; pressing with too much heat, pressure, or oxygen; and improper storage. Destructive storage practices include storing them for excessive periods of time in the presence of light or oxygen (do not leave them uncapped and out of the cupboard or refrigerator) and storing them in plastic bottles or even clear glass bottles that allow light to enter and ruin the oil. EFAs need to be protected from heat, light, and oxygen or they will go rancid and cause more harm than good. Rancid or refined EFAs oxidize easily and then become major factors in creating degenerative disease.

Choosing an Oil

Carnivores have an easier time of finding good sources of EFAs and keeping the Omega 3s and 6s balanced. Fish and Fish oil are readily available. The Omega 3 to Omega 6 ratio of Fish oil, at 12:1, makes it a reasonably good source to balance the plentiful sources of Omega 6s in our society. People using fish, Fish oil, and/or Krill oil still need to keep their Omega 3s and 6s balanced by taking additional sources of good quality Omega 6. For vegetarians, however, the problem of acquiring and balancing EFAs is another matter. Vegetarian sources of the Omega 3 EFA are more difficult to find and are entirely absent from the SAD. Vegetarian sources high in Omega 3 include Black Currant Seed oil (16%), Flaxseed oil (60%), Hempseed oil (19%), Pumpkinseed oil (14%), Soybean oil (8%), Walnut oil (12%), and Chia seeds (49%). Of these six, only one, Hempseed oil, has a near perfect EFA ratio.

Figure 27: High Omega 3 Sources and their Ratios

Ratio	Source	Percentage of Omega 3	Ratio
High	Krill Oil*	27%	15:1
	Fish Oil	36%	12:1
	Flaxseed Oil*	60%	4:1
	Chia Seeds	49%	3:1
Balanced	Macadamia Oil	.28%	1:1
	Hempseed Oil	19%	1:3
	Black Currant Seed oil	16%	1:4
Low	Pumpkinseed Oil	14%	1:7
	Soybean Oil	8%	1:8
	Walnut Oil	12%	1:10

The four oils in the white rows in the table above represent the Four Primary Oils with an over-abundance of Omega 3 and therefore a high Omega 3 ratio. They are most suitable for balancing other oils consumed in the diet that are high in Omega 6s as well as for correcting Omega 3 deficiencies. Of the two oils marked with an asterisk, Flaxseed oil has the highest Omega 3 content.

Flaxseed oil and Krill oil are most suitable for restoring Omega 3 deficiencies. While Krill oil has a lower percentage of Omega 3, it is nevertheless very efficient in building up Omega 3 reserves because its Omega 3s (being attached to phospholipids) are very easily absorbed.

Two criteria for using one or more of these oils as an EFA base from which to build a healthy edible oil regimen include

1. Pick the oil with the ratio you need.
2. Pick the oil with the highest amount of Omega 3.
3. Use any of the above oils in combination with Omega 6 PUFAs.

Among the high Omega 3 sources, Hempseed oil is the best all around choice for Regular use. Hempseed oil has a good amount of Omega 3s, has the best EFA ratio at 1:3, and is also a source of the important EFA derivatives—GLA and SDA. In addition, hempseeds contain all ten of the essential amino acids and are therefore a complete plant-based protein. They are also very vitamin and mineral rich. Hemp, as well as flax, is also a historically viable food source as it has been used historically as a Regular Omega 3 source. Therefore, Hempseed oil can be used as the Regular Omega 3 oil for long-term use, ESPECIALLY for those on a vegetarian diet.

The remaining high Omega 3 oils can be divided into two categories—those that contain a relatively high Omega 3 ratio (Krill oil, Fish oil, Flaxseed oil, and Chia Seeds), and those that have a high Omega 3 content but an insufficient Omega 3 ratio—Pumpkinseed Oil, Soybean Oil, and Walnut Oil. Krill oil, Fish oil, Flaxseed oil, and Chia Seeds have all been used historically as Omega 3 sources in different regions of the globe—Krill oil in the island country of Japan; Fish oil in the Mediterranean region and Pacific islands; Flaxseed oil in the colder, wetter climates of Europe and North America; and Chia Seeds in the hotter, drier climates of the American Southwest and Mexico. Any of these can be used to either reverse Omega 3 deficiency or balance other oils high in Omega 6.

Krill oil is the best oil for these purposes, especially for sick people, because of its extremely high amount of *easily absorbed* Omega 3s. Fish oil is also good because of its high content of Omega 3 derivatives (EPA and DHA). Flaxseed oil is also very good, especially for vegetarians and people living in colder climates. Chia seeds are good, especially for those living in hotter and drier climates and even more especially for vegetarians.

These Primary Four Omega 3 sources can also be used to supplement Omega 3s in the diet when other PUFAs are being used for different reasons, for example, with Grape Seed oil (a high Omega 6) for cooking as it is one of the better oils to withstand high cooking temperatures or for the repair of free radical damage (used raw) in the arteries and skin. The other oils high in Omega 3s but low in the EFA ratio—Pumpkinseed oil, Soybean oil, and Walnut oil—can also be used for variety on occasion in conjunction with the Primary Four Omega 3 sources to bolster their EFA ratios.

Cooking with vegetable oils is another area where some of the high AO Omega 6 oils are useful. Nevertheless, except for the pressing and refining processes, cooking is where edible unsaturated oils get ruined most easily. While we can certainly use these nourishing oils on top of raw and cooked foods, cooking with oils can offer some unique nutritional benefits because cooking with oils can help change the Yin-Yang quality of the foods we eat. Lightly sautéed vegetables sometimes make stronger food for people with more Yin conditions, especially in colder weather. To lower the risk of destroying good oils, however, choose among those with smoke points above 400°F. A partial list of these high smoke point oils includes Macadamia oil (400-450°F), Hazelnut oil (425°F), Coconut oil (450°F), Grape Seed oil (485°F), Rice Bran oil (495°F), and Avocado oil (520°F). Hazelnut oil and Grape Seed oil have the advantage of growing in a temperate climate, but Coconut and Macadamia oils have the advantage in being very low in Omega 3 PUFAs. Their Omega 3s are also in an acceptable EFA ratio. When using Coconut and Macadamia oils you will not have to worry at all about destroying any precious EFAs, and you will not have to worry about throwing your EFA ratios off either.

Figure 28: FA Features of High Smoke Point Oils

Oil	Smoke Point	Omega 3s	Omega 6s	SaFAs	MUFAs
*Macadamia Oil	400-450°F	.28%	2%	17%	81%
Hazelnut Oil	425°F	1%	16%	8%	75%
*Coconut Oil	450°F	0%	2%	90%	6%
Grape Seed Oil	485°F	1%	72%	11%	16%
Rice Bran Oil	495°F	1%	37%	18%	42%
Avocado Oil	520°F	1%	13%	12%	71%
Note: The oils shaded in grey represent the best picks for heat resistance in cooking due to the synergy of high Smoke Point with high AO and/or MUFA and/or SaFA content..					

*The oils marked with an asterisk represent heat resistant cooking oils with a good Omega 3 ratio.

Cooking oils should generally not have too many EFAs because EFAs are so easily destroyed by heat. All of the high Smoke Point oils are virtually void of Omega 3s and need Omega 3 supplementation with the Four Primary high Omega 3 oils mentioned above. All of these oils have a high MUFA content that gives them extra stability during cooking. The one exception is Coconut oil, which is mostly void of all FAs but SaFAs, a feature that makes it potentially even better for cooking as NONE of the more fragile EFAs or even MUFAs are present. Macadamia oil is also good for cooking for similar reasons—it has virtually NO EFAs and those it does have are in the relatively ideal proportion of 1:1. Avocado oil is good because it has a low percentage of Omega 6s AND has the highest Smoke Point of all. Grape Seed oil is also known to be very heat resistant in spite of its high content of the normally fragile Omega 6s (72%), which are protected by its unusually high AO content. Grape Seed oil nevertheless needs to be supplemented with Omega 3s to balance its high Omega 6 content.

Balancing the Omega 3/Omega 6 Ratio
Getting Started

The most important considerations in using edible oils for health are:

1. They provide the optimal AMOUNT of EFAs.
2. The EFAs they contain are in the ideal RATIO of between 1:1 and 1:3.
3. Any oils used for cooking have a HIGH RESISTANCE TO HEAT.
4. Any oils used for cooking have a low amount EFAs so you will not risk their being destroyed by heat.
5. The EFAs in oils used for cooking are also in the ideal ratio of between 1:1 and 1:3. Otherwise, they must be balanced by taking the appropriate amount of additional Omega 3 sources.

The simplest and most foolproof way to satisfy the above requirements is to use Hempseed and Hempseed oil as your Regular Source of balanced EFAs and to supplement this choice with Coconut and/or Macadamia oil for cooking. Hempseed and Hempseed oil are the only adequate sources of Omega 3s that display the ideal ratio of between 1:1 and 1:3. By taking this food as your Regular Source of Omega 3, you will not have to take additional oils for their EFA content to avoid becoming either Omega 3 or Omega 6 deficient. Both Coconut and Macadamia oils have a high degree of heat tolerance and contain very little EFAs so you will not have to worry about destroying them and what little EFAs they do have are already balanced. You can use these three oils with confidence as the basis of your long-range strategy and, for the most part, will not have to worry about neglecting any of the most important factors in using edible oils for health.

Sustaining Your Edible Oil Practice

The drawback to the simplified strategy mentioned above in getting started is that it does not take personal differences, changes in routine, various cooking methods, or the conditions of your health into account. For these, you will have to add more sources that are either high in Omega 3 or in Omega 6 to keep the ratio of EFAs balanced. Many oils high in Omega 6 contain many important AOs and other phyto-nutrients that make them extremely worth using. The only drawback to using them, other than the care it takes to preserve them, is that they need to be balanced with additional sources of the Four Primary oils high in Omega 3—Krill oil, Fish oil, Flaxseed oil, and Chia Seeds.

The examples given in the chart below are to assist you with this balancing act we all need to perform in using the variety of Omega 6s at our disposal. This chart also clearly shows how deficient in Omega 3s we have become as a society and how we can correct this imbalance. This deficiency is even more exaggerated in vegetarian diets because the vegetarian sources containing Omega 3s in excess of the ideal ratio during the twentieth century have been virtually non-existent. If you are a vegetarian, you probably have little to no sources in your diet and are Omega 3 deficient. Every time you take an oil high in Omega 6s, you need to take one of these Four Primary Omega 3s to bring your ratio back in balance.

The same principle holds true in reverse when using the Four Principle Omega 3 oils over a long-range period, especially Krill and Fish oil. The reason is that while many people rely on these oils to provide them with adequate amounts of Omega 3s and their derivatives (EPA and DHA) they do not realize that after their depleted stock of Omega 3s has increased from these sources, their EFA balance gets progressively out of kilter during the process. As long as these Four Primary sources are used, additional oils high in Omega 6 have to be taken in the correct proportion to the Omega 3s to keep their EFA ratio balanced, especially over the long run.

The following chart is based on 100-gram amounts. When you take a given amount of Omega 6s from the shaded left-hand column, choose the proportion you need from the un-shaded columns to the right, depending on which source you want to use, to obtain the ratio you desire. "X" stands for the proportion you need to take to achieve the ratio that amount indicates. For example with Avocado oil, take one half the amount of Krill oil in addition to the Avocado oil to reach the 1:1 ratio; take one eighth the amount of Krill oil in addition to the Avocado oil to reach the 1:3 ratio.

When balancing regular doses of Krill oil and Fish oil, use the same process in reverse and take high Omega 6 oils in the corresponding proportion to bring the Omega 3 ratio down. For example, one measure of Fish oil needs eight measures of Avocado oil to bring the EFA ratio back into balance.

Table 23: Balancing EFAs with Omega 6 Sources

Omega 6 Oil	Krill Oil	Fish Oil	Flaxseed Oil	Chia Seeds
Avocado Oil	x ½ = 1:1 x ⅛ = 1:3	x ⅛ = 1:3	x 1/6 = 1:1 x ⅛ = 1:2	x ⅓ = 1:1 x ⅛ = 1:2
Borage Oil	x 1 = 1:3	x 1= 1:2 x ¾ = 1:2	x ¾ = 1:1 x ½ = 1:2	x ½ = 1:3
Evening Primrose Oil	x 1 = 1:3	x 1= 1:2	x ¾ = 1:2	x 1 = 1:2
Grape Seed Oil	x 1½ = 1:2 x 1 = 1:3	x 1 = 1:2	x ⅔ = 1:2 x ½ = 1:3	x ¾ = 1:2
Hazelnut Oil	x ¼ = 1:2	x ¼ = 1:2 x ⅛ = 1:3	x 1 = 1:1 x ⅛ = 1:2	x ½ = 1:1 x ⅛ = 1:3
Olive Oil	x ½ = 1:1 x ⅛ = 1:2	x ¼ = 1:1 x ⅛ = 1:2	x ⅛ = 1:1 x 1/16 = 1:2	x ¼ = 1:1 x 1/16 = 1:3
Peanut Oil	x ⅔ = 1:2 x ½ = 1:2	x ½ = 1:2 x ⅓ = 1:3	x ¼ = 1:2	x 1 = 1:1 x ⅓ = 1:2
Pumpkinseed Oil	x ½ = 1:1 x ⅛ = 1:2	x ½ = 1:1 x 1/16 = 1:2	x ⅓ = 1:1 x 1/16 = 1:2	x ½ = 1:1 x 1/16 = 1:2
Rice Bran Oil	x ⅔ = 1:2 x ½ = 1:3	x 1 = 1:1 x ½ = 1:2	x ¾ = 1:1 x ¼ = 1:3	x 1 = 1:1 x ⅓ = 1:2
Sesame Oil	x ¾ = 1:2	x 1 = 1:1 x ½ = 1:2	x 1 = 1:1 x ⅓ = 1:2	x 1 = 1:1 x ½ = 1:2
Soybean Oil	x ¾ = 1:2 x ½ = 1:3	x ½ = 1:2	x 1 = 1:1 x ⅓ = 1:2	x 1 = 1:1 x ⅓ = 1:2
Sunflower Seed Oil	x 1¼ = 1:2 x 1 = 1:1	x 1 = 1:2	x ½ = 1:2 x ⅔ = 1:2	x ¾ = 1:2
Walnut Oil	x ¾ = 1:2	x ⅔ = 1:2	x ⅓ = 1:2	x ½ = 1:2
Wheat Germ Oil	x 1 = 1:2	x ¾ = 1:2	x ½ = 1:2	x ½ = 1:2
Cashew Nuts	x ⅓ = 1:2 x ¼ = 1:3	x ¼ = 1:2	x ⅛ = 1:3	x ¼ = 1:2
Pecans	x ½ = 1:2	x ¼ = 1:3	x ¼ = 1:2	x ⅓ = 1:2 x ¼ = 1:3
Pine Nuts	x 1 = 1:2	x ⅔ = 1:2	x ½ = 1:2	x ½ = 1:3
Pistachios	x ½ = 1:2	x ⅓ = 1:2	x ¼ = 1:2	x ⅓ = 1:2

Re-Evaluating Cholesterol

The conventional cholesterol approach is rushing to put everyone with elevated cholesterol on medication regardless of its effect on overall health. The predetermined goals of the conventional approach account for why cholesterol trials have *overlooked* a more significant connection between high cholesterol and heart disease. The most important distinction to make regarding the cholesterol issue is that cholesterol is only an indicator of the disease process and not the cause. Therefore, they have not only missed the opportunity to accurately define which people with high cholesterol ARE at risk for heart disease, they also have failed to identify the more fundamental causes of heart disease, which continues unchecked. On the other hand, nutritional critics of conventional cholesterol theory understand the fundamental causes; they overlook situations when elevated cholesterol and LDL *are* related to heart disease. A more fundamental problem ignored by conventional cholesterol theory is that many studies conclude that LOW serum cholesterol can be more harmful than high cholesterol for good health!

How can BOTH high and low cholesterol levels cause, or be related to, serious health problems like heart disease? Perhaps this problem could be better solved with a cholesterol theory that seeks dynamic changes rather than stasis in cholesterol levels. In acupuncture, the entire basis of health is dynamic change. In contrast, disease is based on stasis, the inability to change, and stagnation. How could the stasis that is related to artificial cholesterol-lowering practices have anything to do with *promoting* health? The scientific literature shows that both high and low cholesterol can cause heart disease. That these two diverging perspectives have remained un-integrated, shows that a more comprehensive cholesterol theory is called for, one in which the need for a dynamic cholesterol range can be understood and practiced.

To do so we need to define which types of people with high cholesterol and which types of people with low cholesterol would be most likely to develop heart disease and which would not. Such a distinction would not only spare most of the public from the unnecessary side effects of medication, but also would also define more accurately what cholesterol levels indicate and therefore provide more reasonable explanations for why conventional dietary approaches do not work. More importantly, the cheap and simple solution we already have could be accepted!

The failure to lower cholesterol adequately and prevent heart disease by lowering the cholesterol content in food in conjunction with lowering SaFAs through conventional dietary practices is well-established even though it is rarely practiced. While the AMA diet limits total fat by 30 percent, saturated fat to less than 10 percent, and total cholesterol intake to less than 300 mg/dL per day, these reductions have not shown long-term improvement in the lowering of triglycerides or the outcome of heart disease, which continues to progress.[147]

While these methods are, nevertheless, still practiced, they will never lower cholesterol sufficiently nor will they prevent heart disease. The simple reason is that the SaFA content of blood has little bearing on cholesterol and even less on heart disease. Instead of rushing towards medication after failing to lower cholesterol through the SAD, as the conventional medical establishment sanctions, it would be more effective to redefine the role of SaFAs, MUFAs, and PUFAs in regulating cholesterol and preventing heart disease, and find a simpler, safer, and more practical solution instead.

Less conventional, though popular, approaches for preventing heart disease, such as the Mediterranean diet, focus on increasing MUFAs. The Mediterranean diet was modeled after traditional diets of the region where heart disease and other chronic disease rates were remarkably low.[148] The Mediterranean diet is a good natural and whole foods diet emphasizing primarily vegetable foods, a small amount of animal foods, and a very high amount of fat (38 percent of total calories) mostly from olives and Olive oil.[149]

In the context of this natural, whole foods diet, the increase of MUFAs lowers cholesterol and LDL levels, and prevents heart disease. However, this approach is not necessarily consistent or reliable when incorporated into the SAD. Other flaws that affect how MUFAs are used are threefold. The first is that the Mediterranean diet does not consider how FAs inter-relate and so does not incorporate the positive and necessary virtues of saturated and polyunsaturated fatty acids. PUFAs are also well known for their ability to prevent and treat heart disease as well as many other health problems. Because PUFAs are largely bypassed in the Mediterranean Diet (with the exception of cooked fish), the widespread Omega 3 deficiency is ignored. MUFA sources like Olive oil contain very little, if any, Omega 3s. The second reason is that that most of the oils used in these diets are now over-heated through refining and over-cooking and are actually deleterious to health. Many so-called Mediterranean recipes that would normally call for good quality Olive oil either fail to distinguish between good and bad quality Olive oil or, even worse, substitute refined and genetically modified Canola oil instead. For example, "choose a fat rich in MUFAs, like olive oil or canola oil, as often as possible"[150] or in spite of the fact that "Canola oil is devoid of phytochemicals…that offer protective health effects…[it] still ranks just below olive oil."[151]

The third reason is that, while the Mediterranean Diet does (to its credit) promote whole foods, important parts of Mediterranean style diets end up being refined as well. Consumers in the US do not fully realize what whole foods are and so are often scammed by labeling practices used by the food industry. Refined foods play a huge part in the creation of degenerative disease! In fact, the biggest drawback in regulating cholesterol through conventional diet is the insistence by the established health-care system on preserving the use of refined and industrialized food in society.

Natural Cholesterol Regulation

Natural cholesterol regulation theory[a] describes a constantly changing flow in cholesterol levels that helps us adapt to a changing environment. Sometimes we need more cholesterol; sometimes we need less. Sometimes we need to concentrate cholesterol at the periphery; sometimes we need to concentrate it deep within. Our ability to change cholesterol levels and directions by adjusting LDL/HDL ratios naturally is what enables us to survive the changing conditions that life presents.

To understand natural cholesterol regulation fully, we have to grasp and synthesize the following five different concepts:

1. Cholesterol and HDL/LDL levels are regulated by the interplay between the Yin-Yang condition at the Peripheral Tissues of the body and the Yin-Yang condition of the Liver Qi
2. The Yin-Yang of the Peripheral Tissues and the Liver Qi is determined by their FA content (SaFAs, MUFAs, and PUFAs)
3. The state of the Liver Qi has more of an effect on cholesterol levels and especially heart disease than any other factor
4. Healthy Liver Qi is created by consuming good quality natural fats and oils
5. Pathological Liver Qi is created by consuming bad quality industrial fats and oils and other types of refined food as well as by environmental toxins and psycho-emotional trauma

Cholesterol is naturally regulated in the body between the Liver, which is more Yin, and the Peripheral Tissues, which are more Yang. The Liver represents the centripetal (inward) Yin side of this polarity. The skin, the cellular and intra-cellular membranes, and the blood vessels (body parts that are characterized by their position at the periphery of the body as well as their hollow and expanded structure) represent the centrifugal (outward) Yang aspect.

The Liver plays the central role in regulating cholesterol because it makes cholesterol, sends cholesterol into circulation, receives cholesterol back into itself, and helps remove cholesterol from the body. The Liver regulates the inward and outward movement of cholesterol through its Yin, Yang, and Balanced functions. These functions parallel the storage of Blood (and increase of HDL) when the Liver is at rest, its Yin mode, and the release of the stored Blood into the general circulation (in conjunction with LDL) during Liver activity, its Yang mode.

When the Liver is balanced, these two Yin and Yang functions are regulated automatically and cholesterol levels can be thought of as "normally responsive." This definition differs from that of conventional medicine, which defines "normal" cholesterol levels in terms of a static numerical value related to

---

[a] Natural cholesterol regulation theory is a physiological not an epidemiological perspective one because the data available from cholesterol studies is so often skewed.

current and one-sided ideas of cholesterol theory but unrelated to the changing physiological functions and environmental conditions that define life. These conventional ideas are based on the theory that because cholesterol is a major ingredient of arterial plaque, it should be lowered to prevent this buildup. The problem with this approach is that it ignores the reasons why cholesterol builds up in arterial plaque (Liver Qi Imbalance), fails to understand the value of cholesterol fluctuations in determining a healthy Body/Mind, and ironically places too much extra burden on the Liver Qi with its artificial cholesterol-lowering methods, especially pharmaceutical drugs.

Natural cholesterol regulation, in contrast, defines "normal" cholesterol levels by examining both sides of the cholesterol flow—the delivery of cholesterol outward from the liver to the Peripheral Tissues and the inward return of cholesterol from the Peripheral Tissues to the liver. By connecting these two sides of natural cholesterol flow, natural cholesterol regulation shows how cholesterol can be regulated wholistically and redefines "normal" cholesterol as having the capacity to automatically respond to different and necessary physiological, psychosocial, and environmental conditions without becoming locked in the stasis of either high or low extremes.

Cholesterol that is locked in statically high levels can indicate global inflammation of the body as well as Liver Qi Inflammation. Each of these situations that can most definitely lead to heart disease. In contrast, if the Liver Qi is stagnant and unable to release cholesterol, especially in times of stress when it is needed to create stress hormones or bolster immunity, low levels of cholesterol can lead to other serious problems including kidney failure and cancer as well as gastrointestinal problems, and respiratory disease, but also heart failure.

The membranes and vessels at the peripheral pole of this equation also play a role in cholesterol regulation depending on the Yin-Yang type of fatty acids of which they are made. Saturated fatty acids are hard and more structurally oriented (Yin) and tend to move cholesterol, which is also hard, out of the Peripheral Tissues and into the bloodstream to make the Peripheral Tissues more flexible and more functionally oriented (Yang). Polyunsaturated fatty acids, in contrast, are soft (Yang). When the Peripheral Tissues are comprised predominantly of PUFAs, they tend to pull cholesterol from the bloodstream into themselves to make them stronger (Yin). The natural movement of cholesterol swings back and forth between the polarities of the Liver and the Peripheral Tissues like the tide and is influenced by the Yin-Yang condition of each.

Different types of Liver disharmony create various extremes in cholesterol regulation. In acupuncture, the Liver corresponds to the spring season and regulates the spreading of Qi (and Blood) to the periphery (the Yang function of the Liver) and back again (the Yin function). These two movements also correspond to the flow of LDL and HDL—the lipoprotein "taxicabs" that shuttle cholesterol back and forth through the bloodstream between the liver and the periphery of the body. Under normal conditions, the Yin-Yang fatty acid balance at the periphery determines whether cholesterol is needed there or not.

In contrast, abnormal conditions produce the greatest demand for elevated serum cholesterol and LDL. These conditions are determined by the degree of free radical damage done to the Peripheral Tissues due to inflammation caused by the oxidation of fatty acids in conjunction with the loss of antioxidants from refined foods and environmental pollutants. Cholesterol is called into these damaged areas for repair.

A balanced and healthy Liver produces LDL (Yang) when the skin, membranes, and vessels at the periphery (Yang) call for more cholesterol from the Liver and Blood. In contrast, a balanced and healthy Liver produces HDL (Yin) when the skin, membranes, and vessels at the periphery (Yang) need to remove cholesterol stored within them to the Blood where it will be directed back to the Liver and be removed from the body.

Figure 29: Cholesterol Regulation Between Center and Periphery

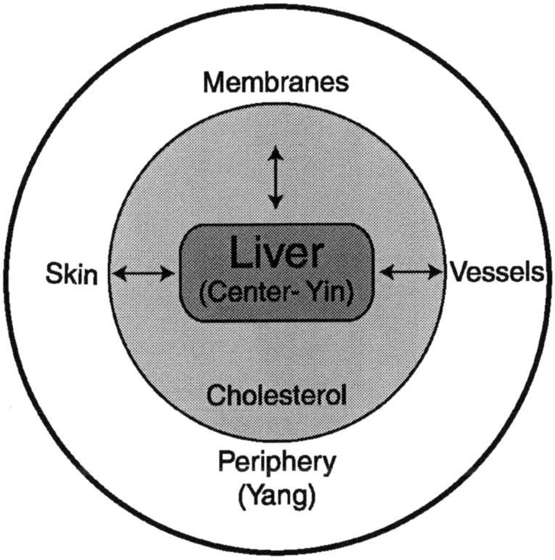

To understand more specifically how this process works, we need to understand how the Yin and Yang fatty acids (SaFAs = Yin, PUFAs = Yang, and MUFAs = Balanced) regulate cholesterol levels at the periphery and also how the various Yin-Yang conditions of the Liver regulate cholesterol levels from the center. But first, we need to examine some basics attributes of Yin-Yang itself.

Yin and Yang

Yang is characterized by light, heat, and outward action. Yin is characterized by dark, cold, and inward action. The Yin-Yang diagram ☯ depicts the relation between these two polarities as they continually interact with each other. Yin changes to Yang and Yang changes to Yin through an infinite and mutually responsive exchange. Yin (the dark half of the diagram) also contains Yang (the light dot within it) while Yang (the light half of the diagram) contains Yin (the dark dot).

Figure 30: Interplay of Yin-Yang Motion

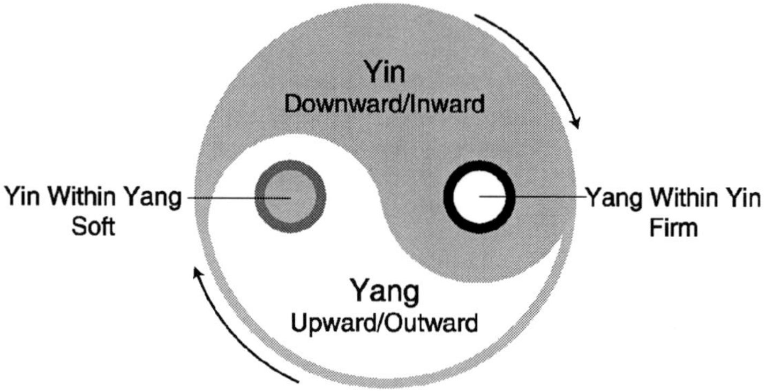

The Yin-Yang diagram depicts these changes by showing how lines of Yin and Yang force constantly change from one direction (clockwise) to the other (counter clockwise) in a way that maintains the integrity of the whole. In these simple changes of direction, one can anticipate the underpinnings of the functional universe as well as the tidal currents of cholesterol flow.

To understand this idea more clearly, imagine tracing the outside of the Yin-Yang diagram in a clockwise direction from the dot on the outer left side (step 1 in the diagram below). After one complete revolution follow the inside "s-shaped" horizontal line (dividing the Yin-Yang diagram into top and bottom halves) from the left-hand side to the opposite right-hand side (step 2) and up around the outside again, but this time in a counter-clockwise direction (step 3). Then continue following the circle counter clockwise back to the starting point on the left side. Resume by following the reversed inside "s-shaped" line to the opposite (right) side again (step 4) and notice that you have reversed direction again by traveling through the circle via the "s-shaped" line. You are now traveling around the circle in a clockwise direction. This reversal depicts the constant change between Yin and Yang, which is symbolized by the figure eight inside of the circle, the symbol of infinite change (step 5). These Yin and Yang changes resemble the permutations of cholesterol as it flows naturally throughout the body between the liver and the Peripheral Tissues. Healthy cholesterol regulation needs to change from an outward to an inward flow and back again in the same way as the changes between day and night!

Figure 31: Yin-Yang Directional Change

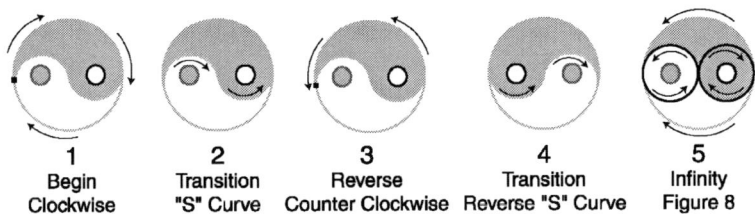

1	2	3	4	5
Begin	Transition	Reverse	Transition	Infinity
Clockwise	"S" Curve	Counter Clockwise	Reverse "S" Curve	Figure 8

Cholesterol Regulation from the Peripheral Tissues

With these Yin-Yang concepts in mind we can now create an association between the Liver (the center) and HDL (the inward-moving lipoprotein) with Yin. Conversely, the Peripheral Tissues including the skin, cell membranes, and blood vessels (as examples of Yang structures) and LDL (the outward-moving lipoprotein) are associated with Yang.

Figure 32: HDL and LDL as the Yin-Yang Function of Cholesterol

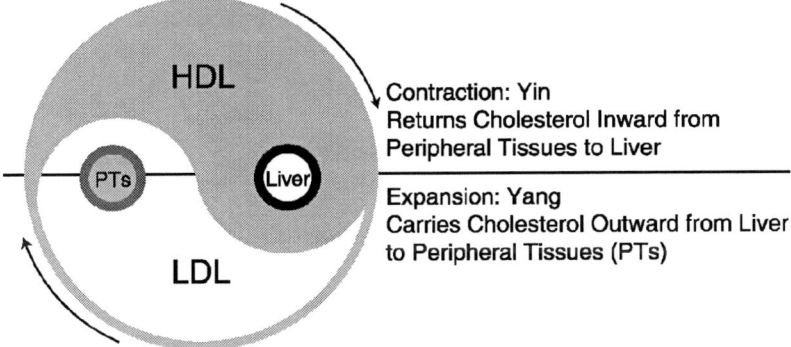

Contraction: Yin
Returns Cholesterol Inward from
Peripheral Tissues to Liver

Expansion: Yang
Carries Cholesterol Outward from Liver
to Peripheral Tissues (PTs)

Now we can add the Yin-Yang polarity between SaFAs and PUFAs to see how they contribute to cholesterol circulation from the periphery. When the Yin (dense, sticky, and hard) SaFAs become a predominant part of the Peripheral Tissues, the similarly hard cholesterol is moved out of the Peripheral Tissues and into the bloodstream where, in a normally healthy Liver Qi situation, it binds with HDL "taxicabs" and returns to the liver. In contrast, when the Yang (light, fluid, and soft) PUFAs become a predominant part of the Peripheral Tissues, the hard cholesterol is called into the Peripheral Tissues for strengthening from the bloodstream and liver via the LDL "taxicabs."[a]

---

[a] In this "Cholesterol Regulation from the Peripheral Tissues" section of this "Natural Cholesterol Regulation" discussion, PUFAs refer ONLY to expeller-pressed, unrefined oils or these quality oils as found in their natural whole

In the figure below, the Yin within Yang protective SaFAs on the left displace accumulated cholesterol in the Peripheral Tissues (PTs), which is then returned to the liver via HDL. SaFAs are dense, sticky, and hard. Their incorporation into the structure of the PTs makes the PTs stronger. In contrast, the Yang within Yin nourishing PUFAs on the right call for more cholesterol from the liver and bloodstream via LDL into the PTs. PUFAs are light, fluid, and soft. When they incorporate into the PTs, the PTs become more functional.

Figure 33: Natural Yin-Yang Cholesterol Conversion

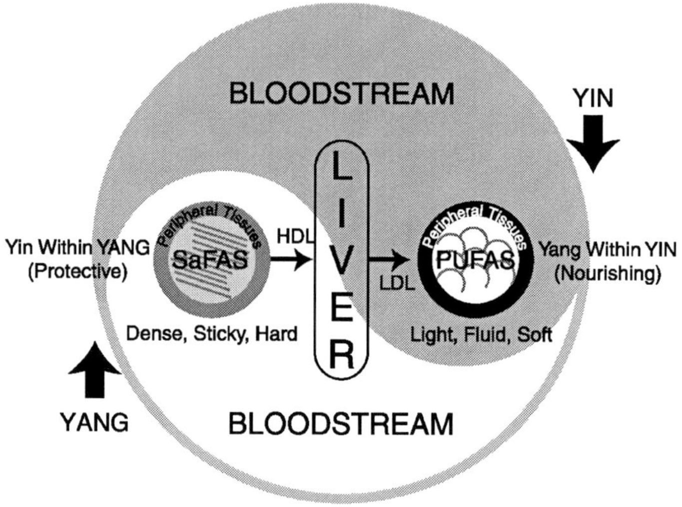

So far we have been discussing normal cycles of cholesterol, those that occur in a healthy state of Liver Qi without Liver Disharmony or artificial drug manipulation. Before continuing, remember that there is really no such thing as "good" and "bad" cholesterol. These are simply terms used by the AHA and the AMA to promote their one-sided agenda and sell drugs. In physiological reality all cholesterol is good in that it provides a function that is necessary and vital for health even when it is involved in the disease process. Even the cholesterol found in atherosclerotic plaque (including oxidized LDL and fatty acids) is used purposefully to heal inflammatory lesions in the arteries formed by free radicals.[a] Cholesterol has one of the most important functions in the body and should not be construed as garbage that gets dumped into the arteries as refuse

---

sources such as in seeds, nuts, fruits, grains, and beans. They do NOT refer to refined, partially hydrogenated, or hydrogenated oils. The effect of these industrial quality oils on cholesterol levels will be examined separately in the following section on "Cholesterol Regulation from Pathological Liver Qi."

[a] See the previous section in the chapter on "The Sterols" called "Cholesterol: A Definition/Function" for a more detailed explanation of the destruction of FAs, LDL, and cholesterol by oxidation and free radicals.

that we must be rid of. Cholesterol plays a pivotal and dynamic role in communicating between various Yin and Yang functions and parts of the body. These include the Yin-Yang interplay of the Liver in relation to the fatty acid composition of the Peripheral Tissues and the balance maintained there between saturated and unsaturated fatty acids. The figure below depicts the normal ebb and flow of cholesterol in the body depending on the SaFA/PUFA content of the membranes and vessels.

Figure 34: Cholesterol Regulation with a Healthy Liver

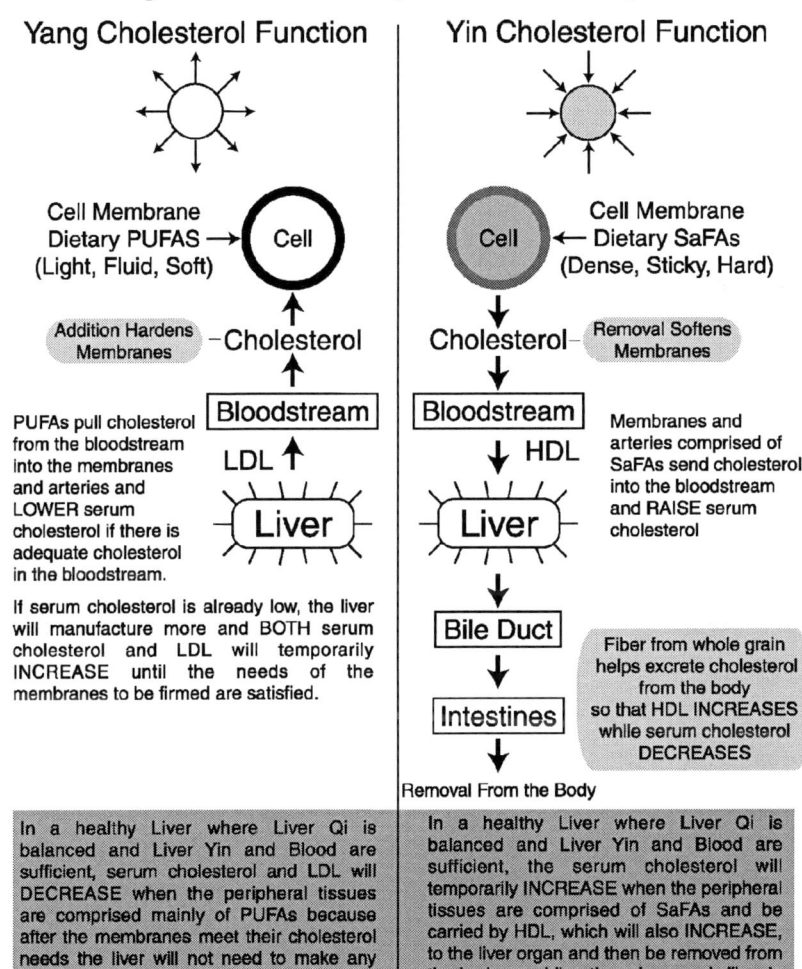

Remember that we are momentarily separating peripheral tissue structure such as the skin, cell membranes, and blood vessels from Liver Qi function in the regulation of cholesterol. By doing so, we are then able to discuss the Yin-Yang influence of Peripheral Tissues separately from those of the Liver. Once these issues are understood, we can put the Yin and Yang of the Peripheral Tissues and Liver Qi back together again to see how they interact. This tactic will help unify the different approaches to cholesterol regulation by creating a more comprehensive and unified perspective.

Triglycerides, [a] as well as cholesterol, are needed to regulate the structure of these Peripheral Tissues. SaFAs and added cholesterol make the Peripheral Tissues hard, strong, and protective while PUFAs make them soft, flexible, and functional. MUFAs are in between. The flexibility of the Peripheral Tissues needs to be constantly regulated in response to the internal and external environment. When the Peripheral Tissues are too hard from a preponderance of SaFAs, cholesterol in them is moved to the bloodstream so that serum cholesterol and HDL are increased. If Liver Qi is well regulated, this elevated serum cholesterol will be transferred to the intestines. If the intestines are well balanced and if there is sufficient fiber in the food supply, preferably from a high percentage of whole grain in the diet, the cholesterol will then be removed from the body.

In contrast, when the Peripheral Tissues are too soft from a preponderance of the softer PUFAs, cholesterol is pulled from the blood stream and into the peripheral structures to strengthen them. From the perspective of the Peripheral Tissues, PUFAs may tend to raise LDL initially depending on the serum cholesterol level and then slightly lower serum cholesterol as it is pulled into the Peripheral Tissues.

MUFAs, which are in between hard and soft, exert more of a homeostatic influence on the direction of cholesterol movement and the balance of LDL and HDL. MUFAs do not place unnecessary demands for cholesterol to be moved into or out of the Peripheral Tissues. Nor do they over stimulate the Yin or Yang functions of Liver Qi. These reasons are why the Mediterranean diet, which is so high in MUFAs, is touted for maintaining healthy cholesterol levels. When MUFAs are added to the diet of those previously eating a predominance of SaFAs, the serum cholesterol and HDL will slightly decrease. For those accustomed to a predominance of PUFAs in the diet, the addition of MUFAs will lower LDL slightly because the Peripheral Tissues will not need as much cholesterol. Remember, these guidelines only hold true from the perspective of the Peripheral Tissues when the overall condition of the Liver Qi is temporarily ignored.

Let us now examine the effect of eating three representative foods from these FA categories on cholesterol levels. Butter is representative of a food high in SaFAs (68%), Olive oil is representative of a food high in MUFAs (72%), and Flaxseed oil is representative of a food high in PUFAs (74%). These amounts are all high levels and are all relatively equal. Imagine then, if you will, three

---

[a] SaFAs, MUFAs, and PUFAs.

different people eating a diet limited to sandwiches comprised of each of these three foods to see how cholesterol levels will be affected. To keep the function of the Liver and intestines optimal, we will make the sandwiches only from whole-wheat bread.

Whole-wheat sandwiches spread with butter (a whole foods diet high in SaFAs) will tend to move cholesterol out of the Peripheral Tissues and into the bloodstream so that both serum cholesterol and HDL are somewhat increased. Because the sandwiches are of whole-wheat though, the serum cholesterol will stabilize in the lower mid-range as the cholesterol is removed by the intestines.

Whole-wheat sandwiches dipped in Flaxseed oil (a whole foods diet high in PUFAs) will temporarily raise LDL but lower serum cholesterol somewhat as the cholesterol moves out of the bloodstream and into the Peripheral Tissues. The slightly elevated LDL with unrefined PUFAs helps strengthen and tone the Peripheral Tissues and helps stimulate immunity and does NOT put one at greater risk for heart disease.

Lastly, whole-wheat sandwiches dipped in Olive oil (a whole foods diet high in MUFAs) will tend to create a slightly moderate serum cholesterol while equalizing LDL and HDL because the Peripheral Tissues will be relatively balanced and will not need to adjust their cholesterol content.[a]

---

[a] While MUFAs have a definite balancing effect on cholesterol levels, they lack the stronger dynamic Yin-Yang range available from SaFAs and PUFAs. Although this balanced characteristic is beneficial in a milder Mediterranean climate, it is not *as* desirable in a temperate climate where variations in the hardness and softness of Peripheral Tissue structure needs to be more varied. In winter, for example, the Peripheral Tissues should be harder and more comprised of SaFAs while in summer they should be softer and more comprised of PUFAs. The Liver helps to regulate the FA content of the PTs naturally providing the FA content of the diet is appropriate to the temperate zone where it is eaten.

Figure 35: Cholesterol Levels from FA Content in Peripheral Tissues

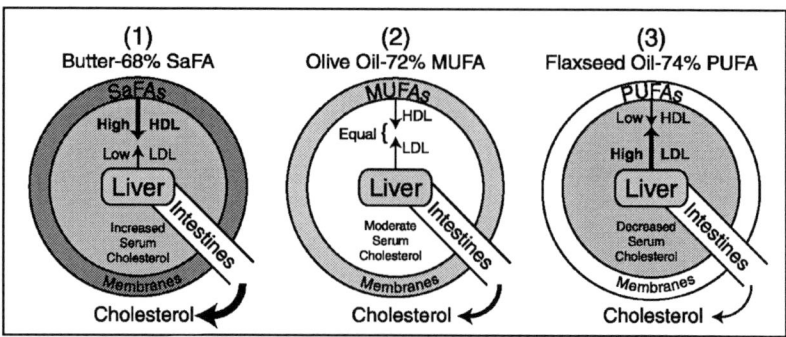

(1) High HDL, Slightly Increased Serum Cholesterol
   (SaFAs Remove Cholesterol from Peripheral Tissues
   While the Liver Moves Cholesterol to the Intestines
   and Out of the Body)
(2) Equal LDL/HDL, Moderate Serum Cholesterol
   (Cholesterol Plays a Lesser Role in Both Peripheral Tissues & Liver)
(3) High LDL, Slightly Decreased Serum Cholesterol
   (Liver Moves Cholesterol from Bloodstream to Peripheral Tissues)

Cholesterol Regulation with Normal Liver Qi

In reality, however, dietary consumption of FAs also affects the balance of Liver Qi. Only when the FA content of Peripheral Tissues is understood in light of Liver Qi imbalance can the effect of diet on cholesterol be fully understood. The three triglycerides have a similar effect on the Liver Qi as they do on the Peripheral Tissues. The hard SaFAs tend to block Liver Qi so that cholesterol can not be easily absorbed by the liver and sent to the intestines where it can be removed from the body. The result is that serum cholesterol is slightly increased. In contrast, the soft PUFAs tend to relax Liver Qi so that the effect by the PUFAs on the Peripheral Tissues in raising LDL is greatly tempered while the serum cholesterol is lowered even more. In the same way that MUFAs tend to balance the flexibility of the Peripheral Tissues, they also tend to balance Liver Qi so that while LDL and HDL are equalized, the serum cholesterol becomes even more moderate.

Figure 36: Regulation of Peripheral Tissue and Liver by FA Content

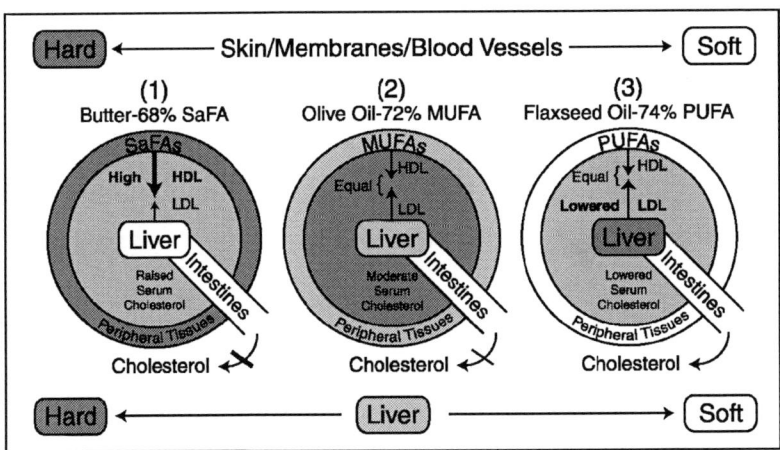

Arrow Length: LDL/HDL Flow as Determined by Membrane Structure
Arrow Width: LDL/HDL Flow as Determined by Liver Response

(1) Elevation of HDL as SaFAs Remove Cholesterol from Membranes
Countered by Liver Response Producing Stagnation Blocking HDL
Overall Effect: Slight Raising of Serum Cholesterol

(2) Moderate Serum Cholesterol
as Cholesterol Stabilizes in the Peripheral Tissues & Liver

(3) Slight Raising of LDL as Liver Sends Cholesterol to Membranes
Countered by Relaxation of the Liver, and Lowering of LDL Production
and Serum Cholesterol

Cholesterol Regulation from Pathological Liver Qi

No matter what the Yin-Yang balance between SaFAs and PUFAs is at the membrane level, abnormal Liver conditions, where the Liver gets stuck in either its Yin or Yang functions, will either RAISE or LOWER serum cholesterol *and* LDL to the most significant pathological degree. The diagram below summarizes cholesterol functions from the previous diagram in terms of the Peripheral Tissues and defines how imbalances of the Liver will affect cholesterol levels.

Figure 37: Cholesterol Regulation with Liver Disharmony

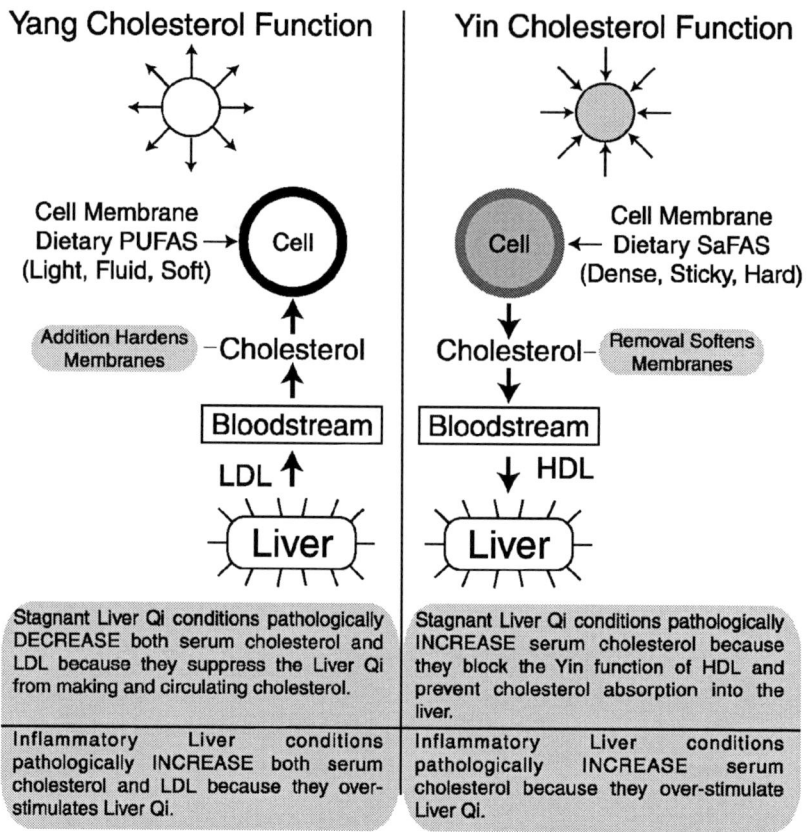

The three main conditions of Liver imbalance relevant to cholesterol levels and heart disease are: Blazing Liver Fire, Arrogant Liver Yang, and Stagnant Liver Qi. Blazing Liver Fire and Arrogant Liver Yang are both inflammatory conditions in the body that over-stimulate LDL production and also create global inflammatory conditions that pathologically increase the need for cholesterol at the local level of the membranes and vessels.[a] Usually, Liver

---

[a] In acupuncture, inflammatory symptoms of Blazing Liver Fire include high fever without cause, restless and agitated sleep, and insomnia; heat sensations in the head with a flushed face; various bleeding symptoms; red, swollen, and painful eyes; conjunctivitis; nose bleeds; coughing with blood; dark, scanty, painful, and sometimes bloody urination (where the Heat moves downwards); urethral discharge; and inflammation of the female sexual organs. Inflammatory symptoms of Arrogant Liver Yang include periodic heat flushes in the head and

Inflammatory conditions are associated with the type of elevated cholesterol that forms atherosclerotic plaque. Blazing Liver Fire is a toxic Full Heat inflammatory condition while Arrogant Liver Yang is a low grade inflammatory condition arising from insufficiency of both Liver Yin and Liver Blood. Both of these inflammatory conditions can be involved in coronary artery disease. Blazing Liver Fire can lead to hemorrhagic stroke while Arrogant Liver Yang can lead to an inflammatory condition of the arterial walls leading to cholesterol deposition and the buildup of plaque. Stagnant Liver Qi conditions block the movement of Blood as well as cholesterol in and out of the Liver. Therefore, serum cholesterol levels pathologically INCREASE with high SaFA diets in conjunction with Stagnant Liver Qi while serum cholesterol and LDL levels pathologically DECREASE with highly refined PUFA diets and Stagnant Liver Qi.

Figure 38: Liver Conditions Associated with Cholesterol Regulation

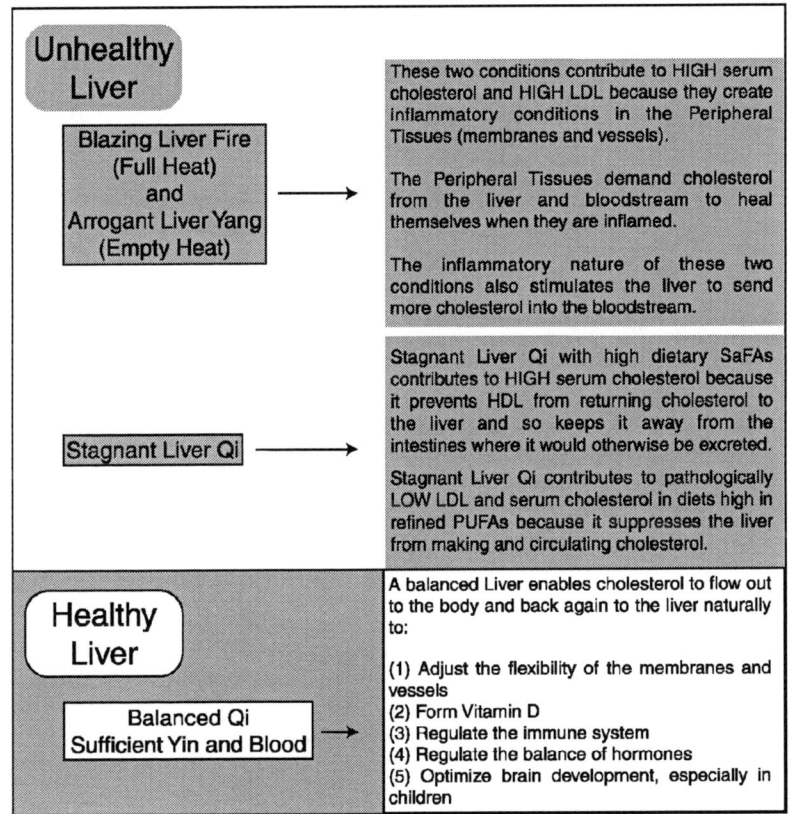

face; reddish eyes; hypertension; ear infections; acute conjunctivitis; hyperthyroidism; bleeding of the upper respiratory tract; and acute nephritis.

Dennis Willmont © 2005; All Rights Reserved   215

While the effect of triglyceride consumption (SaFAs, MUFAs, and PUFAs) on the Peripheral Tissues and Liver Qi function will only have a moderate affect on cholesterol levels,[a] the balance of Liver Qi from other causes will affect cholesterol levels MUCH MORE substantially. Based on the macrobiotic section of the Framingham Study, carnivorous food high in SaFAs will raise serum cholesterol almost 20 percent when added in very modest amounts. Therefore, if you are a vegetarian with a serum cholesterol level of 220 mg/dL (an unlikely high level), carnivorous foods will raise your cholesterol levels to 264 mg/dL. In contrast, if you are a meat eater with a serum cholesterol of 220 mg/dL and switch to a vegetarian based macrobiotic diet, you can expect to lower your serum cholesterol to 176 mg/dL. These differences are based on a moderate addition or subtraction of animal food relative to a vegetarian macrobiotic diet. These "moderate" dietary changes will also apply to a carnivorous diet so that the serum cholesterol differences will be even greater depending on the amount of meat increased or decreased.

Liver Inflammation and Liver Qi Stagnation are the Liver Qi imbalances that affect cholesterol levels the most. Liver Inflammation promotes pathologically HIGH serum cholesterol in BOTH SaFA and PUFA based diets. Stagnant Liver Qi promotes HIGH serum cholesterol with SaFAs and pathologically LOW serum cholesterol and LDL with PUFAs.

In the SaFA scenario discussed above in Figure 34, Liver Inflammation will raise an otherwise minor LDL level and both Liver Inflammation and Liver Stagnation will block HDL from returning cholesterol to the liver. The result will be very high levels of serum cholesterol, especially with Liver Inflammation as it over-stimulates cholesterol production.

In the PUFA scenario, the over-stimulated Liver Qi will significantly raise LDL with Liver Inflammation, while the serum cholesterol will also rise, but not quite as strongly as in the SaFA scenario since the Peripheral Tissues comprised of PUFAs will absorb some of the serum cholesterol excess.[b] Stagnant Liver Qi in a PUFA scenario will suppress LDL and the needed cholesterol so that the Peripheral Tissues will be more susceptible to hypo functioning and infection. They will not be as resistant or protected as they would be with cholesterol in them.

In the MUFA scenario, LDL will also INCREASE but not as much as in the PUFA scenario because the LDL stimulated by the MUFAs is lower to begin with. Expeller-pressed, unrefined MUFAs and PUFAs are, however, unlikely to be associated with pathological Liver Qi because these quality oils

---

[a] This is to say that good quality expeller-pressed, unrefined MUFAs and PUFAs will only have a moderate affect on cholesterol levels.

[b] A natural healing trick to get the skin to absorb and therefore remove cholesterol from the bloodstream is to brush the skin daily from head to toe with a coarse-bristled brush. Japanese vegetable brushes found at Japanese food stores are best.

are healing to the liver. Pathological Liver Qi conditions are more apt to be associated with industrial quality vegetable oils because they are one of the primary agents of Liver Qi pathology.

Rather than thinking "good" and "bad" cholesterol, the more accurate and practical approach is to think "good" and "bad" fats and oils. Good fats are natural, expeller-pressed, and unrefined regardless of whether they are saturated, monounsaturated, or polyunsaturated. Bad fats and oils are industrially refined, hydrogenated, and partially hydrogenated.

Figure 39: Liver Inflammatory Conditions and Cholesterol

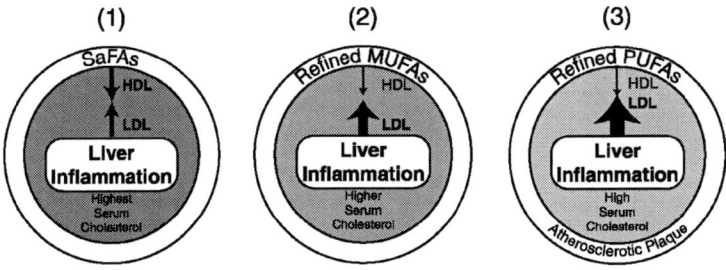

(1) Highest Serum Cholesterol with Equal LDL/HDL
    (Over-Active Liver & Membranes Add Cholesterol to Bloodstream)
(2) Higher Serum Cholesterol and LDL from Over-Active Liver
(3) High Serum Cholesterol with Highest LDL from Most Over-Active Liver

In other words, conditions of pathological Liver Inflammation create the highest levels of serum cholesterol and LDL. The highest pathological serum cholesterol occurs when a diet high in SaFAs interacts with Liver Inflammation. The highest pathological LDL level occurs when the same Liver Inflammation interacts with a diet high in industrial quality PUFAs—these are the "bad" fats and oils. Liver Qi Excess is not likely to occur when natural expeller-pressed unrefined PUFAs are consumed! These are the "good" fats and oils. Liver Qi Excess will most likely occur only when the PUFAs are of industrial quality.[a] Pescatore blames inflammation on an imbalance between Omega 6s and 3s where the 6s outnumber the 3s.[152] The more common and significant way Omega 6s cause inflammation is when they are industrialized or when they become rancid or overheated through cooking. In general, good quality, fresh Omega 6s decrease tissue inflammation. **These Liver Inflammatory conditions are also associated with a high degree of global inflammation. Therefore, they are also MOST responsible for those situations when high levels of serum cholesterol and LDL DO relate to an increase in cardiovascular disease.**

---

[a] Exceptions to this rule are listed in the last Figure of this section, "Causes of Liver Imbalance and De-Regulation of Cholesterol."

217

Good Oils, Bad Oils

In contrast, Stagnant Liver Qi inhibits cholesterol circulation, which then presupposes the body and its organs to hypo-function and infectious disease, imbalances that can lead to gastrointestinal problems, respiratory disease, AND heart failure due to ischemia.

Figure 40: Liver Stagnation and Cholesterol

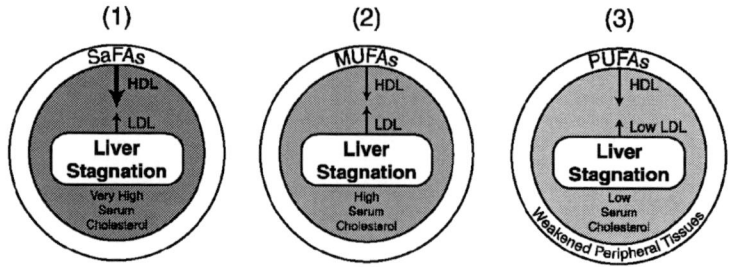

(1) Very High Serum Cholesterol
   (Liver Unable to Absorb Cholesterol from Bloodstream)
(2) High Serum Cholesterol
   (Liver Unable to Absorb Cholesterol from Bloodstream)
(3) Pathologically Low Serum Cholesterol and LDL
   (Stagnant Liver Qi Suppresses Cholesterol Production & Transportation
   Creating High Susceptibility to Stress and Infections)

Figure 41: Liver Dysfunction, Cholesterol Levels, and Cardiovascular Disease

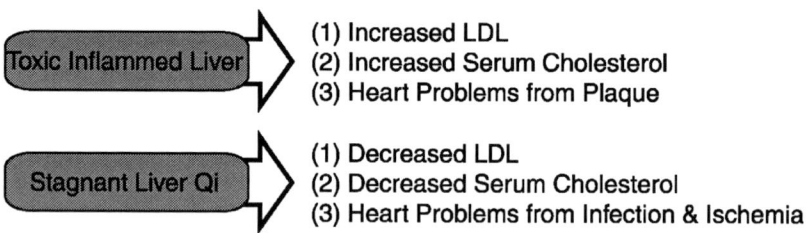

Causes of Cholesterol Imbalance

Other than psycho-emotional trauma and environmental pollution, the overwhelming cause of both cholesterol imbalance and Liver dysfunctions is refined food—the Four Whites. The refining process splits the valuable Yin and Yang components of food into fragmented parts so they are less likely to nourish the body in a sustained and harmonious way. The Yin parts (vitamins and minerals) are usually discarded or sold back to the consumer as nutritional supplements at a profit for the food industry. These contain many of the valuable AOs that normally restrict the Yang functions of food to useful purposes. These Yang parts are called free radicals once they are separated from the organic whole. At this point they now ravage the body causing arterial inflammation and plaque buildup. In addition, some refined food, especially refined vegetable oils, build up excessively and create functional stagnation by inhibiting organic function. In acupuncture, this process is known as Stagnant Liver Qi as discussed above.

Figure 42: Oxidized Food, Cholesterol, and Degenerative Disease

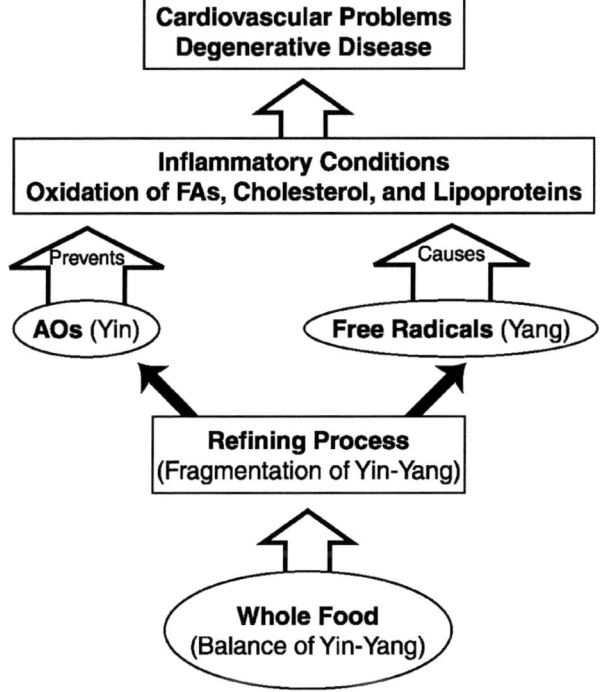

Common causes for these unhealthy Liver conditions and their associated imbalance in cholesterol regulation are given in the figure below.

Figure 43: Causes of Liver Imbalance and De-Regulation of Cholesterol

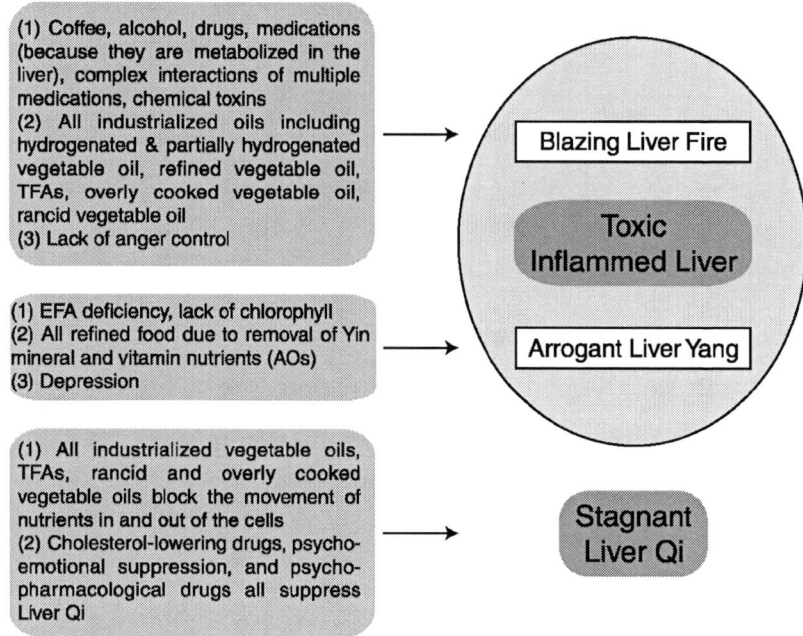

(1) Coffee, alcohol, drugs, medications (because they are metabolized in the liver), complex interactions of multiple medications, chemical toxins
(2) All industrialized oils including hydrogenated & partially hydrogenated vegetable oil, refined vegetable oil, TFAs, overly cooked vegetable oil, rancid vegetable oil
(3) Lack of anger control

(1) EFA deficiency, lack of chlorophyll
(2) All refined food due to removal of Yin mineral and vitamin nutrients (AOs)
(3) Depression

(1) All industrialized vegetable oils, TFAs, rancid and overly cooked vegetable oils block the movement of nutrients in and out of the cells
(2) Cholesterol-lowering drugs, psycho-emotional suppression, and psycho-pharmacological drugs all suppress Liver Qi

Blazing Liver Fire

Toxic Inflammed Liver

Arrogant Liver Yang

Stagnant Liver Qi

Summation

We should realize that within the context of the SAD the amount of dietary cholesterol is not as important in regulating cholesterol levels as is the balance between SaFAs and PUFAs and ESPECIALLY the overall balance of the Liver itself. While the Framingham studies prove conclusively that whole grain, whole food, and vegetarian diets will lower cholesterol substantially, no evidence exists that any modification of the SAD will change cholesterol levels more than a few points and certainly no where near the amount that could account for the tremendous differences of cholesterol levels in the public-at-large. Cholesterol levels range widely from 126 mg/dl for macrobiotic groups to 400+ mg/dl for those with hypercholesterolemia to 220 mg/dl for the average quasi-healthy person on the SAD. Conventional medicine levels set by the National Heart, Lung, and Blood Institute considers a serum cholesterol level above 240 mg/dL to be high; between 200 and 239 mg/dL is considered borderline high; and anything below 200 mg/dL is considered desirable. Most cholesterol levels in the Mediterranean region during the 1960s were below 200 mg/dL.[153] LDL below 130 mg/dL and HDL above 35 mg/dL are considered normal.[154]

Conventional medicine uses genetic variance to account for this difference and ignores the more simple and obvious relation to chemical toxins and industrialized food. This bias is easy to understand once one realizes that the same chemical companies that pollute the environment also run the food industry and the pharmaceutical companies that then control the practice of medicine.

While serum cholesterol levels between normal vegetarians and normal meat eaters may vary,[a] the relevance of these differences to heart disease can be minimized as long as the general diet is based on whole food and plenty of vegetables in a wide variety are included.[b] What accounts for the tremendous range of cholesterol levels among non-whole foods eaters is the SAD itself.[c] People eating the SAD, which is high in refined food and industrial quality fatty acids, in addition to those who over-heat fats and especially vegetable oils in cooking, will most likely develop Liver Qi imbalance that will lead to further imbalances in cholesterol levels. In fact, the primary physiological cause for Liver Qi imbalance IS industrial quality fats and oils (the "bad" oils), which make the Liver Qi polarize into either Yin or Yang extremes. In its Yin (Stagnant) mode, cholesterol levels go pathologically down. In its Yang (Inflammatory) mode, cholesterol levels go pathologically up. Rather than regulating these levels through artificial methods like medication, which lock cholesterol levels in a static direction, suppress Liver Qi, and ignore more fundamental problems, one should strive for cholesterol levels that reflect the ability to change spontaneously according to circumstances because this capacity creates the best foundation for the flexibility and strength we all need in life.

---

[a] Serum cholesterol levels will be lower for vegetarians because the predominance of PUFAs in their diet will pull cholesterol from the bloodstream into the Peripheral Tissues. Vegetarian diets will also relax the Liver Qi so that less cholesterol and LDL will be produced. In contrast, cholesterol levels will tend to be higher in meat eaters because the predominance of SaFAs in their diet will pull cholesterol out from the Peripheral Tissues and into the bloodstream. Carnivorous diets can also contribute to Liver Qi Stagnation so that more cholesterol is contained within the bloodstream.

[b] A whole food diet is one that avoids the Four Whites of refined grain, refined sugar, refined salt, and refined oil.

[c] Non-dietary causes of high cholesterol and LDL levels include over-involvement in the stressful dog-eat-dog mentality that characterizes the extremes of modern life.

Figure 44: Differences in Cholesterol Levels

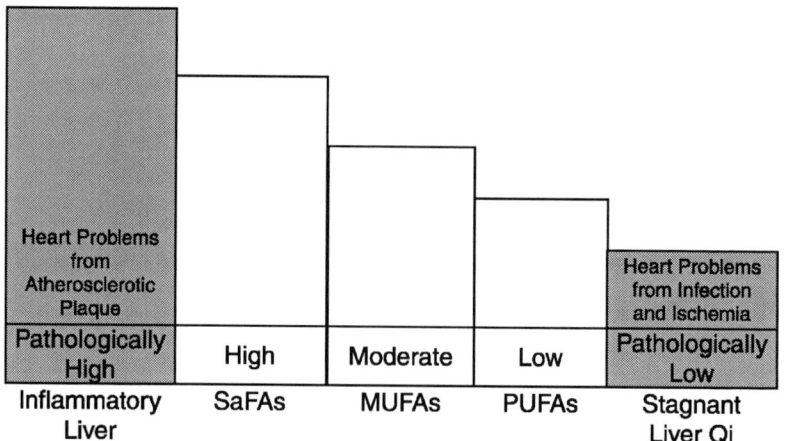

Pathologically HIGH cholesterol levels from Inflammatory Liver Qi represent the true portion of the population at risk for cardiovascular problems because of high cholesterol. Rather than being concerned about cholesterol, either "good" or "bad," these people should focus on removing ALL "bad" fats and oils from their diet as well as replacing refined food with whole food in general. They should also concentrate on INCREASING dietary consumption of chorophyll-rich foods such as sprouted cereal grasses and micro-algae in their diet.

Pathologically LOW cholesterol levels from Stagnant Liver Qi represent the portion of the population at risk for cardiovascular problems because of low cholesterol. These people should also be particularly concerned with removing ALL "bad" fats and oils from their diet, especially those containing hydrogenated and partially hydrogenated oils and *trans*-fats. In addition, these people should INCREASE Omega-3 fatty acids and also heal psycho-emotional trauma either through acupuncture or other natural methods.

Normally high, moderate, or low cholesterol levels will usually NOT present as much risk for cardiovascular problems. A much better insurance for preventing these problems in these populations than cholesterol-lowering drugs would be to INCREASE whole foods in their diet and DECREASE foods that are refined!

Phytosterol Therapy

Phytosterols represent the plant-based polarity within the Sterol class of lipids, in contrast to cholesterol, which is animal based. Phytosterols are currently being used to lower serum cholesterol and LDL. Phytosterols work by delivering cholesterol more readily into the intestines[a] and by inhibiting the re-absorption of dietary cholesterol from the gastrointestinal tract so that cholesterol can be more completely eliminated through the feces.

The amount of dietary cholesterol reduction with phytosterols is however small, with an average of 10% reduction of serum cholesterol and 13% reduction of LDL. This means that phytosterols would only lower a serum cholesterol level of 250 by a negligible 25 points. Because they work at the intestinal level, they can also cause unwanted gastrointestinal side effects including indigestion, fullness, gas, diarrhea, and constipation. Another more serious problem with phytosterols is that they are known to lower serum levels of important nutrients including alpha- and beta-carotene (pro vitamin A), lycopene (an antioxidant thought to help prevent certain cancers, such as prostate cancer, heart disease, and other serious diseases), and vitamin E, by interfering with their absorption. **These nutrients are much more important for health than what can be accomplished by lowering cholesterol levels artificially with phytosterol therapy.** Besides, lowering cholesterol naturally is quite easy while regulating cholesterol naturally is a much healthier goal.

While sometimes available commercially in their unesterified form as capsules, phytosterols are usually esterified (artificially linked to long-chain fatty acids) and made available through undesirable industrial oil products such as margarines, spreads, and salad dressing. Industry likes to esterify phytosterols because they are poorly soluble in their natural state. When they are esterified, their solubility and, therefore, their availability, are increased along with all the TFAs and other undesirable chemicals produced through hydrogenation.

While daily dietary intake of phytosterols ranges from 100 to 300 milligrams, and is higher in vegetarians, they are not easily absorbed. Clinical doses of phytosterols range from 1.12 to 2.24 grams daily for the esterified version and 1-gram daily if they are unesterified. The only natural oil containing enough phytosterols in one serving (1 tablespoon) to equal a clinical dose is Rice Bran oil. A clinical dose can also be obtained with 1½ tablespoons of Sesame oil or 2 tablespoons of Wheat Germ oil. The overall effect, however, would upset the already imbalanced w3:w6 ratio and, therefore, be worse for heart problems than the negligible benefit of the lowered cholesterol obtained from this method. If you take Rice Bran oil, Sesame oil, and/or Wheat Germ oil for their phytosterols to lower cholesterol, you must take additional Omega 3s from any of the Four Primary Omega 3 oils—Krill oil, Fish oil, Flaxseed oil, and Chia Seeds.

---

[a] Bile salts emulsify cholesterol so it can be delivered into the intestines. Phytosterols stimulate the displacement of cholesterol from the bile salts so it can be released more easily into the intestines and removed from the body.

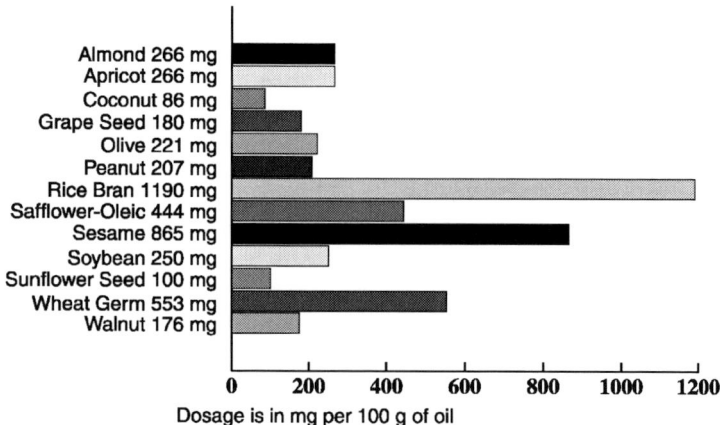

Figure 45: Phytosterols Available in Natural Oils

Dosage is in mg per 100 g of oil

Treatable Conditions

General Strategies

Acupuncture Orientation

In addition to those featured above, treatable conditions responding well to edible oil adjustments range over a variety of areas, including psycho-emotional disorders, immune disorders, skin disorders, musculo-skeletal disorders, brain disorders, eye disorders, digestive disorders, female reproductive disorders, and cancer. These eight different categories can all be grouped together and understood through one overriding pattern in acupuncture theory—Liver Qi dysfunctions. The ten different categories of Liver Qi-related dysfunctions include: Liver Yin Deficiency, Liver Blood Deficiency, Liver Wind, Stagnant Liver Qi, Stagnant Liver Qi Suppressing the Lung, Stagnant Liver Qi Invading the Stomach and Spleen, Blazing Liver Fire, Arrogant Liver Yang, Damp Heat in the Gall Bladder, and Cold Stagnating the Liver Meridian. In addition, the Liver governs different areas and tissues of the body where it is said to open to the eyes, connect to the muscles and tendons, flow through the urinary and reproductive systems, and finalize its particular expression of Qi at the brain where the Liver Meridian ends.

Table 24: Correlation of Wood Phase Categories with Disease Categories

Wood Phase Category	Disease Category
Liver Yin Deficiency	Psycho-Emotional Skin Musculo-Skeletal Brain Eye Female Reproductive
Blood Deficiency	Psycho-Emotional Skin Musculo-Skeletal Brain Eye Female Reproductive
Liver Wind	Skin Musculo-Skeletal Eye Female Reproductive

Wood Phase Category	Disease Category
Stagnant Liver Qi	Psycho-Emotional Musculo-Skeletal Female Reproductive Cancer
Stagnant Liver Qi Suppressing the Lung	Immune
Stagnant Liver Qi Invading the Stomach and Spleen	Digestive
Blazing Liver Fire	Psycho-Emotional Skin Musculo-Skeletal Eye Female Reproductive
Damp Heat in the Gall Bladder	Immune Musculo-Skeletal Digestive
Cold Stagnating the Liver Meridian	Female Reproductive
Opens to the Eyes	Eye
Connects to the Muscles and Tendons	Psycho-Emotional Musculo-Skeletal
Flows Through the Urinary and Reproductive Systems	Female Reproductive
Ends at the Brain	Psycho-Emotional Brain

Liver Yin and Blood Deficiencies

Remember, the Liver belongs to the Wood Phase and the Wood Phase regulates expansive Qi in the Body/Mind/Spirit. Expansion is Yang while contraction is Yin. The Yin nourishing Liver categories, such as Liver Yin Deficiency and Liver Blood Deficiency, control unbridled expansion (Yang) from destabilizing organic function (Yin) and causing inflammation or hyperactivity (Excess Yang), or failure of organic function due to lack of nourishment (Deficient Yin and/or Blood). Psycho-emotional disorders arising from Liver Yin Deficiency and Liver Blood Deficiency include agitation, hyperactivity, nervous tension, depression, and mental debility. Skin disorders include aging skin, wrinkled skin, blemishes, acne, brittle nails, and dry skin. Musculo-skeletal disorders include arthritis, rheumatoid arthritis, and osteoporosis. Brain disorders include lack of nourishment to the brain and insufficient brain development. Eye disorders include impaired vision, spots, and dryness. Female reproductive disorders include insufficient menses, amenorrhea, irregular menses, menopausal problems, miscarriage, obstetric problems, genital herpes, gonorrhea, and syphilis.

Table 25: Deficient Liver Yin and Blood and its Correlations to Disease Categories and Conditions

Disease Category	Specific Conditions
Psycho-Emotional	Agitation, hyperactivity, nervous tension, depression, and mental debility
Skin	Aging skin, wrinkled skin, blemishes, acne, brittle nails, and dry skin
Musculo-Skeletal	Arthritis, rheumatoid arthritis, and osteoporosis
Brain	Lack of nourishment to the brain and insufficient brain development
Eye	Impaired vision, spots, and dryness
Female Reproductive	Insufficient menses, amenorrhea, irregular menses, menopausal problems, miscarriage, obstetric problems, genital herpes, gonorrhea, and syphilis

Liver Fire Conditions

The main over-active Yang Liver categories, Blazing Liver Fire and Arrogant Liver Yang,[a] cause agitation, inflammation, and overactive organ function. Psycho-emotional disorders arising from this toxic over-stimulation include agitation, hyperactivity, volatile anger, mania, and violence. Skin disorders include inflammation and rash. Musculo-skeletal disorders include rheumatoid arthritis, flank pain, and sciatica. Eye disorders include red eyes. Female reproductive disorders may include menopausal problems, miscarriage, obstetric problems, genital herpes, gonorrhea, and syphilis.

Table 26: Blazing Liver Fire and its Correlations to Disease Categories and Conditions

Disease Category	Specific Conditions
Psycho-Emotional	Agitation, hyperactivity, volatile anger, mania, and violence
Skin	Inflammation and rash
Musculo-Skeletal	Rheumatoid arthritis, flank pain, and sciatica
Eye	Red eyes
Female Reproductive	Menopausal problems, miscarriage, obstetric problems, genital herpes, gonorrhea, and syphilis

Liver Qi Stagnation

In between the two extreme Yin and Yang Liver conditions is a group of conditions representing Qi stagnation where either the Qi cannot move easily (such as Stagnant Liver Qi, Stagnant Liver Qi Suppressing the Lung, and Stagnant Liver Qi Invading the Stomach and Spleen), or the Qi moves irregularly and comes and goes inharmoniously, a condition called Liver Wind. Psycho-emotional disorders arising from Stagnant Liver Qi include frustration,

---

[a] Blazing Liver Fire is an extreme condition of liver toxicity while Arrogant Liver Yang is an inflammatory condition resulting from Deficient Yin.

anger, nervous tension, low self-control, manic-depression, juvenile delinquency, suicide, homicide, and schizophrenia. Immune disorders from Stagnant Liver Qi Suppressing the Lung include general immune insufficiency as well as colds and flu, in particular. Skin disorders include most itching skin conditions such as rashes, shingles, eczema, and psoriasis. Musculo-skeletal disorders include trembling, twitching, and spasms; muscular rigidity; numbness and rheumatism, stiff neck, flank pain, and sciatica. Eye disorders include conjunctivitis and cataract. Digestive disorders from Stagnant Liver Qi Invading the Stomach and Spleen include vomiting, stomach ulcers, abdominal pain, gastric discomfort, diarrhea, dysentery, constipation, bowel obstruction, ulcerative colitis, and colon cancer. Female reproductive disorders include menstrual discomfort, dysmenorrhea, menopausal problems, miscarriage, and obstetric problems. Cancer in general is also related to Liver Qi Constraint.

Table 27: Stagnant Liver Qi and its Correlations to Disease Categories and Conditions

Disease Category	Specific Conditions
Psycho-Emotional	Frustration, anger, nervous tension, low self-control, manic-depression, juvenile delinquency, suicide, homicide, and schizophrenia
Immune	Immune insufficiency as well as colds and flu
Skin	Itching skin conditions such as rashes, shingles, eczema, and psoriasis
Musculo-Skeletal	Trembling, twitching, and spasms; muscular rigidity; numbness and rheumatism; stiff neck, flank pain, and sciatica
Eye	Conjunctivitis and cataract
Digestive	Vomiting, stomach ulcers, abdominal pain, gastric discomfort, diarrhea, dysentery, constipation, bowel obstruction, ulcerative colitis, and colon cancer
Female Reproductive	Menstrual discomfort, dysmenorrhea, menopausal problems, miscarriage, and obstetric problems
General	Cancer

Edible Oil Orientation

Liver functions, in both acupuncture theory and modern physiology, correlate directly to the functions of edible oils. In fact, edible oils (depending on their quality, origin, and use) form one of the three major nutrients for the liver along with Vitamin A and chlorophyll. Physiological factors of the liver that connect Liver dysfunction to edible oils include:

1. The storage of fat as well as fat-soluble vitamins
2. The conversion of bile from cholesterol, red blood cells, and salts
3. The breakdown of fats through bile action

4. The regulation of blood sugar through the glycogen/glucose balance by producing glucose from fat or converting excess glucose to fat depending on the body's needs

In addition, the quality of the oils the liver encounters determines whether its functions of distributing Qi (along with important bio-chemicals including cholesterol, prostaglandins, and fat-soluble vitamins) work smoothly.

If these oils are natural, expeller-pressed, unrefined, fresh, oxygen-free, and unheated through cooking or storage, the liver will receive the nourishment from edible oils that it needs to perform these functions. If, instead, the oils are converted through modern industrial processing into harmful chemicals (such as TFAs, unnatural UFA isosmers, cyclic compounds, cross-linked dimmers and polymers, and other altered breakdown products), these functions will not only be impaired but the entire cycle of providing nutrients to the cells and collecting their toxic wastes will be disrupted. Liver Qi controls the membranes, which in turn regulate these processes on the cellular level. **The simple rule is that while good quality natural oils lead to health; bad quality industrialized, chemicalized oils lead to disease!**

Natural edible oils, especially the EFAs, provide much of the nourishment for the Liver that is referred to as Liver Yin in acupuncture theory. In contrast, artificial, industrial edible oils contribute greatly to the toxic overload described as Blazing Liver Fire. These oils also block the distributing function of the Liver and greatly contribute to the various types of Stagnant Liver Qi, especially on the peripheral level of the cell membranes and skin. Thus, the quality of your edible oils will have a fundamental bearing on the health of your skin and your ability to detoxify anywhere in the Body/Mind. All of the refined UFAs and *trans*-fats will disrupt these functions. Even worse are the artificially regulating, Liver Qi constraining, cholesterol-lowering drugs. Rather than prevent disease, they do nothing to alleviate the cause and only help to maintain it in its most insidious form.

Psycho-Emotional Disorders

Psycho-emotional disorders treatable with edible oils relate to the acupuncture syndromes of Deficient Liver Yin and Blood, Blazing Liver Fire, and Stagnant Liver Qi.

Table 28: Psycho-Emotional Conditions Organized by Liver Category

Liver Categories	Conditions
Deficient Liver Yin and Blood	Agitation, hyperactivity, nervous tension, depression, and mental debility
Blazing Liver Fire	Agitation, hyperactivity, volatile anger, mania, and violence
Stagnant Liver Qi	Frustration, anger, nervous tension, low self-control, manic-depression, juvenile delinquency, suicide, homicide, and schizophrenia

Agitation, hyperactivity, nervous tension, depression, and mental debility (the Deficient Liver Yin and Blood conditions) are related to EFA deficiency since EFAs are known to instill calmness. Omega 6, for example, helps produce hemoglobin and directly strengthens the Blood. PGE_1, which is produced from Omega 6, is known for its ability to create a sense of well-being and lower overall tension as well as blood pressure. Depression and mental debility from Deficient Liver Yin and Deficient Liver Blood, in particular, are related to Omega 3 deficiency and known to respond to flaxseed and its oil. For depression, beware of agents that artificially lower cholesterol since they are known to cause depression. For those who are unable to synthesize PGE_1 from Omega 6, Evening Primrose oil, Borage oil, or Black Currant Seed oil can be used. EPO is especially known for treating depression related to alcohol consumption or hyperactivity. For those unable to synthesize PGE3 from Omega 3, use Krill oil. Krill oil is high in Omega 3 derivatives as well as phospholipids. Phospholipids are specific nutrients for the brain.

Agitation, hyperactivity, volatile anger, mania, and violence (the Blazing Liver Fire conditions) are also related to EFA deficiency since EFAs help detoxify the liver. Again, for those who are unable to synthesize PGE_1 from Omega 6, Evening Primrose oil, Borage oil, or Black Currant Seed oil should be used, possibly for a year, two years, or more. Krill oil is good for these conditions as well since it is so strongly anti-inflammatory. Those individuals with sociopathic or homicidal tendencies or even anger management problems should strictly avoid artificial cholesterol lowering agents.

Frustration, anger, nervous tension, low self-control, manic-depression, juvenile delinquency, suicide, homicide, and schizophrenia (the Stagnant Liver Qi conditions) are also related to EFA deficiency since EFAs, especially the balance between Omega 3s and Omega 6s, restore balance to the Liver. Most important for this category is the complete avoidance of artificial cholesterol lowering agents that directly suppress Liver Qi function and, therefore, create and/or exaggerate these conditions. For those people desiring to wean themselves off of psycho-pharmacological drugs, it is essential to completely stop artificial cholesterol lowering agents BEFORE they begin to reduce their dependence on the psycho-pharmacological drugs. Otherwise, these agents may exaggerate withdrawal symptoms of the psycho-pharmacological drugs that can be too difficult to handle. For those wishing to cleanse themselves of these drugs, use caution and proceed slowly and systematically under the supervision of a licensed health-care practitioner.

Table 29: Conditions Corresponding to More Than One Liver Category

Conditions	Liver Category
Hyperactivity	Deficient Liver Yin and Blood Blazing Liver Fire
Depression	Deficient Liver Yin and Blood Stagnant Liver Qi

Immune Disorders

According to acupuncture theory, immune disorders are often caused by Deficient Liver Qi or Stagnant Liver Qi Suppressing the Lung function and the Defensive Qi, which it controls. Immune function is basically the physiological ability to guard the exterior. EFAs regulate this activity at the skin and cell membrane level by enabling the cells to operate at peak function where the cells reach optimal levels of nourishment (reinforcement) and toxin removal (disposal of casualties). EFAs are also known to stimulate immune function through the fat-soluble Vitamin A as well as their ability to prevent infection by concentrating oxygen levels. Omega 3, in particular, is known for its ability to treat infection. It even kills malaria!

Coconut oil is also an important edible oil for strengthening immunity. Coconut oil not only helps form membranes, including the skin, through its content of phospholipids and SaFAs, but its content of lauric and capric acids is directly related to natural antibiotic and antiviral function. Use Coconut oil internally not only for colds and flu, but also to strengthen immunity that has been weakened from taking steroids, immunosuppressive drugs, or artificial antibiotics. For those individuals whose compromised immune system has further weakened digestion to the point where internal dosage is unreasonable, Coconut oil can be applied externally to the large areas of the skin where it will more easily be assimilated. Even with the extreme immune suppression of AIDS, the opportunistic organisms present can be effectively killed by the lauric and capric acids present in Coconut oil.

Skin Disorders

Skin disorders are probably the most obvious conditions related to edible oil consumption. Natural edible oils benefit skin function through their ability to nourish the skin via EFAs and the fat-soluble vitamins they carry, and strengthen and repair skin through the cholesterol it delivers there. In contrast, unnatural oils suppress skin function by failing to deliver proper nourishment to the skin, failing to remove toxins present in the skin (either from natural metabolic activity or from the environment), and creating an extra toxic burden to the already overloaded skin function it suppresses.

Good quality, natural, edible oils make the skin youthful, smooth, and elastic. Many types of marks impairing beautiful skin such as brown spots are simply a result of fatty degeneration created from Vitamin E-deficient refined industrial oils that are then deposited in the skin where their blocking of normal skin function becomes visible. Omega 6-rich fatty acids such as Evening Primrose oil, Borage oil, or Black Currant Seed oil taken internally bring moisturizing fluids (Yin) to the skin and helps to clear skin blemishes and wrinkles due to dryness.

Certain natural edible oils are also well known for restoring healthy skin when applied externally directly to the skin. These include Jojoba oil, Hazelnut oil, Foraha, Coconut oil, and Calendula oil. Use Jojoba oil for dry, flaky skin and facial wrinkles; Hazelnut oil for sun aging; Foraha for smoothing wrinkles; Coconut oil to protect the skin from the sun; and Calendula oil (a mixture of virgin Olive oil and calendula flowers) as a general restorative. Better yet, prepare a blend of these oils by mixing them together in equal amounts and apply them to the skin on a regular basis.

Table 30: Oil Blend for Skin Restoration

Oil	Indications
Jojoba	Dry, flaky skin and facial wrinkles
Hazelnut	Sun aging
Foraha	Wrinkles
Coconut	Sun protection
Calendula	General restorative

For injuries and wounds to the skin, such as abrasions, bruises, swelling, burns, sunburn, insect bites, or scars, prepare a blend of Foraha, Coconut oil, and Calendula oil and take EFAs or Evening Primrose oil internally until the skin is healed.

More serious skin problems can be further grouped according to whether they are hard and dry, inflammatory (red and hot to the touch), pustular (filled with mucous), or itching. Hard and dry conditions like blemishes and eczema are usually a result of Liver Yin/Blood/EFA Deficiency. Take Krill oil, Flaxseed oil, or a combination of Krill oil or Flaxseed oil with Grape Seed oil, Sunflower Seed oil, and Sesame Seed oil; or Hempseed oil; or Evening Primrose oil; or a combination of EPO, Borage oil, and Black Currant Seed oil internally and apply Foraha and Calendula oil externally.

Internal Oils for Inflammatory and Itching Skin
- Krill Oil
- Flaxseed Oil
- Grape Seed Oil
- Sunflower Seed Oil
- Sesame Seed Oil
- Hempseed Oil
- Evening Primrose Oil

Or
- Evening Primrose Oil
- Borage Oil
- Black Currant Seed Oil

Inflammatory conditions such as ulcers, rash, or psoriasis usually result from a toxic build-up in the skin from a history of taking refined oils, *trans*-fats, and other industrially modified oils. Use Evening Primrose oil internally and apply Jojoba oil, Foraha, Coconut oil, and Calendula oil or a blend of them externally on a regular basis.

External Oils for Inflammatory and Itching Skin
- Evening Primrose Oil or Grape Seed oil (Internally)
- Jojoba Oil
- Foraha Oil
- Coconut Oil
- Calendula Oil

Pustular conditions such as abscesses or erysipelas arise from either chronic skin inflammation, an excess of refined oils or animal fats, or infection. Sometimes, as in the case of acne, these conditions are accompanied by EFA deficiency. Use Krill oil, Flaxseed oil, or Hempseed oil; or a combination of Evening Primrose oil, Borage oil, and Black Currant oil internally to clear the deficiency with Coconut oil internally to clear the infection and apply Almond oil, Coconut oil, Calendula oil, or blend of them together externally.

Table 31: Oil Blend for Pustular Conditions of the Skin

Oil	Indications	Application
Krill	Clears Deficiency	Internally
Flaxseed		
Hempseed		
Evening Primrose		
Borage		
Black Currant		
Coconut		
Almond	Heals Skin	Externally
Coconut		
Calendula		

Itching conditions result from Liver Wind and can also be accompanied with infection. Use Evening Primrose oil internally to clear the Liver Wind and apply Coconut oil externally to clear the infection; for scabies apply a 50/50 blend of Foraha and the essential oil of Ravintsara.

Skin cancer is the ultimate result of normal skin function becoming chronically dysfunctional. Chronic skin dysfunction occurs for three reasons: (1) the failure to nourish the skin with the necessary EFAs, (2) the build up of toxins, and, most importantly, (3) the toxic burdening of skin function with the dead carcasses of industrially altered oils. This burden then is unable to be naturally detoxified because of its own destructive function. Too much skin cholesterol from AO-deficient refined food or environmental toxins in combination with an excessive intake of refined UFAs results in skin cancer. You can prevent skin cancer significantly by simply taking a balanced proportion of Omega 3s and 6s, especially using Krill oil with Borage oil and Grape Seed oil regularly.

Musculo-Skeletal Disorders

Musculo-skeletal disorders relating to edible oils are mostly correlated with tension and rigidity in the muscles, tendons, ligaments, and joints due to Stagnant Liver Qi and Liver Wind with an underlying Deficiency of Liver Yin and Liver Blood. Stiff neck, flank pain, and sciatica are common examples and can be prevented and/or alleviated through a balanced intake of EFAs internally accompanied with an external application of Foraha. PGE_1, which is produced in the body from Omega 6, specifically relaxes muscular tension and creates flexibility in the muscles and tendons.

Other forms of musculo-skeletal disorders are frequently developments of this tension over a long period of time. Liver Wind, often caused by EFA deficiency, can result in trembling, twitching, numbness, and spasms. As these conditions develop, they eventually embody themselves more deeply as arthritis and rheumatism. Arthritis is primarily an Omega 6 deficiency because the PGE_1 that Omega 6 produces normally assists the kidneys in removing excess fluid, sodium, and other minerals from the body. When Omega 6 is deficient, these substances build up and accumulate in the joints. PGE_1 also regulates calcium metabolism in order to decrease the overall inflammation response. The more serious rheumatoid arthritis, in contrast, is related to the tension-producing PGE_2s that are derived from arachidonic acid present in foods such as meat and dairy products. Other reasons for rheumatoid arthritis are related to nutrient deficiencies from long-term intake of refined foods (the Four Whites). The simple solution is to restore prostaglandin balance (produce more PGE_1 than PGE_2) by taking good quality Omega 6 regularly, preferably at this stage in the form of Evening Primrose or Borage oil. For rheumatism, add an external application of Foraha.

Osteoporosis (a bone dysfunction) is in polar Yin-Yang contrast to skin cancer. The bones represent the deepest organic tissue while the skin represents the most superficial. The overall Yin-Yang balance of the Liver controls the interplay between these complimentary opposites through its regulation of cholesterol. Excess cholesterol at the skin can cause skin cancer while insufficient cholesterol at the skin level inhibits Vitamin D production and results in osteoporosis. EFAs regulate Vitamin D synthesis and prevent osteoporosis through cholesterol production. They also stimulate the development of teeth and bone through Vitamin A and increase bone density through Vitamin K. Coconut oil also helps to absorb and retain calcium and magnesium and builds healthy bone. Coconut oil's AO-like function also helps to protect bones from free radical destruction often caused by rancid and oxidized UFAs.

Brain Disorders

Brain nourishment, according to acupuncture theory, is one of the functions of Reserve Qi, itself derived in part from adequate reserves of EFAs. Infant brain development is dependent upon cholesterol, an important ingredient in mother's milk. In contrast, infant formulas hardly contain any cholesterol at all. This means that normal brain development is arrested in those infants who were not breast-fed. The fact that non-breast-fed infants represent such a vast percentage of the modern population perhaps reveals that brain development may be lacking in modern times. If so, modern individuals may be at risk of losing their independence because of their over-reliance on technological and other rationalizations in place of common sense. They may get too used to having other people and organizations do their thinking for them. Regular usage of Pumpkinseed oil and Evening Primrose oil for their Omega 3 and GLA content and expeller-pressed, unrefined, non-GEO Soybean oil (because of its lecithin) are useful in preventing and compensating for this problem. Krill oil is the best edible oil to nourish the brain because of its high content of phospholipids, Omega 3s, and AOs, all of which are necessary for brain development. Use Krill oil specifically to prevent and treat senility and Alzheimer's disease.

Eye Disorders

Many eye problems can be prevented or reversed through the appropriate use of natural edible oils because the eyes are controlled by the Liver and benefited by the regular consumption of EFAs. EFAs particularly benefit the eyes because of the large amount of Vitamin A they contain. Vitamin A is one of the most important nutrients for the eyes. Omega 6 is good for the eyes, in part, because it helps produce hemoglobin, which nourishes the eyes. Omega 3 assists this nourishment because, being more Yang than Omega 6, it helps deliver this nourishment out from the Liver, where the Blood is stored, to the eyes. Omega 3 prevents vision impairment because it helps nourish Deficient Liver Yin and Deficient Liver Blood. Weak vision as well as spots in the visual field and even dryness in the eyes most especially relate to these deficiencies and will be prevented by and benefit from regular consumption of EFAs including Flaxseed oil, Black Currant Seed oil, and even EPO.

Visual problems arising from more excessive conditions include red eyes, conjunctivitis, and cataracts. Red eyes stem from either Blazing Liver Fire or Arrogant Liver Yang in conjunction with Deficient Liver Yin. Both of these conditions can result from EFA deficiency. EFA deficiency can sometimes arise from an over-consumption of MUFAs like Olive oil, which in excess can interfere with EFA absorption. EFAs benefit the eyes; Omega 3s detoxify the Liver and reduce inflammation by returning cholesterol and fat-soluble vitamins to the liver. As well, Omega 6 produces PGE_1, which decreases the overall inflammation response. Conjunctivitis is a Liver Wind problem that can also be alleviated with Coconut oil. Cataracts are related to excessive Damp Heat in the Liver and Gall Bladder and result from a serious imbalance between natural edible oils and their industrial twins, the refined oils, *trans*-fats, cross-linked, oxidized, dimerized, and polymerized fatty acids. In addition, artificial cholesterol-lowering agents are associated with a high rate of cataract formation and liver damage.

Digestive Disorders

Digestive disorders related to edible oils are mostly correlated with Stagnant Liver Qi patterns, especially Stagnant Liver Qi Invading the Stomach and Spleen. In terms of Qi, the main idea describing this pattern is that the over-expanding or over-tense Liver Qi interferes with the absorptive and distributive functions of digestion. Most commonly, this pattern results in stomach dysfunctions where the Stomach Qi is forced upwards from its normal downward direction. Indications include nausea, vomiting, gastric discomfort, and stomach ulcers. While a natural diet containing adequate amounts of EFAs and lecithin will strengthen digestion, Coconut oil and/or Calendula oil can be applied externally to the skin of the entire body several times a day when the upset stomach condition prevents internal usage. Most stomach ulcers, including bleeding ulcers manifesting in the vomiting of blood, result from lipid-coated bacteria called helicobacter, which can be killed by the lauric acid contained in Coconut oil without damaging the beneficial intestinal flora. The restorative functions of Krill oil also change the underlying conditions in which these bacteria thrive and thus prevent and treat helicobacter pylori-related digestive problems.

Problems in the lower digestive tract can also be related to Stagnant Liver Qi Invading the Stomach and Spleen and preventing healthy digestive absorption. These problems include abdominal pain, diarrhea, dysentery, ulcerative colitis, bloody stools, constipation, and bowel obstruction. Again, EFAs and lecithin should be consumed in the form of Flaxseed and its oil as well as EPO and Soybean oil in order to strengthen digestion. Hempseed oil has been used medicinally in China over centuries for a wide variety of digestive complaints. Coconut oil is also very useful for these types of digestive problems. Coconut oil is easier to digest because of its MCFAs, which require fewer enzymes, so it does not over burden an already taxed digestive system. Coconut oil can be used effectively even in critical or emergency situations. If these problems are due to microbial infection, Coconut oil will rid the body of them as well.

Colon cancer is the result of a very weakened digestive system compounded with an overload of toxins and Liver Qi Stagnation that seals off this part of the body from the whole. Flaxseed and its oil helps to stimulate the energy that can regenerate the digestive system in general, rid bodily toxins, and reconnect all organic function to its basic Yin-Yang rhythms. Flaxseed and its oil, because it is produced in cold weather climates, stimulates energy production and heat deep inside the body where it can then emanate outward effectively to reconnect with all other parts of the body. Much larger doses of Flaxseed and its oil should be taken in this instance than the normally recommended tablespoon per day per fifty pounds of body weight and should include its use in compresses and enemas.

Obesity Revisited

The explosion seen today with weight problems was mostly non-existent during the 1960s and 1970s when only about 13 to 14 percent of the population was overweight. The trend started in the beginning of the 1980s when the number of overweight adults increased by 8 percent. By the end of the decade, 25 percent of adult Americans were overweight and the number of overweight children tripled.[155] Now the overweight population encompasses half of adult Americans and one in every four children.[156]

Before the 1970s, common sense told us that fat and protein satisfied the appetite. As a result, people were less hungry and less prone to overeating. This simple understanding disappeared when government agencies began to warn against the dangers of fat, especially saturated fat, and the beef and dairy industry began to produce low-fat products.[157] People started to believe that fat in the diet causes weight-gain and heart disease, and that eating cholesterol makes your cholesterol levels rise.[158] Food manufacturers then capitalized on the alarm and flooded the market with man-made fats and other synthetic foods.[159]

In addition to the synthetic poisons these policies dumped into the food supply, most everyone felt an overwhelming compulsion to replace the satisfaction the missing fat provided with something in the diet that would make the food taste good. The substitute was refined sugar, which, however good it tasted, never led to satiation. Consumption of high fructose corn syrup and other variations of processed food rose dramatically.[160]

In 1981, Robert Atkins exposed this fallacy in his book, *Dr. Atkin's Diet Revolution*, by insisting that sugar in the diet, not fat, is what makes people overweight and causes their cholesterol to raise.[161] Since then, studies have proved that "the increased consumption of refined carbohydrates is the primary cause of the obesity epidemic."[162] The fallacious substitution of refined carbohydrates for fat raised triglyceride levels and failed to reduce the risk for heart disease.[163] In fact, refined carbohydrates (and refined oils) are largely responsible for the modern increase in obesity, heart disease, and diabetes.

Diets of simple sugars and refined carbohydrates create short-term energy gain but long-term energy drain. They also weaken the digestive system because they are too easy to digest. Whole-grains, in contrast, are balanced and wholesome. The Iowa Women's Health Study, organized by Dr. David Jacobs and his colleagues, showed that whole-grain based diets decrease the risk of coronary heart disease and that at least one serving of whole-grain foods per day significantly lowers overall mortality.[164] The greater demand that vegetables and whole-grain places on the body increases metabolism so that a greater number of calories can be burned. [165]   Whole-grains work better for the beginning stages of weight-loss (the period when you start to the time when you achieve the desired weight loss) when they are consumed in a smaller amount, roughly 20 percent of each meal by volume). Once the desired weight loss is achieved, this percentage can be increased up to 40 percent for the maximum maintenance of health. Sometimes decreased metabolism is a result of thyroid deficiency, which in turn is a result of iodine deficiency. In fact, up to 90 percent of the population may be iodine deficient. You can correct iodine deficiencies by eating small amounts of sea vegetables, especially Kelp and Kombu on a daily basis.[a]

Fat-restriction diets leave people unsatisfied while very low-carbohydrate diets rely too much on fat so that people feel heavy and uncomfortable after eating.[166] A study in 2004 by Dr. Christine Pelkman and published in the *American Journal of Clinical Nutrition* reported that MODERATE-fat diets emphasizing MUFAs help reduce weight as well as lower the risk for heart disease.[167] MUFAs also regulate LDL and HDL levels as well as lower triglyceride levels.[168] Dr. Pescatore, in his successful whole foods weight-loss diet, the Hamptons Diet, uses Macadamia oil almost exclusively because it is the highest natural source of MUFAs and also because it has a relatively balanced Omega 3:Omega 6 ratio of 1:1. One of the most important factors in succeeding with weight-loss is to completely eliminate all industrial fats including refined or otherwise damaged PUFAs.[169]

For a wholesome, long-term approach to weight-loss, think of understanding foods according to the following categories:

- Sugar (Industrial)—White Sugar, Corn Syrup, Beet Sugar, Fructose, High-Fructose Corn Syrup, Sucrose
- Sugar (Natural)—Stevia, Dried Fruit, Maple Syrup, Brown Rice Syrup, Honey, Cane Sugar
- Fats and Oils (Bad)—Refined, Hydrogenated, Partially Hydrogenated
- Fats and Oils (Good)—Expeller-Pressed & Unrefined) MUFAs (such as Macadamia oil), PUFAs (such as Flaxseed oil), and medium-chain SaFAs (such as centrifuged Coconut oil)
- Animal Food—Eggs, Milk and Cheese, Fish, Chicken, Red Meat, Processed Meat (Bacon, Sausage)
- Fruit—Berries (Raspberry, Strawberry, Mulberry), Melons (Watermelon, Cantaloupe, Honeydew), Stone Fruit (Cherry, Peach, Plum, Nectarine), Seed Fruit (Apple, Pear), Vine Fruit (Grape), Tropical Fruit (Orange, Grapefruit, Banana)
- Nuts and Seeds—Sesame Seeds, Sunflower Seeds, Pumpkin Seeds to name a few

---

[a] One of the best sources of excellent-quality sea vegetables is www.maineseaweedcompany.com or 207-546-2875.

- Non-Starchy Vegetables—Roots (Burdock, Radish, Rutabaga, Salsify, Scorzonera, Turnips), Fruits (Eggplant, Tomatoes), Flowers (Broccoli, Cauliflower), Onions (White, Yellow, Leeks, Scallions), Gourds (Cucumber, Okra, Yellow Squash, Zucchini), Leafy (Arugula, Bok Choy, Cabbage, Celery, Collards, Dandelion Greens, Kale, Lettuce, Mustard Greens, Parsley, Spinach), Shoots (Asparagus, Bamboo Shoots), Sprouts, String Beans
- Starchy Vegetables—Roots (Carrots, Celeriac, Beets, Parsnips), Tubers (Cassava, Jicama, Plantain, Potatoes), Squash (Acorn, Buttercup, Butternut, Hubbard), Sweet Corn
- Legumes—Black-eyed Peas, Fava, Garbanzos, Kidney, Lentils, Peanut, Peas, Tofu and Tempeh.
- Whole-Grains—Brown Rice, Oats, Barley, Millet, Corn, Wheat (Spelt, Kamut), Rye, Quinoa, Amaranth, Teff

When choosing foods from these categories, use the Food Diamond in the figure below. Notice that whole-grains are in the center accompanied by vegetables on top and legumes on the bottom. These categories, especially the whole-grains, correspond to the Soil Phase in acupuncture, which represents the digestive system. Foods from these central categories will strengthen the digestive system when systematically added to the daily diet. They also give the feeling of stability and balance on the physical and psycho-emotional levels, a feeling that can be further enhanced by good quality fats and oils.

The foods in the upper pyramid are more Yang because they increase energy. The refined foods and processed foods at the very top increase energy the most, but they over-stimulate the Body/Mind, which then collapses soon after these foods are ingested. The foods in the lower pyramid are more Yin because they increase structure. At a certain point, consuming these foods causes the Body/Mind to become too dense. The bad oils at the very bottom represent the extreme of this structuralizing tendency because they block functional energy, especially in the Liver and the Peripheral Tissues. This is the point where the creation of structure turns to its opposite and stifles the life force.

Eat foods from the center of the Food Diamond more frequently, usually at every meal, or at least on a daily basis. If your digestive system is healthy and/or you are physically active, consume these foods in a greater proportion. The foods towards the top and bottom of the Food Pyramid should be consumed less frequently and, unless the digestive system is weak or if you are not physically active, in smaller proportion.

Table 32: Food Diamond for Healthy Eating

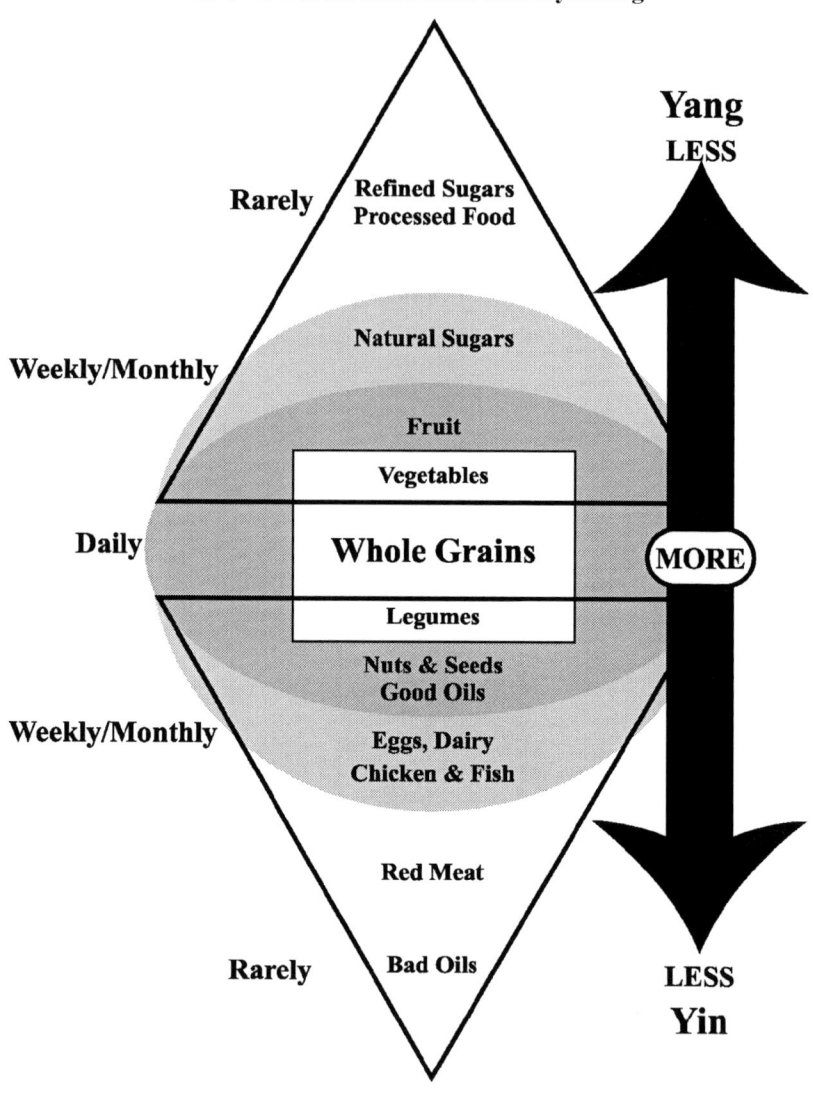

For weight-loss, food selection from the Food Diamond should be adjusted to compensate for the need to restore a weakened digestive system. Use the "Food Chart for Weight-Loss" below instead. Continue to eat foods from the central area daily and preferably at every meal, but eat a smaller percentage of whole-grains in each meal. During the weight-loss adjustment period, greatly reduce or eliminate starchy vegetables. The only exception is to eat raw carrots. Instead, consume more foods from the mid-range of the upper (fruit and vegetables especially) and lower (legumes, nuts and seeds, good oils, and some animal foods if desired) pyramids until the weight-loss goal is achieved. Then begin to choose foods more from the center of the Food Diamond for Healthy Eating as your digestive system improves.

Table 33: Food Chart for Weight-Loss

Eliminate — Refined Sugars / Processed Food

Every Day — Fruit / Non-Starchy Vegetables — Greater Portion

Natural Sugars / Starchy Vegetables

Every Meal { Whole Grains } Smaller Portion

Legumes / Nuts & Seeds / Good Oils

Every Day — Eggs, Dairy / Chicken & Fish / Red Meat — Smallest Portion

Eliminate — Bad Oils

Centrifuged Coconut oil, being a medium-chain SaFA will also increase metabolic rate and burn calories as well as give the feeling of satiation. Because of their sugar content, beer and wine are prohibited during the weight loss period while hard alcohol can be used on occasion.[170] Sugar cravings can be handled with Stevia (a sweetener made from the leaves of the Stevia plant. Stevia is many times sweeter than sugar, but balances and creates healthy blood sugar levels and is also good for the teeth. The amino acid glutamine can also be used for sugar cravings. Take it three times per day and during periods of sugar craving at a dosage of 55 mg each time on an empty stomach.[171]

Men can expect to lose 3-4 pounds per week and women 2-4 pounds per week from this protocol. The more obese you are, the more weight you can expect to lose per week. The less weight you want to lose, the more slowly you can expect to lose it. Even a paltry pound per week adds up to 50 pounds over the course of a year![172]

Female Reproductive Disorders

Female reproductive disorders can also be grouped according to acupuncture patterns. Deficient Liver Yin and Deficient Liver Blood are related to insufficient, absent, or irregular menstrual periods, menopausal problems, and obstetric problems. These patterns are also related to an insufficiency of EFAs in the diet. Omega 6 helps produce hemoglobin, strengthen the reproductive system, and prevent miscarriage. Coconut oil is also effective in relieving amenorrhea possibly because of its content of pregnalone, which converts to progesterone in the body. Pumpkinseed oil, a good source of Vitamin E, prevents menopausal problems. Evening Primrose oil can be used for obstetric problems. Progesterone and estrogen can also be synthesized naturally in the body from cholesterol, a building block of many other important hormones. Therefore, a natural balance of cholesterol in the body, not one artificially induced, is desirable.

Stagnant Liver Qi and Deficient Liver Yin with their accompanying EFA deficiency are also related to female reproductive disorders, especially menstrual discomfort and PMS. Excess of the female hormone prolactin over-stimulates fluid metabolism and aggravates emotional response. The PGE_1 derived from Omega 6 EFAs decreases inflammation response and helps smooth out a woman's menstrual cycle. Sunflower Seed and Sesame Seed oils are useful. In more difficult or extreme cases, use EPO and/or Borage oil. Omega 3s can also reduce inflammation and reverse PMS. Coconut oil and Calendula oil are also known to relieve menstrual discomfort. Krill oil is useful in all types of female reproductive problems. The phospholipid content alleviates the prevalent psycho-emotional aspect; the Omega 3 derivatives decrease pain, inflammation, and constriction; while the super AO content further assists in lowering inflammation. For these purposes, Krill oil can be effectively combined with Borage oil.

Sexually transmitted diseases like genital herpes, gonorrhea, and syphilis are best treated both internally and externally with Coconut oil because of the anti-microbial function of its lauric and capric acids.

Glossary of Abbreviations

AA: Arachidonic acid is one of the main derivatives of the Omega 6 essential fatty acid (linoleic acid) along with PGE_1. The conversion process is as follows: LA $\rightarrow$ GLA $\rightarrow$ DGLA $\rightarrow$ PGE_1 and **AA**, which then produces DPA and PGE_2. PGE_1 and PGE_2 function in polar opposition to one another in the body. PGE_1 relaxes and PGE_2 tightens (promotes platelet aggregation, increases water retention, and increases high blood pressure). Optimal levels of PGE_1 in the body ensure the normally slow conversion of DGLA to AA but can be counteracted by an excessive dietary intake of animal foods, especially pork, eggs, and dairy products, which contain high amounts of AA. Therefore, an over-abundance of AA produced by a diet high in animal products may cause cardiovascular inflammation and constriction as well as kidney disease. PGE_3, which is made from the Omega 3 LNAs, also controls the constricting effects of PGE_2 by preventing the release of AA. PGE_3 is converted from EPA, which is converted from LNA (LNA $\rightarrow$ SDA $\rightarrow$ EPA $\rightarrow$ PGE_3 as well as DHA). Foods rich in EPA, such as the oils from cold-water fish and krill, bypass the conversion process by which EPA is made from LNA and so help to ensure adequate amounts of PGE_3. Foods rich in SDA, such as Black Currant Seed oil and Hempseed oil, while they are one step back in the conversion process from EPA, also help to bypass the conversion process. Nevertheless, reducing animal food consumption can still be important in preventing and reversing these conditions.

AHA: The American Heart Association provides mainstream information to the public concerning heart disease and its prevention.

ALA: See LNA.

AO: Anti-oxidants are associated with Yin in acupuncture in contrast to the free radicals, which are Yang. Anti-oxidants counteract the free radical proliferation found in the development of coronary artery disease and are found in common nutrients such as Vitamin A, C, E, carotene, selenium, and sulfur. Anti-oxidants also appear in natural food sources including Krill oil, Grape Seed oil, Sesame Seed oil, Coconut oil, and Rice Bran oil, as well as the common spices and essential oils of celery, sage, oregano, cumin, cloves, myrrh, and frankincense. All of these sources are depleted of their AOs when refined.

ATP: Adenosine triphosphate is an energy molecule that initially comes from sugar.

CFA: Conjugated fatty acids, while found in insubstantial amounts naturally in meat and milk products, are also industrial by-products of hydrogenation as well as the bleaching stage of the refining process. Conjugated fatty acids are formed by shrinking the double bonds between the carbon atoms. Conjugated fatty acids are also known to interfere with the conversion of PGE_1 from Omega 6 essential fatty acids and cause coronary artery disease. While currently promoted for their AO properties and ability to improve degenerative conditions, the dose of Conjugated fatty acids has to be so high that it counteracts the supposed benefit. While Conjugated fatty acids do have AO functions, there are many more AOs that work more effectively and are also more natural and safe.

DGLA: Dihomo-gammalinolenic acid is converted directly from LA via GLA and goes on to produce both prostaglandins PGE_1 and PGE_2 as well as AA.

DHA: Docosahexaenoic acid, along with PGE_3, is one of the two final stages of conversion from the Omega 3 essential fatty acids (LNA $\rightarrow$ SDA $\rightarrow$ EPA $\rightarrow$ PGE_3 and **DHA**).

DPA: Docosapenetaenoic acid is part of the conversion process of the Omega 6 essential fatty acids. Docosapenetaenoic acid is formed in the last stage of conversion from the Omega 6s from AA (LA $\rightarrow$ GLA $\rightarrow$ DGLA $\rightarrow$ PGE_1 and AA $\rightarrow$ **DPA** $\rightarrow$ and PGE_2).

EFA: Essential fatty acids are comprised of two categories, the Omega 3s and Omega 6s. Essential fatty acids are essential for important life functions, cannot be synthesized, and must be taken regularly and directly in the form of natural food or supplements. As polyunsaturated fatty acids, essential fatty acids soften membranes and will either decrease cholesterol when taken into the membranes in moderate amounts or tend to increase it if taken excessively, especially if they are industrially produced. EFAs are usually reserved for important structural and metabolic functions in the body, especially the creation of the hormone-like prostaglandins.

EPA: Eicosapentaenoic acid is converted from the Omega 3 essential fatty acids to further produce the positive health benefits of the Prostaglandin 3s (LNA $\rightarrow$ SDA $\rightarrow$ **EPA** $\rightarrow$ PGE_3). The PGE_3 derived from EPA prevents AA from being released during the conversion process of the Omega 6s and producing the constricting effects of PGE_2. Both EPA and DHA, which it further produces, are even more easily destroyed by light, air, and heat than LNA; are easily depleted during the winter, especially in combination with excessive intake of SaFAs; and are so highly dispersive and have such low melting points that they will not harden or aggregate. These properties make them very important in preventing stickiness and clogging of the arteries, lowering serum cholesterol level (by 25 percent), lowering LDL, lowering very low-density lipoprotein (by 50 percent), and lowering high triglycerides (by up to 65 percent). For those individuals lacking the enzymes necessary to convert EPA and DHA from LNA, Black Currant Seed oil can be used because it contains the SDA from which EPA is made. A more direct route uses the DHA directly from the oils of krill, cold-water fish and marine animals, as well as brown and red algae such as kelp, kombu, wakame, and dulse as well as from green and blue-green micro-algae.

EPO: Evening Primrose oil contains significant amounts of GLA and can be used to treat LA deficiencies symptomatically.

FA: Fatty acids are lipids; lipids are fats and oils. Fats are lipids that are solid at room temperature, while oils are lipids that are liquid at room temperature. There are three different classes of lipids: sterols, phospholipids, and triglycerides. Sterols, including cholesterol, are very hard and waxy (cholesterol does not even melt until it reaches 300°F). Cholesterol promotes fat digestion; promotes the formation of scar tissue, membranes, and skin; promotes the formation of Vitamin D; promotes the creation of many hormones; and optimizes brain development. Phospholipids, including lecithin, regulate cell membranes, help to transport HDL and LDL, emulsify fat, and facilitate brain and nerve function. Triglycerides insulate the body, regulate sugar metabolism, and form the basis for many other important bodily functions. There are three families of triglycerides including SaFAs, MUFAs, and PUFAs.

GLA: Gamma-linolenic acid is produced in the body from the Omega 6 essential fatty acids (LA → **GLA** → DGLA → PGE$_1$) . About 20 percent of the population cannot convert essential fatty acids into the all-important prostaglandins because of an enzyme deficiency (delta-4,5,6-desaturase) associated with an excessive intake of saturated fats, cholesterol, *trans*-fatty acids, alcohol, anti-inflammatory drugs, insulin deficiency, zinc deficiency, chronic viral infections like herpes, radiation, and cancer. This means that PGE$_1$ is never produced from LA and PGE$_3$ is never produced from LNA, a sure-fire prescription for degenerative disease. A symptomatic remedy for this imbalance is to supplement GLA (for the LA deficiency) and SDA or EPA (for the LNA deficiency) through diet to bypass the beginning stages of EFA conversion and go directly to the production of prostaglandins (both PGE$_1$ and PGE$_2$) . GLA is found separately in Borage oil (20 percent+), Black Currant Seed oil (15 percent), Evening Primrose oil (9 percent), Flaxseed oil (2 percent), and Hempseed oil (1.7 percent). The richest natural food sources of GLA are mother's milk, micro-algae, and cereal grasses. Black Currant Seed oil also contains sufficient amounts of SDA that will convert into PGE_3 and so will address both the PGE_1 and PGE_3 deficiencies (PGE_3 deficiency is more prevalent in our society due to the lack of Omega 3s). Expeller-pressed, unrefined Black Currant Seed oil, though rare, is available. Another alternative is to use the GLA from Evening Primrose oil in conjunction with Krill oil or Fish oil that contain both the EPA, which directly converts to PGE_3, as well as DHA. GLA is very powerful in reducing serum cholesterol formed from *trans*-fatty acids, stopping blood platelets from clumping, lowering high blood pressure, and reducing cancerous cell growth.

HDL: High-density lipoprotein is the misnamed "good" lipoprotein that circulates cholesterol back from the skin and cell membranes to the liver.

LA: Linoleic acid, or Omega 6, along with the Omega 3s, is one of the two major forms of essential fatty acids and helps in the production of hemoglobin. Normal intake of LA should be roughly twice that of LNA, but during the Correction Stage should only be half.

LCFA: Long-chain fatty acids are the most common fatty acids in nature since they provide the most economical form for storage and structure. Long-chain fatty acids contain fourteen to twenty-four carbons and are found in all fats and oils.

LCT: Long-chain triglyceride (see LCFA).

LDL: Low-density lipoprotein is the misnamed "bad" lipoprotein that circulates cholesterol outwards to the skin and cell membranes from the liver.

LNA: Alpha-linolenic acid, or Omega 3, with the Omega 6s is one of the two major forms of essential fatty acids and should technically be called a super-unsaturated fatty acid. Normal intake of LNA should be half that of LA, but during the Correction Stage should be twice as much.

LRC: The Lipid Research Clinics Coronary Primary Prevention Trial of 1984 was the first major study to profess that high serum cholesterol levels were the direct cause of coronary artery disease.

MCFA: Medium-chain fatty acids are a relatively rare saturated fatty acid containing eight to twelve carbons and found naturally in tropical oils such as Coconut oil, Palm oil, and Palm Kernel oil.

MCT: Medium-chain triglyceride (see MCFA).

MRFIT: The Multiple Risk Factor Integration Trial held by the NHLBI in 1982 was the first major study to differentiate between HDL and LDL as important risk factors in the development of coronary artery disease.

MUFA: Monounsaturated fatty acids are unsaturated fatty acids with only one double carbon bond. Olive oil and Peanut oil are the most common examples, while Macadamia Nuts have the greatest MUFA content. Monounsaturated fatty acids are liquid at room temperature but solidify in colder temperatures. Monounsaturated fatty acids, often called Omega 9s, lie between the saturated and polyunsaturated fatty acids in terms of stability and hardness, a fact that makes them more suitable for cooking than the polyunsaturated fatty acids. Like saturated fatty acids, they collect in the external parts of the body and can raise triglyceride levels when taken excessively.

NHLBI: The National Heart, Lung, and Blood Institute of the National Institute of Health conducts conventional surveys concerning lipid research.

NIH: The National Institute of Health conducts conventional surveys concerning lipid research frequently in conjunction with the NHLBI.

OA: Oleic acid is the most common and important of the MUFAs and is found predominantly in Olive and Peanut oils.

PG: Prostaglandins are hormone-like substances created in the body from essential fatty acids and provide much of the foundation for good health.

PGE_1: Prostaglandin 1 is the first of the three important prostaglandins (hormone-like substances regulating local areas of the body) converted in the body from essential fatty acids. The four-stage conversion of Prostaglandin 1 from the Omega 6 linoleic acid (LA $\rightarrow$ GLA $\rightarrow$ DGLA $\rightarrow$ **PGE_1**) is dependent upon enzymes that have become deficient in about one of every five people in modern society. In this case, it is necessary to supplement the diet with oils containing GLA, which is further along in the conversion process. PGE_1 is in polar harmony with PGE_2 and relaxes the Body/Mind. See GLA for specific oils to remedy this enzyme deficient condition.

PGE_2: Prostaglandin 2 is the second of the three important prostaglandins (hormone-like substances regulating local areas of the body) converted in the body from essential fatty acids. The five-stage conversion of Prostaglandin 2 from the Omega 6 linoleic acid is as follows: LA $\rightarrow$ GLA $\rightarrow$ DGLA $\rightarrow$ PGE_1 and AA $\rightarrow$ **PGE_2**. PGE_2 is in polar harmony with PGE_1 and constricts the Body/Mind. In excess PGE_2 will cause platelet aggregation, water retention, and high blood pressure. PGE_2 can also be counter-balanced with PGE_3.

PGE_3: Prostaglandin 3 is the third of the three important prostaglandins (hormone-like substances regulating local areas of the body) converted in the body from essential fatty acids. The five-stage conversion of Prostaglandin 3 from the Omega 3 linolenic acid (LNA $\rightarrow$ SDA $\rightarrow$ EPA $\rightarrow$ **PGE_3**) is dependent upon similar enzymes that have become deficient in the conversion of PGE_1 from LA. Black Currant Seed oil contains sufficient amounts of SDA in order to convert PGE_3. Another alternative is to use Krill oil or cold-water fish and their oils because they contain the EPA that directly converts to PGE_3.

PL: Phospholipids are fatty acids with two chains attached to a common glycerol molecule instead of the three found in the triglycerides. Triglycerides are only fat-soluble. The missing third chain in phospholipids is taken up by a phosphate group, which makes phospholipids both water and fat-soluble. Therefore, phospholipids spread easily over water surfaces and form envelopes around other important substances (especially fats, fat-soluble vitamins, and cholesterol). Phospholipids also help transport these materials in and out of areas in need. Cholesterol, for example, must be coated in phospholipid membranes in order to be soluble in the blood stream. Both LDL and HDL utilize phospholipids as an important element of their structure. Phospholipids are also important components of cell membranes where they help maintain membrane permeability and enable important nutrients and toxins to move easily in and out of the cell. Brain function is also dependent on phospholipids. The best-known phospholipid is lecithin, which forms 22 percent of the composition of both HDL and LDL. The best source of lecithin is non-GMO, expeller-pressed, unrefined soybean oil. Flaxseed, Hempseed, and Rice Bran oils also contain lecithin. Neptune Krill Oil is the best source of phospholipids.

PUFA: Polyunsaturated fatty acids are unsaturated fatty acid molecules comprised of multiple double carbon bonds. Polyunsaturated fatty acids are among the least stable and most fragile of lipids, are liquid at room temperature, and make cholesterol circulate from the body to the membranes in compensation for their softening effect. They are of two types, the more common Omega 6s and the less common Omega 3s.

SAD: The Standard American Diet, as promoted by the AHA, is a result of the political compromise between antiquated nutritional theory and pressure from the food industry. As such, the SAD endorses the public use of refined food thereby contributing significantly to the deterioration of health.

SaFA: Saturated fatty acids are fatty acids with no double carbon bonds and are more common in animal foods. Saturated fatty acids are the hardest, stickiest, and most stable of fatty acids, and are used to build cell membranes. This function displaces cholesterol from the membranes and into the bloodstream where the serum cholesterol level is raised. SaFA consumption should be no more than half of UFA consumption at most, that 30 percent of the total fat intake.

SCFA: Short-chain fatty acids are saturated fatty acids containing just two to six carbons and are only found in nature as vinegar and butter.

SCT: Short-chain triglyceride (see SCFA).

SDA: Stearidonic acid is one of the main derivatives of LNA used by the body to produce the health benefiting Prostaglandin 3s (LNA → **SDA** → EPA → PGE$_3$) . Since many people do not have the required nutrients or enzymes needed to make this conversion, it is necessary to take oils that contain it separately, such as Black Currant Seed oil, Hempseed oil, or other oils that contain acids further down in the conversion chain, such as the EPA and DHA found in Krill oil or cold-water fish and their oils.

SUFA: Super-unsaturated fatty acids refer to the Omega 3 essential fatty acids.

TFA: *Trans*-fatty acids are unhealthy, biologically inactive fatty acids made from industrial processing in order to appease the sensorial appetite and extend shelf life. *Trans*-fatty acids can also be created from the excessive use of heat in cooking and are responsible for much of the development of degenerative disease found today in modern Western society. *Trans*-fatty acids are formed either though excessive heat (they begin to form at + 320°F, form in large quantities at + 392°F, and increase exponentially at + 428°F) or especially through the hydrogenation or partial hydrogenation process by flipping the natural unsaturated fatty acid bond apart and then recombining it into an unnatural saturated bond. This unnatural process, invented to create marketable texture, serves to block the functions of the more necessary and natural forms of UFAs and creates EFA depletion throughout the body. The cellular destruction created by *trans*-fatty acids establishes the foundation for the development of chronic, degenerative disease. TFAs, especially in times of increased activity, stress, or crisis, block the availability of fatty acids from nourishing the heart; interfere with the production of PGs; rapidly increase blood cholesterol levels (up to two to three times more than SaFAs); increase blood fat (up to 47 percent); increase atherosclerotic plaque; increase LDL; and contribute to the creation of free radicals. More than 60 percent of margarines and shortenings contain synthetic *trans*-fatty acids. Natural *trans*-fatty acids differ substantially from their artificial counterparts due to the placement of their double bonds and are found only in minute quantities in the fats of ruminant animals such as antelope, buffalo, cow, deer, goat, and sheep (less than 2 to 5 percent).

TG: Triglycerides comprise one of the three major classes of lipids (including sterols and phospholipids) and are determined by three fatty acid chains linked together by a common glycerol molecule. This "triangular" molecular shape makes them very stable, a characteristic that is further enhanced by the degree of straightness or bend in the particular triglyceride fatty acid chain. The straighter and longer the chain, the more stable it becomes. Therefore, long-chain saturated fatty acids such as those found in beef fat represent the most stable of the triglycerides. This stability is decreased as the chain-length becomes shorter as in the medium-chain fatty acid of coconut oil. Next in lessening degree of triglyceride stability are the monounsaturated fatty acids followed by the polyunsaturated fatty acids, and finally the super-unsaturated fatty acids (a sub-group of the PUFAs), which are the most fragile group of the triglycerides. The stability of triglycerides tends to associate excessive intake of them with over-stickiness of blood cells, which then clump together in order to damage the interior of arteries and increase the risk of heart disease. Triglycerides can also be produced from excessive intake of refined sugars, refined carbohydrates, and their concomitant deficiency of antioxidants. High serum triglycerides can be lowered through exercise and the consumption of whole foods including especially the fragile Omega 3 EFAs (the opposite in polarity to the most stable long-chain saturated fatty acids), which can decrease excess serum triglyceride levels up to 65 percent.

UFA: Unsaturated fatty acids are fatty acids with at least one double carbon bond. Unsaturated fatty acids spread out over surfaces, help provide fluidity in cell membranes, and transport materials in and out of the cells. UFA consumption should be at least twice that of SaFA consumption.

W3: See LA.

W6: See LNA.

Glossary of Fatty Acid Profiles

Table 34: FA Profile of Source Foods (Vegetables)

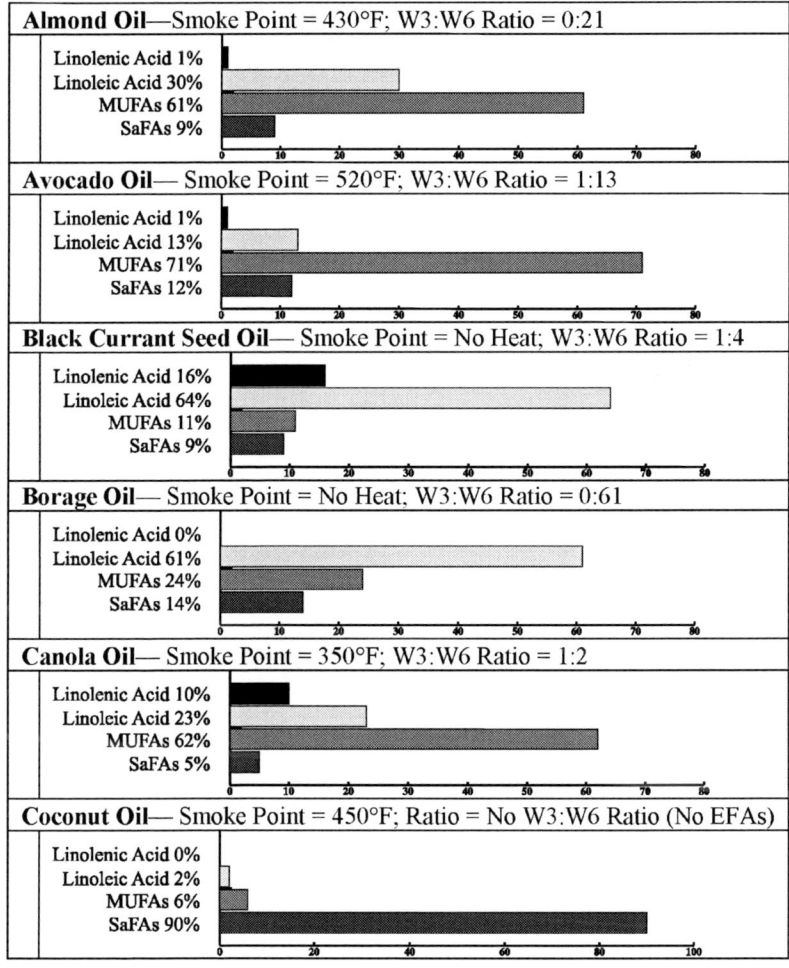

Almond Oil—Smoke Point = 430°F; W3:W6 Ratio = 0:21

Linolenic Acid 1%
Linoleic Acid 30%
MUFAs 61%
SaFAs 9%

Avocado Oil— Smoke Point = 520°F; W3:W6 Ratio = 1:13

Linolenic Acid 1%
Linoleic Acid 13%
MUFAs 71%
SaFAs 12%

Black Currant Seed Oil— Smoke Point = No Heat; W3:W6 Ratio = 1:4

Linolenic Acid 16%
Linoleic Acid 64%
MUFAs 11%
SaFAs 9%

Borage Oil— Smoke Point = No Heat; W3:W6 Ratio = 0:61

Linolenic Acid 0%
Linoleic Acid 61%
MUFAs 24%
SaFAs 14%

Canola Oil— Smoke Point = 350°F; W3:W6 Ratio = 1:2

Linolenic Acid 10%
Linoleic Acid 23%
MUFAs 62%
SaFAs 5%

Coconut Oil— Smoke Point = 450°F; Ratio = No W3:W6 Ratio (No EFAs)

Linolenic Acid 0%
Linoleic Acid 2%
MUFAs 6%
SaFAs 90%

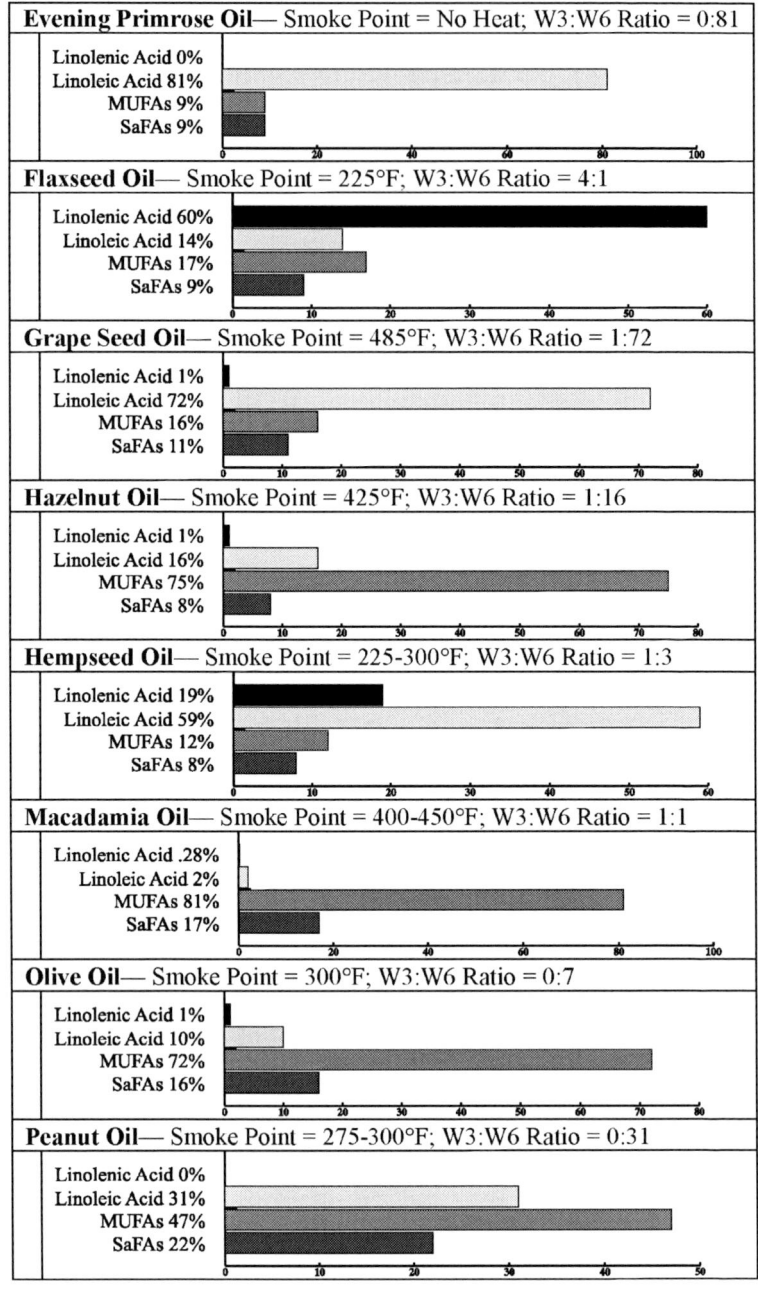

Evening Primrose Oil— Smoke Point = No Heat; W3:W6 Ratio = 0:81

Linolenic Acid 0%
Linoleic Acid 81%
MUFAs 9%
SaFAs 9%

Flaxseed Oil— Smoke Point = 225°F; W3:W6 Ratio = 4:1

Linolenic Acid 60%
Linoleic Acid 14%
MUFAs 17%
SaFAs 9%

Grape Seed Oil— Smoke Point = 485°F; W3:W6 Ratio = 1:72

Linolenic Acid 1%
Linoleic Acid 72%
MUFAs 16%
SaFAs 11%

Hazelnut Oil— Smoke Point = 425°F; W3:W6 Ratio = 1:16

Linolenic Acid 1%
Linoleic Acid 16%
MUFAs 75%
SaFAs 8%

Hempseed Oil— Smoke Point = 225-300°F; W3:W6 Ratio = 1:3

Linolenic Acid 19%
Linoleic Acid 59%
MUFAs 12%
SaFAs 8%

Macadamia Oil— Smoke Point = 400-450°F; W3:W6 Ratio = 1:1

Linolenic Acid .28%
Linoleic Acid 2%
MUFAs 81%
SaFAs 17%

Olive Oil— Smoke Point = 300°F; W3:W6 Ratio = 0:7

Linolenic Acid 1%
Linoleic Acid 10%
MUFAs 72%
SaFAs 16%

Peanut Oil— Smoke Point = 275-300°F; W3:W6 Ratio = 0:31

Linolenic Acid 0%
Linoleic Acid 31%
MUFAs 47%
SaFAs 22%

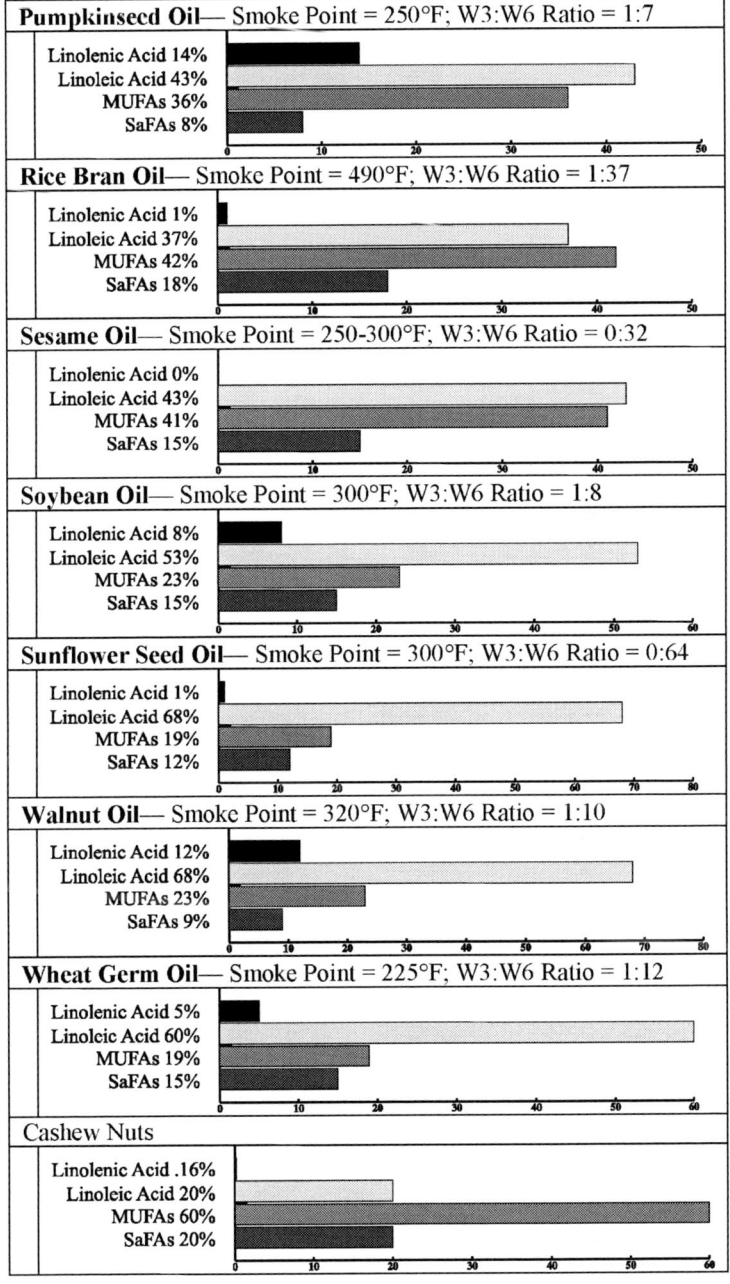

Pumpkinseed Oil— Smoke Point = 250°F; W3:W6 Ratio = 1:7

Linolenic Acid 14%
Linoleic Acid 43%
MUFAs 36%
SaFAs 8%

Rice Bran Oil— Smoke Point = 490°F; W3:W6 Ratio = 1:37

Linolenic Acid 1%
Linoleic Acid 37%
MUFAs 42%
SaFAs 18%

Sesame Oil— Smoke Point = 250-300°F; W3:W6 Ratio = 0:32

Linolenic Acid 0%
Linoleic Acid 43%
MUFAs 41%
SaFAs 15%

Soybean Oil— Smoke Point = 300°F; W3:W6 Ratio = 1:8

Linolenic Acid 8%
Linoleic Acid 53%
MUFAs 23%
SaFAs 15%

Sunflower Seed Oil— Smoke Point = 300°F; W3:W6 Ratio = 0:64

Linolenic Acid 1%
Linoleic Acid 68%
MUFAs 19%
SaFAs 12%

Walnut Oil— Smoke Point = 320°F; W3:W6 Ratio = 1:10

Linolenic Acid 12%
Linoleic Acid 68%
MUFAs 23%
SaFAs 9%

Wheat Germ Oil— Smoke Point = 225°F; W3:W6 Ratio = 1:12

Linolenic Acid 5%
Linoleic Acid 60%
MUFAs 19%
SaFAs 15%

Cashew Nuts

Linolenic Acid .16%
Linoleic Acid 20%
MUFAs 60%
SaFAs 20%

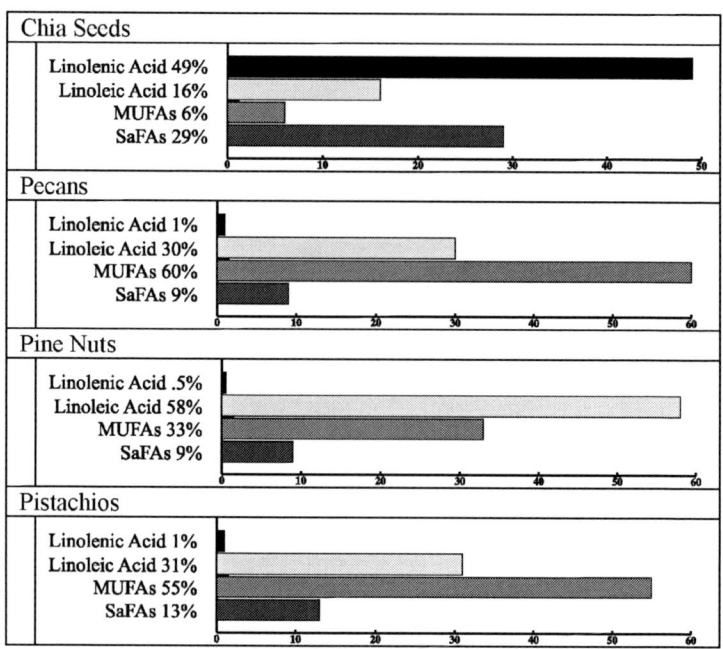

Table 35: FA Profile of Source Foods (Fish)

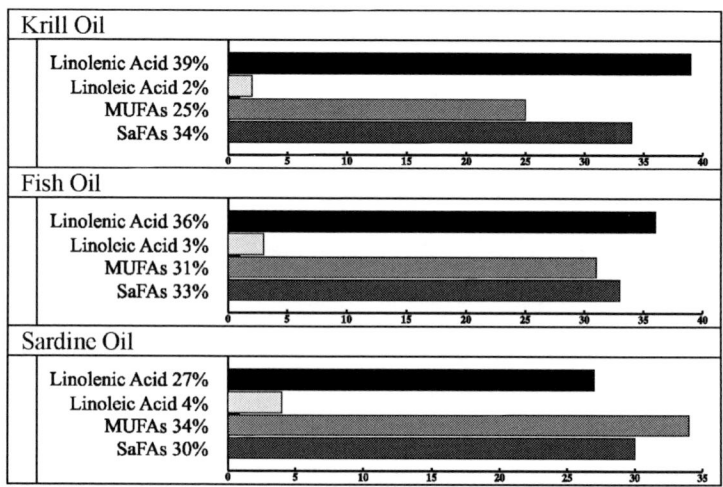

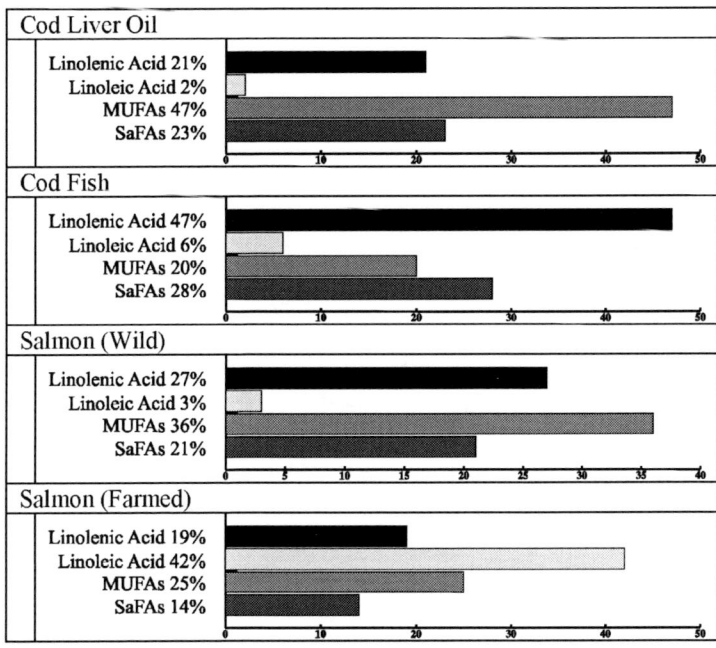

Table 36: FA Profile of Source Foods (Animals)

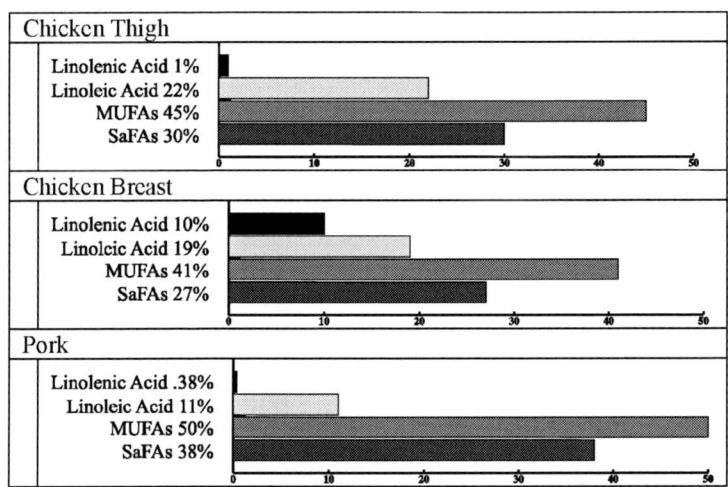

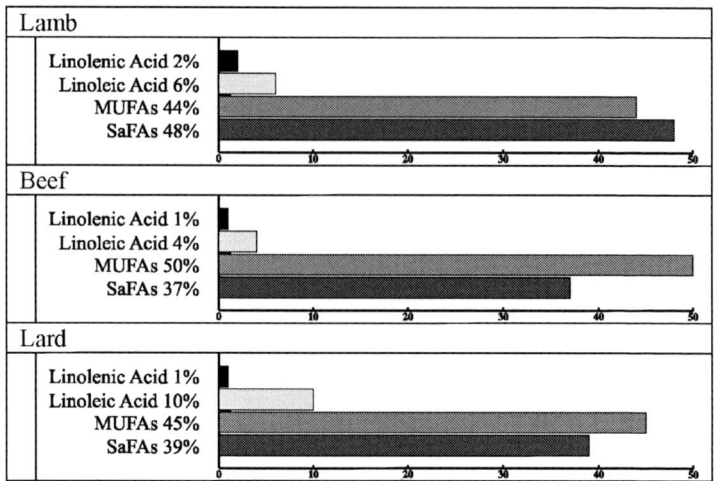

References

Cloutier, Marissa, M.S, R.D. and Eve Adamson. *The Mediterranean Diet*. New York, New York: Avon Books, 2004.

Curran, R.C. M.D., and E.L. Jones, M.D. *Gross Pathology: A Color Atlas*. New York: Oxford University Press, 1974.

Enig, Mary. *Know Your Fats: The Complete Primer for Understanding the Nutrition of Fats, Oils, and Cholesterol*. Silver Spring, Maryland: Bethesda Press, 2000.

Erasmus, Udo. *Fats That Heal, Fats That Kill*. Burnaby BC Canada V5: Alive Books, 1986.

Fife, Bruce. *The Healing Miracles of Coconut Oil*. Colorado Springs, Colorado: HealthWise Publications, 2001.

Goldberg, Burton. *Alternative Medicine: The Definitive Guide*. Tiburon, California: Future Medicine Publishing Company, Inc, 1993.

Kurlansky, Mark. *Salt: A World History*. Penguin Books: New York, New York, 2002.

Kushi, Michio, with Alex Jack. *Diet For a Strong Heart*. St. Martin's Press: New York, 1985.

Kushi and Jack. *The Cancer Prevention Diet*. St. Martin's Press: New York, 1983.

McGee, Charles T., M.D. *Heart Frauds: The Misapplication of Technology in Heart Disease*. MediPress: Coer d'Alene, ID, 1993.

Pescatore, Fred, M.D. *The Hamptons Diet: Lose Weight Quickly and Safely with the Doctor's Delicious Meal Plans*. Hoboken, New Jersey: John Wiley & Sons, Inc., 2004.

Pitchford, Paul. *Healing With Whole Foods: Asian Traditions and Modern Nutrition*. Berkeley, California: North Atlantic Books, 1993.

Ravnskov, Uffe, M.D., PhD. *The Cholesterol Myths: Exposing the Fallacy that Saturated Fat and Cholesterol Cause Heart Disease*. New Trends Publishing, Inc.: Washington, DC, 2000.

Rose, Richard and Brigitte Mars. *HempNut Cookbook*. Book Publishing Company: Summertown Tennessee, 2004.

Scheer, James F. *The Magic of Chia: Revival of an Ancient Wonder Food*. Frog, Ltd.: Berkeley, 2001.

Sheppard-Hanger, Sylla. *Aromatherapy Practitioner Reference Manual*. Self-published, 1995.

References

Index

Index

Index

Endnotes

[1] Mary Enig, Ph.D., *Know Your Fats: The Complete Primer for Understanding the Nutrition of Fats, Oils, and Cholesterol*, (Silver Spring, Maryland: Bethesda Press, 2000) 2.

[2] "Eating Plan For Healthy Americans," Brochure of the American Heart Association, 2001.

[3] Ibid.

[4] Marissa Cloutier, M.S, R.D., *The Mediterranean Diet*, (New York: Avon Books, 2001) 81.

[5] Udo Erasmus, *Fats That Heal, Fats That Kill*, (Burnaby BC Canada V5: Alive Books, 1986) 57.

[6] Cloutier 68.

[7] Fred Pescatore, M.D., *The Hamptons Diet: Lose Weight Quickly and Safely with the Doctor's Delicious Meal Plans*, (Hoboken: John Wiley & Sons, 2004) 30.

[8] Erasmus 33.

[9] Pescatore 4.

[10] Pescatore 6.

[11] Cloutier 79.

[12] Pescatore 27.

[13] Pescatore 11.

[14] Cloutier 87.

[15] Charles T. McGee, M.D., *Heart Frauds: The Misapplication of Technology in Heart Disease*, (Coer d'Alene, ID: MediPress, 1993) 55.

[16] McGee 225.

[17] McGee 7.

[18] McGee 35.

[19] McGee 35.

[20] McGee 33.

[21] McGee 47.

[22] Michio Kushi with Alex Jack, *Diet For a Strong Heart*, (New York: St. Martin's Press, 1985) 116.

[23] Kushi 1985 120.

[24] Kushi 1985 29.

[25] "Controlling Your Risk Factors," Brochure of the American Heart Association, 2001-2003.

[26] McGee 88.

[27] Uffe Ravnskov, M.D., PhD., *The Cholesterol Myths: Exposing the Fallacy that Saturated Fat and Cholesterol Cause Heart Disease*, (Washington, DC: New Trends Publishing, Inc., 2000) 131.

[28] Ravnskov 261.

[29] Ibid.

[30] McGee 74.

[31] Ravnskov 50.

[32] Ravinskov 210.
[33] Enig 78.
[34] Ravnskov 59.
[35] McGee 92.
[36] McGee 77.
[37] McGee 96.
[38] Ravnskov 2.
[39] Enig 187.
[40] Enig 99, 100.
[41] R.C. Curran, M.D., and E.L. Jones, M.D., *Gross Pathology: A Color Atlas*, (New York: Oxford University Press, 1974) 56.
[42] Enig 99, 187.
[43] Enig 99, 186.
[44] Erasmus 333.
[45] Erasmus 69.
[46] Fife 48.
[47] McGee 112.
[48] Kushi 1985 127.
[49] Kushi 1985 130.
[50] Kushi and Jack 1983 40.
[51] Kushi 1985 108.
[52] Kushi 1985 156.
[53] Kushi 1985 107.
[54] Kushi 1985 102.
[55] Pescatore 26.
[56] Pescatore 25.
[57] Enig 85.
[58] Pescatore 26.
[59] Bruce Fife, *The Healing Miracles of Coconut Oil*, (Colorado Springs, Colorado: HealthWise Publications, 2001) 100.
[60] Fife 94.
[61] James South, M.A., *NKO: The Ultimate (Non-Fish) Fish Oil*, (Carson City, NV: Vitamin Research Products) 4.
[62] Richard Rose and Brigitte Mars, *HempNut Cookbook*, (Summertown, Tennessee: Book Publishing Company, 2004) 19.
[63] Tina Sampalis, M.D., Ph.D., "Neptune Krill Oil Part I, II, III," In *The Vitamin Research News*, (Carson City, NV: Vitamin Research Products) 5.
[64] Sampalis 11.
[65] South 1.
[66] Sampalis 2.
[67] South 1.
[68] Sampalis 8.
[69] Sampalis 7.
[70] Sampalis 3.
[71] Sampalis 3.

[72] Sampalis 4.
[73] Sampalis 4.
[74] Sampalis 8.
[75] Sampalis 9.
[76] Sampalis 11.
[77] Sampalis 9.
[78] Sampalis 10.
[79] Sampalis 11.
[80] Sampalis 4.
[81] Sampalis 11.
[82] South 2.
[83] South 5.
[84] Sampalis 4.
[85] Cloutier 186.
[86] Pescatore 23.
[87] Mark Kurlansky, *Salt: A World History*, (New York: Penguin Books, 2002) 68.
[88] Kurlansky 71.
[89] Erasmus 279.
[90] Erasmus 281.
[91] Rose 19.
[92] Rose 20.
[93] Rose 35.
[94] Rose 9.
[95] Rose 8.
[96] Rose x.
[97] Rose 10.
[98] Rose 9.
[99] Rose 9.
[100] Rose 30.
[101] Rose x.
[102] Rose 5.
[103] Rose ix.
[104] Rose 3.
[105] Rose 5.
[106] Rose 4.
[107] Rose 3.
[108] Rose x, 3.
[109] Rose 4.
[110] Rose 23.
[111] Rose 23.
[112] Rose 22.
[113] Rose 5.
[114] Rose 23.
[115] Rose ix.

[116] Rose 6.
[117] Rose 1.
[118] Rose 6.
[119] Rose 7.
[120] Rose 8.
[121] Rose 31.
[122] Rose 33.
[123] Rose 26.
[124] Rose 31.
[125] Rose 28.
[126] Rose 26.
[127] Rose 21.
[128] Rose 25.
[129] Rose 24.
[130] Patricia Kane, Ph.D., "It's All in the Fat: The Role of Essential Fatty Acids in Health."
[131] Rose 25.
[132] Rose 28.
[133] Burton Goldberg, *Alternative Medicine: The Definitive Guide*, (Tiburon, California: Future Medicine Publishing Company, Inc, 1993 56.
[134] Sylla Sheppard-Hanger, *Aromatherapy Practitioner Reference Manual*, (Self-published, 1995) 133.
[135] Erasmus 202.
[136] Erasmus 140.
[137] Erasmus 135, 139.
[138] Erasmus 203.
[139] Erasmus 75-76.
[140] Erasmus 125.
[141] Erasmus 428.
[142] Erasmus 157.
[143] Erasmus 199.
[144] Erasmus 201.
[145] Cloutier 67.
[146] Erasmus 236.
[147] Pescatore 21.
[148] Cloutier 67.
[149] Cloutier 7.
[150] Cloutier 81.
[151] Cloutier 84.
[152] Pescatore 8.
[153] Cloutier 77.
[154] Cloutier 78.
[155] Pescatore 9.
[156] Pescatore 21.
[157] Cloutier 8.

[158] Pescatore 9.
[159] Pescatore 10.
[160] Pescatore 10.
[161] Pescatore 3.
[162] Pescatore 29.
[163] Pescatore 29.
[164] Pescatore 97.
[165] Pescatore 67.
[166] Pescatore 31, 32.
[167] Pescatore 5.
[168] Pescatore 27.
[169] Pescatore 35.
[170] Pescatore 96.
[171] Pescatore 102.
[172] Pescatore 62.

Publications Available From Willmountain Press

Energetic Physiology in the Acupuncture Pointnames (611 pp.)

The acupuncture points are the doorway of the Body, Mind, and Spirit. Ancient practitioners gave each of these points up to twenty-four different names. These names go beyond mere descriptions of the points. They lend their original perspective to modern understanding by illuminating the world-view from which acupuncture was produced. The study of these names, therefore, constitutes one of the most important ways to understand; not only the acupuncture points, but acupuncture itself.

Energetic Physiology in the Acupuncture Pointnames is an in-depth study of all 894 pointnames of the 361 points of the Main Meridians of acupuncture. These names describe the Actions, Effects, and Spirit of the acupuncture points through symbols derived from various aspects of early Chinese culture including: the Chinese characters, philosophy, religion, mythology, alchemy, astrology, astronomy, architecture, fengshui, sexology, political structure, city planning, etc.

All of these symbols are here tied together with the energetics of the point to produce a rich and unified picture of each point's meaning and how it can be used. This book is well illustrated with over 125 drawings and diagrams, and bound for convenient study and clinical use.

The Twelve Spirit Points Of Acupuncture (264 pages)

The human spirit incarnates into the human body in Four Stages of Three Aspects each, making Twelve Aspects in all. Each of these Twelve Aspects is represented by an acupuncture point. In each Stage the Spirit has the opportunity to become comfortable with its physical abode. When life experience disrupts the natural progression of this evolution, the Twelve Spirit Points can be used as a group treatment, or together in various combinations to restore the Body, Mind, Spirit unity appropriate to the Stage or Aspect associated with this disruption.

The *Twelve Spirit Points* is a state of the art study of the acupuncture pointnames as they relate specifically to the development of the *Shen*/Spirit in human evolution. After first examining the nature of this evolution, in general, each of the twelve points is discussed in detail in terms of its role in the integration of Body, Mind, and Spirit. All of the relevant issues of ancient Chinese culture are fully explored in order to fully understand the symbolic impact of these names, and their significance to healing on the Spirit level. The reader will then gain an appreciation of the importance of Spirit in healing, as well as its place in ancient Chinese society.

Natural Healing with Essential Oils (512 pages)

This book presents aromatherapy from the perspective of Chinese herbalism and acupuncture for both the layperson and the professional in a way that shows great insight into understanding how to create natural healing with essential oils on the levels of the Body, Mind, and Spirit.

Part I covers basic application techniques as well as various categories for organizing essential oil knowledge including: 1) Essential Oil Chemistry, 2) the Functional Categories of Disease, 3) the Five Phases, 4) the Seven Chakras, and 5) the Twelve Spirit Points of Acupuncture. Part II covers ninety essential oils in depth and includes sections on essential oil contents, properties, functions, uses, blends, contraindications, and discussions of character types and plant signatures. It also covers important Carrier Oils and forty-four Synergies analyzed by function. Part III covers how to use essential oils for health and disease and includes extensive chapters on Psycho-Emotional Disorders; Heart and Circulatory Disease; Healing the Body, Mind, and Spirit; Breast Cancer; Prostate Cancer; Children's Disorders; Respiratory Disorders; Musculo-Skeletal Disorders; as well as a full spectrum of other disease categories from addictions to urinary problems.

This book is designed to read either from cover to cover for a greater depth of insight into natural healing issues, or simply as a reference manual. It contains over two hundred fifteen charts, graphs, and figures that make it easy to understand, use, and remember the concepts that are presented in the text as well as over sixty beautiful illustrations of the plants used in the art of aromatherapy.

Fat Chance: Surviving the Cholesterol Controversy and Beyond (284 pages)

This book explains and demystifies fats and oils and the different terms used for them in order to inform the public about the immense value of natural fats and oils and the grave danger of their unnatural industrial twins. Fats and oils are then discussed in relation to relevant disease categories including liver, heart, and circulatory disease and the false and dangerous modern cholesterol theory of coronary artery disease.

Finally, the importance of fats and oils is discussed in relation to Chinese Medicine. Acupuncturists know that Liver conditions adversely affect more organs and tissues in the body than any other condition. Good fats and oils nourish the Liver while bad fats and oils create pathological Liver conditions that create havoc throughout the Body/Mind. Learning about good and bad quality fats and oils will teach you more about taking care of your health than any other single thing you can do.

Price List

Code	Title	Price	Shipping
100	*Energetic Physiology In The Acupuncture Pointnames*—COIL BOUND	$100.00	$13.00
200	*The Twelve Spirit Points Of Acupuncture* COIL BOUND	$50.00	$12.00
300	*Natural Healing With Essential Oils* COIL BOUND	$90.00	$13.00
350	*Fat Chance: Surviving the Cholesterol Controversy and Beyond* PERFECT BOUND	$30.00	$8.00

All prices subject to change without notice

**Willmountain Press
496 Pine Street
Marshfield, MA 02050
781-837-3455
Willmountain.com**

Order Form

Please print out the form below, fill it in completely and include it with your order. Please make all checks payable to Willmountain Press.

Ship To:
Name: _____
Address: _____

City/State/Zip: _____

Phone: _____

Email Address: _____

Code	Qty	Unit Price	Total
		SUBTOTAL:	
		Shipping/Handling:	
		TOTAL COST: